To Allan a[nd] [...]
with love from
Rose x

The most amazing royal places in Britain

The most amazing royal places in Britain

PUBLISHED BY
THE READER'S DIGEST ASSOCIATION, INC.
LONDON • NEW YORK • SYDNEY • MONTREAL

Contents

INTRODUCTION 6–7
RULING BRITANNIA 8-11

SOUTHWEST ENGLAND 12–35
Cornwall 14–21
Devon 22–23
Dorset 24–27
Somerset 28–33
FEATURE: **THE LEGENDARY KINGDOM OF ARTHUR PENDRAGON 30–31**
Channel Islands 34–35

SOUTHERN ENGLAND 36–75
Bedfordshire 38
Berkshire 39–43
Buckinghamshire 44–45
Hampshire & Isle of Wight 46–53
FEATURE: **OF CAPTAINS AND KINGS 54–55**
Hertfordshire 56–57
Kent 58–63
Oxfordshire 64–65
Surrey 66–67
Sussex 68–73
Wiltshire 74–75

LONDON 76–111
Inner London 78–101
FEATURE: **CROWNED IN GLORY 96–97**
Outer London 102–111
FEATURE: **THE PERILS OF POWER 106–107**

EAST ANGLIA 112–129
Cambridgeshire 114–115
Essex 116–119
FEATURE: **ROYAL TREASURE – LOST AND FOUND 120–121**
Norfolk 122–127
Suffolk 128–129

CENTRAL ENGLAND 130–157
Derbyshire 132–133
Gloucestershire 134–136
Herefordshire 137

FEATURE: **TUDOR TRANSFORMATION 138–139**
Leicestershire & Rutland 140–141
Lincolnshire 142–145
Northamptonshire 146–147
Nottinghamshire 148
Shropshire 149
FEATURE: **FLIGHT OF THE UNCROWNED
KING 150–151**
Staffordshire 152
Warwickshire 153–155
Worcestershire 156–157

NORTHWEST ENGLAND 158–169
Cheshire & The Wirral 160–161
Cumbria 162–165
Lancashire, Liverpool & Manchester 166–169

NORTHEAST ENGLAND 170–181
Durham & Teesside 172
Northumberland & Tyneside 173–175
Yorkshire 176–181

WALES 182–195
North & Mid Wales 184–191
FEATURE: **KINGDOM OF CASTLES 186–187**
South Wales 192–195

SCOTLAND 196–215
Southwest Scotland 198–199
Fife & Southeast Scotland 200–206
FEATURE: **THE PALACE OF
HOLYROODHOUSE 202–203**
Central & Northeast Scotland 207–212
North Highlands & Islands 213–215

INDEX 216–223
ACKNOWLEDGMENTS 223

Introduction

Over the past 1,000 years, an elite minority of men and women have had an extraordinary impact on the British landscape. Now you can walk in the footsteps of these kings and queens with this guide to the most amazing royal places in Britain.

Our heritage is inextricably bound to the story of our rulers, the kings, queens and princes of England, Scotland and Wales. We see everywhere the sumptuous pleasure palaces they commissioned, the formidable castles they raised, the gardens they laid out and the deer parks they enclosed. We see, too, the battlegrounds upon which some met their end and the towers in which others languished.

All the best and worst traits of Britain's kings and queens, princes and princesses, found expression in what they created. Their munificence, enlightenment, playfulness and artistic vision made their mark. In the same way, their megalomania, greed and paranoia left a legacy. Stout fortresses and crumbling remains recall Edward I's military adventures across borders. Magnificent ruins stand as reminders of Henry VIII's Dissolution of the Monasteries – an act of such extreme vandalism that in the space of five years the British landscape was changed forever. While he wrecked the religious houses, Henry instigated great building projects, too – splendid noble mansions and strongholds that guard our south coast, the latter a testament to how much he had to fear from Catholic Europe.

In towns, cities and in the countryside, the story of royalty can be read in stone. And it is an ongoing tale, as the tradition and pageantry that surround the royal family and their magnificent palaces and estates link past with present, reinforcing Britain's national identity and drawing visitors from the world over.

How to use this book

The book is divided into nine regions (see map, right) which are sub-divided by county or, in the case of Scotland and Wales, by area. Each chapter opens with a map of the region. Numbers on the map show the location of each featured place. Directions by road – or in the case of London by public transport –

are listed at the end of each entry, together with the postcode for satnav users.

Almost all featured places are open to the public for part or all of the year: some are free to enter, others charge a fee. Check opening hours on dedicated websites or by phone before visiting as times and access may be subject to change according to year and season. Where places or properties are privately owned, always respect the owners' privacy and don't stray on to private land to view or photograph the site.

A timeline with dates of Britain's kings and queens, plus a brief history of the royal houses and influential rulers, is featured on pages 8–11.

Useful websites

Many British palaces, castles, houses and areas of the countryside are owned or managed by the heritage organisations listed below. The abbreviations have been used throughout this book at the end of the relevant entries. Check websites for opening times, entry fees and events.

● English Heritage (EH)
www.english-heritage.org.uk

● The National Trust (NT)
www.nationaltrust.org.uk

● Cadw (CADW)
www.cadw.wales.gov.uk

● The National Trust for Scotland (NTS)
www.nts.org.uk

● Historic Scotland (HS)
www.historic-scotland.gov.uk

SCOTLAND
196-215

NORTHWEST ENGLAND
158-169

NORTHEAST ENGLAND
170-181

WALES
182-195

CENTRAL ENGLAND
130-157

EAST ANGLIA
112-129

LONDON
76-111

SOUTHWEST ENGLAND
12-35

SOUTHERN ENGLAND
36-75

Channel Islands

Ruling Britannia

Early times

After the Romans left Britain in AD 410, more than 300 years of peace came to an end. Troubled times began as the peoples of Britain endured successive waves of invasion from northern Germany and Denmark, erasing almost all Roman culture.

Anglo-Saxons & Viking Kings

In the 5th century AD, Saxon invaders from northwestern Europe began to settle in Britain. Before long they established kingdoms in the south. Wessex emerged as the most powerful of these Anglo-Saxon kingdoms and the kings of Wessex became the overlords. From the late 700s, Viking raiders scourged the land until in 1013, Swein Forkbeard became the first Viking king of Britain. The Anglo-Saxon line was restored when Edward the Confessor succeeded Hardicanute as king in 1042.

802-839	EGBERT
855-860	AETHELBALD
860-866	ATHELBERT
866-871	ATHELRED
871-899	ALFRED *the Great*
899-925	EDWARD *the Elder*
925-940	ATHELSTAN
940-946	EDMUND *the Magnificent*
946-955	EARDRED
955-959	EADWIG *All Fair*
959-957	EDGAR *the Peaceable*
957-978	EDGAR *the Martyr*
978-1016	AETHELRED *the Unready*
1016	EDMUND *Ironside*
1013	SWEIN *Forkbeard*
1016-1035	CNUT *Canute the Great*
1035-1040	HAROLD I
1040-1042	HARDICANUTE
1042-1066	EDWARD *the Confessor*
1066	HAROLD II

Early Scottish kings

By the late 6th century, Picts from Ireland controlled southeastern Scotland. In 839, Vikings routed the Pictish clans. At this time Kenneth Mac Alpin emerged as leader of all the Scots, adding Pictland to his kingdom of Dal Riatan. He named his new kingdom Alba. The early Scottish kings were all descended from Mac Alpin.

843-858	KENNETH I *Mac Alpin*
858-862	DONALD I
862-878	CONSTANTINE I
878-879	AEDH
879-889	EOCHAID

889-900	DONALD II
900-942	CONSTANTINE II
942-954	MALCOLM I
954-962	INDULF
962-966	DUB *or Duff*
966-971	CUILEAN *or Colin*
971-995	KENNETH II
995-997	CONSTANTINE III
997-1005	KENNETH II
1005-1034	MALCOLM II

ALFRED *the Great*

By 878 Britain was once again in peril from Viking invaders. A tale of Alfred letting cakes burn while charged with watching them is almost certainly apocryphal, but it reflects the problems he faced. Alfred saw that he must never allow himself to be caught unprepared. Displaying an enormous attention to detail, he organised his army so that half was always battle-ready. He built a navy and established burbs (fortified communities). He unified the land culturally and politically, and displayed great humanity in all his actions.

EDWARD *the Confessor*

Window: Chester Cathedral

Edward grew up in Normandy in exile during Viking rule of Britain. He returned in 1041 and was soon declared king. Edward married Edith, the daughter of a powerful earl, Godwine, but the marriage was childless because Edward allegedly remained celibate. Godwine challenged Edward's authority but the king managed to avoid civil war. Godwine was dead by 1053. The remainder of Edward's reign was stable and prosperous seeing the completion of Westminster Abbey. A cult associated with Edward's saintliness grew after his death and he was canonized in 1161

around 2,000 years ago
Britian is made up of several tribes, each led by a warior chief.

43-410
Romans invade and conquer most of Britian, except for the Scottish tribes, who they refer to as Picts.

250

from 450
Saxon raiders invade and begin to settle in the south and east of Britain.

around 500
The Scots, a tribe from Ireland, invade territory in the west of Scotland.

500

from 757 to 796
Offa, King of Mercia, holds sway over most of southern Britain.

750

789
Vikings launch their first raids on Britian.

by 870
Vikings occupy the north and east of England and parts of Scotland.

by 878
England is divided between the Anglo-Saxon kingdoms in the south and Viking territory called the Danelaw in the north.

959
Edgar is crowned king – the first coronation of which a full account survives.

1000

1013-1014
Danish king Swein Forkbeard invades Britain. He dies six weeks later.

1066
Edward the Confessor names Harold his heir on his deathbed.

House of Normandy

William of Normandy embarked for England in 1066 to claim his kingdom, alleging that Edward the Confessor had named him as his heir in 1051. Victorious at Hastings, William quickly established control. Two of his sons succeeded him but when his grandson, Stephen, took the throne, civil war followed. Stephen fought his cousin Matilda, who had been named heir by her father, Henry I, until she agreed to her son, Henry, succeeding Stephen.

1066-1087	WILLIAM *the Conqueror*
1087-1100	WILLIAM II *Rufus*
1100-1135	HENRY I *Beauclerc*
1135-1154	STEPHEN

House of Dunkeld

Taking its name from Duncan I's father, this Scottish house ruled until 1290 when Edward I was asked to name Margaret's successor after she had been drowned; trouble ensued.

1034-1040	DUNCAN I
1040-1057	MACBETH
1057-1058	LULACH
1058-1093	MALCOLM III
1093-1094	DONALD III
1094	DUNCAN II
1094-1097	DONALD III
1097-1107	EDGAR
1107-1124	ALEXANDER I
1124-1153	DAVID I
1153-1165	MALCOLM IV
1165-1214	WILLIAM
1214-1249	ALEXANDER II
1249-1286	ALEXANDER III
1286-1290	MARGARET
1290-1292	*Interregnum*
1292-1296	JOHN BALLIOL
1296-1306	*Interregnum*

Plantagenet kings

Angevin, Plantagenet, York and Lancaster are the four royal houses of the Plantagenet line beginning with the Angevin Henry II, son of Geoffrey Plantagenet and Matilda, Henry I's daughter. He and his son, Richard I, spent much of their reigns in foreign wars. John's barons answered his misrule with the Magna Carta in 1215. Henry III survived further baronial revolt. Edward I was a warrior king, but his weak son, Edward II, was murdered. Edward III started the Hundred Years War with France. His grandson, Richard II, was usurped by his Lancastrian cousin who ruled as Henry IV. Unrest followed leading to the Wars of the Roses, between the houses of York and Lancaster, ending with the death of Yorkist Richard III.

1154-1189	HENRY II *Curtmantle*
1189-1199	RICHARD I *the Lionheart*
1199-1216	JOHN *Lackland*
1216-1272	HENRY III
1272-1307	EDWARD I *Longshanks*
1307-1327	EDWARD II
1327-1377	EDWARD III
1377-1399	RICHARD II
1399-1413	HENRY IV *Bolingbroke*
1413-1422	HENRY V
1422-1461	HENRY VI
1470-1471	
1461-1470	EDWARD IV
1471-1483	
1483	EDWARD V
1483-1485	RICHARD III

House of Bruce

A ferocious warrior, Robert the Bruce was chosen king of the Scots in 1306 as Edward I fought for control of Scotland. In 1314, Robert's army drove the English from their land.

1306-1329	ROBERT I
1329-1371	DAVID II
1332-1341	EDWARD BALLIOL *with interruptions*

EDWARD I

Edward was an impressive and energetic warrior, earning the soubriquet 'Longshanks' because of his tall stature. On crusade when his father died, he returned and set about strengthening his royal authority. Next he sought to subjugate Wales and Scotland. In Wales, he crushed the Welsh princes and made his son the first Prince of Wales. In Scotland, Edward became known as the 'Hammer of the Scots' because of his continuous attempts to bring the Scots under English rule.

Statue: Burgh-by-Sands, Cumbria

1066
William of Normandy invades England defeating the last Anglo-Saxon king Harold.

1078
William I orders the building of the White Tower in London.

1086-87
William I commissions the Domesday Book to obtain a full census of his kingdom.

1120
Matilda, Henry I's daughter is left his only heir after his two sons, William and Richard, are drowned in the wreck of the White Ship.

1193-94
Richard I is taken prisoner in Germany on his return from the Third Crusade and held for ransom.

1215
The Barons revolt against John and force him to add his seal to the Magna Carta, curtailing his power as the monarch.

1314
Edward II's army loses the Battle of Bannockburn and the English are driven from Scotland.

1320
Scottish independence is declared in the Declaration of Arbroath.

from 1337 to 1453
Start of the Hundred Years' War between England and France.

from 1348 to 1370s
Outbreak of the Black Death. Between one third and one half of the population dies.

1415
Henry V is victorious at the Battle of Agincourt.

from 1455 to 1485
Start of the Wars of the Roses. The rival royal houses of York and Lancaster each seek to gain the Crown.

1461
Lancastrian Henry VI is deposed and Yorkist Edward IV becomes king.

1485
The Yorkist Richard III is slain at the Battle of Bosworth. The Lancastrian Henry Tudor takes the Crown as Henry VII.

1000

1100

1250

1450

House of Stewart

The dynasty of Stewart descended from Robert the Bruce's daughter Margaret and her husband Walter the Steward. Even though many Stewart kings succeeded as minors, the line prospered for 300 years until James VI became James I of England, uniting the kingdoms of England and Scotland.

1371-1390	**ROBERT** II
1390-1406	**ROBERT** III
1406-1437	**JAMES I**
1437-1460	**JAMES II**
1460-1488	**JAMES III**
1488-1513	**JAMES IV**
1513-1542	**JAMES V**
1542-1567	**MARY, QUEEN OF SCOTS**
1567-1625	**JAMES VI (JAMES I OF ENGLAND)**

House of Tudor

On gaining the throne, the Lancastrian Henry VII married Elizabeth of York, thus ending the bitter Wars of the Roses. He left a full treasury for his son, Henry VIII, who beguiled all until his need for a male heir became overriding. Henry reduced papal power in England, leading to the Reformation. His son Edward VI's reign was short. Mary, his daughter, restored papal supremacy, reviving ancient heresy laws to ensure Catholicism's return. Her half-sister, the astute Elizabeth, established a secure Church of England.

1485-1509	**HENRY VII**
1509-1547	**HENRY VIII**
1547-1553	**EDWARD VI**
1553-1558	**MARY I**
1558-1603	**ELIZABETH I**

House of Stuart

The Stuart dynasty ruled from 1603 to 1714 and saw a tumultuous period of civil wars, plague, fire, religious debate and radical politics. A civil war between the Crown and Parliament ended with Charles I's execution and a short-lived republic. Charles II's triumphant Restoration in 1660 was followed by his Roman Catholic brother James II who, before long, was desposed. The 'Glorious Revolution' swiftly followed which saw William III and Mary II, James II's daughter, as joint monarchs and defenders of Protestantism.

1603-1625	**JAMES I OF ENGLAND**
1625-1649	**CHARLES I**
1649-1659	**THE COMMONWEALTH**
1660-1685	**CHARLES II**
1685-1688	**JAMES II**
1685-1688	**WILLIAM II & MARY II**
1702-1707	**ANNE**

Window: Bristol cathedral

HENRY VIII

Raised, unusually for the time, in the company of women, Henry was not supposed to succeed to the throne until the death of his elder brother, Arthur, cast him to the fore. Highly educated, cultured and always delighting in hunting, he pursued his own interests early in his reign. The lack of a legitimate male heir saw his rule change for the worse – as his retinue of wives shows. Always affectionate to his children, he died leaving an ailing son, childless daughters, religious ferment – and danger ahead.

CHARLES II

Known popularly as the 'merrie monarch', the very tall, witty and good-humoured Charles was very merry indeed allegedly fathering 16 children from a succession of mistresses, although his marriage sadly lacked any legitimate issue. His youth had been shaped by the harrowing events of the civil war and his father's execution, and his own perilous escape into exile. As king, he presided over a glittering court, working with Parliament only as much as it suited his needs. Charles favoured religious tolerance yet Parliament threw out his efforts to achieve this. But when there were moves to exclude his Catholic brother James from the succession, Charles dissolved Parliament.

1509
Henry VIII marries his brother's widow, Catherine of Aragon.

1534
Henry cuts ties with the Roman Catholic church becoming supreme head of the Church of England.

from 1536 to 1540
The Dissolution of the Monsteries begins. Henry seizes the Church's lands, buildings and riches.

1553
Edward VI dies. Lady Jane Grey is queen for nine days. Mary Tudor, with a force of 20,000 men, quickly claims the throne.

1571
Elizabeth restores Protestant practice. The Thirty-Nine Articles lay down doctrines and practice of the Church of England.

1587
Mary, Queen of Scots, is implicated in a plot against Elizabeth's life. Mary is executed.

1588
Elizabeth's fleet disperses the Spanish Armada.

1603
James I succeeds uniting the English and Scottish thrones.

1642-1651
Relations between Charles I and Parliament disintegrate. Civil war ensures.

1649
Charles I is put on trial and executed. Parliament abolishes the monarchy by statute.

from 1649 to 1659
Interregnum (English Commonwealth). First Parliament and then Oliver Cromwell hold power.

1660
Charles II is restored to the English throne.

1685
The Duke of York succeeds as James II. He converted to Roman Catholicism in 1668.

1688
William of Orange lands at Torbay. James II flees England.

1689
James II deposed. A Bill of Rights obliges the monarch to govern with Parliament's assistance. No Catholic can be monarch. William III and Mary II are declared co-rulers.

1690
William III defeats James II at the Battle of the Boyne.

1500

1600

1700

House of Hanover

When George I, the first Hanoverian, came to the throne his claim was distant – he was 52nd in line. The dull, German-speaking George was, however, the direct Protestant heir according to the Act of Settlement of 1701. Jacobite supporters continued to foster unrest. Nevertheless the Hanoverian line proved enduring, with only six monarchs in nearly 200 years during a period that saw glorious military victories, revolutions overseas, industrial revolution – and the expansion of a mighty empire.

1714-1727	**GEORGE I**
1727-1760	**GEORGE II**
1760-1820	**GEORGE III**
1820-1830	**GEORGE IV**
1830-1837	**WILLIAM IV**
1837-1901	**VICTORIA I**

House of Saxe-Coburg-Gotha

On the marriage of Victoria to Prince Albert in 1840, Saxe-Coburg-Gotha became the name of the royal house. When he succeeded to the throne in 1901, Edward VII became the only king of the House of Saxe-Coburg-Gotha. His mother Victoria, like many other Hanoverian monarchs, did not like her heir and had not involved him in learning about a sovereign's duties. But Edward proved to be a skilled diplomat and used this talent to great effect.

1901-1910	**EDWARD VII**

House of Windsor

In 1917, during World War I, George V changed the German-sounding title Saxe-Coburg-Gotha to Windsor, and this is the name the royal family holds to this day. After Edward VIII succeeded his father in 1936, he abdicated 11 months later and his younger brother Albert, Duke of York succeeded. As George VI he ruled for 16 years before he was succeeded by his 25-year old daughter Elizabeth II.

1910-1936	**GEORGE V**
1936	**EDWARD VIII**
1936-1952	**GEORGE VI**
1952-present	**ELIZABETH II**

VICTORIA

A strong-willed 18-year old woman learned that she had succeeded to the throne of the United Kingdom in the early hours of June 20, 1837. Two years later her German cousin Albert came to pay her court. She was smitten and proposed to him within days. Nine children followed before Albert's death in 1861. A widow at 42 years old, she dressed in black for the remainder of her life. Her 63-year reign, saw Victoria became the Empress of India, sovereign to ten Prime Ministers, and her children marry into the ruling royal houses of Europe.

Statue: Leamington Spa

GEORGE VI

A quiet though sometimes irascible soul, undermined by a debilitating speech impediment, George VI felt ill-equipped to be king and emperor when his elder brother abdicated in December 1936. Public opinion of the new king quickly increased as he found staunch reserves of moral strength within himself when war broke out in 1939. With his wife and two daughters at his side, he became the outstanding monarch of the 20th century. The resilience he showed during World War II united the king with his subjects. His premature death in February 1952 was deeply mourned.

THE HANOVERIANS

SAXE-COBURG-GOTHA

WINDSOR

1700

1800

1900

2000

1694
George I divorces his wife Sophia imprisoning her in a castle in Hanover for the rest of her life.

1717
Speaking little English, George I rarely attends Cabinet meetings and depends increasingly on his ministers.

1745
George II's reign is threatened by Charles Edward Stuart, the Young Pretender. He is defeated at Culloden. The Jacobite threat to the throne is at an end.

1760
George III surrenders the Crown Estate to parliamentary control in return for a Civil List annuity to pay for royal household and civil expenses.

1811
Poryphria causes George III to become mentally unfit to rule. His eldest son becomes the Prince Regent.

1829
George IV's ministers force him to agree to Catholic Emancipation against his will.

1856
Victoria institutes the Victoria Cross, the highest decoration for valour. The medals are cast from Russian canon captured in the Crimea War.

1877
Victoria becomes Empress of India.

1903
Edward VII's diplomatic skills pave the way for the Entente Cordiale with France, which extends to include Russia in 1907.

1914-1918
World War I

1917
George V changes the name of the royal house from Saxe-Coburg-Gotha to Windsor.

1936
Edward VIII succeeds to the throne in January. By December, he abdicates to marry Mrs Wallis Simpson. George VI succeeds.

1939-1945
World War II

1952
Elizabeth II succeeds to the throne on her death of her father.

2012
Elizabeth II celebrates her Diamond Jubilee, 60 years since she succeeded to the throne on February 6, 1952.

Southwest England

KEY
- **1** Main entry
- County boundary
- Motorway
- Principal A road

Ilfracombe **2** A39

Barnstaple

Bideford

1

A39

Bude

A386

A377

DEVON
22-23

Okehampton • A30

A39

12

11

Launceston

16

4

A386

Dartmoor
National
Park

Padstow

A39

Bodmin
Moor

A30

14

Tavistock

Bodmin •

15 Liskeard

13

Newquay

CORNWALL
14-21

10

A390

A38

19

18 Plymouth A38

17

St Austell

A390

8

9

Truro

Falmouth

7

6

St Ives

4

A394

Penzance •

1 **2**

Helston

3

5

England's southwestern peninsula is steeped in Arthurian legend. Tudor fortresses guard a once-vulnerable shoreline, and historic inns and noble houses found fame sheltering a fleeing future king.

Bristol

A38

A37

6 7 8
Bath

Weston-super-Mare

Mendip Hills

Frome

A361

Minehead

Exmoor National Park

1 A39

Somerset Levels

4 A361

Bridgwater

Glastonbury

3

A361

2 **SOMERSET** A37
28-33

A303

Taunton M5

5

Shaftesbury

A303

Yeovil

2
A30 **3**

7 **9**

A350

A354

A361

A396

3 Tiverton

Honiton

A30

A35

A37

Blandford Forum

12
11 **10**
A31

A348

A338

DORSET
24-27

Exeter

Lyme Regis

1

A35

Dorchester

A35

Poole

Bournemouth

13

Exmouth

4

A36

A380

Weymouth

8
Swanage

5

6

Torquay

A385

5

tmouth

6

6 Alderney

Guernsey   Herm

5 St Peter Port

Sark

7

CHANNEL ISLANDS
34-35

Jersey

2 **4** **3**

1 St Helier

CORNWALL

Long before the Dukes of Cornwall held court here, this was the realm of the legendary King Arthur. Henry VIII built defensive castles, while in more peaceable times Queen Victoria's children paddled in the sea.

❶ King Ricatus's Cross

Visitors to the art gallery in the Victorian Penlee House will find something more ancient and enigmatic in the grounds – a 10th-century stone cross inscribed with the words *regis ricati crux* (The cross of King Ricatus). The cross is now rough and weathered, but drawings made of it in 1929 reveal two carved figures, knotwork panels and vestiges of further inscriptions. It is said that the last true Celtic king of Cornwall was Doniert (see page 20), but the 'crown' may belong to Ricatus. Nothing is known of him, but here is evidence that he lived and ruled – although whether as a king or a chieftain no one can say.
▶ *TR18 4HE. On A30, 8 miles E of Land's End.*

❷ St Michael's Mount

This tiny islet, little more than a mile around and crowned by a medieval church and castle, has lived through history on an epic scale. To the Benedictine monks of Mont Saint Michel who came here after the Norman conquest, it was perfect for the contemplative life, but it was also a perfect natural fortress. In 1193, it was taken for the future King John by Henry La Pomeray, whose men came ashore disguised as pilgrims. In the Wars of the Roses, in 1473, the Earl of Oxford held the island for six months against Edward IV's troops. In the Civil War, the islanders fought off the Parliamentarians from 1642 and on the surrender of the Mount in 1647, Colonel John St Aubyn was appointed its governor. The St Aubyns have lived in the castle ever since, although they were not at home when Victoria and Albert paid an impromptu visit in 1846. The island was better prepared in January 2011 when the Prince of Wales and the Duchess of Cornwall came by. Casts were made of their shoes, to join those of Queen Victoria (a dainty size 3), and of Edward VII, who was here in 1902.

Visitors can cross by boat, or on foot at low tide, then climb rocky paths to the church and castle and look down on sub-tropical terraced gardens. Cream teas are served in the café.
▶ *TR17 0HT. S of A394, 4 miles E of Penzance. Reached on foot via causeway at low tide or ferry (not winter) at high tide. NT.*

❸ Loe Pool

Is this where the young King Arthur received his sword Excalibur from the hand of the Lady of the Lake? The 'loe' (or loch) is separated from the sea by the bank of Loe Bar. As with everything about King Arthur, the identity of the lake is a matter of conjecture, but Alfred, Lord Tennyson seems to have had Loe Pool in mind in his *Idylls of the King*, with his references to 'waste sand', 'waste sea' and a 'death white mist over sand and sea'. Then there is this: 'He, stepping down/By zigzag paths, and juts of pointed rock,/Came on the shining levels of the lake./There drew he forth the brand Excalibur …' The surrounding Penrose estate with its zigzag paths teems with wildlife.

The National Trust describes Loe Pool as 'one of Cornwall's glorious surprises'. Its main rival for the location of the lake is Dozmary Pool on Bodmin Moor (see page 20).
▶ *1½ miles S of Porthleven. Paths from car park on B3304 on NE edge of Porthleven or from car park near Porthleven Sands. NT.*

ST MICHAEL'S MOUNT

❹ Godolphin

The family home of the Godolphins once gave shelter to a fleeing prince. Sir William Godolphin was a soldier under Henry VIII. His grandson Sidney was Queen Anne's Lord Treasurer from 1702 to 1710, when she dismissed him – although upon his death in 1712 she wept, blaming their estrangement on his association with the Duke of Marlborough. The queen's friendship with the duke's wife had ended after the duchess arrived at court with a bawdy poem, hinting at an improper relationship between Anne and a woman of the bedchamber, Abigail Hill. No matter for the Goldolphins, who continued to prosper, as Sidney's son married Marlborough's daughter, and Sidney was made an earl. The house's main claim to royal fame, however, is the King's Room, where the future Charles II is said to have rested on his flight to France, after his father's defeat at Naseby. This fascinating Tudor and Stuart granite mansion with Elizabethan stables is romantically set deep in ancient woodland, surrounded by formal gardens little changed since the 16th century.
▶ *TR13 9RE. 5 miles NW of Helston on minor roads, off B3302. NT.*

❺ Kynance Cove

'Break, break, break,/At the foot of thy crags, O Sea!' The landscape of the Lizard Peninsula, the most southerly point on mainland Britain, and particularly this rugged cove, held great appeal for wealthy Victorians, among them the poet Alfred, Lord Tennyson. Prince Albert brought his children here in 1846, and one of the giant rock stacks is named 'The Albert Rock'. The family party would not have seen Tennyson's 'cold grey stones' or repined for 'the touch of a vanished hand', but, visiting in summer, would have scrambled over sun-warmed outcroppings and paddled in a turquoise sea.
▶ *Paths from car park at end of minor road off A3083, 1 mile N of Lizard. NT.*

❻ Pendennis Castle

In the autumn of his reign, having defiantly split with Rome, Henry VIII feared invasion by forces from Catholic Europe, so he set about creating Fortress Britain. The king commissioned more than 20 strongholds to defend ports and estuaries along the south coast, known as the 'Henrician' or 'device' castles. Pendennis Castle and its 'sister', St Mawes, were built in 1540–45 on either side of the River Fal estuary. This simple but stout keep within a curtain wall was approached by dry moat and portcullis. In the reign of Elizabeth I, in 1598, an outer wall was added after Spanish raids on Cornwall, amid fears of a second Armada.

The Spanish never came but the future Charles II did, taking refuge here on his flight to safety. In 1646 the castle was besieged from both land and sea. For five months Sir John Arundel held out against Oliver Cromwell's Parliamentarian troops. 'I resolve that I will bury myself before I deliver up this Castle to those who fight against his Majesty,' declared the 70-year-old Sir John. He very nearly had to, and was reduced to eating horse and dog before near starvation forced him to surrender. Only Raglan Castle held out for longer – by two days.

▶ *TR11 4LP. Pendennis Head, 1 mile SE of Falmouth. EH.*

❼ St Mawes Castle

Another link in Henry VIII's defensive chain, Pendennis's prettier, more fragile sister occupies a hillside plateau on the eastern shore of the Fal estuary. It is a superb example of Tudor military architecture, elaborately decorated with gargoyles and window details, and with the royal coat of arms carved into the stonework above the door. A hexagonal guardhouse and stone bridge on the landward side gave access to a central tower with wooden carvings of the Tudor rose, cherub, monk and fleur-de-lys. Inscriptions in Latin extolled Henry and his son Edward, swearing allegiance to the crown. Around the central tower were added three circular bastions, so that, from a seagull's eye view, it resembled a trefoil.

The cannons remained trained upon the water and on the Spaniards who failed to show, but it was from land that the invasion finally came during the English Civil War. While Sir John Arundel, at Pendennis across the water, held the Parliamentarians at bay, the Royalist commander of St Mawes – lacking Sir John's mettle, his patriotism, his hilltop vantage and his fatalistic sense that 'my age of 70 calls me hence shortly' – surrendered without a shot being fired.

▶ *TR2 5DA. At end of A3078, 10 miles S of Truro. EH.*

⑧ St Austell, the Eden Project

On a visit to Cornwall, Henry VIII described St Austell as a small village surrounding a central church. John Leland, the poet and 'father of English local history', found much the same thing, noting in his *Itineraries* of 1538–43 that 'at S Austelles is nothing notable but the paroch chirch'. Things looked up when Elizabeth I granted a charter for a weekly market, and opened the copper mines in 1580. The Duke and Duchess of Cornwall – later George V and Queen Mary – visited the china clay works in June 1909. The Queen and the Duke of Edinburgh arrived by train in 2006 on the way to the Eden Project – and here is St Austell's claim to royal fame, a global garden on the site of a disused clay quarry. Prince Charles visited this other Eden in 2001 to lend support, returning in 2011 to mark the 10th anniversary with a personal video message for a 'daring and fascinating idea' that has 'grown into one of Britain's biggest assets'.

▶ *St Austell at junction of A390 and A391. Eden Project, PL24 2SG, 2½ miles NE of St Austell, off A390.*

⑨ Fowey and Place House

Sir Francis Drake and Sir Walter Raleigh both set sail from Fowey's deep harbour. Its annual Royal Regatta was attended on occasion by Queen Victoria and Prince Albert, and has also been graced by the present queen. In 1846, Victoria and Albert visited Place House at the top of the town. Visitors today approach it by the same steep, winding streets.

Seat of the Treffry family since the 13th century, the house was rebuilt and fortified in the early 1500s, after fighting off the French in 1475. The 16th-century poet and chronicler John Leland recorded how 'the wyfe of Thomas Treury the 2, with her men, repellid the French out of her house in her housebandes absence' whereupon Thomas 'buildid a right fair and stronge embatlid towr'. This tower would have been what Victoria first saw of Place House, dominating the harbour. As Leland further said, the manner of its rebuilding 'made it a castelle: and onto this day it is the glorie of the town building in Faweye'.

▶ *5 miles E of St Austell on A3082.*

PLACE HOUSE – 'THE GLORIE OF THE TOWN'
FOWEY HARBOUR

RESTORMEL CASTLE

⑩ Restormel Castle

In springtime the banks around the ruins of this 13th-century shell-keep are a sea of daffodils, just as they would have been when Edward, the Black Prince, held court here in 1354. However, 'that young Mars of Men' was probably too preoccupied with plans to lay siege to Aquitaine to give his mind to wild flowers. Edmund, Earl of Cornwall, built the castle in the late 1200s, on a spur beside the Fowey. After the Black Prince's sojourn, it had been abandoned and was in disrepair when the Parliamentarians took it over during the Civil War. It was recaptured by Royalists in August 1644.

Perfectly circular, it resembles nothing so much as a crown, a surprisingly well-preserved shell. When Victoria and Albert came to Fowey, they went to the castle, and visited nearby iron mines, even going below ground to meet the queen's subjects, whom Victoria judged 'intelligent, good people'. She and Albert got into a truck and were dragged into the tunnel by miners wearing 'curious woollen dress'.

▶ *PL22 0EE. On A390, 13 miles SW of Liskeard and 6 miles NW of St Austell. Castle N of Lostwithiel town centre. EH.*

⑪ Slaughterbridge

In a leafy roadside streambed lies a 6th-century stone, said to mark the spot where King Arthur met his nemesis. It was here, some believe, that he was mortally wounded by the poisoned blade of his dying nephew, the usurper Mordred, at the Battle of Camlann in AD 537. Popularly known as 'King Arthur's Stone', it was first recorded in 1602 by the antiquary Richard Carew, a thousand years after it was inscribed in Latin and rare Ogam Celtic script with the legend 'Latinus son of Macarus lies here'. 'The olde folke thereabouts,' wrote Carew, 'will shew you a stone, bearing Arthur's name.'

In 1848, Alfred, Lord Tennyson stood at the spot and was inspired to tell the tale in his *Idylls of the King*: 'Then Mordred smote his liege/ Hard on the helm which many a heathen sword/ Had beaten thin; while Arthur at one blow,/ Striking the last stroke with Excalibur,/ Slew him, and all but slain himself, he fell.' Stirring stuff!

The stone is more than 2.75m (9ft) long, and the Latin inscription has been interpreted in many different ways over time. Nearby is the Arthurian Centre with exhibitions, gift shop and tea rooms.

▶ *Stone just N of B3314 at Slaughterbridge, 1 mile N of Camelford. The Arthurian Centre, PL32 9TT.*

⑫ Tintagel Castle

Romantic ruins sit high on Cornwall's rugged north coast, guarding their mystery. The remains of a Celtic fortress built by Richard, Earl of Cornwall, they date from the 13th century, but the story of Tintagel goes back much further, to the 5th or 6th century and the birth of the Celtic prince Arthur of Camelot. We owe to Geoffrey of Monmouth's *History of the Kings of Britain* much of what we know – or think we know – of the fabled king. He tells us that Arthur was born here, the son of Uther Pendragon and Igraine, wife of Duke Gorlois of Cornwall. Uther had been transformed by the magician Merlin to resemble Gorlois to the life. Below the castle is 'Merlin's Cave'. Geoffrey of Monmouth was writing in the 12th century in a period of anarchy and civil war. Perhaps he was trying to create a hero and role model for the British people. But recent excavations have revealed a monastic site, far earlier than the fortress, on a promontory behind the castle – a possible stronghold of a Celtic king, lending substance to Arthurian legend. One truth can be firmly stated: this is a magical place.

▶ *PL34 0HE. Signed off B3263 between Boscastle and St Teath. EH.*

⑬ St Mawgan in Pydar Church

'We are so highly sensible of ye extraordinary Merits of our County of Cornwall of their zeal for ye Defence of our Person & ye Just Right of our Crown ...' So began a letter written by Charles I to his Cornish subjects from his camp at Sudeley Castle in the Cotswolds, dated September 10, 1643. Most of Cornwall was behind the monarch in his struggle with the Parliamentarians, and many communities displayed the Stuart coat of arms until the defeat of the Royalists, when discretion proved the better part of valour. More remarkable were copies of the king's thank-you message, displayed in many churches and destroyed on Cromwell's victory. At the Restoration, more copies were made, some paper, some painted, and a number can be seen today. There is one on the north wall of this historic church, in an English village so picture-perfect that it was chosen by the BBC as the location for their Miss Marple television series. The large, low-built church is impressive, offering much of interest to visitors. In its tower, dating from the 13th and 15th centuries, hangs a priceless medieval bell. In the churchyard, a boat-shaped memorial recalls the names of local sailors who died at sea in tragic circumstances.

▶ *TR8 4ER. 6 miles NE of Newquay, off B3276.*

⑭ Dozmary Pool

Does King Arthur's sword Excalibur lie at the bottom of these silvery waters, returned there by Sir Bedivere as his liege lay dying? Was Dozmary ('drop of the sea'), high on Bodmin Moor, home to the Lady of the Lake? It is one of several contenders, including Loe Pool (see page 14). This is a wild, mystical and wonderful place to visit, whatever lies beneath the water's surface.
▶ *Beside minor road, 2 miles S of Bolventor, on A30 running across Bodmin Moor.*

⑮ King Doniert's Stone

On the southeastern side of Bodmin Moor, in a roadside enclosure, stand what remains of two early medieval granite crosses. 'Doniert's Stone' is the decorative pedestal of a memorial cross, extravagantly carved on three sides with an interlaced pattern, while the fourth side bears an inscription, *Doniert rogavit pro anima* (Doniert begs [that this be made] for the sake of his soul). Beneath this and its companion, 'The Other Half Stone', excavations have uncovered a rock-cut passage, although how it relates to the crosses has not been explained. The *Annales Camriae* refer to a King 'Dungarth' or 'Dwingarth', the last documented king of Cornwall, who drowned in around AD 875 and from whom has passed down a quotation, melancholy and haunting: 'Sorrow comes from a world upturned.'
▶ *1 mile NW of St Cleer, off B3254, 3 miles N of Liskeard. Layby parking. EH.*

⑯ Launceston Castle

At this rugged castle, Prince Charles's investiture as Duke of Cornwall took place in 1973. Launceston wears its castle jauntily. A high drum tower and curtain wall make it seem less like a crown than a ten-gallon hat, belying its use for years as an assize court, prison and place of execution. It was built by Robert of Mortain, half-brother of William I, in the motte-and-bailey style. Stone replaced timber in the 12th century. When Edward III created the Duchy of Cornwall in 1337, Edward, the Black Prince, became duke and ordered repairs. During the Civil War, the town was loyal to Charles I. His son, the future Charles II, stayed here on his way to join Royalist troops. Parliamentarians captured the town in 1643 but could not rout the Royalists, who forced Cromwell's army back across the Tamar.

As Dukes of Cornwall, both George V and the Duke of Windsor visited, in 1909 and 1921. George VI made a state entrance in 1937, when

he was presented with his feudal dues – set out by Richard, Earl of Cornwall in a charter of 1230 – and including 100 shillings and a pound of pepper.
▶ *PL15 7DR. On A30 18 miles SW of Okehampton, 22 miles NE of Bodmin. EH.*

⑰ Mount Edgcumbe House and Country Park

'There were crowds where we landed, and I feel so shy and put out without Albert,' wrote Queen Victoria in her journal when she came here on a yachting tour one hot and hazy August day in 1846. She was met by Lady Mount Edgcumbe, her ladyship's two sons and her sisters and nieces. 'I got into a carriage with the children and Lady Mount Edgcumbe …' she recorded. 'We had a lovely drive along the road which overhangs the bay, commanding such beautiful views on all sides.' The unexpectedly shy Victoria was not the first royal visitor. Queen Adelaide, wife of William IV, was here in 1827. Queen Adelaide's Grotto, an 18th-century cave used as a watch house and enhanced with a stone arch, marks the occasion.

The house, dating from the mid-16th century, was gutted by a German bomb in 1943. Its 18th century interiors have been restored to showcase period furniture, porcelain, paintings and

tapestries. The Earl's Garden, laid out in the 1700s, contains some rare trees and a classical garden house, and the views over Plymouth Sound are breathtaking. A special garden was created in 2002 to commemorate the Queen's golden jubilee.
▶ *PL10 1HZ. 10 miles from Torpoint at end of B3247.*

⑱ Antony

A portrait of a sad-eyed Charles I at his trial hangs in the hall of this beautiful 18th-century mansion. His look is a reproach, the visitor might feel, to the descendants of John Carew, who was among those to sign the king's death warrant in 1649. The estate has been in the Carew family for 600 years. This house was built by Sir William Carew in 1711–21 between the estuaries of the Tamar and the Lynher, lapped by the sea at its southern edge. It remained in the Carew Pole family until 1961, when it was given to the National Trust. In 2008, film director Tim Burton was looking for 'a perfect pocket-sized mansion ... beautifully symmetrical, with intimate interiors, wide views and landscaped gardens', in which to film *Alice in Wonderland*. He found Antony and looked no further. As for John Carew, who had cried, in so many words, 'Off with his head!', after the Restoration he was tried for regicide, sentenced to death, and hanged, drawn and quartered on October 15, 1660.
▶ *PL11 2QA. 2 miles W of Torpoint on A374. NT.*

⑲ Trematon Castle

When Sir Francis Drake docked in Plymouth in 1580, after circumnavigating the globe, he stashed gold, silver and emeralds here, until the treasures could be moved to the Tower of London. Three centuries later, Queen Victoria, sailing by, noted in her journal, 'Trematon Castle to the right, which belongs to Bertie as Duke of Cornwall ... [is] extremely pretty'. The present Queen visited the ruins in July 1962. Trematon – thought to have been founded by Robert, Count of Mortain, half-brother of William I – is owned by Prince Charles and is not open to the public. The public, though, may see it, as military historian Sir Charles Oman tells us, 'high aloft, on one of the summits of the rather chaotic group of hill-tops which lie behind Saltash and its daring modern bridge'. Extensive parts of the Norman walls remain, so that the original form – the oval keep, the rectangular gatehouse – can be discerned.
▶ *1 mile S of Saltash town centre, off A38.*

DEVON

Richard I went crusading from Dartmouth and ever since, Devon's sheltered harbours have attracted royal attention, not least from William of Orange, who landed at Brixham to kickstart a revolution.

❶ Hartland Abbey

The last monastery in the county to fall to Henry VIII's Dissolution nestles in a wooded valley a mile from north Devon's rugged coast. The king presented Hartland to the aptly named William Abbot, his Sergeant of the Wine Cellar at Hampton Court, whose descendants, the Stucleys, live here today.

The Augustinian monastery was built in 1157 and consecrated in 1160. During the 18th and 19th centuries it was given the *House and Garden* treatment by Sir George Gilbert Scott and John Meadows – the visitor will see medieval, Queen Anne, Georgian, Regency and Victorian interiors, including Gothic revival. The Emperor Haile Selassie visited in 1938 while in exile from Ethiopia after Mussolini's invasion. The chair on which he sat is displayed in St Nectan's church in Stoke by Hartland, a place of pilgrimage for Rastafarians. Peacocks and guinea fowl roam the abbey grounds, donkeys and sheep graze the Old Deer Park. There was a rumour that this may have been where Prince William held his pre-wedding party in April 2011. 'Our mouths are zipped,' said Hartland's chatelaine, Lady Angela Stucley, when questioned by the press.
▶ *EX39 6DT. On minor road off B3248, 2 miles W of Hartland, 20 miles W of Bideford.*

❷ Chambercombe Manor

Lady Jane Grey, the ill-fated 'nine-day queen', once stayed at this ancient manor. It was owned from around 1162 by the Champernon family, and became the property of Jane's parents, Henry, Duke of Suffolk and Lady Frances Brandon, the daughter of Henry VIII's younger sister Mary. It is charming rather than grand, with a Tudor frieze and barrel ceiling, and furniture from Elizabethan to Victorian times.

Although no shade of Jane remains, in the 18th century the owner discovered a hidden chamber adjoining the room in which she slept, and the skeleton of a woman lying on a bed. Her ghost is believed to be one of a number of non-paying guests to reside here indefinitely. Any visitor chilled by a paranormal close encounter can find comfort in a cream tea at Ye Old Manor Buttery.
▶ *EX34 9RJ. 1 mile SE of Ilfracombe town centre, off A399.*

❸ Tiverton Castle

Katherine Plantagenet was something of a bartered bride. The youngest legitimate daughter of Edward IV, she was promised by her father to Juan of Aragon, and by her brother-in-law, Henry VII, to James Stewart, second son of James III of Scotland. With her father's death from riotous living, and that of James III at the Battle of Sachieburn, those best-laid plans went awry. Instead, in 1495, she married William Courtenay, praised by Tudor historian Polydore Vergil for his bravery and manly bearing. He became Earl of Devon, and she became mistress of the castle. Local tradition recalls her as a 'quiet, proud, gentle lady' who used to walk about town with her daughter, Margaret.

Originally built in 1106 by Richard de Redvers, on the orders of Henry I, the castle was rebuilt and enlarged in the 13th and 14th centuries. In the Civil War, it was taken by the Parliamentarians when a shot hit a chain and brought down the drawbridge. It was slighted to prevent further military use, and fell into neglect. Yet it stands in considerable and dignified ruins on a hilltop, partly obscured by modern buildings, beside a splendid Perpendicular church. At its 16th-century heart it is a private home, in which may be seen – and even tried on – Civil War arms and armour, as well as antique furniture and paintings. A tour guide tells of secret passages and friendly ghosts, and there is a battlemented walk along what survives of the curtain wall.
▶ *EX16 6RP. Tiverton lies at junction of A361 and A396, 8 miles W of Junction 27 of M5. Castle in town centre.*

❹ The King's Way

Dartmoor, once a royal hunting ground, is traversed by the King's Way. This is the Tavistock–Okehampton section of the London–Plymouth coaching route, used to deliver the king's mail (believed to be Charles I). The route is marked by wayside crosses, of which a previously unrecorded example was found in September 2011, set into a 'corn ditch wall'. These barriers were designed to keep the king's deer off cultivated land.
▶ *Runs E of A386 between Tavistock and Okehampton.*

❺ Torbay

Here the Protestant William of Orange came ashore in 1688 to march on London and seize the crown from his father-in-law, Catholic James II. The 'Glorious Revolution' – or the 'Bloodless Revolution' – resulted in William and his wife Mary ascending the throne as William III and Mary II, the only royal couple to have reigned over Britain as joint monarchs.

Queen Victoria sailed to this part of the English Riviera in August 1849, and again in 1852. The red rocks and wooded hills gave her an idea of an imagined Italy (since she had never been) 'or rather of a ballet or play where nymphs are to appear – such rocks and grottos, with the deepest sea, on which there was not a ripple'. She would have gone ashore had it not started to rain, so instead she encouraged her daughter Vicky to read aloud the story of England's past – perhaps to learn that Brixham in Torbay was where William landed and changed the course of English history.

▶ *Torbay is fringed by towns of Torquay, Paignton and Brixham at junction of A380 and A385.*

❻ Dartmouth

'Notwithstanding the rain, this place is lovely, with its wooded rocks and church, and castle at the entrance,' wrote Queen Victoria in her journal. 'It puts me much in mind of the beautiful Rhine, and its fine ruined castles and its Lurlei.' Bad weather having forced them to dock, the royal family and their entourage had come ashore and were charmed, as the visitor is today by this ancient picture-postcard town and deep-water port. It stands on the River Dart, and indeed has much in common with the landscape of the Rhine, where the Lorelei sat upon her rock and lured sailors to their deaths.

Victoria donated £25 and Albert £20 for three rowing races, the prizes to be competed for by the sailors of Dartmouth, and the queen bestowed upon the town's regatta the title 'Royal'. In 1147, 164 ships left from here on the Second Crusade, and in 1190, Richard I set sail for the Third Crusade with 37 ships.

▶ *At junction of A379 and A3122, 12 miles SE of Totnes.*

'SUCH ROCKS AND GROTTOS'
TORBAY

DORSET

A solid castle, a safe house, a holiday home, a love nest and an eco-village – following murder and intrigue at Corfe, succeeding rulers have found Dorset more than ready to accommodate them.

❶ Lyme Regis

'I remember, how boldly abundance of men talked for the Duke of Monmouth when he first landed. If half of them had as boldly joined him sword in hand, he had never been routed.' So wrote Daniel Defoe about Monmouth's failed rebellion (see page 29). That hapless duke, illegitimate son of Charles II, came ashore here in 1685, bent on taking the crown. The 'rout' at Sedgemoor by the army of the arrogant James II led to the arrest of 99 local men and the execution of 12 of them on the beach.

Although Lyme gloried in its regal name, granted by Edward I in 1284, this was not its first clash with monarchy. 'That heretic town', as Mary Tudor called it, was strongly Parliamentarian in the Civil War. In 1644, it held out against Prince Maurice, nephew of Charles I, inflicting great losses, until he withdrew, with a sour-grapes dismissal of 'this little vile fishing town defended by a small dry ditch'. The 'vile fishing town' is, in fact, a characterful resort and a magnet for fossil hunters on the dramatic Jurassic Coast. Its Cobb harbour wall is instantly recognisable.
▶ *On A3052 16 miles SE of Honiton.*

❷ St Andrew's Church, Trent

The bells, the bells! There was no sleeping for a royal guest at Trent Manor. After the Battle of Worcester in September 1651, the fugitive Prince of Wales, the future Charles II, stayed in a series of safe houses as he made his way to the coast *en route* to France. In Trent, he was offered sanctuary by Colonel Francis Wyndham, a Royalist officer, and remained for 16 days in Lady Wyndham's room, which offered a hiding place under the roof in case of a raid. At one point the incessant clangor of the church bells drove him to distraction. Grave insult was added to this injury when he learned that the jubilant pealing was a response to the rumour that he had been found and killed. When he was restored to the throne in 1660, he remembered Wyndham's loyalty and kindness with a gift of £1,000 'for the buying of a jewel for his great and eminent service'. The colonel and his wife are buried in the neat and pretty churchyard.
▶ *DT9 4SL. On minor roads between A30 and A359, 4 miles NE of Yeovil.*

❸ Sherborne Castle

'Shirburne castle, park, manor etc, did belong (and still ought to belong) to the Church of Sarum. Sir WR begged it as a Bon from Queen Elizabeth.' John Aubrey, Sir Walter Raleigh's biographer, was writing of the day when, on a trip to Plymouth, Raleigh saw Sherborne Castle and, falling in love with it, begged it as a gift from Elizabeth I. He did not then live in the 12th-century castle, but built himself on the estate what Aubrey describes as 'a delicate Lodge in the Park of Brick; not big: but very convenient … A place to retire from the Court in Summer time, and to contemplate, etc.'

While Raleigh was imprisoned in the Tower, charged with treason, James I leased Sherborne to Robert Carr. It was sold to Sir John Digby, 1st Earl of Bristol, in 1617. In the Civil War, the Digbys were Royalist. The old castle was twice under siege, and in 1645, Parliamentary forces demolished it. Now it stands a ruin in the grounds of the 'New Castle', Raleigh's lodge. Prince William of Orange was entertained here; so was George III in 1789.

Through all his travels, Raleigh had an abiding love for the place, writing to his family, in his Bible, on the eve of his execution in 1618, 'Beg my dead body, which living is denied you; and bury it either in Sherbourne or Exeter Church.' His final resting place is St Margaret's, Westminster.
▶ *DT9 5NR. On A30 5 miles E of Yeovil. Castle E of Sherborne town centre.*

❹ Poundbury

His Modernist critics poured scorn upon it, but Prince Charles's model village, polemic in stone, is loved by its residents. An extension of Dorchester, this eco-village, begun in the 1990s, was mocked for its Toy Town aesthetic. It is built on land owned by the Duchy of Cornwall, to accord with The Prince's vision for a scheme that would demonstrate how traditional architecture and modern town planning could combine to create a thriving community, with people living and working in close proximity. It is scheduled for completion in 2025, and, despite some murmurs of discontent, most of the inhabitants are very happy to have moved here.
▶ *W of Dorchester town centre, off A35.*

WEYMOUTH

The *grateful* Inhabitants
To GEORGE THE THIRD
On His entering the 50th Year
Of His REIGN.

❺ Weymouth

'Think but of the surprise of His Majesty when, the first time of his bathing, he had no sooner popped his royal head under water … than a band of music struck up God save great George our King.' This was the diarist and novelist Fanny Burney on George III's visit to Weymouth in 1789, a year after his first bout of madness. Burney was at the time Second Keeper of the Robes to Queen Charlotte. George suffered from porphyria, the symptoms of which can include hallucinations and paranoia. His doctor recommended salt water and sea air, hence his trip to the coast, where he took a dip, using one of the new-fangled bathing machines. The king enjoyed the town and bought Gloucester Lodge for a holiday home. His patronage gave Weymouth a great boost. The Georgian seafront buildings date mostly from his reign, and he is celebrated by a fine statue.

▶ *8 miles S of Dorchester on A354.*

❻ Portland Castle

Standing sentinel over Portland Harbour is one of Henry VIII's finest coastal defences. Henry had reason to fear the wrath of Europe after divorcing Catherine of Aragon and creating a schism with Rome. But like so many of the forts Henry built along the coast from Kent to Cornwall, Portland stood largely unmolested until the Civil War, when it was occupied by Parliamentarians, then by Royalists, and served as a jail for the enemies of Oliver Cromwell. It is built of the highest quality Portland limestone, known as ashlar, and has stood up magnificently to the ravages of time. Visitors can explore the Great Hall, the kitchen, the gun room and heritage garden.

▶ *DT5 1AZ. 5 miles S of Weymouth, off A354. EH.*

❼ Shaftesbury

This historic hilltop town was founded by King Alfred in AD 880, and is a testament to his true greatness. Shaftesbury is one of four Dorset towns documented in the 'Burghal Hidage', a list of Wessex's fortified 'burhs', which were designed for the defence of the kingdom against the ruthless Vikings. There were 33 in all, forming a cohesive system, ensuring that nobody in Alfred's kingdom was ever more than 20 miles from a place of refuge.

Alfred was a scholar and a man of vision, who not only introduced this centralised initiative, but established the navy and reorganised the army. His dynamic approach to defence assured most burhs of military, economic and social success. Most, like Shaftesbury, thrived, and are still thriving. Thomas Hardy called this 'the city of dreams' and 'one of the queerest and quaintest spots in England … breezy and whimsical'.

▶ *20 miles W of Salisbury at junction of A30 and A350.*

❽ Corfe Castle

The downfall of this once mighty castle in the Civil War was an inside job. The castle was owned by the Bankes family, supporters of Charles I, who fought off the Parliamentarians twice – with her husband, Sir John, absent, 'Brave Dame Mary' Bankes was left literally to hold the fort. But despite Dame Mary's courage, the castle fell victim to a turncoat, who let in the besieging army, and the Parliamentarians proceeded to blow up the towers and ramparts, leaving the beautifully ragged remains we see today.

The stone keep was built for Henry I in the 12th century, and its commanding position and gleaming towers could not have failed to impress. An earlier castle on this same hilltop was the scene in AD 978 of the murder of the Saxon King Edward (the Martyr), probably by his stepmother, Elfrida, after a reign of less than three years. 'The boy king' was declared a martyr and buried in Shaftesbury Abbey. Edward II was held prisoner here. King John used the castle to imprison those who crossed him, including his niece and two Scottish princesses, who were consigned to the dungeon, from which there was no escape.

The historic high status of Corfe Castle has only recently been more fully understood. In 2006, an 'appearance door' designed for Henry I was discovered, where he would have stood before his subjects.

▶ *BH20 5EZ. 4 miles S of Wareham on A351 Swanage road. NT.*

❾ Shaftesbury Abbey

A Benedictine abbey on this site collapsed under the weight of history. It was largely destroyed by Henry VIII's vandals, ending a long, sometimes unhappy association with royalty. These began with its founding in AD 888 by King Alfred as the first abbey solely for women. His daughter Aethelgifu was its abbess. When Alfred's great-great grandson, King Edward (later known as St Edward the Martyr), was murdered at Corfe Castle in AD 978, his body was first buried in Wareham but two years later reinterred here, and the abbey became a place of pilgrimage.

In 1035, the abbey received the heart of the Danish King Cnut (Canute). Within its walls were imprisoned Elizabeth de Burgh, wife of Robert the Bruce, and Marjorie, his daughter, as Scotland's warrior king battled the forces of Edward I. With the Dissolution in the 16th century the abbey was demolished. In 1931, a lead casket of bones was unearthed among the ruins, assumed to be the remains of Edward the Martyr.

The visitor today will find what Thomas Hardy called 'vague imaginings' of its former glory. A museum, dramatically decorated in medieval colours, houses a collection of carved stonework, statuary and illustrations from ancient manuscripts. In the gardens are plants that would have been used by the nuns for dyes, as well as medicinal and culinary herbs, including Aethelgifu's Herb Collection.

▶ *SP7 8JR. Shaftesbury town centre.*

⑩ Wimborne Minster Church

King Alfred's brother, Aethelred I, killed in battle by Danish Vikings, was buried on this site, where a Benedictine nunnery had been founded in AD 705. It was dedicated to St Cuthburga, sister to Ina, King of the West Saxons, and destroyed by the Danes in 1013. The imposing twinned towered church is largely Norman. In 1318, Edward II declared this a 'Royal Peculiar', which meant that it belonged to the monarch, not the diocese, and so it remained until 1846. Some centuries earlier, in 1496, Lady Margaret Beaufort, the mother of Henry VII, founded a small chapel here, to which a priest was attached and charged with teaching grammar to all comers.

Visitors can see Aethelred's brass memorial plaque next to the altar and the Chained Library, where rare books from the 15th and 16th centuries are displayed.
▶ *BH21 1HT. 10 miles NW of Bournemouth.*

⑪ Kingston Lacy

For centuries, rumours circulated that a palace of the kings of Wessex had once stood here, yet no trace of it could be found. After his father Sir John Bankes was routed from Corfe Castle in the Civil War, Sir Ralph Bankes built a mansion on this estate and found no evidence of that fabled 'fair maner place'. It was not until a storm in 1990 uprooted trees that the land gave up its secrets and the remains of a medieval manor were discovered. Once part of a Saxon royal estate, this had been the home of one of the most significant figures in medieval England, John of Gaunt, 2nd Duke of Lancaster, third surviving son of Edward III. The house was built in the 13th century – and by the 15th had been all but obliterated. Account rolls at Dorset Record Office show that Kingston Lacy played host to John of Gaunt's son and grandson, Henry IV and Henry V. The 'fair maner place' begun by Sir Ralph in 1663 was remodelled in the 1830s by Sir Charles Barry. It contains a fine collection of paintings and antiquities amassed by William Bankes at that time. The visitor blinks upon stepping into the Spanish Room, its walls hung with gilded leather. The house and dramatic formal gardens are set in wooded parkland.
▶ *BH21 4EA. 2 miles NW of Wimborne Minster, S of B3082. NT.*

⑫ Badbury Rings

Another layer of history uncovered on the Kingston Lacy estate comes in the form of the Iron Age earthworks known as the Badbury Rings. These are the remains of a hillfort, constructed on a site that had been occupied in the Bronze Age. It is said that this is Mount Badon, scene of a great 6th-century battle in which King Arthur trounced the Saxons.
▶ *4 miles NW of Wimborne Minster, N of B3082. NT.*

⑬ The Red House

The Langtry Manor Hotel on Bournemouth's East Cliff, formerly the Red House, was once the love nest of a prince and his 'Jersey Lily'. Albert Edward, the future Edward VII, made no secret of his affair with Lily Langtry, parading her at Goodwood, Ascot, Henley and Cowes. But the couple also valued their seclusion, and she threw herself into designing this quiet retreat for the two of them. Her initials 'ELL' (Emilie Le Breton Langtry) were inscribed on the foundation stone and carved into the inglenook. The mottos *Dulce domum* (Sweet home) and *Stet Fortuna Domus* (Good fortune to those who dwell here) still adorn the walls of the house, now an Edwardian-themed boutique hotel, and beneath the minstrels gallery is the defiant statement: 'They say What say they? Let them say.' A stained-glass window commemorates the birth to Lily of a daughter, Jeanne Marie, in Paris in 1881 under the care of the prince's private physician. Rumour had it that the father was, in fact, Prince Louis of Battenberg, with whom she also had an affair. They say What say they? Let them say!
▶ *BH1 3QB. Bournemouth at junction of A35 and A338. Hotel E of town centre.*

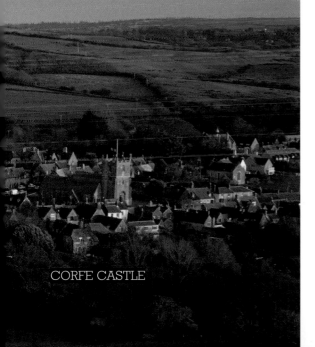

CORFE CASTLE

SOMERSET

Alfred burnt the cakes, Arthur breathed his last and the Monmouth rebellion came to a sticky end – but all was well by the time of the Regency when the children of George III took Bath to their hearts.

❶ Dunster Castle

The words 'God save the King!' inscribed on a warming pan recall the time when the future Charles II slept here. The castle had not always been a royalist bastion. In 1376, Dunster was sold to Lady Elizabeth Luttrell, a granddaughter of Edward I. For the next 600 years it passed in and out of Luttrell hands, as the whirligig of history spun the family around. Support for the Lancastrians in the Wars of the Roses resulted in their estate being confiscated, but it was restored to them by Henry VII. In the Civil War, the castle passed back and forth between Parliamentarians and Royalists before it was slighted, its defences destroyed, on the orders of Oliver Cromwell. The castle was spared as a dwelling. What had been built up over centuries was undone in just 12 days in August 1650 by 300 workmen.

In 1868, the castle was remodelled to reflect its medieval origins. The pragmatic Luttrells had survived great adversity. Their family motto – 'Gained by strength, held by skill' – says it all. The castle, Gothic and picturesque on its wooded hilltop, commanding panoramic views, is now a lavish country house, surrounded by 6ha (15 acres) of gardens. These include the national collection of strawberry trees. The medieval gatehouse and a ruined tower remain as reminders of its colourful past.

▶ *TA24 6SL. Dunster 2 miles E of Minehead at junction of A39 and A396. Castle in town centre. NT.*

❷ Isle of Athelney

A hilltop monument marks the site of a monastery built by King Alfred to give thanks for victory. For 20 years the Vikings had raided Britain, sacking, seizing, plundering – and then they came to stay. With all but Wessex fallen, the country was now as good as theirs. For nine years Alfred, King of Wessex, had fought them, but in AD 878 he disappeared – gone, it was supposed, to Rome, or to a monastery. Meanwhile, in the boggy, brooding 'island' of Athelney, a humble man lodged with a herdswoman and, in deep distraction, allowed her cakes to burn. From this hideaway, Alfred sent messengers to the people of Somerset, bidding them prepare. St Cuthbert, appearing to him, assured him, 'All Albion is given to you and your sons.'

In May, he called upon his 'secret army' to rise up, and they marched under the banner of a Golden Dragon. Others flocked to join them. In one battle, at Eddington, the Danes were vanquished and Alfred became king of 'all Albion', although he would confess, 'this earthly power never will please me, nor did I altogether very much yearn after this earthly authority.' The Danish Guthorm, having been so let down by Odin, Thor and all his gods, became a Christian and was baptised by Alfred. Athelney Abbey survived until the Dissolution of the Monasteries, when it was razed, and the rubble valued at £80.

▶ *Monument just N of Athelney, off A361, 9 miles NE of Taunton.*

SEDGEMOOR BATTLEFIELD

❸ The Battle of Sedgemoor

The same marshy countryside that gave shelter to King Alfred was the downfall of a rebel and his followers. This was the scene of the last great battle to be fought on English soil, in 1685, between the supporters of the charismatic James Scott, Duke of Monmouth, illegitimate son of Charles II, and the forces of his uncle, James II (see page 24). The young duke's cavalry were defeated not only by James's troops, but by the 'rhynes', or ditches, which the horses struggled to cross when the desperate Monmouth launched a night attack. The rebels numbered 3,600, but many were armed only with scythes, pitchforks and Protestant conviction. They were no match for 2,600 highly trained soldiers led by Louis de Duras, 2nd Earl of Feversham. In three hours, on July 6, 1685, the royal army lost 80 men, the rebels perhaps 1,000. Monmouth fled, disguised as a peasant, but was captured, taken to the Tower and clumsily beheaded. A memorial stone near the village of Westonzoyland recalls the mayhem.

▶ *Battlefield along track from Westonzoyland, on A372, 4 miles SE of Bridgwater.*

❹ Glastonbury Abbey

Is this the last resting place of Arthur, 'the once and future king'? The tale is told that the dying Arthur was brought from Slaughterbridge across the water to the Isle of Avalon. At the site where it is claimed Arthur was buried with Guinevere, a notice tells how, in 1191, monks dug deep to find beneath a stone a leaden cross inscribed *His iacet inclitus Arturius in insula Avalonia* (Here lies King Arthur, buried in Avalon) and a coffin containing the bodies of a man and a woman. Her hair was still golden, but crumbled at a touch. In 1278, when the king, Edward I, paid a state visit, the bones were placed in a casket in a black marble tomb in the abbey church, where they stayed until the Dissolution in 1539. The 'proof' is tenuous, the notice board prosaic, but the abbey ruins are among the most evocative anywhere in Britain.

▶ *BA6 9EL. Glastonbury 6 miles S of Wells on A39. Abbey in town centre.*

❺ Cadbury Castle

An Iron Age hillfort, known locally as 'Arthur's Palace', is said to be the site of Camelot, where King Arthur held court. From the summit the visitor looks over to Glastonbury Tor, 12 miles distant. Excavations in the 1960s brought to light evidence of periodic occupation between 3000 BC and late Saxon times. This, said the archaeologists, had been the site of a fortress of some great king, its large timber hall built between AD 460 and 500. An entire army could have been contained within the castle walls. However, as always on the trail of Arthur, proof evades us.

▶ *On minor roads 2 miles E of A359, 9 miles N of Yeovil.*

The legendary kingdom of Arthur Pendragon

Ancient tales of a superhero echo through the ages; whether or not they contain a grain of truth, the magic lives on.

Arthur was born the son of King Uther Pendragon and the Lady Igraine, later his queen, with a little help from Merlin, and numerous chroniclers, fabulists, fabricators, poets, pseudologists and romantics over centuries. Although Arthur evades historians and guards his mystery, all over Britain, and especially in Celtic regions – Scotland, Wales, Ireland and Cornwall – he has left his footprint.

An English monk, Gildas (AD 500–70), was first to tell, in *The Ruin and Conquest of Britain*, of a great leader of the 5th to 6th century, who vanquished Saxon invaders, but he did not name him Arthur. Not until AD 830, did that king appear, in the *Historia Brittonum* of the Welsh monk Nennius: 'Then in those days Arthur fought against them with the kings of Britons, but he was commander in those battles.'

Making of a myth

After the trauma of the Norman conquest of 1066, the Celts took refuge in magical thinking, mythmaking and verse. They told wishful, lyrical tales of Celtic Britons rising up in triumph against their new overlords, extolling Nennius's Arthur as a hero.

It was Geoffrey of Monmouth, Bishop of St Asaph (Flintshire), however, who 70 years later raised that dashing king to the status of demigod, with his *History of the Kings of Britain*. He claimed that the work derived not just from the writings of Gildas and Nennius, but from 'a certain very ancient book', a secret Celtic manuscript loaned to him by Walter, Archbishop of Oxford, which Geoffrey alone could study. If there was ever such a book, no one has seen it. What price if it should ever come to light?

Geoffrey was the first to give a full account of Arthur's life, from his supernatural conception and birth. He describes Arthur's accession to the throne, his battles, his death after being betrayed, and his final resting place at Avalon. Geoffery wrote a vivid, action-packed narrative, of the wizardry of Merlin, of the wonders of Camelot, of the treachery of Mordred, Arthur's nephew, who seized the crown and Queen Guinevere. In Geoffrey's day annalists enjoyed the freedom to embellish fact with fiction, and he called upon his imagination to create a legend so epic and enduring that it still captivates today. He must have had a higher motive than hoax, for in the telling of the tale, he restored the British people's self-belief, endowing

them with a sense of nationhood and a mythological status to rival that of the Norman oppressors.

Soon the stories spread through Celtic northern France. At the court of the French-born English king Henry II and Eleanor of Aquitaine, troubadours sang of Arthur's exploits and he passed into French legend. Indeed, a Frenchman, Chrétien de Troyes, was the greatest writer of Arthurian romances of the Middle Ages, telling of the quest for the Holy Grail.

Pendragon prestige

By the Tudor era many fictions had been spun about the golden age of chivalry, and King Arthur and the Knights of the Round Table. English and French renderings cross-fertilised one another, as English authors sought to reclaim Arthur. Thomas Malory's *Le Morte d'Arthur*, in 1486, became one of the first books to be printed in England. Not for nothing was Henry VII's first son christened Arthur, at Winchester (Geoffrey's Camelot) although he did not live to be king. At Winchester Castle is the Round Table, or so it is claimed, upon which prince Arthur's younger brother Henry VIII ordered the painting of his image when he entertained the Holy Roman Emperor Charles V there. The legendary Arthur had become hot property, and the boast that he had once slept at this castle, or fought a battle in that field, must have conferred the status of a blue plaque.

In Victorian England there was a massive surge of interest in Arthur Pendragon and all things medieval. Alfred, Lord Tennyson was moved to write his *Idylls of the King* by the sight of King Arthur's Stone at Slaughterbridge in Cornwall, where Arthur is said to have fallen. Pre-Raphaelites thrilled to the drama. Sir Edward Burne-Jones painted *The Last Sleep of Arthur at Avalon*; Dante Gabriel Rossetti, *The Damsel of the Holy Grail*; Arthur Hughes, *Sir Galahad*.

Sacred places

For lovers of Arthurian legend the fascination never wanes. They seek him here, they seek him there. In Cornwall, Geoffrey tells us, Tintagel was his birthplace. The ethereal Dozmary Pool vies with Loe Pool as the lake where Arthur received Excalibur. The Iron Age hillfort of Cadbury Castle in Somerset, known as 'Arthur's Palace', is a putative site of Camelot. Glastonbury Abbey allegedly stands on the site of

Avalon, where the king was buried with Guinevere. Intriguingly, historians have identified a 5th-century warrior prince called Arthur, a shadowy figure who died in battle with the Scottish Picts. And teasingly, whenever the whole thing is in danger of being dismissed as a ripping medieval yarn, something will turn up at an Arthurian site – never compelling proof, but a scintilla of supporting evidence. And somewhere – at Sewingshield Crags in Northumberland, maybe, or Alderley Edge in Cheshire – 'the once and future king' and his knights lie, not dead but sleeping, and they will rise up at Britain's hour of need.

Arthur's mystique permeates the land of his birth, blurring the line between myth and reality.
TINTAGEL

❻ Bath Abbey

Edgar the Peaceable was crowned the first King of all England in Bath Abbey in AD 973. The ceremony is commemorated in the Edgar Window in the abbey church, which was founded in 1499. Peaceable he may have been, but virtuous Edgar was not. He took various wives and concubines and, allegedly, abducted the abbess of Wilton, whom he made pregnant. He had reigned for 14 years before his friend and advisor Dunstan, Archbishop of Canterbury, judged his conduct so improved that he merited the crown. The ceremony designed by Dunstan set a precedent for every coronation since then.

Henry VIII, as was his divine right, sold off the abbey in the Dissolution of the Monasteries. Elizabeth I granted a licence to raise funds for its restoration. A stone in the floor commemorates the day in 1973 when the Queen visited to celebrate a thousand years of British monarchy. The cruciform abbey church of St Peter and St Paul is one of the largest exemplars of Perpendicular Gothic in the West Country. It was restored in the 1860s by George Gilbert Scott, and beneath its spectacular fan-vaulted ceiling there is seating for 1,200 people. A heritage museum is housed in the vaults.
▶ *BA1 1LT. Bath town centre.*

❼ Bath

'As for Bath,' wrote William Thackeray, 'all history went and bathed and drank there' – and so it sometimes seems. The Romans came for rest and relaxation, but a settlement existed around the hot springs millennia before they arrived. However, what really put Bath on the social map was a visit by the future Queen Anne in 1688. By the 18th century the Bath season rivalled that of London, with concerts and balls in the new Assembly Rooms – 'the most noble and elegant of any in the kingdom' – organised by the dandy Beau Nash. People flocked to bathe in and drink the waters, and the town was transformed into a vision of Georgian loveliness. The Royal Crescent acquired the prefix after Prince Frederick, son of George III, lived there in the late 1700s. Not everyone was impressed. Thomas Rowlandson's watercolour cartoons of *The Comforts of Bath* inspired derision. Undeterred, Queen Charlotte, consort of George III, took up residence in 1817 at 93 Sydney Place; her son the Duke of Clarence, the future William IV, moved in at 103. In 1830, Princess Victoria, the future queen, arrived with her mother to open the park named in her honour. Their stay is marked by a plaque on a wall in the Royal Hotel. At the Art Gallery that bears her name there is a statue of Victoria as queen. Prince Charles's Highgrove shop sells produce directly from, or inspired by, his Cotswolds estates. Princess Anne and Camilla, Duchess of Cornwall, often visit local charities.
▶ *12 miles SE of Bristol.*

❽ Bath Pump Rooms

Queen Anne was a martyr to gout – at her coronation she was carried in a sedan chair, with an open back to accommodate her train. It was in the hope of a cure that she came several times to England's only hot springs, to bathe in and drink the waters. The water was not palatable. According to the journal of Celia Fiennes, daughter of Lord Saye of Sele, in 1678: '… it's very hot and tastes like the water that boyles eggs, has such a smell, but the nearer the pumpe you drink it the hotter and less offencive and more spiriteous.'

A new Great Pump Room was built in the 1790s, when, in the course of excavating the foundations, the remains of a Roman Temple of Minerva were uncovered. In the year before her death in 1818, Queen Charlotte, the popular German wife of George III, visited the Pump Room. 'She daily passed in a sedan chair,' it was related, 'and graciously as well as gracefully acknowledged the obeisances of those who assembled to behold her.' The beautiful building, in honeyed Bath stone, is Grade I listed.
▶ *BA1 1LZ. Abbey Churchyard, town centre.*

EDGAR WAS CROWNED THE FIRST KING OF ALL ENGLAND
BATH ABBEY

CHANNEL ISLANDS

Historic castles and fabulous scenery worked their magic on Victoria and Albert – Jersey's Lily Langtry had the same effect on their eldest son – and later another royal couple left footprints of their own.

❶ St Helier, Jersey

'A simply splendid day. I never saw a more beautiful deep blue sea; quite like Naples.' This was September 3, 1846, and Victoria and Albert were visiting Jersey, admiring the view before coming ashore. The royal couple were welcomed with wild enthusiasm. 'We landed … amid the cheers of the numberless crowds, guns firing, and bands playing,' wrote Victoria in her journal. 'Were received by all the ladies of the town … gaily dressed, who, strewing flowers on our way, conducted us to the canopy, where I received the address of the States and of the militia.'

▶ *S coast of Jersey.*

❷ Elizabeth Castle, Jersey

A defensive stronghold and homage to a queen, this castle was named Fort Isabella Bellissima by Walter Raleigh, governor of Jersey from 1600 to 1603. 'The Beautiful Elizabeth', standing on the rocky tidal islet of St Aubin, is surrounded by sea for seven out of every 12 hours. The fortress was begun in the 1590s when Mont Orgueil Castle was deemed incapable of withstanding cannon fire from sea-borne invaders. Under George Carteret, it was the last bastion to resist the Parliamentarian onslaught, which destroyed a medieval abbey church at its heart.

Having sailed by with Albert on their yacht in 1846, Victoria recorded that Elizabeth Castle was 'a picturesque fort on a rock, with the town of St Helier behind it'.

▶ *JE3 3NU. Accessible at low tide by foot or by ferry.*

❸ Mont Orgueil Castle, Jersey

One of Britain's best-preserved castles occupies a rocky promontory, protected on three sides by steep cliffs and sea. It was built on the orders of King John in the 13th century and served as a fortress, a prison and a seat of government. The granite on which it stood made it impossible to undermine, and it must have seemed almost impregnable, until new weaponry in the 16th century left it vulnerable to attack from ship-mounted cannons. By the 1600s it had been usurped by Elizabeth Castle as the island's primary defence, but the islanders were proud that Mont Orgueil had never been breached.

Victoria and Albert visited Mont Orgueil in 1846, and Victoria recalled that it was 'beautifully situated, completely overhanging the sea … from one of the batteries you command the bay, and the French coast was distinctly seen, only 13 miles away.' Ceremonies were held at Mont Orgueil to welcome George V in 1921, and Elizabeth II; inscriptions mark the occasions.

▶ *JE3 6ET. 4 miles E of St Helier, close to Gorey Pier.*

④ St Saviour's Church, Jersey

A more recent of Jersey's claims to fame is as the birthplace, in 1853, of Emilie Charlotte Le Breton, known as Lily Langtry, the 'Jersey Lily'. On moving to London, she became the mistress of the future Edward VII – Albert Edward, Prince of Wales. She died in 1929, having led a very racy life, and was buried here in the graveyard of St Saviour, where she is commemorated by an Art Deco sculptured bust.
▶ *1½ miles NE of St Helier.*

⑤ Victoria Tower, Guernsey

Sunday, August 23, 1846: 'Albert thought we might perhaps manage to see one of the Channel Islands ... Accordingly, he sent for Lord Adolphus Fitzclarence, and it was settled that we would go to Guernsey, which delighted me, as I had so long wanted to see it.' Thus it was decided that Victoria and her consort would pay an almost impromptu visit to the second largest of the Channel Islands, leaving their hosts with little time to prepare. Ten days later, Jersey would be ready to greet them with rapture. In Guernsey, some time after the visit, the Victoria Tower was commissioned to commemorate the occasion. It is a prominent St Peter Port landmark, symbolising Guernsey's link to the British crown.
▶ *Arsenal Road, St Peter Port.*

⑥ Alderney

The only railway in the Channel Islands, the 'Orient Express', was opened by Queen Victoria and Prince Albert in 1847. The third largest of the Channel Islands, at just a mile wide and 3½ miles long, Alderney had the first nationalised railway. It was run by the Admiralty and is one of the oldest lines in the British Isles. Built to carry stone from the eastern end of the island to be used in the construction of a breakwater and some forts, the train now carries people. On August 8, 1854, Victoria and Albert were the first official passengers, conveyed by horse-drawn tender. Almost a century later, in 1949, the entire population of the island turned out to welcome Princess Elizabeth and the Duke of Edinburgh, in a mood of pure jubilation after grim years of German occupation.
▶ *Ferry from St Peter Port, Guernsey.*

⑦ Sark

The smallest of the four main Channel Islands, Sark was not left out when Princess Elizabeth and the Duke of Edinburgh visited in 1949. They were officially welcomed by the Dame of Sark, Sibyl Hathaway, and her husband, Bob Hathaway. The Duke opened the Maseline Harbour, and at the Seigneurie – home of the Seigneurs of Sark since 1730 – the royal couple signed the visitors' book, writing their names a few pages after those of the occupying officers. The Dame, ever dignified in adversity, had insisted that the German soldiers must be treated and behave as visitors.
▶ *Ferry from St Peter Port, Guernsey.*

ELIZABETH CASTLE, JERSEY

KEY

1 Main entry
County boundary
Motorway
Principal A road

Banbury

Buckingham
1
A422

Milton Keynes
A421

Bedford
A428

BEDFORDSHIRE
38

Biggleswade

A6

A421

A1

1
2
M1
A5

Leighton Buzzard
A505

Luton

A1(M)

Steven

1

Hertfo

A602

Witney
A40

A44

A34

A41

Aylesbury
2

BUCKINGHAMSHIRE
44-45

Tring

HERTFORDSHIRE
56-57

A41

St Albans
2

A413

5

3

Watford

3

M25

Oxford
4 **5**

OXFORDSHIRE
64-65

1

2

Didcot
A34

3

High Wycombe
4

The Chilterns

M40

Maidenhead

A419

A429

Swindon
3

M4

BERKSHIRE
39-43

Reading
12

1

Windsor
9
10
6
5 **6** **7** **8**
11
A322

6

1

Chippenham
A350

Marlborough
A346

2 **1**

Newbury
4

A339

1

2
A33

M3

Woking

SURREY
66-67

2

Devizes

Trowbridge

WILTSHIRE
74-75

A361

A338

A303

Andover
A34

Basingstoke
2

A31

Guildford
3
4

A3

Dorking
3
5

M25

Reigat

A24

A303

Warminster
4

A36

Farnham

HAMPSHIRE
and
Isle of Wight
46-53

Haslemere

A3

Crawley

A264

A3

A354

Salisbury
1

2 **3**
A36

M27

Winchester
3 **4**

5 **6**

Petersfield

1

A272

Haywards Heath

A24

11
12

Southampton

South Downs National Park

SUSSEX
68-73

A16

Ringwood

New Forest National Park
13

14

M27

8

A3(M)

Chichester
2 **3**

A27

5

Worthing

Brighton
7

6

Lymington
15

19 **22**
23 **20** **21**
18 Newport
17 **24**

9
10

Portsmouth

Bognor Regis
4

Isle of Wight

Southern England

Defensive strongholds stand sentinel along the coast; dream castles and lavish stately homes enrich the countryside. From splendid Windsor Castle to the fantastical seaside Pavilion built for the Prince Regent, each residence tells its own royal story.

- Gravesend
- Rochester **8** **7**
- **6** Chatham
- The North Downs
- M26 M2
- A249
- A299
- Margate
- **9** **10** **11**
- A253
- **12**
- Canterbury
- **4** Maidstone
- A21 A26 A20
- A228
- M20
- **5**
- A2
- **13**
- **14**
- **1** **2** Royal Tunbridge Wells
- A28
- **15**
- **3**
- A229
- KENT 58-63
- Ashford
- A2070
- Dover
- A259
- Folkestone
- **16**
- Crowborough
- A26
- A229
- A21
- A259
- Rye
- **12**
- **13**
- A26 A22
- **9** **10**
- A27
- Bexhill-on-Sea
- Hastings
- **11**
- Eastbourne

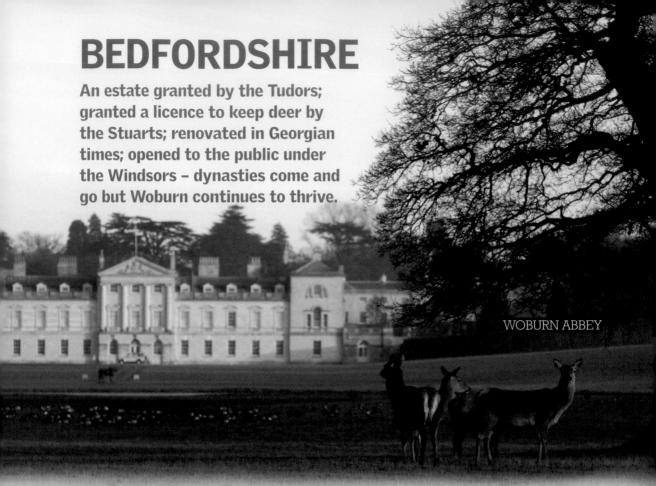

BEDFORDSHIRE

An estate granted by the Tudors; granted a licence to keep deer by the Stuarts; renovated in Georgian times; opened to the public under the Windsors – dynasties come and go but Woburn continues to thrive.

WOBURN ABBEY

❶ Woburn Abbey

The story of how a 12th-century Cistercian monastery became the ancestral home of the Dukes of Bedford begins with Henry VIII's Dissolution of the Monasteries. Passion Week in 1538 found Abbot Robert Hobbes a deeply unhappy man. His body was racked with 'stranguillion'. His conscience 'grudged' him daily for having sworn an Oath of Supremacy to the king and erased the pope's name from all service books. He wished he had died – and soon he would do so. The abbey was confiscated and the abbot, having made his feelings too well-known, was hanged from an oak tree at the gate. In 1547, the property was granted to John Russell, later 1st Earl of Bedford, by Edward VI. Elizabeth I visited at short notice in 1572. The 2nd Duke wrote anxiously to Lord Burghley, 'I pray God, the rowmes and lodging there may be to her majesties contentation … If I could make them better upon such a sodayn, then would I.'

The mansion of today was rebuilt by Henry Flitcroft for the 4th Duke in 1747. Humphry Repton landscaped the park in 1802. The 13th Duke inherited a building falling into ruins and set about massive renovations. In 1955 he opened his doors to the paying public – who arrived that first day in two cars and on a bicycle.

One of England's finest art collections includes works by Gainsborough, Reynolds, Van Dyck and Canaletto, as well as etchings by Queen Victoria and Prince Albert.

▶ *MK17 9WA. Woburn 8 miles SE of Milton Keynes close to junction of A4012 and A5130*

❷ Woburn Deer Park

Francis, Duke of Bedford, was granted a licence to keep deer in 1690, but by the turn of the century stocks were low, and in 1703 he was forced to borrow, from the Duke of Rutland, the obligatory two bucks to send to Trinity College, Cambridge. A century later, the park had been so well replenished that Archduke John of Austria wrote in 1815 that 'we had never seen a park so full of deer'. Herbrand, the 11th Duke of Bedford, as president of the Royal Zoological Society, introduced many exotic deer – nine species now roam Woburn's 1,200 or so walled hectares (3,000 acres). 'Hatband' was less successful in improving the house. His first attempt to install electricity resulted in a fire; the second was hampered by his distaste for the sight of workmen, who had to hide when he came by.

▶ *MK17 9WA. Woburn 8 miles SE of Milton Keynes close to junction of A4012 and A5130.*

BERKSHIRE

Monarchs have chosen to pursue their everyday lives here, building homes, planting gardens, founding schools – and one queen formalised the sport of kings, to the evident delight of her successors.

❶ Hungerford

A battered brass horn is said to have been given to the town by a royal patron. On the death of her older sister, Maud, the manor of Hungerford passed to Blanche of Lancaster and her husband, John of Gaunt, son of Edward III. His gift of a horn was an affirmation of the townspeople's right to fish the River Kennet, but a written charter stated that entitlement was lost in the reign of Elizabeth I. In 1574, with the right under threat, an appeal was made directly to the queen, who graciously responded that 'the said inhabitants should hereafter have use and enjoy without interruption all such liberties and profits and benefits heretofore time out of mind and remembrance of man they had used and enjoyed'. And so they did. The diarist John Evelyn, passing by Hungerford in the summer of 1654, remarked that this was 'a town famous for its trouts'. A Hocktide punch is still drunk here after Easter in John of Gaunt's honour and he is remembered in the names of a school and an inn. The westernmost town in Berkshire, Hungerford is within the North Wessex Downs Area of Outstanding Natural Beauty.
▶ *At junction of A4 and A338, 3 miles S of Junction 14 of M4.*

❷ Bear Hotel

One of the country's most historic inns, at 'the Crossroads of England', has signifcant royal connections. The atmospheric 13th-century hostelry was once named the Bear and Ragged Staff. In the 15th century it bore the badge of the Earls of Warwick. Henry VIII gave the property to his fourth wife, Anne of Cleves, and later to his sixth, Catherine Parr. In the Civil War, before the second Battle of Newbury, Charles I stayed here and held councils of war. In 1688, William, Prince of Orange, stayed for two nights, having landed at Brixham, Devon, and marched his army upon London. On the morning of December 8, William sat down with three emissaries of James II – Lords Halifax, Nottingham and Godolphin – to discuss his challenge to the throne. James subsequently fled to France, and William reigned jointly with his wife and cousin, Mary.
▶ *RG17 0EL. Town centre, Hungerford.*

❸ Ashdown House

This exquisitely beautiful, Dutch-style 17th-century house was built for a Stuart romantic heroine by her most ardent admirer. Elizabeth was the eldest child of James I and Anne of Denmark. For her christening at Holyrood were ordered 'violers and taborers to make music' and 63 ells of scarlet 'London cloth' for the attendants. The king wore new socks of crimson and gold velvet in her honour. She grew up to be 'the most beautiful princess in Europe', and on St Valentine's Day 1613, she married Frederick V, Elector of the Palatinate of the Rhine. In 1619 she became Queen of Bohemia, but her husband's rule was brief: the couple were exiled in 1620 and she was nicknamed 'the Winter Queen'.

Elizabeth outlived Frederick by 30 years, and in the early 1660s travelled to London to visit her nephew, Charles II. Her admirer, William, 1st Earl of Craven, hearing that she 'longed to live in quiet', commissioned the Dutch-born architect Captain William Winde to build this house for her on the site of a medieval deer park, but she died in 1662 before it was completed, and it is 'consecrated' to her.

An extraordinary chalk-block Dutch-style building, it was compared by the architectural historian Nikolaus Pevsner to a dolls' house. With its cupola, flanking pavilions and immaculate parterres, it is quintessentially feminine, isolated amid the rolling Berkshire Downs. The grounds were landscaped by Capability Brown in the 1770s. A maze, woodland walks and wild deer add to the charm.
▶ *RG17 8RE. On B4000 10 miles E of Swindon.*

❹ Bucklebury

In February 2011, gold-embossed invitations began arriving at addresses in this pretty Berkshire village. Among those on the guest list to attend Westminster Abbey for the marriage of a local girl, Catherine Middleton, to Prince William, were the postman, the pub landlord, the butcher and the couple who kept the general store – where William would look in from time to time to buy a Vienetta ice cream.
▶ *On minor roads 6 miles NE of Newbury.*

❺ Windsor Castle

It took 250 fire-fighters 15 hours to put out the blaze that ripped through Windsor Castle on a cold November morning in 1992. The Queen was devastated to hear of the fire at her favourite residence – the largest and oldest occupied castle in the world. But by a near miracle most of the treasures were spared, and with them 900 years of history.

The castle has been used by monarchs since the reign of Henry I. In the Civil War it served as a military HQ for Parliamentarians and a prison for Charles I. Charles II had much of it rebuilt, creating lavish baroque interiors. Under George III and George IV, the State Apartments received the full Georgian treatment. In winter, visitors can see George IV's richly decorated quarters.

While the scale of the castle overwhelms, there is a wonder, too, in miniature, in the dolls' house created by Sir Edwin Lutyens in 1921–24 for Queen Mary, consort of George V. Some 1,500 artists, craftsmen and manufacturers contributed to it. Its miniature library is stocked with works penned by Rudyard Kipling, Thomas Hardy, J.M. Barrie and Sir Arthur Conan Doyle, there is wine in the cellar supplied by Berry Bros & Rudd, electricity, running water and a flushing lavatory. Queen Mary described it as 'the most perfect present that anyone could receive'. The dolls' house was shown at the British Empire Exhibition of Arts and Manufacturing, where 1.6 million jaws dropped at the sight of it.
▶ *SL4 1NJ. Windsor S of River Thames, 1 mile S of Junction 6 of M4.*

❻ Windsor Great Park

Queen Victoria loved her daily walk with Albert in the parkland around Windsor Castle. After his death in 1861, she found solace in those idyllic acres. The park was first established as a hunting ground by William the Conqueror on a vast tract of Windsor Forest. In 1753, Prince William Augustus, youngest son of George II, ordered the creation of the lake named Virginia Water, surrounded by a naturalistic landscape. It would set a style for grand garden design, and acquired the name of 'The Royal Landscape'. The shaping of the park continued under George III: a statue depicts him astride his horse. George IV installed the Leptis Magna ruin – a folly built of columns from the Roman city site in Libya – beside Virginia Water. The two-mile Long Walk provides a breathtaking approach to Windsor Castle.
▶ *TW20 0UU. S of Windsor. Access from A332.*

❼ Frogmore House and Mausoleum

'All is peace and quiet and you only hear the hum of the bees, the singing of the birds.' Queen Victoria loved this 17th-century house and gardens within Windsor Great Park. The original house was built by royal architect Hugh May for his nephew Thomas, and in 1792 was bought by George III for his German wife, Queen Charlotte. Her passion for botany found expression in laying out the borders with rare plants and in floral interior decorations. Victoria gave Frogmore to her mother in 1841, and when Prince Albert died of typhoid, on December 14, 1861, she commissioned a mausoleum to be built here. The walls are of Scottish granite and Portland stone – recalling those heady days when the royal couple travelled in the Highlands and sailed around the West Country. Bronze angels at the entrance bear a sword and trumpet. The tomb was the last work of Baron Carlo Marochetti, and has marble effigies of the queen and prince consort. All is peace and quiet now for Victoria and her prince among men.
▶ *TW20 0UU. 1 mile S of Windsor Castle in Home Park.*

❽ St George's Chapel

This beautiful ecclesiastical building within Windsor Castle is the last resting place of numerous monarchs. Edward IV, who commissioned the chapel in 1475, was buried here in 1483, rather than in Westminster Abbey. Among those who joined him were Henry VIII and his third wife, Jane Seymour, George V and Queen Mary, and George VI. This is the church of the Most Noble Order of the Garter, the highest order of chivalry in England, founded in 1348 by Edward III as a 'society, fellowship and college of knights'.

Was Charles I interred here also? A black marble ledger stone in the quire states that he lies beneath it – but there are conflicting accounts about the fate of his remains. In 1813, in the presence of the Prince Regent, Sir Henry Halford opened the coffin alleged to be Charles's, to find within it a body and a 'loose' head that had been severed by 'a heavy blow inflicted by a very sharp instrument'. This may not be proof enough for conspiracy theorists, but, as the Knights of the Garter would say, *Honi soit qui mal y pense* (Evil to him who evil thinks). In 2005, the Prince of Wales and Camilla Parker-Bowles had their civil marriage blessed in the chapel.
▶ *Windsor Castle, SL4 1NJ.*

ST GEORGE'S CHAPEL

ETON COLLEGE

❾ Eton College

'The King's College of Our Lady of Eton besides Wyndsor' was founded by Henry VI in 1440. Here, 70 boys would have the benefit of free education and move up after a year to the new King's College, Cambridge. With the school came a community of secular priests, a pilgrimage church, almshouse and a collection of holy relics that included fragments of the True Cross and the Crown of Thorns. The church was not entirely built when, in 1448, it was pulled down to make way for a grander one, which in turn was not completed when the Lancastrian Henry VI was deposed by the Yorkist Edward IV and the college's effects were removed to St George's, Windsor. Not until 1482 was the church – the chapel of today – completed. It is a fine building in the Perpendicular Gothic style, although falling far short of the king's ambition for it. In other ways, however, his vision has been royally fulfilled. 'The chief nurse of English statesmen', Eton has educated 19 prime ministers, including David Cameron. Guided tours are available, and a Museum of Eton Life is open from April to October. The college was used as a location for the filming of *The Madness of King George*.
▶ *SL4 6DW. Eton on N side of Thames opposite Windsor, close to Junction 6 of M4.*

❿ Ankerwycke Yew

Could this venerable tree have cast its shade over King John as he sealed the Magna Carta? In 1215, John sat down to sign an extensive bill of rights designed to curtail his freedoms and excesses. The king was encamped at Wraysbury on the north bank of the Thames; his feudal barons were based across the river at Runnymede. Perhaps symbolically, or for each side's natural protection, they were to meet on what was then an island. A few hundred years later, George Simon Harcourt, lord of the manor and high sheriff of the county, referred to this as 'Magna Carta Island', and in 1834 he rebuilt a fisherman's cottage on the spot, to house an octagonal slab on which it is believed the charter was signed and sealed. The stone had been preserved in Ankerwycke House until Harcourt removed it, and some historians believe that a 2,000-year-old yew tree in the grounds of the ruined Benedictine Ankerwycke Priory was where John actually put seal to parchment. Whatever the truth, the yew is an incredible sight, some 9.5m (31ft) wide. According to tradition, Henry VIII courted Anne Boleyn in its shade.
▶ *1 mile S of Wraysbury, off B376.*

⓫ Royal Ascot

In 1711, Queen Anne bought land close to Windsor Castle on which would be run the world's most famous horse races. Her uncle, Charles II, had held private races before Newmarket became racing's first public venue, but these were between two horses and in Anne's reign several horses competed. At Ascot, 'Her Majesty's Plate' carried a prize of 100 guineas and the horses had to carry at least 76kg (12 stone).

The first Ascot Gold Cup, run on Ladies' Day 1807, set the tone for Ascot as we know it today. The five-day event, each June, is steeped in pageantry and begins with the royal procession, in which the Queen and her party parade along the track in horse-drawn landaus. Only members can enter the exclusive royal enclosure, where the dress code is rigid – and hats are preposterous.
▶ *SL5 7JX. 4 miles E of Bracknell at junction of A329, A330 and A332.*

⓬ Reading Abbey

The abbey at Reading was built for one King Henry and surrendered to another. Henry I founded the abbey in June 1121 'for the salvation of my soul, and the souls of King William, my father, and of King William, my brother, and Queen Maud, my wife, and all my ancestors and successors'. After his death in France in 1135, his body was brought to Reading and buried before the high altar in the still unfinished church, which was consecrated in 1164, by Thomas Becket, in the presence of Henry II. Here John of Gaunt married Blanche, daughter of Henry Plantagenet, in May 1359. The abbey fell victim to Henry VIII's Dissolution. In 1539, its abbot, Hugh Cook Farringdon, was executed for refusing to acknowledge the king's religious supremacy. The monks were expelled and part of the building was used as a palace.

In 1550, Edward VI granted the abbey church to his uncle Edward Seymour, eldest brother of his mother Jane Seymour, Henry VIII's third wife. Seymour, Lord Protector of England, plundered it for materials for the rebuilding of St Mary in Reading. Henry I's tomb was broken up and his bones dispersed. The Lady Chapel in turn was stripped to furnish the Poor Knights' Lodgings at Windsor Castle, and so the destruction continued, leaving substantial ruins – now subject to repairs – and the gateway outside which the abbot met his death. This was restored by the architect Sir George Gilbert Scott, after partial collapse in 1861.
▶ *Access Reading from Junctions 10, 11 and 12 of M4. Abbey in town centre.*

SOUTHERN ENGLAND

BUCKINGHAMSHIRE

In this leafy county, stylish gardens were once enjoyed by Tudor monarchs, towns held steadfast to their principles, and a prime minister's esoteric mansion provided restful interludes for his queen.

❶ Buckingham

Henry VIII often visited what was then a village, and it is said that his first queen, Catherine of Aragon, introduced the inhabitants to the craft of lace-making. She is remembered by a devotional crucifix in the town's Old Gaol Museum. Henry's Protestant Reformation found little support in Buckingham, and when his son, Edward VI, tried to pursue it further, there was a Catholic uprising in the area. On Edward's death, Catherine's daughter, the Catholic Mary Tudor, became queen. In gratitude for local support, Mary issued a royal charter in 1554, establishing Buckingham as a borough to be governed by a bailiff. For its Royalist stand in the Civil War, 'The Loyal and Ancient Borough of Buckingham' was granted a second charter by Charles II in 1684.

▶ *15 miles W of Milton Keynes on A421.*

❷ Aylesbury

This ancient town became the object of Henry VIII's fickle favour when he courted Anne Boleyn. Henry had been all for Buckingham in the early years of marriage, when the people took his queen, Catherine of Aragon, so much to their hearts. But when he set his sights on the daughter of Thomas Boleyn, Lord of

HUGHENDEN MANOR

the Manor of Aylesbury, Buckingham lost its status as county town. An Aylesbury man, Sir John Baldwin, was appointed as chief justice, and the assizes were moved here. In another vagary of history, Aylesbury's support for Parliament in the Civil War earned it the disfavour of Charles II, who smiled benignly upon Buckingham.

▶ *At junction of A41 and A418, 15 miles NE of Junctions 8 and 8A of M4.*

❸ Great Kimble

Does the pretty parish of Kimble derive its name from Cymbeline, an ancient warrior king? Also known as Cunobelinus, Cymbeline was king of the territory of the Catuvellauni, an ancient Celtic tribe of pre-Roman Britain. He reigned around AD 10 to 41 and was a master of diplomacy, successfully staving off Roman invasion while extending his power in the southeast of Britain. Earthworks on Beacon Hill are believed to be the foundations of his castle, and coins have been found bearing his name.

The manor of Great Kimble had been owned by the Hampden family from the 14th century when John Hampden called a parish meeting in St Nicholas' Church and refused to pay Charles I's ship tax. The church still has the roll of the names of those who met to affirm their opposition.

▶ *HP17 0XS. 6 miles S of Aylesbury on A4010.*

❹ Hughenden Manor

Queen Victoria was a staunch supporter of her Prime Minister Benjamin Disraeli, and often visited him at his country retreat.
'Dizzy' and his wife, Mary Anne, bought a late-18th century stuccoed mansion of modest design in 1848, engaging Edward Buckton Lamb to remodel and 'dramatise' it. Disraeli was thrilled with 'the romance many years realising', although a century or so later architectural historian Nikolaus Pevsner judged the resulting baronial

A FINE PLACE TO ENTERTAIN A SOVEREIGN

redbrick edifice 'excruciating'. It was a fine place for Disraeli to entertain a sovereign with whom he would grow very close. On the death of Prince Albert it seemed to Victoria that Disraeli was 'the only person who appreciated the Prince'. In a letter to the queen he ventured to touch on 'a sacred theme'. To have known Albert had been 'one of the most satisfactory incidents of his life: full of refined and beautiful memories'. He made Victoria Empress of India – she made him Lord Beaconsfield. Many of the Disraelis' books, paintings and furniture remain in the house. The gardens have been restored to Mary Anne's own design. She and Benjamin were a devoted, childless couple. When he once remarked that he had married her for money, she riposted, 'Ah, but if you had to do it again, you would do it for love.'

▶ *HP14 4LA. 2 miles N of High Wycombe on A4128.*

❺ Chenies Manor

This 15th-century manor, previously known as Chenies Palace, played host to both Henry VIII and Elizabeth I and their courts.
The manorial rights were granted to the Cheyne family in 1180 by Edward III. At its heart, the house today is a part-fortified brick manor, built by Sir John Cheyne in the mid 1400s. The building was extended by John Russell, Earl of Bedford, in the 16th century, when it came to him through marriage. The antiquary John Leland found it 'so translated that little or nothing of it yn a maner remaynith untranslated … a great deale of the House in ben newly set up made of Bricke and Timber.' Russell lost an eye when he was shot with an arrow while fighting for Henry at Morlaix in Brittany in 1522. He was knighted for his heroism. Architectural historian Nikolaus Pevsner, in his book *The Buildings of England (1951–74)*, perhaps still reeling from the 'excruciating' Hughenden Manor, found it 'beautifully mellow under the trees by the church, and architecturally a fascinating puzzle'. In summer, the gardens are resplendent.

▶ *WD3 6ER. 4 miles E of Amersham on A404.*

❻ Holm Island

Walkers on the Thames path above Penton Hook Lock, near Staines, can see the island where Edward VIII and Wallis Simpson had a love nest. Holm Island is connected to the north bank by a footbridge, and the couple stayed in a house appropriately named 'The Nest'.

▶ *1½ miles S of Staines town centre, off B376.*

HAMPSHIRE & ISLE OF WIGHT

Among ancient woodlands and seaside towns, castles, fortresses, manors and stately homes encompass great swathes of history, while a small island remains indisputably the realm of Victoria and her family.

❶ Stratfield Saye

Victoria and Albert would often visit the 1st Duke of Wellington at the country home that was his reward for the defeat of Napoleon at Waterloo. The duke had stood by Victoria's baptismal font, and was godfather to her seventh child, Prince Arthur. For his military success, he was granted a fortune to build himself a palace to rival Blenheim (see page 65). The Iron Duke, however, settled on the estate of Stratfield Saye, home of the Pitt family and instead commissioned alterations to the 17th-century house. A conservatory and outer wings were added, as were water closets in many rooms, and central heating (Victoria found the place too hot). Among the duke's effects on show are his spectacles and slippers, and paintings including one of his charger, Copenhagen. The horse carried him for 18 hours in his most decisive battle. An exhibition in the stables includes the duke's massive, ornamental funeral carriage, cast in bronze from cannons captured at Waterloo.
▶ *RG7 2BT. 10 miles S of Reading on minor roads, off A33.*

❷ The Vyne

Henry VIII's Lord Chamberlain, William, the 1st Lord Sandys, built the original house from a group of medieval structures, and the king visited with his first wife, Catherine of Aragon, then his second, Anne Boleyn. Elizabeth I came to see the 3rd Lord Sandys, and from here wrote a letter commanding the Earl of Huntingdon to take Mary, Queen of Scots into custody.

From 1650, for 350 years, the Vyne was home to the Chute family, who, among many alterations, added a classical portico by John Webb, talented pupil of Inigo Jones. Impressive interiors include the carved Oak Gallery. The house, set in gardens and meadows, is filled with textiles, tiles, carvings and paintings. In the Tudor Gothic chapel, stained-glass images of both Henry and Catherine have a peculiar brilliance. Although Sandys was distressed when the king divorced Catherine, he was obliged to receive Anne when Henry brought her to visit – as he would later be obliged to escort her to imprisonment in the Tower.
▶ *RG24 9HL. 3 miles N of Basingstoke on minor roads, off A340. NT.*

❸ Winchester Castle

After Winchester's surrender to William the Conqueror in 1066, he ordered the building of a castle, and here it was that the future Henry III was born in 1207. Henry was just nine years old when his father, John, died and he ascended the throne. He was crowned in Gloucester, because Winchester and London were under the control of Prince Louis of France – and with the circlet worn by his mother, Isabella of Angoulême, since the crown jewels had been lost in the Wash – but in 1222 he was back in Winchester and began to modernise his castle. The Great Hall that he built was the scene of Sir Walter Raleigh's trial for treason (that time, Raleigh was reprieved).

In the Civil War, the city fell to the Parliamentarians, and in 1651 most of the castle was destroyed by Cromwell's men. In 1665, Charles II engaged Sir Christopher Wren to design a palace to rival Versailles, to be built on an adjoining site, but he did not live to see the King's House completed. It was gutted by fire and demolished in 1894.

The great heroic survivor here amid the ruins is the 13th-century Great Hall, which houses an 1897 bronze statue of Queen Victoria. Here, too, is the symbol of medieval mythology, the round table of King Arthur – on which Henry VIII had his image painted, when he entertained the Emperor Charles V, in 1522.
▶ *SO23 8UJ. Off High Street, city centre. Access Winchester from Junctions 9, 10 and 11 of M3.*

❹ Queen Eleanor's Garden

Within the walls of Winchester Castle, just outside the south door of the Great Hall, the medieval garden of Queen Eleanor – in fact, two Eleanors – has been recreated. The first was Eleanor of Provence, wife of Henry III, the second, her daughter-in-law, Eleanor, Queen of Castile, wife of Edward I. As the seat of British royalty in its day, the castle was home to both. This faithful representation of a garden of that time has turf seats, bay hedges, a fountain, flower borders and herbs both decorative and medicinal. It was opened by the Queen Mother in 1986.
▶ *SO23 8UJ. Off High Street, Winchester city centre.*

❺ Winchester Cathedral

William the Conqueror built this soaring Romanesque edifice on the site of the first Christian church in Winchester, known as Old Minster, burial place of King Cnut (Canute). It was begun in 1079 and served royalty down the centuries. The future Henry III was baptised here in 1207. In 1486 it was the scene of the christening of Henry VII's first son, Arthur – and in 1538, his second son, Henry VIII, ordered his commissioners to destroy St Swithun's shrine in the cathedral, at the same time as dissolving the city's three monastic institutions. In 1554, Mary Tudor, Henry's daughter by Catherine of Aragon, wed Philip of Spain at the cathedral. In the Civil War, Roundheads ransacked the building. What could not be destroyed was the aura of serenity, which visitors can still sense today.

▶ *SO23 9LS. Access from Junctions 9, 10 and 11 of M3. Cathedral in city centre.*

❻ Alfred's Statue, Winchester

In Saxon times, Alfred the Great chose Winchester as the capital of England, and it was home to royalty for centuries.
An impressive bronze statue of Alfred by Hamo Thornycroft was commissioned and erected in 1901 by the City Corporation to mark the millennium anniversary of the king's death. On its high Cornish granite base, the 4.5m (15ft) tall, 5-tonne figure grasps a cross-hilted sword – symbol of Christianity – and with his helmet and flowing cape, Alfred appears every inch a king.

▶ *Broadway, by Abbey House, Winchester city centre.*

❼ Avington Park

Charles II used to entertain his beloved Nell Gwyn at the home of George Brydges, his Groom of the Bedchamber. The estate of 'Afintun' belonged to Winchester Cathedral until it was granted to Edmund Clerke by Henry VIII. When Brydges acquired the house, he enlarged and improved it to make it fit for a king and his mistress. It was not the only time it would accommodate illicit royal lovers. When the Duke of Buckingham and Chandos inherited the property, he played host to George IV and the widowed Maria Fitzherbert, a Catholic, whom the king married in secret, in contravention of the Royal Marriages Act. Avington today is a splendid Georgian manor with classical portico surmounted by statues, sweeping lawns, a lake, and gilded, painted and mirrored interiors.

▶ *SO21 1DB. 5 miles NE of Winchester, off B3047.*

ALFRED'S STATUE, WINCHESTER

❽ Portchester Castle

For centuries, from the reign of Henry II, this stalwart medieval castle within an ancient Roman fort was a royal possession, an important departure point for missions to France. Henry often stayed here. King John used it as a base for hunting. Edward II, in fear of French invasion, ordered repairs and reinforcements. What survives of the royal apartments today was built for Richard II in the 1390s. It was here in 1415, that another Henry, preparing to invade France, uncovered the 'Southampton Plot' to overthrow him. The tale, related in Shakespeare's *Henry V*, tells of 'three corrupted men', Richard, Earl of Cambridge, Henry, Lord Scroop of Marsham, and Sir Thomas Grey, knight of Northumberland, who had 'for the gilt of France – O guilt indeed! Confirm'd conspiracy with fearful France; And by their hands this grace of kings must die …' In the end, it was the plotters who died.

By 1441, a survey found the castle 'right ruinous and feeble'. When Henry VIII came with Anne Boleyn in 1535, it was the first time in more than a century that a monarch had set foot in it. Elizabeth I, with a wary eye on Spain, had it fortified once more and so remodelled that she could hold court here. Only when Charles I sold it in 1632 did it finally pass out of royal hands.
▶ *PO16 9QW. 6 miles N of Portsmouth, off A27. EH.*

❾ Portsmouth Dockyard

The oldest dry dock in the world has been a key part of these islands' defences since 1495 when it was built by Henry VII. The first warship to be built here was the *Sweepstake,* in 1497, but the most famous was the carrack *Mary Rose*, between 1509 and 1511, in the reign of Henry VIII. It capsized in 1545, was raised in 1982, and the hull will be on show in a new museum from mid 2012. A great favourite with the king, *Mary Rose* was one of the first ships able to fire broadsides. Seven broadside guns were found on the starboard deck, and there would probably have been as many on the port side.

As an army is said to march on its stomach, so it seems Tudor naval crews sailed on theirs. By 1565, 23 years before the fleet took on the Spanish Armada, regulations stated that each sailor must receive in a week, 7lb of biscuits, 7 gallons of beer, 8lb of salt beef and three-fifths of a pound of cheese. Among the many ship's artefacts found were wooden bowls, plates, tankards and knives.
▶ *PO1 3LJ. Access Portsmouth by M275 from M27 and A27.*

❿ Southsea Castle

This castle was barely completed – in just six months, in 1544 – when the *Mary Rose* sank within sight of it. Another link in Henry VIII's chain of coastal defences (see page 62), it stands four-square and spruce on guard over the entrance to Portsmouth Harbour, and, like its fellows, was never called upon to repel French or Spanish invaders. But it was seized by the Parliamentarians in the Civil War, and damaged by an explosion in 1759. In the 19th century it was rebuilt, to serve as a military prison.
▶ *PO5 3PA. At S end of Portsea Island.*

⓫ Romsey Abbey

When Henry VIII's henchmen were ravaging the monasteries in the 1530s, this jewel of Norman architecture was threatened with demolition. It was saved for use as a parish church on payment of £100 raised by the townspeople, although the abbey was suppressed and the nuns evicted. The bill of sale with the king's seal is displayed in the south choir aisle.

The abbey church has its origins in a nunnery founded in AD 907 and re-founded for the Benedictines in around 960 by King Edgar. As part of her devotions, the second abbess, Ethelflaeda, would wade naked into the River Test at night to chant psalms. Towards the end of the 11th century, a half-Saxon Scottish princess, Edith, was sent to live in the care of the abbess. She married Henry I, took the name Matilda and later became known as 'Good Queen Maud'. She died in 1118, and the present abbey building was begun two years later, perhaps by Henry. In the Civil War, Parliamentarians rooted out the pews and smashed the organ, and Puritan worship was imposed by Cromwell. Lord Mountbatten of Burma, the uncle of Prince Philip, is buried in the south transept.
▶ *SO51 8EP. Romsey 8 miles NW of Southampton at junction of A3057 and A3090. Abbey in town centre.*

⓬ Broadlands

This stately home was an idyllic and romantic honeymoon retreat for Princess Elizabeth and the Duke of Edinburgh. Prince Charles and Princess Diana also spent part of their honeymoon here at the invitation of the owner, Lord Mounbatten, Charles's 'honorary grandfather'. He had first introduced the young Princess Elizabeth to his nephew Philip in 1939.

The original manor belonged to Romsey Abbey, and was sold by Henry VIII in 1547. In 1736 it became the home of Henry Temple,

CALSHOT CASTLE

1st Viscount Palmerston, who swept away the formality of the grounds to create a 'gentle descent' to the River Test. Capability Brown and architect Henry Holland created the Arcadian park and Palladian manor that the visitor will see when refurbishment is complete in summer 2012.

Broadlands was home to Anthony Ashley Cooper, 7th Earl of Shaftesbury, a social reformer and opponent of child labour, known as 'the poor man's earl'. On December 6, 1861, he wrote in his diary, in dismay: 'Heard at Ringwood this morning that the Prince [Consort] was dead! … The desolation of the Queen's heart and life; the death blow to her happiness on earth! … To me they, both of them, were very kind.'
▶ *SO51 9ZE. Just S of Romsey town centre.*

⑬ New Forest

This verdant forest – anything but 'new' – was taken as a park for deer hunting by William the Conqueror in 1079. At that time, the word 'forest' defined an area where deer and boar were protected for the monarch's sport. Severe punishments were imposed upon anyone who infringed the king's exclusive right to his 'beasts of the chase' and their food, or 'browse'. Even today, byelaws are in place, and although less stringent than of old, they are applied by a unique Verderers' Court in the Queen's House in Lyndhurst. An apparently natural landscape of woodland pasture, heaths and bogs has been shaped over nine centuries by kings and queens, who used the forest for recreation and as a source of timber for ships of war and exploration. Captain Frederick Marryat's *Children of the New Forest*, a bestseller of 1847, set in the time of the

Civil War, the rule of Oliver Cromwell and the Restoration, held its young readership in thrall to the history and the scenery, as it would today.
▶ *S of Southampton, access from A35 and A337.*

⑭ Calshot Castle

Here is an illustration of how the purposes of monarchs shaped the New Forest. This circular, three-storey, stone artillery fort was built by Henry VIII to repel the French or Spanish should they venture on Southampton Water (see page 62). Entrance was across a drawbridge and through the gatehouse. The castle was damaged by fire in the reign of Elizabeth I, and 127 of the forest's oaks were felled to repair it. Although no military action took place in Tudor times, it came into its own in both world wars. In 1913, Calshot Naval Air Station opened here – and Winston Churchill, First Lord of the Admiralty, took his first seaplane flight from it.
▶ *SO4 1BR. Calshot 2 miles SE of Fawley. Path from car park at end of B3053 in Calshot. EH.*

⑮ Hurst Castle

Another Henrician castle, this one was built on a shingle spit in the turbulent reign of Henry VIII to stand guard over the Solent. It was one of the most advanced artillery forts of its day and has stood up well to time and tide. Charles I was among the prominent figures to be imprisoned here, in 1648, before being taken to London for trial and execution. On a clear day, from the castle, the Isle of Wight is visible.
▶ *Milford on Sea SO41 0TP. 3 miles S of Lymington, off A337. EH.*

16 The Rufus Stone

An iron-clad stone in the New Forest marks the spot where William II was fatally wounded by a stray arrow while hunting. The third son of William I, the red-headed and flamboyant Rufus was out with his noblemen in 1100 when Sir Walter Tyrrell loosed an arrow at a stag. He was one of the king's finest archers, yet he missed and the arrow, glancing off an oak tree, pierced William's lung and killed him. Whether or not this was a genuine accident, Sir Walter, a Frenchman, fled back to Normandy, while a charcoal burner named Purkis loaded the body on to his cart and trundled it to Winchester Cathedral for burial. An inscription tells the tale.
▶ *1 mile NW of Minstead, just N of A31.*

17 Carisbrooke Castle, Isle of Wight

The desperation of Charles I can only be imagined when, imprisoned within these walls, he tried in vain to squeeze between window bars in a bid to escape. The king had sought sanctuary on the Isle of Wight, only to be incarcerated by the governor, who had declared for Parliament, in 1647.

Carisbrooke Castle was begun in 1100 when the island was granted to the de Redvers family, who built the stone shell-keep on a high mound. It was rebuilt in 1262 on the orders of the indomitable Countess Isabella de Redvers. Aged 11 or 12, she had become the second wife of William de Fortibus, Count of Aumale in Normandy. On his death, and that of her brother, she had come into vast wealth. In her mid-twenties, she would have been a catch for Simon de Montfort junior, who acquired the right to her hand in 1264, but she went into hiding and evaded him – even as, in 1265, the Simons de Montfort, father and son, captured Henry III at the Battle of Lewes, and briefly took over the kingdom. The countess further refused to marry Edmund Crouchback, third son of Henry III. She dug herself in at the castle with her copy of the statutes of the realm, and fired off lawsuits for infringements real or imagined. She held off Edward I, who coveted the island, finally selling it to him on her deathbed in 1293.

In 1898, a year after she became island governor, Princess Beatrice, youngest daughter of Queen Victoria, founded Carisbrooke Museum in the castle's gatehouse, as a memorial to her husband, Prince Henry of Battenberg. Some of the castle's older buildings are ruins, but other parts, including the Great Hall, are open to the public. The Constable Chamber, used by Princess Beatrice as a dining room, was where Charles I slept for 14 months. The chapel of St Nicholas has been rebuilt as a national memorial to that unfortunate king.
▶ *PO30 1XY. 1 mile SW of Newport. EH.*

18 St Mary's Church, Isle of Wight

This ancient church, dating from the 11th and 12th centuries, counted Princess Beatrice among its worshippers when she lived at Carisbrooke, from 1913–38. When she entered for matins with her lady in waiting on a Sunday morning, the congregation would get to their feet and sing the national anthem. Elderly island residents can recall how as children they would cluster in the porch after a service and offer her bunches of flowers that they had picked. As they waved her off, she would wave back, calling to them, 'See you next week.' She made a present to the church of an antique processional cross and supported local causes.
▶ *PO30 1NR. High Street, Carisbrooke. 1 mile SW of Newport.*

19 St Mildred's Church, Isle of Wight

In this church, Princess Beatrice was married with great ceremony – and now lies buried with the husband she so loved. This small but beautiful Victorian church has many royal associations. It was built in 1854–5 by Albert Jenkins Humbert, although Prince Albert may have contributed. A font dating from 1860, a gift from Queen Victoria, was designed by Princess Louise, her fourth daughter. A reredos, or altar structure, depicting the Last Supper was presented in memory of Victoria by Edward VII.

The greatest royal occasion ever held at the church was the wedding in 1885 of Princess Beatrice to Prince Henry Maurice of Battenberg. The streets were lined by the Argyll and Sutherland Highlanders, wearing crimson and tartan. The church floor was spread with crimson cloth and oriental rugs. Beatrice, in white satin and with diamonds in her veil, was attended by ten royal bridesmaids. It was a glorious start to a marriage that produced four children. In 1889, Henry became the island's governor but he died of malaria in 1896, in Ghana, while fighting in the fourth Ashanti War. Beatrice, at 38, stepped in as governor. She now shares a marble sarcophagus with her prince in the Battenberg Chapel.
▶ *PO32 6LP. 1 mile S of East Cowes.*

HERE STOOD
THE OAK TREE,
ON WHICH AN ARROW
SHOT BY
SIR WALTER TYRRELL
AT A STAG,
GLANCED AND STRUCK
KING WILLIAM
THE SECOND,
SURNAMED RUFUS,
ON THE BREAST,
OF WHICH HE
INSTANTLY DIED,
ON THE SECOND
DAY OF AUGUST,
ANNO 1100.

OSBORNE HOUSE

⑳ Osborne House, Isle of Wight

'A Sicilian palazzo with garden terraces, statues and vases shining in the sun, than which nothing can be more captivating.'
Benjamin Disraeli, Queen Victoria's favourite prime minister, had been enraptured by a visit to her seaside retreat. In 1845, Victoria and Albert had bought an estate overlooking the Solent. An existing Georgian house was demolished and, with the help of the fashionable architect Thomas Cubitt, Albert designed this grand Italianate villa with two campaniles, mixing Roman, Florentine and Palladian styles. A grand marble corridor linked the Family Pavilion to a wing intended for visitors and members of the household. The family spent many of their happiest days here. Victoria would walk with Albert in the grounds as he whistled to the nightingales. It was an idyll that ended in 1861 with his death, when the house took on an air of mourning.

There were, however, further developments at Osborne. After Disraeli made Victoria Empress of India, an Indian hall was added in 1890–1, decorated by Indian craftsmen, with Moghul-style plasterwork. Called the Durbar Room, it was designed by Bhai Ram Singh with advice from John Lockwood Kipling, father of Rudyard. Above were apartments for Victoria's youngest daughter, Beatrice, and her family. Victoria died at Osborne in January 1901, with her children and grandchildren around her. Edward VII gave the house to the nation in 1902.
▶ *PO32 6JX. 1 mile SE of East Cowes, off A3021. EH.*

㉑ The Swiss Cottage, Osborne House, Isle of Wight

'This was a place of supreme enchantment, quite one of my dearest recollections. A little house of dark wood, built in rustic Swiss-chalet style, a low-drooping roof with stones on the top and a balcony around the upper storey.' To Marie, Queen of Romania, Queen Victoria was 'Grandmama'. Her father, Alfred, was the second son of Victoria and Albert, and she would never forget the holidays she spent as a girl on the Osborne Estate, or this playhouse built for Alfred and his eight siblings. In the lower part of the cottage, there was a 'museum' in which were kept treasures collected by Victoria's offspring. Children today are no less entranced by the Swiss Cottage with its child-size furniture and emphasis on fun while teaching domestic skills.
▶ *PO32 6JX. 1 mile SE of East Cowes, off A3021. EH.*

㉒ Norris Castle, Isle of Wight

Victoria knew the Isle of Wight from childhood, when she used to stay at this castle, built by James Wyatt in 1790, in the Norman style, for Lord Henry Seymour. From her granddaughter, Marie of Romania, we have a lyrical account of this place, leased one summer by her aunt the Empress Frederick, her father's sister and mother of the Kaiser. 'It was closer to the sea than Osborne House; it was a large place built in grey stone in the same style as Windsor, it seemed to me … I thought it extraordinarily beautiful … There were peacocks strutting about in all their glory on the terraces. It was the first time I heard peacocks calling, and ever since, the call of the peacock has reminded me of Norris Castle.' Today, it is in private hands, but visitors can have a wonderful view of it from the Solent.
▶ *PO32 6AZ. 1 mile E of East Cowes.*

㉓ Cowes, Isle of Wight

The world's largest sailing regatta is based at Cowes, and dates from the reign of George IV, who was a great yachting enthusiast. It takes place in August and follows Goodwood and the 'Glorious 12th' (start of the grouse-shooting season) in the social calendar. The first-ever regatta, held on August 10, 1826 under the flag of the Royal Yacht Club, later the Royal Yacht Squadron, offered the prize of a 'Gold Cup of the value of £100'. The Duke of Edinburgh was another keen yachtsman. His granddaughter, Zara Phillips, took part in a charity race in 2011, competing against actor Ewan McGregor in one of the other four yachts.
▶ *Reach Cowes by ferry from Southampton.*

㉔ Newport Minster, Isle of Wight

In the north aisle of this Victorian church is a memorial to a broken-hearted princess. A figure of a young woman, in white marble, is seen lying with her cheek upon a bible. Above hangs a grating, suggesting that she was once a prisoner, but the bars are broken; she is free! The Princess Elizabeth Memorial was presented to the church by Queen Victoria, to honour the second daughter of Charles I, who was imprisoned with her brother Henry in Carisbrooke Castle, after their father was captured and beheaded. It is said that she died of grief. She was buried in the Chancel of St Thomas. Prince Albert laid the church foundation stone in 1854.
▶ *PO30 1JU. Newport 4 miles S of Cowes.*

Of captains and kings

Ever since Alfred took to the waves, succeeding monarchs have relied on naval prowess to safeguard these shores.

In *Richard II*, Shakespeare has John of Gaunt describe the 'silver sea' that surrounds Britain as a defensive moat 'against the envy of less happier lands'. Across that 'moat' came the Romans, Angles, Saxons, Jutes and Vikings, and then in 1066 the Normans. In the 9th century, Alfred the Great had been the first to launch longships to combat Viking raids on the south coast. Without a seaborne fighting force no king or queen could feel secure upon the British throne. In 1155, Henry II granted a Royal Charter to the 'Cinque Ports' to maintain ships on stand-by for the Crown. For this service, Hastings, New Romney, Hythe, Dover and Sandwich were granted tax concessions, autonomy, and the right to levy tolls, detain and punish criminals, and claim flotsam, jetsam and floating wreckage.

Marine traffic was not all one way, of course. The Navy was not just defensive, and British ships made frequent forays as aggressors – invading France, waging Holy War in distant lands. Indeed, the size and composition of the Navy reflected the mindset and ambitions of different monarchs.

A reformation of the 'Navy Royal' began under the Tudors. To Henry VIII, the Channel must have looked less like a moat than an open door. After the king's divorce from Catherine of Aragon, fearing attacks from Catholic France or Spain, he commissioned a mighty chain of artillery forts along the coast, and the building of 27 new ships, funded by the sale of the monasteries and their treasures. He even used

stone from the religious houses, for example at Deal Castle in Kent, which was designed by the brilliant, eccentric military architect Stephen von Haschenperg to resemble a Tudor rose. It stands perfectly intact, embodying materials from a Carmelite priory at Sandwich. A formal naval administration was set up to manage the expanded fleet of 'Great Ships' of a new design, bristling with guns, such as the modestly named *Henry Grace à Dieu* (*Henry Grace of God,* also known as the *Great Harry*) and *Mary Rose*. The *Mary Rose*, overloaded with insubordinate men, sank as the king watched, dismayed, from the shore, during an engagement with the French fleet. 'I have the sort of knaves I cannot rule,' lamented the Vice Admiral. She was one of the first ships to fire a broadside, and one of Henry's favourites.

Edward VI and Mary I took little interest in the Navy, but for Elizabeth I it was a priority. She antagonised Spain by condoning the piracy of sea dogs, such as Francis Drake and John Hawkins, who

preyed on Spanish merchant ships for silver and gold, and for supporting a Dutch revolt against Spanish occupation. The 'invincible' Armada set sail in July 1588, despatched by Philip II to overthrow the heretic queen. He was her brother-in-law, having been the reluctant consort to Mary I, but there was no love lost between them. The Armada had been two years in preparation, while at Chatham British shipwrights had been busy on a new class of swift galleons – *Nonpareil*, *Golden Lion*, *Hope*, *Revenge*, *Tremonata* – to repel the enemy.

Under Charles II, diarist Samuel Pepys gave such distinguished service at the Admiralty that he became known as 'the right hand' of what was now the Royal Navy. For the next century or so, the fleet engaged in a protracted struggle with France, winning four wars between 1688 and 1763. In 1802 the British and French signed the treaty of Amiens but George III regarded the uneasy peace as an 'experiment'. When war resumed in 1803, he wrote to Bishop Hurd, 'We are here in daily expectation that Bonaparte will attempt his threatened invasion ... Should his troops effect a landing, I shall certainly put myself at the head of mine.' Fortunately, in Horatio Nelson his Navy had a supremely able commander to prevent that landing. France's last challenge came in 1805 when they were vanquished at Trafalgar. Nelson had resisted pleas by his flag captain Sir Thomas Hardy to remove the conspicuous decorations on his uniform that would identify him, but he was hit by a musket shot and fell, breaking his back. He died below deck on *HMS Victory*, reassured by Hardy that the British had the French on the run.

The crown and the navy

The 'HMS' prefix, 'On His/Her Majesty's Service', bears witness to the enduring links between Crown and Navy. The Queen's father, George VI, as a sub-lieutenant, was the last British sovereign to see active service at sea, in the battle of Jutland in May 1916. Prince Philip, now Lord High Admiral of the Fleet, served with the Royal Navy, gaining the rank of commander, and in 1941 was mentioned in despatches. The Prince of Wales holds the rank of admiral and took command of his own ship in 1976. Prince Andrew was part of the task force that sailed to the South Atlantic to regain the Falkland Islands in 1982. He holds the rank of captain and is commodore-in-chief. Prince William is a sub-lieutenant and commodore-in-chief for Scotland and submarines.

HERTFORDSHIRE

The ancient church of St Albans was a place of pilgrimage until brought down by a cardinal and a king. Some years later, at a retreat nearby, a king's daughter discovered that she would inherit the crown.

❶ Knebworth House

Elizabeth I was among the distinguished visitors to grace this stately home, which has been in the Lytton family since 1490. The original house was built of red brick to a quadrangle design, but by the time it passed to Edward Bulwer-Lytton in 1843, only the west wing was standing. Bulwer-Lytton, a former MP, was the author of historical fiction, and the saying that 'the pen is mightier than the sword'. He engaged H.E. Kendall Junior and John G. Crace, architect and decorator, to create a Victorian Gothic fantasy with towers, pinnacles, heraldic beasts and gargoyles, while the gardens were laid out in Italianate fashion. Knebworth's links with royalty today are tenuous – it appears that one of Bulwer-Lytton's ancestors on the maternal side was an aunt of Henry VII's.

In modern times, Knebworth has become famous as a music venue, 'the stately home of rock', but it has had musical associations since the 1760s, when Leonora Lytton married Sir James Oswald, Scottish composer of such catchy numbers as 'the Knebworth Jig'.

▶ *SG3 6PY. Access Knebworth from Junction 7 of A1(M).*

❷ St Albans Cathedral

On Holy Innocent's Day, 1115, Henry I was present to see the consecration of a Norman abbey that had been completed more than 25 years earlier. In fact, the history of St Albans goes back much further than that. It is the oldest site of continuous Christian worship in Britain. Offa II of Mercia founded a Benedictine abbey at this site in the 8th century but its beginnings lie in Roman times, with the martyrdom of Alban, who was beheaded for embracing the faith.

Like all ancient churches, St Albans has been much altered over the centuries, but a great part of the layout and proportions of the building that the visitor sees today dates from the first abbot, Paul of Caen, in the late 11th century. By the time the abbey was surrendered to the Crown in 1539, during Henry VIII's Reformation, it had already been stripped of most of its treasures by Cardinal Wolsey, who, in nine years as absentee abbot, removed gold and silver, altar clothes and tapestries. Even iron and lead were taken, and

what Wolsey had left was snapped up for the Crown. St Albans no longer welcomed pilgrims or royal visitors, and no longer did its abbey bells ring out. The building fell into a state of collapse until the great Sir George Gilbert Scott was appointed architect to restore it in 1856. It was a project dear to his heart and he worked on it until his death in 1878 – a year after Queen Victoria granted St Albans city status and the abbey became a cathedral.

▶ *AL1 1BY. St Albans city centre.*

❸ Hatfield House

Elizabeth Tudor was sitting reading in the shade of an oak tree in the park of her childhood home when they brought her the news – the queen was dead, long live the queen! Hatfield House began life in 1485 as Hatfield Palace, built for the Bishop of Ely. Henry VIII, in seizing church properties, took it over as a home for his children, Mary, Elizabeth and Edward. At Hatfield, more than anywhere else, visitors have a sense of the young Elizabeth. Although the house is not as she knew it, the Great Hall in which she held her first Council, in 1558, survives, along with her portrait, gloves, stockings, and an illuminated parchment in the library, which fancifully traces her lineage back to Adam and Eve. In the Great Hall she enjoyed masques, being entertained by a play, bear-baiting and the singing of a boy soprano, until a stern reproof from her half-sister Mary, as queen, warned against such 'frivolity'.

When James I inherited Hatfield, he did not much care for it, and proposed to Robert Cecil, chief minister of the Crown and later 1st Earl of Salisbury, that he exchange it for his home, Theobalds (today a hotel and conference centre). Cecil can't have much cared for it, either. In 1607 he demolished three sides, and rebuilt it to designs by Robert Lyminge, modified by others, among them perhaps a young Inigo Jones. Hatfield is now the home of the 7th Marquess and Marchioness of Salisbury. Visitors find a stupendous Jacobean manor. As well as the old Great Hall and library, there is an armoury, and in what was originally the King's Great Chamber, a life-sized statue of James I, finished to look like bronze, by the French sculptor Maximilian Colt.

▶ *AL9 5NQ. Hatfield signed from Junction 4 of A1(M).*

HATFIELD HOUSE

KENT

Fortified castles, working harbours and historic dockyards show how much royal attention has been paid to defending a vulnerable part of the coastline, while inland, the shade of Anne Boleyn persists.

❶ Hever Castle

The childhood home of Anne Boleyn is an idealised dream of a castle, moated, crenellated and complete with drawbridge and portcullis. In 1451, the 13th-century fortress of William de Hever was bought by Sir Geoffrey Bullen, whose grandson, Thomas Boleyn, would become an ambassador and treasurer for Henry VIII. Thomas and his wife, Elizabeth Howard, had two daughters, Mary and Anne. Both became ladies in waiting at court, Anne to Queen Catherine of Aragon. And wait she did, in her role as Henry's mistress, for the day when he would divorce Catherine. The marriage she had so desired lasted just three years and produced a daughter and future queen, Elizabeth. On May 19, 1536, at Tower Hill, Anne Boleyn commended her soul to God and laid her head on the block. Two years later, upon Thomas Boleyn's death, Hever was taken by the Crown. On his divorce from his fourth wife, Anne of Cleves, Henry gave her the castle as part of her settlement. It was bought in 1903 by William Waldorf Astor, the American millionaire, who landscaped and extended the grounds. In the castle are Anne Boleyn's two prayer books, both signed in her own hand.
▶ *TN8 7NG. 10 miles NW of Royal Tunbridge Wells on minor roads.*

❷ Penshurst Place

The Elizabethan poet, soldier and courtier Sir Philip Sidney was born in this house, the most complete surviving example of 14th-century architecture in England. The original house was transformed into a country mansion by Sir Stephen de Penchester in around 1340, and in the 1390s it was fortified against a feared invasion by the French. In the 15th and 16th centuries it was owned by the Dukes of Buckingham, and upon the execution of the 3rd Duke, in 1521, the estate, as property of a traitor, was seized by the Crown. Henry VIII stayed here when he was wooing Anne Boleyn at Hever Castle. His son, Edward VI, granted it to his childhood friend Sir Henry Sidney, whose father had been tutor to the bookish Edward. Sidney's wife, Mary, was the sister of Sir Robert Dudley, Earl of Leicester, a favourite of Elizabeth I. The

queen visited often and the Queen Elizabeth Room is named in her honour. In the State Dining Room is a painting of her being whirled off her feet by Dudley as they dance the Volta. The Great Hall has been described as one of the world's greatest rooms, and the Elizabethan gardens have been spared later remodelling.
▶ *TN11 8DG. 6 miles NW of Royal Tunbridge Wells at junction of B2176 and B2188.*

❸ Royal Tunbridge Wells

'11th August 1663. I to the 'Change, where I met Dr Pierce, who tells me the King comes to towne this day, from Tunbridge, to stay a day or two and then fetch the Queen from thence.' Thus diarist Samuel Pepys records a visit by Charles II and his wife Catherine of Braganza to the wells, where the waters must have picked her up wonderfully, since the queen had 'grown a very debonair lady'. From the discovery of Chalybeate Spring in 1606, this genteel town in the Weald became a favourite resort for royalty and aristocracy. Charles II's mother, Henrietta Maria, came to recover from a miscarriage, and attributed his birth to her stay. Princess Victoria came several times with her mother, staying in the sandstone mansion that is now the Hotel du Vin. She would have admired so much fine Regency architecture, and rode on the common on her donkey, Flower. Edward VII bestowed the 'Royal' prefix in 1909.
▶ *15 miles S of Junction 5 of M25 at junction of A26 and A264.*

❹ Knole

'It has a deep inward gaiety of some very old woman who has always been beautiful, who has had many lovers,' wrote poet and novelist Vita Sackville-West of the family home. Henry VIII was one who took a shine to the old lady. The huge 15th-century country house was the creation of Thomas Bouchier, an Archbishop of Canterbury, who acquired the Knole estate in 1456 and created a grand episcopal palace, home to five archbishops before it was taken by the king in 1538. In 1566, Elizabeth I gave Knole to Thomas Sackville, 1st Earl of Dorset. He transformed it into a Renaissance mansion. In the late 17th century, the 6th Earl amassed a collection of Stuart furniture and textiles, and in the 18th, John Sackville, 3rd Duke of Dorset, hung the house with Old Masters from Italy, as well as portraits by English artists, such as Reynolds and Gainsborough. The grey Kentish ragstone building presented to some a gloomy aspect. The 17th-century diarist John Evelyn was brought low by this 'greate old fashion'd house', while in the 18th century, MP and art historian Horace Walpole concluded that it had 'neither beauty nor prospects'. Vita saw it through different eyes, recording: 'It has the tone of England; it melts into the green of the garden turf, into the tawnier green of the park beyond, into the blue of the pale English sky.' It was the setting for her 1930 novel *The Edwardians*.

▶ *TN15 0RP. 2 miles SE of Sevenoaks. NT*

⑤ Leeds Castle

What better gift for a king to give his queen than one of the loveliest castles in the world? The 12th-century fairytale castle is itself very beautiful, but its island location,

lapped by and mirrored in an artificial lake, is what makes it so magical. The first stone castle on the site was built by Robert de Crèvecoeur on land given to his father by William the Conqueror. In 1265 the family was dispossessed after Robert's great grandson sided with Simon de Montfort against Henry III.

Crèvecoeur means 'heartbreak', and many a heart has been broken at this castle. Edward I and his beloved queen, Eleanor of Castile, adored Leeds and stayed often. He brought his second wife, Margaret of France, to Leeds for their honeymoon. Richard II, in his turn, gave the castle to Anne of Bohemia, and spent time here after her death in 1394. Henry IV gave the castle to his second wife, Joan of Navarre. On his death, her stepson, Henry V, had her confined at Pevensey for alleged sorcery, and gave the castle to his wife, Catherine of Valois. Henry VIII transformed the castle into a palace for Catherine of Aragon – but kept it for himself. It is now run by the Leeds Castle Foundation.

▶ *ME17 1PL. 6 miles E of Maidstone. Close to Junction 8 of M20.*

THE KING'S BED, KNOLE

❻ Chatham Dockyards

William Camden's *Britannia* of 1607 records how, on the foaming Medway, was built 'the finest fleet the sun ever beheld, and ready on a minute's warning'. The role of Chatham in the defence of Britain begins, as Camden tells us, with the commissioning of ships by 'our gracious sovereign Elizabeth for the security of her subjects and the terror of her enemies'. The archenemy at that time was Spain, and the shipwrights at Chatham prepared the queen's warships to face the mighty Armada. The fleet slipped out of harbour in March 1588, under the command of the Lord High Admiral, Lord Howard of Effingham, and sailed for Plymouth.

Although the original Tudor docks were closed in 1613, and the 32ha (80-acre) site is no longer a working dockyard, there are museum galleries that recall 400 years of Royal Naval history, and the visitor can see such important buildings as the restored Commissioner's House, and the working ropery, which is a quarter of a mile long. The Commissioner's House is the dockyards' earliest surviving building, dating from the reign of Queen Anne (1702–13). Nelson's flagship, HMS *Victory*, was built at Chatham, fitted out as a reserve ship and launched on May 7, 1765. Chatham is one of the world's most complete examples of a dockyard from the age of sail.

▶ *ME4 4TZ. Access Chatham from Junctions 2, 3 and 4 of M2.*

❼ Upnor Castle

'Britannia rules the waves!' proclaimed Elizabeth I on a visit to the only castle she commissioned in her reign. This small, turreted artillery fort on the banks of the Medway, fronted by a water bastion, was built in 1559 to protect the ships moored at Chatham dockyards. It failed to do so in June 1667, when the Dutch, under the command of Admiral de Ruyter, sailed up the river and attacked. Charles II's economies meant that the fleet had been reduced and the 'big ships' laid up, leaving the country vulnerable. Diarist Samuel Pepys, chief secretary of the Navy Board, heard from a neighbour up from Chatham that he had seen 'the *Royal James*, *The Oake*, and *London* burnt by the enemy with their fire-ships; that two or three men-of-war come up with them, and made no more of Upnor Castle's shooting than of a fly.'

To Pepys, a revolution and an end to Charles's reign seemed inevitable. 'All our hearts do ake; fore the newes is true, that the Dutch have broke the chaine and burned our ships ... I do fear that the whole kingdom is undone.' Charles survived as king. England survived. Britannia ruled the waves.

▶ *ME2 4XG. 3 miles N of town centre. EH.*

UPNOR CASTLE

❽ Rochester Castle

Bishop Gundulf, in his service to William the Conqueror, was the first King's Engineer, and is regarded as the father of the Corps of Royal Engineers. He supervised the building of the White Tower at the Tower of London (see page 100), and in the first year of the reign of William Rufus, 1087, he rebuilt Rochester Castle in stone to defend the Medway crossing of the road from London to the Kent coast. Henry I granted it to William de Corbeil, Archbishop of Canterbury, in 1127, who commissioned a towering square keep with soaring turrets, fearsome without, luxurious within. In 1215, the castle was garrisoned by rebel barons, and King John and his army used stone-throwing engines to bombard it. For two months the onslaught continued until the king's men undermined the southeast angle, shoring it up with pit props and burning them with pork fat, to bring the southeast tower down. In 1264, the castle was badly damaged by Simon de Montfort's men in the uprising against Henry III. Now, after centuries of rebuilding and neglect, the interior of the keep is little more than a shell but still inspires a sense of awe.

▶ *ME1 1SW. Town centre. Access Rochester from Junctions 2 and 3 of M2.*

❾ Canterbury Cathedral

'Will no one rid me of this turbulent priest?' Henry II's frustrated lament led to murder most foul. Having made Thomas Becket Archbishop of Canterbury in 1162, the king expected loyalty from him. Instead, Becket sided with the pope in disputes over power within the Church. Railing against 'miserable drones and traitors', bemoaning the 'shameful contempt of a low-born cleric', he uttered the fateful cry, which four of his knights took for an order. On December 29, 1170, they entered the cathedral during vespers and killed Becket as he knelt in prayer. He was canonised in 1173. Canterbury became a place of pilgrimage. His shrine was destroyed in Henry VIII's Dissolution. In the Civil War, Cromwell's Puritans stabled horses in the nave. Yet today it is an awe-inspiring example of English Perpendicular Gothic. Columns soar heavenward to meet in vaulted arches. Stained-glass windows depict miracles that began three days after Becket's death. The Romanesque crypt dates from the 11th century. The effigy of Edward, the Black Prince, who died in 1376, is made from burnished latten and is startlingly beautiful. Opposite lie Henry IV and his queen, Joan of Navarre.

▶ *CT1 2EH. Canterbury city centre.*

SOUTHERN ENGLAND

61

❿ Canterbury Castle

This great stone castle, dating from the reign of William the Conqueror, has a long and rather grim history as a prison. A new keep was begun in the reign of William II and completed by Henry I. Louis, Dauphin of France, seized it in 1216, but then departed. In 1290, Edward I issued an edict to expel all Jews from England, and Jewish citizens of Canterbury were held here before being exiled. Thomas Cromwell, 1st Earl of Essex, enthusiastically supporting Henry VIII's Reformation, had two priests incarcerated for permitting the pope's name to appear in their books. Henry's daughter, as Queen Mary, had 40 or more people imprisoned and executed for rejecting Catholicism. By the 17th century, the castle was abandoned and derelict. In 1730, a County Session House was built on the site of the Great Hall, and in the 19th century the castle served as a coal and coke depot. What was described in 1901 as 'a most miserable, discoloured ruin, its Cyclopean walls begrimed with soot and filth', has since been restored to a more aesthetically pleasing ruined state.
▶ *CT1 2PR. SW of Canterbury city centre.*

⓫ Canterbury Statues – Ethelbert and Bertha

Pagan Saxon king Ethelbert of Kent and his Christian bride, Bertha, granddaughter of Clovis of France, are commemorated with 21st-century statues by the Ramsgate sculptor Steve Melton. They were unveiled by Princess Michael of Kent in May 2006. The lifelike figures, more than 2m (7ft) tall, stand on Lady Wootton's Green, and have been placed so that they appear to be engaged in dialogue. An inscription tells how Ethelbert met a Christian mission from Rome in AD 597, led by Augustine, the first Archbishop of Canterbury, and a saint in the making.
▶ *E of Broad Street, Canterbury city centre.*

⓬ Ramsgate Royal Harbour

This bright and breezy seaside town owes its royal kudos to the warmth of its people – and to the pique and malice of an intemperate king. The marriage of the Prince Regent, later George IV, to his cousin Caroline of Brunswick was made in hell. At the time of his coronation in 1820 they had already been estranged for many years. He was outraged when she arrived at Dover to be a part of the show, and 'multitudes met her on the beach with loud acclamations, banners and every sign of popular enthusiasm'. His new title of King of Great Britain and Hanover obliged him to visit Hanover, and in 1821 he chose to snub Dover and sail from Ramsgate. George was a gluttonous, licentious drunk, but he was also the king, and the welcome he received so pleased him that he 'denominated' Ramsgate to be a Royal Harbour – still the only one in Britain. He spent a night with his friend Sir William Curtis in Cliff House, overlooking the West Pier. The tycoon made, among other things, ships' biscuits but despite his business acumen, he was not highly literate, and unwittingly endowed the language with the phrase 'the three Rs' – 'reading, riting and rithmetic'. The obelisk erected to mark the king's visit was soon known as 'the royal toothpick'.
▶ *CT11 9LQ. Ramsgate 17 miles NE of Canterbury.*

⓭ Deal Castle

One of the earliest and most elaborate of Henry VIII's coastal artillery forts was designed by Stefan von Haschenperg, a Moravian military engineer, to resemble a Tudor rose or double clover. At its centre is a circular tower, around which are smaller circular bastions. It is built of Kentish ragstone and Caen stone plundered from the dissolved religious houses in the region. Together with the castles of Walmer and Sandown, which no longer exists, its purpose was to protect against invasion from the French and Spanish. The three 'Castles of the Downs' did not see action until the Civil War, when they suffered grave damage. They were held first for Parliament then the king. The Roundheads, under Colonel Rich, were fought off for three months. Despite being repaired and refortified, Deal has had no defensive role since the end of the Napoleonic wars in 1815, although it was home to a Captain of the Castle until World War II.
▶ *CT14 7BA. 8 miles N of Dover on A258. EH.*

⓮ Walmer Castle

The long sandy beaches of the East Kent coast were vulnerable to attack from just across the water. Henry VIII had reason to fear invasion by Catholic Europe. It was not from pure paranoia that he commissioned his series of defensive forts, known as 'Henrician' or 'device' castles, along the coast. With Deal and Sandown, Walmer was designed to repel the French and Spanish, who never came. The three castles were built by press-ganged labour with stone from monasteries, including the Carmelite priory in Sandwich. Earth bulwarks linked them into a single defensive system. Walmer was built to a

concentric plan around a circular keep, with access via a drawbridge to the northern bastion. By the time it was completed, the threat of foreign incursions had diminished. From 1708 it served as the official residence of the Lords Warden of the Cinque Ports, a ceremonial office often held by prime ministers or members of the royal family. Their influence tempered the castle's military image. William Pitt and the 2nd Earl Granville created the lovely gardens. The 1st Duke of Wellington was warden from 1829 until his death in 1852. His bedroom is much as he left it, including the armchair in which he died, and a pair of boots. The Queen Mother was warden until her death in 2002 and loved to stay at Walmer in the summer. Some of her rooms are open to the public. One of the gardens, designed by Penelope Hobhouse, within the 19th-century walled garden was a gift for her 95th birthday.
▶ *CT14 7LJ. 1 mile S of Deal. EH.*

⑮ Dover Castle

This massive stone castle on Dover's white cliffs was begun by Henry II on the site of an Iron Age fort. William the Conqueror had the fort converted into a timber stockade in the space of eight days in 1066. Henry I and his Plantagenet successors created a medieval stone fortress that was garrisoned for nine centuries. The imposing Great Keep was designed by Maurice the Engineer and erected between 1180 and 1185. It is a daunting edifice, 25m (83ft) tall, with walls in parts 6.5m (21ft) thick. It was intended to serve not just as a defence but as a symbol of the king's might, and as a ceremonial palace where Henry could hold court. After his former friend Thomas Becket was killed by his knights, the king entertained important guests here, who were making pilgrimages to Becket's shrine at Canterbury Cathedral. Although he had not actually ordered Becket's murder, Henry had done penance for it, and then exploited Canterbury's popularity as a religious destination. The addition of the Great Tower was an assertion of his royal authority.

The castle played host over the centuries to Henry VIII, Elizabeth I and Henrietta Maria, wife of Charles I. At 5 o'clock on December 27, 1539, Lady Anne, daughter of the German Duke of Cleves, stepped ashore at Dover on her way to London to become the fourth Mrs Henry VIII. 'I like her not!' was Henry's verdict on first seeing the woman whom he afterwards derided as 'the Flanders mare'
▶ *CT16 1HU. E of Dover town centre. Access Dover from A2 and A20. EH.*

⑯ Westenhanger Castle

The ruined Rosamund's Tower in the north wall of this partly derelict castle was scene of trysts between Henry II and his mistress, Rosamund de Clifford. She was a famous beauty, known as 'the fair Rosamund' and 'Rose of the world'. The affair became public knowledge in 1174 and ended when she retired to a nunnery two years later. The quadrangular castle had been built in the 14th century and by the mid-1500s had been greatly extended to include suites for royalty. Elizabeth I used it as a command centre for Kentish troops to defend the coast against the Spanish Armada. By the mid-1600s, it had become one of the principal houses in Kent. Much of it was demolished in 1701, and it fell into neglect. Now a reconstructed house and impressive medieval barns set in 6ha (14 acres) of meadowland are occasionally open to the public.
▶ *CT21 4HX. 3 miles W of Hythe off A20.*

THE DUKE'S FAMOUS BOOTS
WALMER CASTLE

OXFORDSHIRE

Among the dreaming spires of Oxford, Henry VIII designated a college and a cathedral. Its castle has a grimmer history. To the north, the magnificent Blenheim Palace emphasizes the significance of war.

❶ Wantage

Alfred the Great was born in the 9th century in the royal palace at the Roman settlement of Wanating – now Wantage, a small market town of narrow streets and half-timbered buildings. On July 14, 1877, the Prince and Princess of Wales unveiled a statue of Alfred in the marketplace, commissioned and paid for by Colonel Robert Loyd-Lindsay, and executed by Count Gleichen (Prince Victor of Hohenloh-Langenburg). Sculpted from Sicilian marble and set upon a granite block, it depicts Alfred with a battle-axe in one hand and parchment in the other. A plaque reads: 'Alfred found learning dead and he restored it, education neglected and he revived it, the laws powerless and he gave them force, the church debased and he raised it, the land ravaged by a fearful enemy from which he delivered it. Alfred's name shall live as long as mankind shall respect the past.' Nobody knows what Alfred looked like, and it is said that the statue's face resembles none more so than Colonel Robert Loyd-Lindsay.

▶ *18 miles SW of Oxford at junction of A338 and A417.*

❷ Abingdon

Mute swans have been the property of the monarch since the 12th century, when swan was served at royal banquets. In Tudor times, roast swan was particularly popular for a wedding centrepiece – as in the feast to celebrate the marriage of Henry VIII and Catherine of Aragon. Even today, The Queen has ownership of mute swans in the UK, except in the Orkney Islands where that right was challenged. In the third week of July a census of swan populations is conducted on the Thames between Sunbury in Surrey and Abingdon. Under the Act of Swans 1482, it became the responsibility of two Livery Companies of the City of London, the Vintners and the Dyers, to round up, mark and count the birds. It is the duty of the sovereign's Swan Marker to count the cygnets, to ensure that swan populations are not depleted. In 2009, the Queen as 'Seigneur of the Swans', travelled up the river to witness the ancient ceremony of Swan Upping for the first time.

▶ *7 miles S of Oxford at junction of A415 and A4183.*

SWAN UPPING, ABINGDON

❸ Henley Royal Regatta

Since Prince Albert first lent his support to the regatta in 1851, the reigning monarch has been patron of this international event. The annual regatta has been held in smart Henley-on-Thames every year since 1839 apart from during the two world wars. It takes place over five days in late June/early July and is often attended by royalty.

▶ *RG9 2LY. 8 miles NE of Reading at junction of A4155 and A4130.*

❹ Christ Church, Oxford

Cardinal Wolsey built Cardinal College in 1524 on the site of St Frideswide's monastery, which he had suppressed. Wolsey was Henry VIII's Lord Chancellor and at the height of his powers. In his role as absentee abbot of St Albans Cathedral, he stripped its treasury to help fund his college. He had a passion for wealth, grand houses and the high life, but fell from favour when he failed to secure a papal annulment of the king's marriage. He was accused of treason and, in 1529, Henry took over his property. As part of his reorganisation of the Church of England, the king re-founded the college in 1546, and appointed the old monastery as cathedral of the diocese of Oxford. The institution of cathedral and university college was named *Aedes Christi* (House of Christ).

In the Civil War, Charles I lived in the Deanery, holding Parliament in the Great Hall and worshipping in the cathedral. Charles II rewarded the college for its loyalty. 'The Dean, Chapter and Students of the Cathedral Church of Christ in Oxford of the Foundation of King Henry the Eighth', to give it its formal title, is the only college in the world that is also a cathedral, and the seat of the Bishop of Oxford.

▶ *OX1 1DP. St Aldates, city centre.*

❺ Oxford Castle

Robert D'Oilly was a comrade-in-arms of William the Conqueror, fighting alongside him in the Norman Conquest. Robert began building this castle in 1071 on the western edge of the Saxon town, and for most of its existence it has been a prison. According to legend, Princess Matilda, daughter of Henry I and known as the 'Empress Maud', was held here by Stephen, Henry's nephew, in 1135, as the two struggled for the throne in the period known as the Anarchy. Matilda escaped from the castle and fled across the frozen Thames, unseen in her white nightdress.

The castle was garrisoned by Royalists in the Civil War and destroyed by Cromwell's men. The prison buildings were extended, however, and until 1996 convicted criminals were held here at Her Majesty's pleasure. Now the 2ha (5-acre) site in the city centre has been opened up, and includes restaurants, cafés, a hotel and art gallery. To former inmates, it must be unrecognisable. The Saxon St George's Tower and the Norman Castle Mound have survived the centuries of destruction and rebuilding.

▶ *OX1 1AY. Just W of Oxford city centre.*

❻ Blenheim Palace

John Churchill, 1st Duke of Marlborough, was a mean, avaricious man, intent upon his own advancement. Yet he was a great general, a military genius and leader of men. In 1678, he married Sarah Jennings, one of Princess Anne's attendants and her intimate. When Anne came to the throne in 1702, Churchill became one of the most powerful men in England, imposing his views on the ailing queen through his meddlesome wife. In a letter to the duke, expressing gratitude for victory at the Battle of Blenheim in 1704, the queen wrote that it 'will not only humble our enemyes abroad but Contribute very much to ye Putting a Stop to ye ill designs of those at home'. More tangible was the gift of the royal estate at Woodstock, on which to build a palace. John Vanbrugh was commissioned, and a model was presented to the queen at Kensington. Sarah, who would have chosen Sir Christopher Wren, lamented 'the madnesse of the whole Design … I opposed it all that it was possible for me to doe.' In spite of her cavilling, Vanbrugh, together with Nicholas Hawksmoor, set out to build a baroque mansion in the highest style.

At court, meanwhile, the duchess overstepped the mark with Anne, and the Marlboroughs, falling from favour, went into temporary exile. In 1712, work stopped, but the house was eventually completed at the duke's own expense. Vanbrugh declared it a work of 'beauty, magnificence and duration'. Above all, it is triumphal. On the ceiling of the Great Hall, Sir James Thornhill painted a map of Blenheim battlefield. Heroic murals celebrate military might. At the end of an avenue stands a 41m (134ft) Column of Victory. For Sarah, who dreamt of a comfortable country house, it was indeed 'madness'. In November 1874, the most famous Churchill of them all, Winston Spencer Churchill, was born here.

▶ *OX20 1PP. 8 miles NW of Oxford on A44.*

SURREY

Monarchs have been royally entertained in the palaces and mansions of Surrey, but one king was forced to relinquish his ancestral rights here, and 700 years later another chose to abandon the throne.

❶ Fort Belvedere

What began life as an elaborate folly was to be the scene of one of the most momentous events in the recent history of British royalty.
When Prince William Augustus commissioned Fort Belvedere in 1750, it was to be essentially picturesque, its only practical purpose that of a summerhouse. In 1828, Sir Jeffrey Wyattville enlarged the structure, adding an octagonal room in which George IV would dine. In 1911 it was converted into a residence – presented, in 1929, by George V to his son Edward, Prince of Wales. Even as king, Edward VIII stayed frequently, and it was here, on December 10, 1936, that he renounced the throne to marry an American divorcee, Wallis Simpson. In 2011, letters came to light, written by Wallis to Ernest, the husband she was divorcing, which reveal that she still loved him. She had enjoyed being the king's mistress – but had not dreamt that she would marry 'Peter Pan'. She wrote, 'None of this mess and waking emptiness is my doing.' An abdication of responsibility, one might say.

The house, on Shrubs Hill in Windsor Great Park, is in private hands.
▶ *SL5 7SD. 8 miles S of Windsor close to junction of A30 and A329.*

❷ Nonsuch

Visitors enjoying Nonsuch Park could for centuries only fantasise about the palace that once stood here. Henry VIII ordered it to be built in one of his great hunting grounds to celebrate the birth, in 1537, of his long-awaited son and heir, Edward. Even by Henry's standards the project was ambitious. The palace was the height of ostentation – Henry's intention was to overshadow the palace of his rival, François I of France. One overawed foreign visitor commented, 'This which no equal has in art or fame, Britons deservedly do Nonsuch name.' The building cost £24,000 and was incomplete when Edward VI ascended the throne. Just four paintings were made of it before it was given by Charles II to one of his many mistresses, Barbara Palmer, the Duchess of Cleveland, in 1670. The foul-tempered and promiscuous duchess, described by diarist John Evelyn as 'the curse of the nation', had the place dismantled and sold the materials to pay her gambling debts. Now, in the service wing of Georgian Nonsuch Mansion, at the heart of the park, the public can see a large and beautiful model, created by Ben Ruthven-Taggar from research conducted by Professor Martin Biddle over 50 years. Perfectly to scale, and astounding in its detail, it was unveiled in October 2011.
▶ *SM3 8AL. Just NE of centre of Ewell.*

❸ Polesden Lacy

The illegitimate daughter of an Edinburgh brewer created a fabulously grand house here in which to entertain royalty. In 1906, Captain the Hon. Ronald Greville acquired for his new bride, Margaret McEwan, a regency villa designed by Thomas Cubitt. Mrs Greville engaged Charles Mewes and Arthur Davis, the architects of the Ritz, to create opulent Edwardian interiors, with an additional suite of rooms to accommodate Edward VII. After the death of her husband in 1908, Margaret continued to cultivate friends in high places. She grew very close to Queen Mary, consort of George V, and to Elizabeth Bowes-Lyons, future wife of George VI (the couple spent part of their honeymoon here). After Mrs Greville's death in 1942, Elizabeth wrote to Osbert Sitwell, 'She was so shrewd, so kind and so amusingly unkind, so sharp, such fun, so naughty, altogether a real person, a character, utterly Mrs Ronald Greville and no tinge of anything alien.' To photographer Cecil Beaton she was 'a greedy, snobbish old toad'. Her jewellery collection included the Empress Josephine's emeralds and a diamond ring that once belonged to Catherine the Great. To her friend Elizabeth she left Marie Antoinette's necklace. Among her bequests, £500 went to Sonia Keppel, daughter of Alice Keppel, last mistress of Edward VII and great-grandmother of Camilla, Duchess of Cornwall. The greatest bequest of all was of this spectacular house and grounds to the National Trust.
▶ *RH5 6BD. 4 miles SW of Leatherhead, off A246. NT.*

❹ The Loseley Estate

When James I stayed at Loseley he was so well pleased that he commissioned portraits of himself and his queen, Anne of Denmark.
They are by his court painter, John de Critz, and

hang in the Great Hall, where the panelling comes from Henry VIII's lost pleasure palace, the incomparable Nonsuch. The house was built in the 1560s as a place to entertain Elizabeth I, when she deemed an earlier house inadequate, and has been in the More-Molyneux family for 500 years. The drawing-room ceiling was commissioned especially for James I's visit. The fireplace, carved from the local chalk, is to a design by Holbein; cushions are said to have been worked by Elizabeth I herself. Here are such curiosities as George IV's coronation chair and panels carved for Henry VIII's banqueting tents. The visitor has a sense of both pride of possession and the impulse to share. Within the walled gardens, a series of 'rooms' display plantings of roses, herbs and vegetables.

▶ *GU3 1HS. 2 miles SW of Guildford.*

❺ The Silent Pool

Legend has it that in the 12th century, in the clear waters of this spring-fed pool, a woodcutter's daughter was bathing when a nobleman rode by. Dismounting, he approached and tried to entice her out. She, in panic, waded out of her depth and cried for help. As her brother ran to her aid, the nobleman leapt into the saddle and galloped away, dropping his hat as

he went. Neither the girl nor her brother could swim well, and both drowned. The dropped hat bore the crest of Prince John, who would be crowned king in 1199. The ghost of the girl, Emma, is said to haunt the pool.

▶ *Near Albury. Just S of A25, 5 miles E of Guildford.*

❻ Runnymede

Here is where 'the greatest constitutional document of all time' was sealed by King John in 1215 ... or was it? He didn't want to do it. Magna Carta (or 'Great Charter') was forced upon the king by his feudal barons in an effort to curtail his abuses of power and privilege. The charter granted liberties for the British people, and established the principal, still in force today, that no 'freeman' could be punished other than through the law of the land. In this peaceful setting stands the Magna Carta Memorial by Sir Edward Maufe. The Fairhaven Memorial Lodges, matched by twin kiosks, are by Sir Edwin Lutyens.

The debate about whether the charter was actually sealed here or under the aged and huge Ankerwycke yew remains unresolved (see page 43).

▶ *TW20 0AG. 4 miles SE of Windsor on A308. NT.*

THE SILENT POOL

SUSSEX

The coast of Sussex was once a site of invasion and rebellion, as castles and battlefield sites bear witness. Peaceful opulence was more to the Prince Regent's taste, and the traditional royal love of the turf.

❶ Cowdray Park

The home of British polo for more than a century, Viscount Cowdray's 6,475ha (16,000-acre) estate is internationally renowned. Grooms and players start to arrive in April for the start of a season that lasts through to September, with some 450 matches being played. The club was founded in 1910 by Harold Pearson, whose father, Sir Weetman Dickinson, an industrialist and engineer, was made a viscount in 1919. In the 1950s, Princess Elizabeth came to watch her husband, Prince Philip, participate, after he was encouraged to take up the sport by his uncle, Lord Louis Mountbatten. Prince Charles followed in his father's hoof prints, coming to Cowdray to play in 1979, and in 1980 he brought Lady Diana Spencer. He continued to play here until 2003, and now the sport is enjoyed by his sons, William and Harry.
▶ *GU29 0AQ. Just NE of Midhurst town centre.*

❷ Goodwood House

The beautiful French courtier Louise de Keroualle was one of Charles II's many mistresses, and in 1672 she bore him a son. In 1675, Charles heaped titles upon the boy, also called Charles – Duke of Richmond (in Yorkshire), Earl of March and Baron Settrington, and in Scotland, Duke of Lennox, Earl of Darnley and Lord of Torbolton. The young Charles was also given Richmond Castle in Yorkshire.

He was a sporty lad who grew up to love hunting and gambling, and he visited Goodwood from the age of 17 to ride to hounds. When he bought and enlarged this Jacobean house on the Sussex Downs in 1697, it was for use as a hunting lodge. The 'old house' was extended in the 18th century, with the addition of a Palladian-style, Portland-stone south wing. The north wing that followed was partly demolished 50 years ago because of dry rot. James Wyatt added Regency state apartments and a round tower. Goodwood might have never measured up in the eyes of Louise de Keroualle, Duchess of Portsmouth, whose rooms at Whitehall were praised for being 'ten times' richer and more sumptuous than the queen's, but it is nonetheless one of England's finest stately homes and one of the most unusual.
▶ *PO18 0PX. 6 miles NE of Chichester.*

❸ Goodwood Racecourse

'The world's most beautiful racecourse' began life in the early 19th century when the Duke of Richmond offered land on his estate for that purpose. A racecourse was laid out and the first meet was very informal, but the next year the duke's horse, Cedar, went neck and neck with Trumpator, owned by the Prince of Wales, who was later crowned George IV. Now 'Glorious Goodwood', in July, is one of the highlights of the sporting calendar. Here Edward VII set a new trend, eschewing the morning suit and top hat of Ascot, and wearing the linen suit and panama still fashionable today. Goodwood is controlled by the family of the Duke of Richmond, whose seat is Goodwood House.
▶ *PO18 0PX. 4 miles NE of Chichester.*

❹ Bognor Regis

'The time is approaching when His Majesty's removal to sea air will be advantageous,' read a circumspect statement issued from Buckingham Palace in 1929. Some elderly Bognorians can still remember the excitement when, in February that year, George V and Queen Mary came to stay while he convalesced after a lung operation. The royal couple spent 13 weeks at the resort, to be visited over that time by members of their family. The queen was often seen about the town, in her car, on foot, attending church, even popping into Woolworth's. The sea air proved efficacious, as expected, and the king and queen were waved off with great cheers from crowds lining the seafront.

The visit proved advantageous to Bognor, also. The town not only enjoyed its spell at the centre of the Empire and a consequent tourist boom, but could also add 'Regis' to its name. The king, when asked to grant that accolade, responded to his private secretary, Lord Stamfordham, with a snort and the words 'B★★★★★ Bognor!' Stamfordham conveyed George's reply in more diplomatic terms: 'His Majesty has been graciously pleased to accede to your request.' Bravo, Bognor!

Once a fishing village, these days Bognor is a traditional seaside town with a promenade, parks and gardens and a museum.
▶ *7 miles SE of Chichester at junction of A29 and A259.*

ARUNDEL CASTLE

❺ Arundel Castle

For 850 years this has been the stately home of the Dukes of Norfolk, who have found themselves throughout the centuries in the very thick of history. The 2nd Duke was Lord Howard of Effingham, who with Sir Francis Drake fought off the Spanish Armada in 1588. The 3rd Duke was an uncle of both Anne Boleyn and Catherine Howard, the second and fifth wives of Henry VIII – both of whom were beheaded, as was the duke's son Henry Howard, 'the Poet Earl', and, in his turn, the 4th Duke.

The castle was badly damaged in the Civil War, when it was besieged first by Royalists, then by Parliamentarians. Some two hundred years later, in 1846, Victoria and Albert spent three days here. Bedroom and library furniture were specially commissioned for their stay. Today's castle is largely a Victorian re-creation by Henry, 15th Duke of Norfolk. It was completed in 1900 and although it may not be genuinely medieval, it is wonderfully easy on the eye. Among a wealth of treasures are portraits by Van Dyck, Reynolds and Gainsborough, tapestries, clocks and some personal possessions of Mary, Queen of Scots.

The Duke of Norfolk is the 'Premier Duke', the title bestowed upon Sir John Howard by Richard III in 1483. With the dukedom comes the hereditary office of Earl Marshal of England, and responsibility for state ceremonial, such as the coronation and funeral of the sovereign.

▶ *BN18 9AB. Arundel 8 miles E of Chichester, off A27.*

BRIGHTON ROYAL PAVILION

❻ Brighton Royal Pavilion

George, Prince of Wales, was not a man to stint himself, and when it came to creating a palace for himself, he went the whole hog. In the mid-1780s, he rented a small farmhouse in Brighton, where the climate and the practice of 'dipping' in sea water were said to be therapeutic. In 1787 he commissioned Henry Holland to transform the house into a villa, calling it the Marine Pavilion. It was a modest indulgence of his love of art and architecture – and nothing compared with what was to come. In 1811, when his father George III's bouts of insanity left him unfit to rule, George was sworn in as Prince Regent, and four years later he commissioned John Nash to turn the villa into an oriental fantasy. Tented roofs, minarets, domes and pinnacles were added, the interior lavishly decorated and furnished. Of the great dome over the banqueting hall, the writer and cleric Sydney Smith remarked that it 'looked for all the world as if the Dome of St Paul's had come down to Brighton and pupped'.

The Pavilion was the purest expression of George's personality, his love of beauty and excess. Flamboyant Marie-Antoine Carême, the first celebrity chef, created extravagant banquets for him, once making him a 1.2m (4ft) high Turkish mosque out of marzipan. Whatever his faults, the prince not only endowed Brighton with this unique architectural caprice, but brought the town prosperity, while the beautiful Regency seafront squares and crescents exist entirely thanks to his presence. He became George IV in 1820, but his health, so taxed by his unrestrained lifestyle, was failing, and after the Pavilion was completed in 1825, he made just two further visits.
▶ *BN1 1EE. City centre. Access Brighton by A23.*

❼ Corn Market and Dome

If the prince must live in Brighton in architectural splendour, so should his horses. The magnificent rotunda building was designed by William Porden in 1804, in the 'Hindoo' style. The Corn Exchange alongside was modelled on its namesake in Paris. The stables building set the Islamic style for the estate – indeed, it was only when Porden's creation overshadowed his villa that the prince called in John Nash to renovate it in so spectacular a manner. The stables were converted to a concert hall in 1867. In 1934–5, Robert Atkinson removed an inner ring of columns and made the interior over in cine-modern style. The complex is today a vibrant arts and entertainment venue.
▶ *BN1 1EE. City centre. Access Brighton by A23.*

❽ Fletching

Beside the ancient, beautiful village of Fletching, Simon de Montfort, 6th Earl of Leicester, and his rebel barons set up camp in May 1264. From this secret location, described only as '*in bosco juxta Lewes*', the barons sent peace proposals to Henry III, in the near certainty that he would refuse. Receiving an angry response, they prepared for the bloody battle of Lewes (see page 72). The village produced bows and arrows, and armed many of Henry V's bowmen for victory at Agincourt in 1415. The word 'fletching' describes the aerodynamic stabilisation of arrows by the use of feathers (from the French *flèche*). Strangely, it was the cavalry and infantry, armed with slings rather than the arrows, who decided the day at Lewes.
▶ *4 miles NW of Uckfield on minor roads.*

❾ Lewes

If William de Warenne were to return to Lewes today to see the castle and priory he founded, he would recognise neither, the one being substantially rebuilt, the other substantially destroyed. William was one of the nobles advising William of Normandy on his invasion. De Warenne fought at Hastings and was rewarded with the territory of Lewes, where he built a castle to the north, high on a mound above the River Ouse, and founded a Cluniac priory to the south. The castle, remodelled over the centuries, remains largely intact. The priory, demolished in the Reformation, stands in ruins.

The ancient town nestles on gently rolling land beside the Ouse where it cuts through the South Downs. William Morris described it as 'lying like a box of toys under a great amphitheatre of chalky hills'. The core of the town follows a street plan established under Alfred the Great. A 15th-century Wealden hall house was part of the settlement that came the way of Anne of Cleves on her divorce from Henry VIII. The annulment of the marriage must have suited her. Three months after it was signed and sealed, the French Ambassador was pleased to relate that 'Madame of Cleves has a more joyous countenance than ever'. 'The luckiest Queen', she escaped not just with her life but with a fortune. Many others fared less well under the Tudors. A Martyrs Memorial in Lewes commemorates the burning to death of 17 Protestants during the reign of Henry's daughter, the fanatical Mary I, for refusing to renounce their faith.
▶ *Anne of Cleves House, BN7 1JA. Lewes 8 miles NE of Brighton and Hove on A27.*

SOUTHERN ENGLAND

⑩ The Battle of Lewes

'Come out Simon, thou devil!' In the thick of battle, Henry III's men spotted Simon de Montfort's carriage under his great banner and assailed it. The king's men, flying the dragon standard, assumed that they had their archenemy at their mercy. They tore open the vehicle and hacked to death four unfortunate occupants – opponents of the rebel barons, whom de Montfort had taken captive in London. This was symptomatic of the chaos and mayhem of that day, May 14, 1264.

The battle was fought between the town and the top of Offham Hill, a mile to the northwest, where de Montfort's men had taken their position that morning, having marched from Fletching. The rebel forces were outnumbered but better prepared. The very landscape in which Lewes is couched – a hilltop advantage, the presence of marshland, the river – served their purposes. De Montfort, having run the king and his son Edward to ground at the priory, took over the kingdom as *de facto* ruler, calling the first directly elected parliament in medieval Europe. What seemed like a decisive victory in reality proved less conclusive. We have to go to Evesham, page 156, to find out what happened next.

▶ *1 mile W of Lewes town centre.*

⑪ Pevensey Castle

With the benefit of hindsight, Harold Godwinson would not have neglected the Saxon stronghold that stood within the Roman fort of Andarida. The fort was of oval design, shaped for the peninsula on which it stood. The castle we see today is four miles inland, but in 1066 the sea washed the fortress's footings, and it was here, on September 28, 1066, that Duke William of Normandy came ashore with his men, bent on conquest. Since Godwinson's accession to the throne in January, as Harold II, the nation had been bracing itself for invasion from France. Defences were being prepared – but not this one. The new king was busy in the north, fighting off the Norwegian Harold Hardrada, who was also intent on claiming the English crown. When he heard that the Normans had landed and were laying waste to the countryside, he marched south to confront them, meeting with William near Hastings on October 14 – and the rest, as they say, is history.

Upon his victory, William gave Pevensey to his half-brother, Robert, Count of Mortain, who fortified and extended the structure. The stone tower keep was probably added after his death.

Over the centuries, a moat and drawbridge were also added, and in the 13th century, a gatehouse. The castle was badly damaged by King John in 1216, but was refortified in 1588 amid fears of a Spanish invasion. As the sea receded, so the castle was left high and dry and it fell into substantial ruin. However, its deep significance, and the survival of so much that is Roman, make it uniquely interesting.

▶ *BN24 5LE. Pevensey 5 miles NE of Eastbourne, close to junction of A259 and A27. EH.*

⑫ Battle Abbey

'So beggary a house I never see, nor so filthy stuff.' In the summer of 1535, Battle Abbey received an unwelcome visitor. Richard Layton came to inspect the premises and make an inventory for the Crown, only to find this supposedly prosperous Benedictine abbey run down and impoverished. Had the abbot stripped the place before Henry VIII's men could? How ruthless was the king that he did not spare even this monument to momentous history!

The abbey was begun by William I to honour those who died at the Battle of Hastings – in the year 1066, as every schoolchild knows. It was founded in 1070 with monks from the Loire and quantities of Caen stone. The high altar marked the spot where King Harold fell, shot through the eye with an arrow, ushering in the Norman era. In the 13th century, the abbey was rebuilt and enlarged. In the 1330s, the addition of a vast gatehouse signified its defensive role in the face of French invasions. A more insidious invader arrived 20 years later – *Yersinia pestis*, the Black Death, and killed many of the monks.

Upon the Dissolution, the estate was granted to Sir Anthony Browne, who flattened the magnificent church and used the stone to convert domestic buildings into a mansion. Today, a stone marks the place of the high altar, crypts have been excavated, and the visitor can see the undercrofts of the east range, including the Novices' Room, with beautifully crafted columns, lancet windows and carved corbels. The mansion has been a school since 1922. Traces of the original vaulting on the façade can be seen across the cloister.

▶ *TN33 0AD. Battle 7 miles NW of Hastings. EH.*

⑬ Camber Castle

There are three peculiarly intriguing aspects of this 'Henrician' castle, which was built to defend the coast against French or Spanish invaders. The first – why is it so far inland? – is explained by silting, which by 1637 had rendered the castle obsolete. At the heart of this unusually well-preserved artillery fort is a tower built in 1512–14 by Sir Edward Guildford, Lord Warden of the Cinque Ports, to protect a shallow harbour called the Camber. Around this were added four towers, to which, in turn, were added bastions for gun platforms. As the shoreline receded, Sir Edward's tower was raised in order to maintain cannon range.

The second source of intrigue is the tower's designer, Stefan von Haschenperg, a gentleman of Moravia, armourer, architect and spy. In 1541, he was made surveyor of works at Carlisle, but his service to the king ended when he was sacked. In 1545 he wrote to Henry from Antwerp to beg

for his job back, proposing various inventions. One was included in a scheme to bring fresh water to the king's Ewell residence (see page 66) – 'an art unknown to Vitruvius, Archimedes and Ctesibius, a horse-driven, water-pumping mill, a marvel fit for Non-Such Palace'. This last was accompanied by a drawing of the device.

The third intrigue concerns the identity of a man named Sir Edward Guildford and a theory, advanced in 1995, that the boy princes were not murdered in the Tower by their uncle, Richard III, but grew to manhood under assumed identities, and that Guildford was none other than Edward V.

▶ *TN31 7TD. Camber 1 mile S of Rye. EH.*

PEVENSEY CASTLE

WILTSHIRE

The scene of a Shakespeare first night and a trend-setting stately home whet the appetite for a visit to Salisbury, beloved of the Stuarts, where a king's illness triggered his overthrow.

❶ Wilton House

'One cannot be said to have seen anything that a man of curiosity would think worth seeing in the country and not have been at Wilton House ... the seat of that ornament of learning and nobility the Earl of Pembroke.' So wrote Daniel Defoe, 17th-century pamphleteer, novelist and author. The 12th-century Benedictine abbey was seized and given to William Herbert by Henry VIII, and has remained in the family ever since. Elizabeth I visited in the summer of 1574. After a fire in 1647, John Webb was contracted to extend the house in the Palladian style, creating the grandest rooms in England of that period. James I loved Wilton and was among the audience for the first performance of *As You Like It*, staged here on December 2, 1603, when Shakespeare himself may have been present. Sir Philip Sidney stayed in 1581 and drew inspiration for his prose romance *Arcadia*. Amid all the grandeur, what most visitors remember above all is the Palladian-style bridge across the River Nadder, which flows through the grounds. Scenes for *The Madness of King George* and *Mrs Brown* were filmed here.
▶ *SP2 0BJ. 3 miles W of Salisbury, off A36.*

❷ Salisbury Cathedral

'The people of Salisbury are gay and rich, and have a flourishing trade; and there is a great deal of good manners and good company among them.' Daniel Defoe also noted that the cathedral's spire, 'is without exception the highest, and the handsomest in England, being from the ground 410 foot, and yet the walls so exceeding thin'.

The cathedral was begun in 1220, and took almost 40 years to complete. In the Civil War great damage was done and not until the late 18th century was there radical rebuilding by James Wyatt. In the Chapter House is the best preserved of four remaining exemplars of the Magna Carta, sealed with such reluctance by King John on June 15, 1215 in acquiescence to his barons. In the cathedral is an effigy to John's half-brother, William Longspee, who urged the king to accept the barons' terms.
▶ *SP1 2EJ. Access Salisbury from A36, A338 and A354. Cathedral in city centre.*

❸ Bishop's Palace

A royal indisposition at this home of bishops helped to shape the course of history. The original palace was among the first residential buildings to be completed in Salisbury's Cathedral Close, in time for the consecration of the altars in 1225. Bishop Beauchamp (1450–81) commissioned a new Great Hall. James I stayed often, as did his son, Charles I, who loved Salisbury. In the Civil War, the palace was let out as apartments. A wealthy Dutchman turned the ground floor into an ale house, and the damage was so great that Beauchamp's hall had to be demolished.

In 1689, James II was preparing to set off from here to join the army and fight the advancing William of Orange. However, he was confined to bed for three days, during which time his generals switched sides. He returned to London before fleeing to the Continent – having suffered perhaps the most fateful nosebleed in history.
▶ *Just S of Salisbury Cathedral.*

❹ Longleat

Sir John Thynne was a former Shropshire farmer's son made good, made bad, made good. After the Reformation, in 1540, Thynne bought the medieval Augustinian priory of Longleat for a grand country home. Almost at once it burnt down. Thynne was twice imprisoned in the Tower by Edward VI. Nothing daunted, on his release and return to Wiltshire, he built one of the greatest 'prodigy houses' – palatial dwellings to host royalty – in 1567. When Elizabeth I visited in 1575, it stood two storeys tall. The third storey was almost certainly added by Thynne's son John. Apart from a few baroque embellishments, the exterior is little changed. The Small Gallery was built in 1663 for a visit by Charles II, who granted his host the title of Lord Weymouth. Many of the rooms were redesigned in the late 19th century.

Longleat was the first house in England to reflect the Italianate style. In 1947 it became the first stately home to welcome the paying public. In 1966 it opened the first drive-through safari park. Its character today is influenced by the eccentric and flamboyant Alexander Thynn, Marquess of Bath.
▶ *BA12 7NW. 4 miles W of Warminster.*

SALISBURY CATHEDRAL
WITH FONT BY WILLIAM PYE

SOUTHERN ENGLAND

Enfield

Harrow•

Hampstead
Heath

see panel opposite

Barking

OUTER LONDON
102–111

Richmond
upon Thames

8 9
10
7   2
1 **Richmond
Park**
6   5

Kingston
upon Thames

3
4

Bromley•

Croydon•

13 12 17
14   11
15

16

Thames

KEY

1 Main entry
County boundary
Motorway
Principal A road

M25
A110
M1
A10
A1
A410
A406
A409
M11
A5
A406
A10
A180
A40
A4020
A13
M4
A102
A4
A4
A316
A30
A308
A3
A2
A205
A3
A24
A217
A21
A222
A232
A23
A243
A22
A23
A233

London

In this city shaped by England's monarchy, kings and queens have been crowned, acclaimed, married, housed in luxury, entertained – and sometimes imprisoned to await a brutal end.

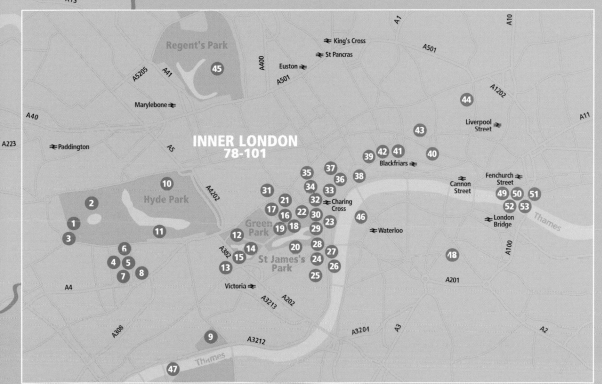

A12

A12

A127

A12

M25

A13

A13

Regent's Park

A5205   A441

45

A400

King's Cross

St Pancras

A501

A1

A10

A501

Euston

Marylebone

A44

A1202

A40

INNER LONDON
78-101

A5

Liverpool
Street

A11

A223

Paddington

A43

A4202

10

Hyde Park

39 **42** **41**
Blackfriars

40

Cannon
Street

Fenchurch
Street

2

35 **37** **36** **38**

43

49 **50** **51**

1

31   **34** **33**

32 Charing
Cross

52 **53**

Thames

3

11

17

21

22 **30**

23

46

London
Bridge

Green
Park

16

19 **18**

29

Waterloo

A100

6

12

14

20

28

27

18

4 **5**

15

St James's
Park

24

26

A201

7 **8**

13

25

A4

Victoria

A3213   A202

A3204   A3   A2

A308

9

A3212

47

Thames

INNER LONDON

Britain's royal heritage is part of the very fabric of this vast and vibrant city. Magnificent palaces, churches and parks are matched by a cultural legacy of museums, art galleries and concert halls.

❶ Kensington Palace

Before her wedding to Prince William, Kate Middleton fell in love with the 'wonderful peace' of the palace apartment, once home to the late Princess Margaret, and The Queen promised it to her. Another William, and his wife Mary, were the first monarchs to live at this Jacobean mansion, which was built in 1605. The joint monarchs bought it in 1689 because the village of Kensington had 'esteem'd very good Air', which relieved the king's asthma. George II was the last reigning monarch to live here. On the death of Queen Caroline, in 1737, he let much of the building fall into disuse. Horace Walpole, antiquarian, art historian and Whig politician, complained that 'though there are so many vacant chambers, the King hoards all he can, and has locked up half the palace'. Caroline was the real power behind the throne; George must have been lost without her.

His grandson, George III, chose Buckingham Palace over Kensington, and not until 1798 was the king's fourth son, Edward, Duke of Kent, granted the former king's apartments. They had been unoccupied for 28 years, and the duke commissioned James Wyatt to bring them back to life. In 1818 he married Victoria, Dowager Princess of Leiningen. Their daughter, Princess Victoria, was born here on May 24, 1819. Edward died nine months later, but the duchess and her daughter stayed until Victoria's accession to the throne, in 1837, when she moved to Buckingham Palace. Kensington was home to Diana, 'the People's Princess', from her wedding day, July 29, 1981. On August 31, 1997, as news of her death broke, the gates stood amid a sea of flowers. Some rooms and displays are open to the public.
▶ *W8 4PX. Kensington Gardens. High Street Kensington tube.*

❷ Kensington Gardens

'I was able to take the aire, as far as Kensington, where I saw the house ... & the plantation about it, to my great admiration and Refreshment.' John Evelyn, the 17th-century diarist, believed that 'the air and genius of gardens operate upon human spirits towards virtue and sanctity'. The one that so impressed him was once a part of Hyde Park. When William and Mary bought the palace, they began to create formal gardens around their new home. Mary's sister, Anne, who came to the throne in 1702, took a further 12ha (30 acres) and commissioned Henry Wise and George Loudon to create an English-style garden. She added the beautiful Orangery, now a café-restaurant. But it was Caroline of Ansbach, consort of George II, whose vision shaped the park we see today, encompassing yet another 120ha (300 acres). On her instruction, Charles Bridgeman designed the Round Pond, with avenues of trees radiating from it. He created the Long Water by damming the Westbourne stream. Instead of separating park and gardens with a hedge, a ditch was dug to form a boundary, known as a 'ha-ha' – representing the cry of surprise on encountering such an obstacle. Sharing her bounty, Caroline opened the gardens on Saturdays to anyone 'respectably dressed'.

The Italian Gardens were added in the Victorian era, and a sunken garden in the reign of Edward VII. Victoria's tribute to her beloved husband, the Albert Memorial, a high-Gothic, gilded extravaganza, stands on the edge of the gardens. In 2000, a playground was opened in memory of Diana, Princess of Wales, who was so loving to all children.
▶ *W8 4PX. W of Hyde Park, bounded on N by Bayswater Road and on S by Kensington Road. High Street Kensington or Queensway tube.*

❸ Maggie Jones

The rather cheeky name of this studiedly old-fashioned restaurant celebrates a royal customer. The late Princess Margaret, younger sister of The Queen, lived for nearly 42 years at Kensington Palace, and it is claimed that she would come here with her photographer fiancé, Antony Armstrong Jones, now Lord Snowdon. Little has changed since the 1960s. Candles in bottles, high-backed settles, mismatched chairs and bare floorboards set the style for the princess, who once said, 'My children are not royal; they just happen to have The Queen for their aunt.' The food is very British. Wild boar sausages, venison terrine and game in season recall the days of Henry VIII's great chase, when Hyde Park was enclosed for the king's beasts.
▶ *W8 4PL. Old Court Place, off High Street Kensington. High Street Kensington tube.*

MAGGIE JONES

❹ Albertopolis

Prince Albert of Saxe-Coburg-Gotha, Queen Victoria's husband and cousin, was not immediately popular with the British public
and yet his gift to them was immense. Against powerful opposition, he masterminded the Great Exhibition of 1851, to celebrate the advances of the industrial age and the expansion of an Empire upon which 'the sun never set'. His critics were confounded when, between May 1 and October 15, six million people visited, generating an unexpected profit of £186,437 (£16.2 million today). With this surplus, Albert proposed that neglected land in what is now South Kensington should be home to 'institutions that would further the general aims of the Exhibition and extend the influence of Science and Art upon Productive Industry'.

The area owes its cultural richness to Albert's vision. An astonishing array of institutions includes the Victoria and Albert Museum, Natural History and Science museums and Royal Colleges. Albert was a great reformer and innovator, and a fierce opponent of slavery and child labour. The people, despite adopting the satirical nickname, increasingly saw the point of 'the foreign Prince'. In 1857, after 17 years of marriage, he was dignified with the title Prince Consort. With his death in 1861, from typhus, aged just 42, the nation lost a man who had been 'to all intents and purposes King'.

▶ *S of Kensington Gardens and Hyde Park; Exhibition Road runs through the area. South Kensington tube.*

❺ Royal College of Music

'Class can no longer stand apart from class ... I claim for music that it produces the union of feeling which I much desire to promote.' With these fine words, Edward, Prince of Wales, the future Edward VII, opened this college in 1883. The eldest of Victoria and Albert's nine children, the prince was a deep disappointment to his parents, flunking the rigorous education that Albert had devised for him, then indulging in a playboy lifestyle. Yet, as Disraeli said, he was 'informed, intelligent and of a sweet manner'; he was a skilled public performer and great patron of the arts.

The college that he founded is opposite the Royal Albert Hall. The fine redbrick building, dressed with buff-coloured Weldon stone, dates from 1892-4. It was designed by Sir Arthur Blomfeld in the Flemish Mannerist style, and is truly Blomfeld's crowning achievement. Visitors can take a tour of this world-renowned conservatoire, which includes a museum of more than 1,000 rare instruments and artefacts, from the earliest surviving stringed instrument to a glass armonica and trombones played by the composers Elgar and Holst. Since its founding, the college has always had close links with royalty. The Queen is its patron, Prince Charles its president. There is a 400-seat theatre and recital rooms. In all, the college is a fitting tribute to its founder who loved wine, women – and song.

▶ *SW7 2BS. Prince Consort Road. South Kensington tube.*

LONDON

⑥ Royal Albert Hall

Queen Victoria's sense of loss upon the death of Albert found public expression in the decorative memorial at Kensington Gardens. Here is his practical memorial. He had nurtured the idea of a hall to promote the understanding and appreciation of the arts and sciences. Progress was slow, his time ran out, and it was left to Henry Cole, one of his collaborators in the Great Exhibition, to drive the project forward. The building was begun by Captain Francis Fowke, a Royal Engineer, and completed, on Fowke's death, by Lt Col Henry Darracott Scott. A vast auditorium with glazed dome and wrought-iron girders is at the heart of the hall. The exterior, comprising six million bricks and 80,000 tonnes of terracotta, drew inspiration from Italy. Above a 24m (80ft) terracotta frieze of allegorical figures engaged in artistic, scientific and cultural endeavours, the legend declares: 'This Hall was erected for the advancement of the Arts and Sciences and works of industry of all nations in the fulfilment of the intention of Albert Prince Consort.' When Victoria opened the hall in May 1867, she was too overcome to speak – beyond saying that it reminded her of the British constitution – and the Prince of Wales had to step in. Today, this music and entertainment venue is home to an annual eight-week season of 'Promenade concerts'.

▶ *SW7 2AP. Kensington Gore. South Kensington tube.*

ROYAL ALBERT HALL

❼ Natural History Museum

On a visit to the London Zoo in 1842, Queen Victoria remarked, 'The orang-utan is too wonderful ... frightfully, painfully and disagreeably human.' She was on to something! At the time of the Great Exhibition in 1851, almost nothing was known of human evolution. Not until 1859 did Charles Darwin publish *On the Origin of Species*, provoking Disraeli to ask, 'Is man an ape or an angel? My Lord, I am on the side of the angels. I repudiate with indignation and abhorrence these new-fangled theories.'

The debate was still raging when 'The animals' Westminster Abbey' opened in 1881. The museum traces its origins to the extensive collections of Sir Hans Sloane, who left them to George II for the nation in 1753. They were housed in the British Museum at first, but as other collections were added, the superintendent, Sir Richard Owen, pressed for a dedicated new building for the natural history exhibits – and what a building! It was to be the work of Captain Francis Fowke, who had also begun the Royal Albert Hall, but with his death in 1865, it passed to Alfred Waterhouse, who altered the design from Renaissance to German Romanesque. The huge façade, the high, spired columns and rounded arches are worthy of a cathedral.

Here is the largest and most important natural history collection in the world, with more than 70 million specimens gathered over 400 years, from microscopic spores to the bones of a woolly mammoth. In September 2009, Victoria's great-great-great-great grandson Prince William attended the grand opening of a modern new wing, the Darwin Centre. Disraeli's question had been settled on the side of the apes.

▶ *SW7 5BD. W of junction of Cromwell Road and Exhibition Road. South Kensington tube.*

❽ Victoria and Albert Museum

With the success of the Great Exhibition of 1851, Prince Albert seized the initiative. He saw to it that some of the profits went to establish the Museum of Manufactures with the purpose of educating working people and inspiring British design and industry. The institution was renamed the South Kensington Museum when it moved to its present site in 1857, expanding its collection of metalwork, furniture, fabrics, paintings, drawings, prints and sculptures. New buildings were added as required. With their iron frames and glass roofs they were intended to be semi-permanent exhibition halls, but all have survived. In 1899, Victoria laid a foundation stone for a new building that would give the museum a grand façade, a grand entrance and a grand royal name, the Victoria and Albert Museum, or the V&A as it is now known.

Despite the international scope of the collections, Britain is strongly represented. Among the royal portraits are many by Cecil Beaton, including a number of the Duke and Duchess of Windsor, the former Wallis Simpson, for whom the duke gave up the throne. Beaton photographed Edward and Wallis on their wedding day – she appears less than radiant. Here, too, are photographs, of the widowed Victoria, matronly and dour in her black silk, bombazine and crepe, and Edward VII, hung with medals and looking particularly fine. A prettily composed wedding group features George V and Mary of Teck (of whom it was said, 'Her appearance is formidable; her manner ... well, it was like talking to St Paul's Cathedral'). Prince Charles is a small boy again, with his mother, at Clarence House, and the Queen Mother comes alive before the visitor's eyes. In a lithograph by John Brandard, a sprightly Victoria and Albert dance the polka. Vases, brooches, commemorative plates and photographs of historic royal events make fascinating browsing. And it is the essential humanity of royalty, not their 'otherness', that hits the observer with such force.

▶ *SW7 2RL. E of junction of Cromwell Road and Exhibition Road. South Kensington tube.*

❾ Royal Hospital

Charles II commissioned Sir Christopher Wren to build a home for the 'succour and relief of veterans broken by age and war'. In gratitude, he is remembered every year on Royal Hospital Founder's Day, when the veterans, the Chelsea Pensioners, are usually reviewed by a member of the royal family.

Founder's Day is held on, or close to, May 29, Charles II's birthday and – what a birthday gift! – the date of his restoration as king in 1660. It is also known as Oak Apple Day, commemorating Charles's escape after the Battle of Worcester in 1651, when he hid in an oak tree to evade capture by Parliamentarians. For the celebrations, the gilded statue of Charles II, which stands in Figure Court, is decorated with oak leaves, and all participants in the parade, wearing their scarlet uniforms, sport sprigs of oak, as do many of the spectators. The veterans are proud to give guided tours of their fine accommodation, by arrangement, and visitors and small groups are welcome to drop by.

▶ *SW3 4SR. Royal Hospital Road. Sloane Square tube.*

LONDON

⑩ Hyde Park

In January 1540, Abbot William Boston of Westminster and his 24 monks furnished Henry VIII with another hunting ground.
The monks signed a deed of surrender, giving up to the king, his heirs and successors in perpetuity, all their possessions – including the abbey grounds. Hyde Park remained a royal hunting ground until the reign of James I, when he graciously allowed the public limited access. His son, Charles I, went further, opening it entirely to the public in 1637. This was, said diarist John Evelyn, where the noblesse went to take the air. He went himself to watch a coach race, and 'collationed in Spring Garden'.

Things took a depressing turn under Oliver Cromwell. In April 1653, Evelyn found that 'every coach was made to pay a shilling, and every horse sixpence, by the sordid fellow who had purchased it of the state, as they called it'. How jubilant, then, was the mood in May 1660, when Charles II returned to London in triumph! On July 3, Evelyn saw at the park 'His Majesty and abundance of gallantry'.

In 1814, the Prince Regent organised a spectacular fireworks display here to celebrate the end of the Napoleonic Wars, and, of course, Hyde Park was the scene of Prince Albert's pet project, the Great Exhibition of 1851, when the 'Crystal Palace' was built upon it. It remains today a Royal Park and one of London's finest landscapes.
▶ *Bounded on N by Bayswater Road, on E by Park Lane and S by Knightsbridge. Kensington Gardens lie to the W. Marble Arch, Hyde Park Corner or Knightsbridge tube.*

⑪ Rotten Row

From their home in Kensington Palace, William and Mary laid down one of the most fashionable avenues in London. The mile-and-a-half track along the southern length of Hyde Park was a relatively safe way into town. However, with the exposure of a Jacobite plot to assassinate the joint monarchs in 1696, they must have felt a little vulnerable, and to add to their security, 300 lamps were hung from trees along the way, making it the first road in England to be artificially lit.

Soon all society followed the sovereigns' route, and it became a place to stroll and ride, to show off in fancy carriages, much as Parisians did in the Bois de Boulogne. Some say the name derives from *route du roi* (the king's road). Antiquary John Timbs suggested in 1855 that the name comes from 'rotteram', to muster, adding: 'It is for saddle

HYDE PARK

horses who can gallop over its fine loose gravel without danger from falling, and it is crowded with equestrians between 5 and 7pm.' Today, it is used by the Household Cavalry from the Knightsbridge Barracks to exercise their horses, and for their daily trot to Horse Guards.
▶ *W2 2SB (Hyde Park Stables, Bathurst Mews). S side of Hyde Park. Hyde Park Corner or Knightsbridge tube.*

⑫ The Green Park

Charles II created a royal park on land formerly enclosed by Henry VIII, laying out the main walks and building an ice house.
The park was the scene of a spectacular event in the reign of George II, when, on April 27, 1749, a royal firework party was held here to celebrate the end of the War of Austrian Succession. Handel was commissioned to compose Music for the Royal Fireworks. The proceedings went with quite a bang: an enormous timber building – designed for the musicians by Jean-Nicolas Servan, French decorator and scene-painter – caught fire after the collapse of a bas relief of the king.

The Green Park lies between Hyde Park and
St James's Park. With Kensington Gardens and the
grounds of Buckingham Palace, these green acres
form an almost uninterrupted stretch. Unlike its
neighbours, the Green Park has no buildings or
lakes. In contrast, its wooded meadows have a
feeling of countryside, a refuge from the bustle
of the surrounding city. Beneath the east side are
government offices, and, below ground level,
corridors with glass roofs link the royal palaces.
These may have been converted from tunnels built
as part of the Cabinet War Rooms in World War II.
▶ *Bounded by Piccadilly and Constitution Hill.*
Green Park tube.

⑬ Royal Mews

**The palatial quarters of the royal horses
also house a fairytale golden coach and 'the
Royal Fleet' of streamlined motor cars.**
One of the finest working stables in the world lies
behind a giant entranceway flanked by Roman
columns. Within, the Riding House dates from
1760; the mews itself was built for George IV by
John Nash 60 years later. A pedimental carving,
Hercules Capturing the Thracian Horses, was
added in 1859 by William Theed. It depicts
Hercules going about his eighth labour, and was
one of the first sculptures in Britain to show the
influence of the newly acquired 'Elgin' or
Parthenon Marbles. Also known as the Mares of
Diomedes, the four horses were untameable,
maddened by their diet of human flesh. The
horses in the mews have impeccable manners,
thanks to more suitable fare. These gorgeous
Cleveland Bays and Yorkshire Greys can be seen
out and about, being exercised on the streets and
in Hyde Park, and pulling the brougham that
delivers mail from Buckingham Palace to
St James's Palace. They also swing by St James's
Palace, pulling a covered brake, to collect the
Yeomen of the Guard for investitures at 'Buck
House', and turn out for such pageants as
Trooping the Colour. A great attraction of the
mews are the miniature carriages designed for
Queen Victoria's children, among them the Prince
of Wales and future Edward VII, the first member
of 'the firm' to ride in a motorcar – a Daimler
belonging to Lord Montague. By the time of his
coronation he had no fewer than four of them.
▶ *SW1W 1QH. Buckingham Palace Road.*
Victoria tube and rail.

LONDON

⑭ Buckingham Palace

George III bought the modest and secluded Buckingham House in 1761 for his German wife, Charlotte. Fourteen of their 15 children were born here. The king extended the building to include four libraries for a vast collection of rare books, including an original Gutenberg Bible. This collection was gifted, as he always intended, to the nation, and is in the British Museum. His son, George IV, planned to knock the building down and start again, but Parliament stinted him, so he engaged John Nash to remodel it. Like his Pavilion at Brighton, Buck House was to be a showpiece, since his court must 'quite eclipse' Napoleon's in Paris. It was a work in progress when George died in 1830, and Edward Blore was called in to complete it. The verdict of Whig politician Thomas Creevey: 'It has lost a million of money and there is not a fault which has not been committed in it … The costly ornaments of the state rooms exceed all belief in their bad taste and every species of infirmity. Raspberry coloured pillars without end that quite turn you sick to look at it.' The Portland stone façade the visitor sees today was created in 1913 by Sir Aston Webb. The London headquarters of the royal family is colossal, with 775 rooms. The State Rooms are opened every year, and show nothing to turn a visitor sick. The Changing of the Guard takes place daily on the forecourt.

▶ *SW1A 1AA. At junction of The Mall and Constitution Hill. Victoria, Green Park or Hyde Park Corner tube or Victoria rail.*

BUCK HOUSE WAS TO BE A SHOWPIECE
BUCKINGHAM PALACE

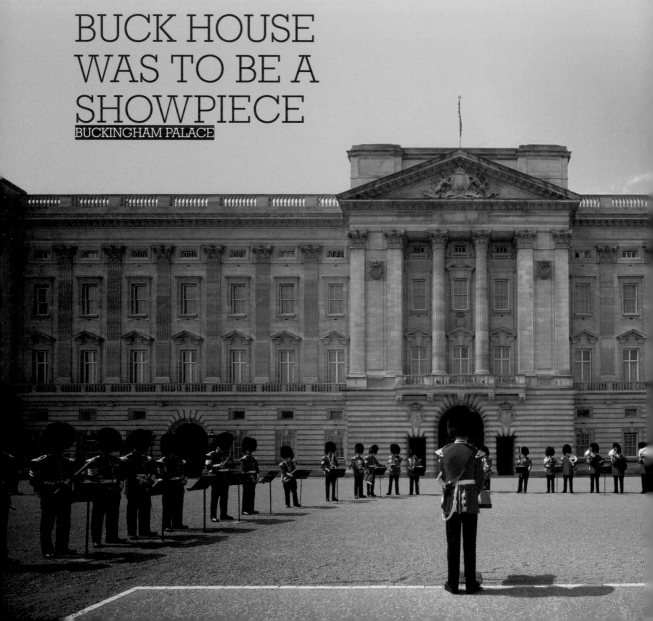

ⓕ Queen's Gallery

Here are treasures amassed by kings and queens over more than five centuries. Paintings by Rembrandt, Leonardo, Van Dyck, Canaletto and Stubbs, Fabergé eggs, Sèvres porcelain, miniatures, chinoiserie, armour, fans and clocks are on display in regularly changing exhibitions. The gallery, on the southwest side of Buckingham Palace, began life as a chapel designed by John Nash, and has been developed from its bombed-out shell. It opened to the public in 1962 and closed for remodelling in 1999. A Doric entrance portico was added and new rooms. It was opened by The Queen in May 2002 to coincide with the Golden Jubilee.

▶ *SW1A 1AA. Entrance in Buckingham Palace Road. Victoria, Green Park or Hyde Park Corner tube or Victoria rail.*

ⓖ Queen's Chapel

This elegant little chapel was conceived for a princess and built to be fit for a queen. It was designed by Inigo Jones as an integral part of St James's Palace, and was intended for Maria Anna, the Infanta of Spain, on whom James I had his eye as a suitable match for his son, the future Charles I. However, the promise of a chapel of her own, in the architect's signature Italianate style, was not enough to persuade the Infanta to marry a Protestant. So it was built for Henrietta Maria of France instead – a Catholic with a more relaxed religious view. Construction took place in 1623–5. The chapel had stucco walls, stone quoins, a simple pediment and England's first Venetian window at its eastern end. It remains one of the facilities of the British monarch's personal religious establishment.

Although it was originally an adjunct to the palace, when adjacent apartments burnt down in 1809 they were not replaced. Instead, in 1856–7, Marlborough Road was laid down between palace and chapel, so that it now seems more a part of Marlborough House. Here, on her death in March 2002, the body of Queen Elizabeth, the Queen Mother was placed in preparation for her lying-in-state in Westminster Abbey. The public can attend services between Easter and the end of July, on Sundays and some weekdays. The bronze memorial on red granite on the road beside the building is by Alfred Gilbert, the sculptor of Eros. On the plinth of this ethereal, allegorical work is written: 'Faith, Hope, Love, The Guiding Virtues of Queen Alexandra.'

▶ *SW1Y 5HX. At junction of Pall Mall and Marlborough Road. Green Park tube.*

ⓗ Spencer House

The only surviving 18th-century aristocratic family palace in London was built for the 1st Earl Spencer, a forebear of Diana, Princess of Wales. Ranging in style from Rome to Athens, the house was begun in 1756, the builder working to a Palladian design by John Vardy. The exterior, including the façade with its decorative pediment and seven upper bays split by Tuscan columns, along with the ground-floor interiors, are Vardy's work, but in 1758 sculptor and architect James Stuart, newly returned from Greece, stepped in to work on the upper floor.

After the death of the 1st Earl, the 2nd Earl ordered some remodeling by Henry Holland, the architect of nearby Brook's Club, who added Ionic columns and laid out the garden. Some of the state rooms – the Morning Room, the Music Room, the Ante Room (the Spencers' 'Little Eating Parlour') and the Library – although very grand, have the authentic feeling of a family home. Recently, the glory that was Greece and the grandeur that was Rome have been revived for visitors to see on most Sundays, by arrangement and by guided tour.

▶ *SW1A 1NR. St James's Place. Green Park tube.*

LONDON

ST JAMES'S PALACE

⑱ Clarence House

On June 25, 1830, Prince William Henry went to bed as Duke of Clarence – and awoke as William IV. When the news reached him in the morning that his profligate elder brother, George IV, had died, he went straight back to bed with his wife, Adelaide of Saxe-Meiningen, for the thrill of sleeping with a queen. Clarence House was built for the duke in 1825-7, to designs by John Nash. This was the London home of Elizabeth, the Queen Mother, from 1953 until 2002. It was also home to Princess Elizabeth and the Duke of Edinburgh upon their marriage in 1947. It is the town residence of the Prince of Wales and the Duchess of Cornwall. In 2012, it will reopen to the public in summer, when visitors will be able to join a tour of the ground floor and see part of the Royal Collection.

▶ *SW1A 1AA. Stable Yard Road, off The Mall. Green Park or St James's Park tube.*

⑲ St James's Palace

'When I am dead and opened, you will find Calais written on my heart.' It was at St James's Palace, in 1558, that Queen Mary signed the treaty surrendering the last English possession in Europe. From here, too, Elizabeth I set out to address her troops at Tilbury, as Britain faced the threat of the Spanish Armada. The palace was built for Henry VIII, father of both Mary and Elizabeth. It would be home to kings and queens for 300 years, and even today is the senior palace of the sovereign.

Much survives of the original redbrick building, including the Tudor gatehouse and turrets and the Chapel Royal. The chapel was built in honour of Henry's brief marriage to Anne of Cleves, and was decorated by Hans Holbein. Mary I's heart was buried beneath the choir stalls, with 'Calais' metaphorically written on it. Here Elizabeth I prayed for the defence of the realm against the Spanish, and Charles I received Holy Communion before his execution.

Later extensions covered the Ambassadors Court, Engine Court, Friary Court and Colour Court. By tradition, the accession of a new sovereign is proclaimed by the royal herald and trumpeters from the balcony of Friary Court. On the Gatehouse is the cipher of Henry VIII, an 'HR' topped by a crown. In his *Dictionary of London* in 1879, Charles Dickens junior, son of the great novelist, wrote of the palace that 'its cramped and inconvenient rooms have been found highly impracticable for the more important … functions, and Her Majesty's drawing-rooms have been removed to Buckingham Palace, where the fight for priority of admission to the royal presence is not embittered by quite such close packing.'

▶ *SW1A 1DH. N of The Mall. Green Park tube.*

⑳ St James's Park

December 1, 1662: 'Having seen the strange and wonderful dexterity of the sliders on the canal in St James's Park, performed before their Majesties by diverse gentlemen and others with skates …' Diarist John Evelyn had made his way by river to an ice show, and marvelled at the skaters 'with what swiftness they pass, how suddenly they stop in full career'.

The oldest of London's royal parks – a hunting ground for Henry VIII, a place of pageant and pomp for Elizabeth I – had been opened to the public by Charles II. He came often to feed the ducks and to mix with his subjects. No doubt he thought a lot about his father, who had been permitted a last walk around the park with his pet dog on the cold, grim morning of his execution.

In the Hanoverian period, Horse Guards Parade was created, and is the scene every June, on the Queen's official birthday, of the ritual Trooping the Colour, with Her Majesty in attendance to take the salute. In the 19th century, John Nash redesigned the park in a more romantic style, transforming the canal into an apparently natural lake. The Ornithological Society of London made a present of some birds in 1837 and a delightful cottage was built for a bird-keeper – a position still held today.

▶ *Bounded on N by The Mall, on E by Horse Guards Road and on S by Birdcage Walk. St James's Park tube.*

㉑ St James's

Royal warrants abound in this smart part of town, so close to the palaces. On St James's Street, the shoemakers John Lobb hold warrants from the Duke of Edinburgh and the Prince of Wales. Floris, 'Perfumers to Her Majesty the Queen', held a warrant from George IV as makers of combs. Paxton and Whitfield were first appointed royal cheese-makers by Queen Victoria. Berry Bros & Rudd on St James's Street have supplied wine to the royal household since the reign of George III. The smallest order they filled must surely have been for the miniature Queen Mary's Dolls' House at Windsor Castle.

▶ *Lies between Piccadilly and The Mall. Piccadilly Circus or Green Park tube.*

㉒ The Mall

Like a great red carpet, this avenue rolls out from Buckingham Palace to Admiralty Arch and Trafalgar Square. It was created for Charles II as part of the landscaping of St James's Park, and in the early 1900s was transformed into its present state as the ceremonial route from the palace to Whitehall. The red pigment was obtained from synthetic iron oxide. The Queen accompanies visiting heads of state as they are escorted, by carriage, up the Mall. On these occasions, the route is hung with Union flags and the flags of the visitor's country. The royal family makes its traditional appearances on the palace balcony, overlooking the Mall and Sir Aston Webb's 'wedding cake' Queen Victoria Memorial, which includes the marble statue of Victoria and the figures of Victory, Courage and Constancy. On June 4, 2002, there was a parade down the Mall in honour of the Queen's Golden Jubilee. Among the 20,000 who took part were a 5,000-strong gospel choir and 4,000 people representing Commonwealth countries. A million people gathered here on June 3 and 4 to watch Jubilee festivities.

▶ *Runs between Buckingham Palace and Trafalgar Square. Charing Cross tube and rail.*

㉓ Banqueting House

'I shall go from a corruptible to an uncorruptible Crown, where no disturbance can be.' With such dignity did Charles I make his farewell before signalling to the executioner and laying his head upon the block outside Whitehall Palace in 1649. Within the Banqueting House are nine works that Charles commissioned from Peter Paul Rubens to celebrate the life and rule of his father. Among them is *The Apotheosis of James I*, confirming the divinity of Stuart kings. They are enormous pieces, painted on canvas and fixed to the ceiling, and they are still the crowning glory of the only surviving building from the palace, which burnt down in 1698.

It had been designed for court entertainments, and many of the masques that were performed here were by Ben Jonson. Today, Inigo Jones's Palladian masterpiece is open to all. As well the Rubens paintings, the lavish grandeur of the building may be admired – a revelation at a time when Tudor brick and timbering still prevailed. The wonderfully atmospheric vaulted basement, the Undercroft, was used as a drinking den by James I, and by Charles II to hold lotteries.

▶ *SW1A 2ER. Junction of Whitehall and Horse Guards Avenue. Westminster tube.*

THE AVENUE ROLLS OUT LIKE A GREAT RED CARPET

THE MALL

㉔ Westminster Abbey

For the wedding of Prince William and Catherine Middleton in April 2011, Westminster Abbey appeared as radiant as the couple themselves. Down the long aisle walked the bride, between soaring columns, beneath the highest Gothic vault in England – how different from the funerals of Diana, Princess of Wales, and Queen Elizabeth, the Queen Mother, when it was hushed, solemn, magnificent.

Its associations with royalty give this building a tenacious hold upon the English imagination. For some it is above all a 'national Valhalla', a vast mausoleum for princes and poets. The relics of its founder, St Edward the Confessor, were enshrined in the sanctuary by Henry III, when he rebuilt the abbey. From Henry himself in 1272 to George II in 1760, most British kings and queens were buried here. Henry VII built the Lady Chapel, where he shares a vault with his queen, Elizabeth of York, and James I. Described as 'a culminating masterpiece of the English Perpendicular Gothic' and, by the antiquary John Leland as 'the wonder of the entire world', this chapel is adorned with Tudor roses, portcullises, fleurs-de-lys, greyhounds, lions, dragons, and 95 statues of saints. In its north aisle is the tomb of Elizabeth I and Mary I.

The abbey of today is essentially that of Henry III, although Sir Christopher Wren and Nicholas Hawksmoor made alterations in the 1700s. It was always intended that there should be a spire, which would unify the mass and lift it heavenward. From 2009 this was again under discussion, but for now the abbey remains a glorious unfinished symphony.

▶ *SW1P 3PA. Westminster tube. Open Monday to Saturday; Sunday for services only.*

㉕ St John's, Smith Square

The tale is told of how Queen Anne, when asked how she would like this church to look, kicked over a stool and said, 'Like that'. The architect was Thomas Archer, the story is apocryphal, but the building, with a tower at each corner, became known as 'Queen Anne's Footstool'. Music exalts this English baroque masterpiece in Westminster's political heartland. Its wonderful acoustics and airy space attract musicians from all over the world. It was rebuilt to be used as a concert hall after being gutted by an incendiary bomb in World War II, and was described by architect Sir Hugh Casson as being 'as cool and evocative as the inside of a seashell'.

▶ *SW1P 3HA. Off Millbank. Westminster tube.*

LONDON

㉖ Westminster Hall

Charles I was tried in this ancient hall as a 'tyrant, traitor and murderer; and a public and implacable enemy to the Commonwealth of England'. The hall was packed with soldiers to keep the public out as the king was condemned to death. Upon the Restoration of the Monarchy, the head of his nemesis, Oliver Cromwell, was stuck on a spike above the hall, his body having been exhumed and hanged. In 1899, shortly after the 300th anniversary of his birth, a statue of Cromwell by Hamo Thornycroft was erected in front of the House of Commons. His head is bowed, in order, it is said, to avoid looking at Charles I's bust opposite.

The largest hall in Europe in its time, Westminster was built for William II, son of the Conqueror, in 1099. In the 14th century, Henry Yevele, England's first named architect, took away supporting pillars and created a hammerbeam roof of unprecedented proportions, using 650 tonnes of English oak. When there were law courts here as well as market stalls, it must have been a rowdy place. Parliament sat here for a while and was surely just as rowdy.

▶ *SW1A 0AA. Houses of Parliament. Westminster tube.*

㉗ Houses of Parliament

Once a year the Queen arrives here from Buckingham Palace, escorted by the Household Cavalry. She passes through the Sovereign's Entrance and proceeds to Augustus Pugin's high-Gothic Robing Room, where she dons the Imperial State Crown and robe, before processing through the Royal Gallery to the Chamber of the House of Lords, to take the throne for the State Opening of Parliament. This

is the ceremonial highpoint of the parliamentary calendar, and is set about by arcane ritual. The cellars are searched by the Yeomen of the Guard, in case of a modern-day Gunpowder Plot, and a hostage is held at Buckingham Palace, to assure the sovereign's safe return. 'Black Rod', sent to summon the Commons, has the door slammed in his face until he knocks on it with his staff of office. The MPs follow him and the Commons Speaker to stand behind the Bar of the House of Lords to hear the Queen's Speech. No monarch has entered the Commons since Charles I did so in January 1642, to arrest five MPs for high treason, and was defied by Speaker Lenthall.

In 1834, a catastrophic fire ripped through the building. The interior reflects the preoccupation with the Gothic revival style at the time of its rebuilding (1837–60). William Dyce's paintings of Arthurian legends adorn the walls.

▶ *SW1A 0AA. Westminster tube.*

㉘ Parliament Square

Richard I, known as Lionheart, sits astride his elegant, high-stepping steed outside Parliament. The tall and handsome warrior king has the reputation of having been a great monarch, a folk hero, but as the son of French-born Henry II and Eleanor of Aquitaine, he spoke little English and spent just a few months of his reign (1189–90) in Britain. While crusading abroad, he left his grandmother, Matilda, in charge of Normandy, and his mother in charge of England. In 1199, he was fighting to win back lost territories in France when he was wounded by an arrow and died of an infection.

The statue was originally modelled in clay by Baron Marochetti, a favourite of Victoria and Albert's, and it won an award at the Great Exhibition of 1851. Public subscription paid for its casting in bronze. When Richard's sword was bent by shrapnel in 1940, it was portrayed in a radio broadcast as a symbol of strength that would not break under attack. In 2009, the statue was stripped of a coating of black wax to reveal the original dark brown.

▶ *SW1P. Westminster tube.*

㉙ Cenotaph

One of the most moving and dignified royal ceremonies is enacted here each year on Remembrance Sunday, when tribute is paid to the 'glorious dead' of two world wars and later conflicts. 'Cenotaph' means 'empty tomb' in Greek, and Edwin Lutyens' Portland stone monument, unveiled in 1920, is a memorial to those who fell in the Great War. An air of deep solemnity attends proceedings as the Queen lays the first poppy wreath at the foot of the pillar, followed by members of her immediate family, one by one, bowing if in civilian dress, saluting if in military uniform. Next it is the turn of the prime minister, then the leader of the opposition, and many more. The march-past of war veterans is stirring.

The stone column replaced a temporary structure of timber and plaster. Lutyens later recalled the public pressure for a permanent replacement, expressed in the daily laying of fresh flowers. 'Thus,' he wrote, 'it was decided, by the human sentiment of millions, that the Cenotaph should be as it now is, and speaking as the designer, I could wish for no greater honour, no more complete and lasting satisfaction.' None can remember the carnage of World War I, 'the war to end all wars' – and none should ever forget.

▶ *SW1A 2BX. Whitehall, just S of junction with Downing Street. Westminster tube.*

LONDON

㉚ Horse Guards

What more beautiful backdrop for a wedding procession could a couple ask than William Kent's Palladian-style Horse Guards building? As the coverage of the marriage of Prince William and Catherine Middleton was beamed around the world on April 29, 2011, London appeared at its dazzling best, with Horse Guards playing a starring role in the event. Amid the clatter of horses' hooves and the tossing plumes and scarlet coats of the Household Cavalry, the gilded state carriages crossed Horse Guards Parade, bound for Buckingham Palace and the crowd-pleasing balcony scene. It was quite a pageant – but, then, every day is a pageant here.

The building, which dates from 1751, stands on the site of the guardhouse of the former Whitehall Palace. From 10am to 4pm, two mounted troopers flank the central arch, the formal entrance on the Whitehall side to St James's and Buckingham Palace. At 4 o'clock there is a dismounted parade of the guardsmen. On the Parade – once Henry VIII's tiltyard – on the other side of the building, a guard-changing ceremony is staged every weekday at 11am, and at 10am on Sundays. It is also used for grand ceremonial occasions, in particular for Trooping the Colour on The Queen's official birthday.

▶ *SW1A 2AX. Whitehall. See Horse Guards Parade from Horse Guards Road. Westminster or Charing Cross tube or Charing Cross rail.*

㉛ Royal Academy of Arts

'An enthusiastic if undiscriminating patron of the arts', George III founded this academy in 1768. Sir Joshua Reynolds was its first president and laid down in his *Discourses* the conception of the Academy by which it lives today, as a body of professionals that, 'besides furnishing able men to direct students', would form 'a repository for the great examples of the Art'. The RA's first show, in 1769, was attended by author and lexicographer Dr Johnson, who recorded: 'The Exhibition is eminently splendid. There is contour and keeping and grace and expression, and all the varieties of artificial excellence.' Thus was established the RA's Summer Exhibition, which today attracts some 10,000 works for selection by Academicians.

The Royal Academy began life in Somerset House and in 1867 arrived at its present home in Burlington House. This was built by Sir John Denham, Charles II's Surveyor of the Office of Works, in 1664–5, and has since been extended and remodelled. Burlington House alone is worth a visit for its contour and grace and expression, not to speak of all the varieties of artificial excellence that it contains. There is a café, and a restaurant where the visitor can dine as well as Samuel Johnson did at the inaugural banquet, when he 'sat over against the Archbishop of York'.

▶ *W1J 0BD. Burlington House, Piccadilly. Green Park or Piccadilly Circus tube.*

㉜ Statue of Charles I

'Comely and calm, he rides/Hard by his own Whitehall:/Only the night wind glides;/No crowds, nor rebels, brawl.' The 19th-century poet Lionel Johnson was describing the equestrian monument to Charles I (1625–49) just south of Trafalgar Square, which seems to want to gallop down the road to reclaim Parliament. It was commissioned from the sculptor Hubert Le Sueur, in 1633, by the 1st Earl of Portland, for his garden in Roehampton. Le Sueur came to England with the retinue of Henrietta Maria upon her marriage to Charles I, and introduced the art of bronze sculpture to these shores. When Parliament sequestered the Roehampton estate, the statue was sold to St Paul's, Covent Garden, before Cromwell's Puritans ordered its destruction. A Holborn brazier, John Rivett, was ordered to melt it down, but instead hid it in his garden. Upon the Restoration, he was rewarded by Charles II with the title of King's Brazier.

The placing of the statue at this spot was charged with symbolism. It was erected in 1673 on the site of a medieval monument that had been destroyed by the Puritans, the Eleanor Cross (see below). This is the very centre of London, from which all distances are measured. Charles is set high on a plinth made by Joshua Marshall, the king's Master Mason. He looks defiantly towards the Palace of Westminster and the Great Hall, where he was tried, past the Banqueting House, the scene of his beheading.

▶ *WC2N 5DN. Junction of Whitehall and Northumberland Avenue, S of Trafalgar Square. Charing Cross tube and rail.*

㉝ Charing Cross

Edward I was a man of war who so loved his wife that she travelled with him on his campaigns. He was 15 when he was married, by arrangement, to the 10-year-old Eleanor, Infanta of Castile. Celebrations were lavish, but the couple did not live together for a few years. When they did, they became inseparable. She bore him 16 children, of whom six survived to adulthood. In November 1290, she was taken ill,

dying at Harby in Lincolnshire. After her burial in Westminster Abbey, Edward commissioned a series of Eleanor Crosses to mark the 12 places where her cortege had rested overnight, to remind passers-by to say a prayer for 'the Queen of Good Memory … whom living we dearly cherish, and whom dead we cannot cease to love'. His Master Mason created a basic design for the tiered monuments, which would bear heraldic shields, coats of arms and statues of his queen. The last cross was erected at Whitehall, on what was part of the Royal Mews, where Charles I now sits astride his horse. It was the grandest and the largest, made of marble. The 21m (70ft) Eleanor Cross on the forecourt of Charing Cross station is a replica built by the South Eastern Railway Company. Most of the originals were destroyed by Puritans during the Civil War. It is a romantic but false notion that the name is a corruption of *chère reine* (beloved queen).
▶ *WC2. Strand. Charing Cross tube and rail.*

㉞ National Portrait Gallery

Queen Victoria was delighted to approve the grant of £2,000 agreed by the House of Commons, towards the establishment, in 1856, of a 'British Historical Portrait Gallery'. Philip Henry Stanhope, backed by Thomas Babington Macaulay and Thomas Carlyle, was the driving force behind the initiative to bring together portraits of famous British men and women. As the 5th Earl Stanhope put it to the House of Lords, there should be for the nation 'a gallery of original portraits, such portraits to consist as far as possible of those persons who are most honourably commemorated in British history as warriors or as statesmen, or in arts, in literature, in science'. It was established on the principle, still applied today, that the status of the sitter, rather than the art, would be paramount, yet art there is of a most affecting kind – although not all the characters depicted are honourable.

The gallery has occupied Ewan Christian's Florentine-Renaissance-style building since 1896, and the busts of the three eminent Victorian founders are set in the wall above the entrance. By the time the gallery opened, it was already too small to house the collection, and it has been subject to extension ever since. The view from the rooftop restaurant is one of the best in London – diners look out past Nelson's Column and the statues of Charles I, James II and George IV, across Whitehall to Parliament, where the fate of King Charles I was sealed.
▶ *WC2H 0HE. St Martin's Place. Charing Cross tube and rail or Leicester Square tube.*

LONDON

35 National Portrait Gallery – royal portraits

George IV and Caroline of Brunswick could not live together in life, but in death they share a room. They hang in the first of the Weldon Galleries, designed by Piers Gough in 1996, in an exhibition of 'Royalty, Celebrity and Scandal'. It covers the period of George's Regency (1811–19) and his reign (1820–30). He cuts quite a dash in Field Marshal's uniform in Thomas Lawrence's paintings – made in 1814 and 1815, before the great debauchee ran to fat. Lawrence's portrait of Caroline shows her defiant in a dress of red velvet. Thomas was rumoured to be among her many lovers, and the work challenges George's view that she was no oil painting. Sir George Hayter's epic *The Trial of Queen Caroline* from 1820 depicts a parliamentary debate on a bill contrived to grant the king a divorce after a scandal over Caroline's affair with an Italian valet.

These are among a great variety of paintings and photographs of royalty. Here is Henry VIII by Hans Holbein, and Catherine of Aragon, Anne Boleyn and Catherine Parr. The visitor can see Daniel Myten's Charles I and Robert Walker's Oliver Cromwell; Sir Peter Lely's James II and his William III. Behind every one there is a tale, and these portraits bring alive great characters from history – the good, the bad and the ugly.
▶ *WC2H 0HE. St Martin's Place. Charing Cross tube and rail or Leicester Square tube.*

36 Rules

Edward VII, as Prince of Wales, wined and dined his mistress Lily Langtry at this venerable establishment. She usually wore her trademark black dress. Today, Rules is the oldest restaurant in London. The present building was designed for Benjamin Rule, fishmonger and oyster-bar proprietor, in 1873, but as long ago as 1798 Thomas Rule had an oyster stall on Maiden Lane. Paintings and prints, busts and bronzes, red plush seats, stained glass and theatrical relics set a romantic scene. The Greene room is a shrine to the author Graham Greene, who often celebrated birthdays here. Rules appears in some of his novels, including *The End of the Affair*. For Langtry, the end of the affair – one of many for both Lily and Edward – came in 1880 (for happier times see page 27). It has been said that the prince deplored her bad behaviour at a dinner party, but the fact was that Lily was upstaged by actress Sarah Bernhardt when she arrived in London in June 1879.
▶ *WC2E 7LB. Maiden Lane, off Strand. Covent Garden tube.*

37 Royal Opera House

Prince Charles's love of classical music is well known. He is patron of the Royal Opera, and it seems that his daughter-in-law, the Duchess of Cambridge, shares his appreciation of the art. The two of them have paid visits to both the opera and the ballet here, and watched a performance of *Alice's Adventures in Wonderland*.

Sir Edward Middleton Barry's 19th-century colonnaded building is the third theatre on the site. The first was the Theatre Royal, built with funds raised by actor/manager John Rich, which opened in December 1732. At that time, Covent Garden and Drury Lane still enjoyed almost sole rights to present drama in London – granted almost 70 years before by Charles II, whose mistress Nell Gwyn was the most famous Restoration actress of all time. A performance of Handel's 'The Messiah' attended by George II began the tradition of holding oratorio performances at Lent. Handel bequeathed his organ to Rich, but it was lost in a fire that destroyed the building in 1808.

The foundation stone for the second theatre was laid by the Prince of Wales, later George IV, in December 1808. One of the largest theatres in Europe, it opened with that famous tale of a king of Scotland, *Macbeth*, and this building, too, fell victim to fire. Barry's building dates from 1857–8. In the 1990s £216 million was lavished on it, to make it one of the most exciting public spaces in the capital, with restaurants and bars. 'Velvet, Gilt and Glamour' tours afford a glimpse of the royal retiring room, which is still used by royal patrons today.
▶ *WC2E 9DD. Junction of Bow Street and Floral Street. Covent Garden tube.*

38 Somerset House

According to the vision of George III, this was to be 'a great public building ... an object of national splendour'. So why did he at first commission an underling, a clerk at the Office of Works named William Robinson, to undertake the project? He must have been mad! In the end, Sir William Chambers, the king's favourite architect, created the design. Chambers' neoclassical building – wing extensions were added in Victorian times – was to accommodate not just the Royal Academy of Arts, the Royal Society and the Society of Antiquaries, but government departments, the Navy Board and the King's Bargemaster. It would require direct access to the Thames. Indeed, it stood right on the river until the construction of the Embankment and the driving through of a new road under the modernising Victorians cut if off, so that its watergates looked upon a carriageway. Chambers did not live to see the completion of his building. He resigned in March 1795, pleading 'infirmities incident to old age' and died within the year. He would not have been pleased to see his great creation turned over to bureaucracy in 1849 when the Inland Revenue moved in.

Today, it is at the very heart of the capital's cultural life – and home to the Royal Society of Literature. It is, at last and as Chambers intended, devoted to 'the reception of useful learning and polite arts'. The visitor stepping through the gateway on a cold December evening enters a winter wonderland where skaters glide around a temporary rink in the light of flaming torches. In summer, in this grandly conceived classical urban space, fountains play and so, sometimes, do musicians and films.
▶ *WC2R 1LA. Between Strand and Victoria Embankment by Waterloo Bridge. Temple tube.*

㊴ Royal Courts of Justice

'Jarndyce and Jarndyce drones on. This scarecrow of a suit has, in the course of time, become so complicated that no man alive knows what it means.' Charles Dickens had a poor view of the workings of the Court of Chancery in the Victorian era, and satirised proceedings in his 1852 novel *Bleak House*. Later, the headquarters of the Chancery Division were moved to the Royal Courts of Justice, and are still there.

The building, opened by Queen Victoria in 1882, is a grey-stone edifice by George Edmond Street, which harks back in style to the 13th century. Behind its iron gates and elaborately carved porches lies 'London's last great secular building of the Gothic revival', displaying the scale and grandeur of a cathedral. Within, the atmosphere is solemn, majestic, overawing. The Great Hall is 24m (80ft) high, and has Italian marble mosaic flooring, and heraldic devices in the tall windows. Civil litigants – the injured, the divorced, the aggrieved, the disinherited, the traduced, the libelled, the wronged and the wrongdoer – must feel that the law is mighty. Those with less of an investment can simply appreciate the glorious scale, the fine detail, the craftsmanship – then catch some real-life human drama. The Criminal Division of the Court of Appeal hears advocacy on behalf of those detained 'at Her Majesty's pleasure'.
▶ *WC2A 2LL. Strand, E of junction with Aldwych. Temple tube.*

㊵ St Paul's Cathedral

On July 29, 1981, Prince Charles broke with royal tradition to marry Lady Diana Spencer in St Paul's Cathedral, rather than in the usually favoured Westminster Abbey, and 600,000 people thronged the streets of London. Diana arrived in the glass coach to take the three-and-a-half-minute walk up the aisle, which was duly red-carpeted for the event, with the 7.6m (25ft) train of her gown flowing behind her.

Sir Christopher Wren's immense 17th-century church stands at the top of Ludgate Hill, the highest point in the City. Its stupendous dome, topped by a cross 111m (365ft) above the ground, is comparable to that of St Peter's in Rome. Its ceiling, decorated with scenes from the life of St Paul by John Thornball, is false, a matter of architectural aesthetics best appreciated from the perspective of the Whispering Gallery. Such are the acoustics here that a *sotto voce* murmur on one side can be heard by someone putting an ear to the wall 30m (100ft) away on the far side of the dome. Embellishments of the interior include choir stalls and iron gates, fashioned by Grinling Gibbons and the French master metal worker Jean Tissot. The ceiling mosaics and the single painting, William Holman Hunt's *The Light of the World*, arrived in the late 19th century.

This is the fifth cathedral to stand on the site since AD 604, and the first built after Henry VIII's Reformation. It was begun in 1675, after the previous building was destroyed in the Great Fire of 1666, and completed in 1710, in the reign of Charles II. Queen Victoria marked her diamond jubilee here in 1897. Although Prince Charles chose the cathedral over Westminster Abbey for his wedding to Diana, it was to the abbey that she was brought for her funeral on September 6, 1997.
▶ *EC4M 8AD. St Paul's Churchyard. St Paul's tube.*

㊶ Mary Queen of Scots House

Perched high in a niche in the elaborate façade of Mary Queen of Scots House is a statue of that ill-fated queen – right above a branch of a popular sandwich shop. Born at Linlithgow Palace in 1542, Mary became queen when she was just seven days old, on the death of her father, James V of Scotland. Her life was one of turmoil and she was executed in 1587 on the orders of her close relative, Elizabeth I (see Holyroodhouse, pages 202-203). On Elizabeth's death in 1603, Mary's son, James VI of Scotland, became James I of England.
▶ *EC4A 2BP. Fleet Street, just W of Ludgate Circus. Blackfriars tube.*

LONDON

THE TOMB OF HENRY VII AND ELIZABETH OF YORK

Crowned in glory

Coronations, weddings, funerals – Westminster Abbey has been the scene of many a royal rite of passage.

A coronation is always an occasion for public celebration, but the eve of the crowning of Charles II on April 23, 1661 was marked by delirious rejoicing. Diarist John Evelyn tells us that the fountains of London ran with wine, church bells peeled and speeches were made at triumphal arches. Nearly a year had passed since the king's return from exile in France after the death of Oliver Cromwell and the failure of his Commonwealth. The coronation the next day would be a lavish spectacle but also symbolic. The fabric of Westminster Abbey is great and glorious, and of such momentous events is its ethos made. The sense of the past hangs heady as incense.

Gothic masterpiece

The abbey has been the place of coronation for 38 kings and queens over almost 1,000 years. William of Normandy, upon his victory at Hastings in October 1066, marched his army to London and was crowned here on Christmas Day. He stood at the high altar upon Edward the Confessor's gravestone, to assert his claim that Edward had appointed him as successor.

The establishment of Westminster Abbey as the place of coronation fundamentally influenced its transformation under Henry III in the 13th century. It must be a glorious theatre to accommodate assemblies of the great and good to witness each coronation, and also burial. Henry's religious fervour, passion for art and habitual prodigality found expression in the ambitious rebuilding of the abbey. He had been crowned at Gloucester at a time when London was under the sway of Prince Louis of France – but he could at least be buried here. The project was not complete upon his death, when his son Edward I became the first to hold his coronation, and that of his queen, Eleanor of Castile, in the Gothic

> Henry III had seen the great cathedrals of France. Now England must have one as grand, for the anointing of each new monarch, and as a 'place of royal sepulture'.
> WESTMINSTER ABBEY

marvel. The Stone of Scone, which he had brought from Scotland, was fitted into a wooden throne – 'King Edward's Chair' – and he was crowned upon it, sealing his claim to be 'Lord Paramount' of Scotland.

The coronation service used to be in Latin, but by 1603, when James I came to the abbey, the liturgy was entirely English. If history had taken a different course, the coronation of Charles I in February 1626 might have been the last. It was indeed the last time that the ancient regalia were worn, and the first time that the anthem *I Was Glad* was sung. This draws on verses from Psalm 122, and is essentially a prayer for peace and prosperity in Jerusalem. The peace so longed for was not to hold. The Civil War resulted in victory for Oliver Cromwell 23 years later, and the severing of the head that had worn the crown. Parliamentarians destroyed most of the regalia and the crowns, prising off the precious stones, melting down the metal to sell. The coronation chair was removed to Westminster Hall and Cromwell sat upon it in December 1653. The king was dead; long live the lord protector. A second throne was built for William III and Mary II in 1689, and is now in the abbey museum.

Majestic ceremonial

The character of the monarch was at times reflected in proceedings. The flamboyant George IV spent a fortune on the spectacle. William IV, his retiring younger brother, wanted little fuss at what was dubbed 'the penny coronation'. Since the coronation of Queen Victoria in 1838, however, there has been a profound understanding of the significance of the event, not just in Britain but abroad, attracting dignitaries from all over the world. When the Queen was crowned in 1953, televisions beamed the proceedings into people's homes.

Although diarist Samuel Pepys came to witness the coronation of Charles II, he wrote that 'to my great grief, I and most of the Abbey could not see'. John Evelyn fared better and was able to report: 'The Archbishop placed the Crown Imperial on the altar, prayed over it, and set it on his Majesty's head, at which all the Peers put on their coronets. Anthems, and rare music, with lutes, viols, trumpets, organs, and voices were then heard, and the Archbishop put the ring on his Majesty's finger.

Still an exalting place of worship, Westminster Abbey is ineffably 'royal', a treasure house of art – and above all a rich repository of the chequered history of Britain's kings and queens.

LONDON

㊷ St Dunstan's-in-the-West

Just a short stroll from her cousin Mary, Queen of Scots is the only statue made of Elizabeth I in her reign. It stands within the gates of St Dunstan's-in-the-West in Fleet Street, and dates from 1586. It used to stand in the gate of Ludgate Prison, but the building was gutted in the Great Fire of 1666, and in 1760, the year of George III's succession, the gate was taken down. Elizabeth's statue was consigned to a pub cellar, where Mary would no doubt have been happy for it to languish for ever. It was forgotten, but eventually found by workmen in 1839, in the course of demolishing the building. Now it is in an alcove, sharing the church courtyard with the mythical sovereign, King Lud.

Mary was always a problem to Elizabeth. Her arrival in England, a fugitive from Scottish Protestants, posed a real and present threat that Catholics would back her in her bid to take the English throne. There were many who believed that Elizabeth's father, Henry VIII, had married her mother, Anne Boleyn, illegally. Certain factions would have liked to see her deposed – as deposed she was, if only from her gateway.

▶ *EC4A 2HR. Fleet Street. Temple tube.*

㊸ St Bartholomew's Hospital

Above the entrance to St Bartholomew's Hospital stands London's only public statue of Henry VIII, in gratitude for a rare act of magnanimity. A hospital and priory were founded here in 1123 by Rahere, a former courtier to Henry I, although the oldest building on the site today dates from the 1730s. The priory was closed in 1539, during the Dissolution of the Monasteries and the future of the already ancient hospital was in doubt. A plea to the king from Londoners, who feared an outbreak of the plague, caused him to issue a signed agreement granting the hospital to the City, and letters patent endowing it with properties and income. The hospital museum still holds the deed of agreement for the refounding of 'Barts'.

The first superintendent was Thomas Vicary, Sergeant-Surgeon to Henry VIII and to his children, Edward, Mary and Elizabeth. His position at court enabled him to advance the status of the surgeon. A painting by Holbein shows the king handing to Vicary the 1540 charter of the Act of Union between barbers and surgeons. Vicary was 'but a meane practiser in Maidstone' – until the king advanced him 'for curing his sore legge'.

▶ *EC1A 7BE. At front of St Bartholomew's Hospital, West Smithfield. Barbican tube.*

ST BARTHOLOMEW'S HOSPITAL

㊹ Armoury House

The large drill hall of this veritable castle is named the Prince Consort Room after Prince Albert, who was Captain General of the Honourable Artillery Company. The present Captain General is The Queen and her portrait hangs with those of her predecessors in the dining room, known as the Long Room. The company's battlemented HQ building dates from 1735 and has been much added to over the years. Besides being a fighting force, the company has three ceremonial roles – as guards of honour to the royal family (they fire the royal salutes from the Tower of London and Hyde Park); as the Company of Pikemen and Musketeers, in which role they wear uniforms of Charles I's time for the Lord Mayor's show; and as a mounted light cavalry. Gun salutes are a mark of respect and celebration, and occur on the Queen's actual and official birthdays, Coronation Day, the birthdays of the Duke of Edinburgh and the Prince of Wales and the State Opening of Parliament. Royal births and visits from heads of state are also marked in this way.

▶ *EC1Y 2BQ. City Road, S of junction with Old Street. Old Street tube.*

㊺ Regent's Park

In 1538, as was his divine right, Henry VIII seized from the Abbess of Barking a great acreage of the forest of Middlesex, a trot and gallop from Whitehall Palace. Around 'Marylebone Park', a ditch and rampart were built to keep in deer for the chase. The land was later sold and turned over to farming until 1811, when it reverted to the Crown, at which point the Prince Regent commissioned John Nash to create 'the Regent's Park'.

Nash's original plan was typically theatrical – a grand double circle with a domed royal residence at the centre to be linked to St James's Palace by a processional route. However, the prince's wings were clipped, and the flight of fancy was limited to the creation of a circular pleasure garden, with a lake and canal. Eight villas were built on the park, of which two remain, and grand Regency terraces rose up around it. The park was closed to all but royalty and the 'carriage set' who lived there. It wasn't until 1835, in the reign of William IV, that it was opened to the public – for just two days a week.

▶ *N of Marylebone Road. Regent's Park tube.*

㊻ Royal Festival Hall

On May 3, 1951, a ceremonial concert attended by George VI and Queen Elizabeth marked the opening of a new concert hall. Three years earlier, Clement Attlee's Labour government had announced plans for a Festival of Britain, a 'tonic to the nation' at a time of post-war austerity. A new concert hall would replace the Queen's Hall, which had been destroyed by an incendiary bomb in 1941. Attlee himself laid the foundation stone in October 1949. The building cost £2 million and took scarcely more than 18 months to erect.

In March 1967, the Queen opened the new Queen Elizabeth Hall and Purcell Room, right next to the Royal Festival Hall. There is something optimistic about the light, airy and accessible building – the tonic effect is still at work. Concerts in the main hall can be inexpensive, and the smaller Purcell Room and Front Room allow for a variety of performances.

Together, these venues are now known as the Southbank Centre. The foyer has a bar and café and there is often something happening, including free Sunday music in the Clore Ballroom, and exhibitions of photographs or paintings in the basement gallery.

▶ *SE1 8XX. S bank of Thames by Hungerford Bridge. Waterloo tube and rail.*

㊼ Albert Bridge

The 'Trembling Lady', London's prettiest bridge, was built at the urging of Prince Albert, to link Chelsea on the north bank of the Thames to Battersea on the south. It opened in 1873 as a toll bridge (the octagonal tollbooths are still in place) but it was never commercially viable. The bridge was designed by Rowland Mason Ordish, a leading architectural engineer, and was built according to his patented Ordish-Lefeuvre principle – an early form of cable-stayed bridge design. It had to be strengthened between 1884 and 1885 – a project overseen by that great Victorian engineer Sir Joseph Bazalgette – incorporating some of the elements of a suspension bridge.

However, the bridge was never designed for heavy traffic. Notices at either end warned marching soldiers from Chelsea Barracks to break step so as not to damage the structure. Due to its fragile condition, the bridge was closed in February 2010 for major restoration work, and it reopened in December 2011. Its attractive appearance is partly functional. Shades of pink and green ensure its visibility to river traffic in murky weather, and at night it is enchantingly lit with 4,000 low-voltage bulbs for the same purpose.

▶ *Lies between Battersea and Chelsea bridges. Sloane Square tube.*

㊽ Trinity Church Square

Here can be seen one of the oldest free-standing statues in London. Its provenance is unknown, and even the identity uncertain, although a reference to it from 1830 confidently claims that this is Alfred the Great. From behind, the 9th-century King of Wessex doesn't look so great, and the lack of detail at the back, compared with the fairly elaborate front, suggests that it might have been made to stand in a niche. The original was made of stone, but a repairer has used artificial stone. There is some speculation that this was one of a group of eight medieval statues from Westminster Hall, five of which disappeared when Sir John Soane rebuilt the north front in 1819–22. Perhaps Soane gave this one to William Chadwick, an acquaintance, who laid out the garden here in 1822.

King Alfred (AD 871–99), an enlightened patron of the arts and a master tactician, became known as 'King of the English' for routing Danes from the kingdoms they had conquered.

▶ *SE1 4HU. Trinity Church Square, between Borough High Street and Great Dover Street. Borough tube.*

LONDON

㊾ Tower of London: White Tower

William the Conqueror built the Tower not for London but against it. He had won a victory at Hastings, but as his troops marched on the capital, they were attacked by citizens who did not wish to bow to a foreign invader. The rebels were swiftly put down and the king ordered the building of three timber fortifications to suppress and terrify a 'huge and brutal populace'. When fire destroyed these structures, a stone castle was begun in 1077. The building took 20 years to complete, and was like none that had been seen in England before. It was mainly of Kentish ragstone, but incorporated cream-coloured stone from Caen. Alien, ominous, it rose up against the skyline – a royal residence that was also a fortress and a symbol of power. Even today the White Tower, with its four distinctive turrets, is the dominant aspect of the Tower complex.

In March 1240, the Keeper of the Works was ordered by Henry III to whitewash the building inside and out, so that it 'smote the eye'. The ancient heart of the Tower has evolved over centuries but the ethos of menace has never entirely dissipated. For many visitors, it is exciting and intriguing, although others share the view of the writer V.S. Pritchett, for whom there was 'no grimmer sight in England than this terrible building'. Anne Boleyn, Lady Jane Grey and Sir Walter Raleigh were beheaded here. Princess Elizabeth, the future queen, was imprisoned here by her sister, Mary I. Most notoriously, this was where 'the Princes in the Tower', Edward V and Richard of Shrewsbury, were incarcerated by their uncle, Richard Duke of Gloucester, Richard III. In around 1483 they disappeared, and it is assumed that they were murdered, but nobody really knows.

The small, stern, bare Chapel of St John is of a solid purity that expresses the strength of Norman faith – in Pritchett's words, 'the austerity is cold yet elating'.
▶ *EC3N 4AB. Tower of London, on N bank of Thames by Tower Bridge. Tower Hill tube.*

㊿ The Jewel House

This is the room in the Tower of London where the crown jewels are kept, well guarded but on public display. Westminster Abbey, April 23, 1661: 'The crowne being put upon his head, a great shout began.' Diarist Samuel Pepys did not have a good view of the coronation of Charles II, but the cries of jubilation can be imagined. What a day it was

that solemnised the Restoration of the Monarchy! And what a day was June 2, 1953, when the same crown was set upon the head of Elizabeth II! This is St Edward's crown, a replica of the one worn by St Edward the Confessor at Christmas 1065 (see right), and it is quite a party hat. The centrepiece of the world's greatest 'working' collection of crown jewels, it is made of solid gold, with velvet cap and ermine trim, spangled with 444 precious stones and weighing 2.2kg (4lb 12oz). The original was destroyed by Oliver Cromwell. He broke it up with the rest of the crown jewels. The present crown has been remodelled for the various monarchs who have worn it, although Queen Victoria preferred the lighter imperial crown.

Among today's treasures are the crowns of sovereigns, consorts and Princes of Wales, sceptres, orbs, rings, swords, spurs, bracelets … The value of the collection has been hazarded at billions, but for its potent symbolism it is priceless. The Koh-i-Noor diamond, the 'Mountain of Light' presented to Queen Victoria on a silk cushion in 1851 as a symbol of the Raj, is set in Victoria's favoured imperial crown, which was worn by the late Queen Mother, as a consort, at both her husband's and her daughter's coronation – literally, the jewel in the crown.
▶ *EC3N 4AB. Tower of London, on N bank of Thames by Tower Bridge. Tower Hill tube.*

⑸ Wakefield Tower

This medieval building, part of the Tower of London complex, is where Henry VI, the last Lancastrian king, probably met his bloody end in 1471. Now the famous ravens are lodged next to it. According to popular theory, Charles II was the first monarch to insist that the ravens at the Tower must be protected. The king's astronomer, John Flamsteed, had, according to the tale, complained that these dark birds of ill omen, harbingers of death, interfered with his work at the Royal Observatory in the White Tower. They would have been removed, but a soothsayer warned that the day they disappeared, England would fall.

The seven ravens at the Tower today – a requisite six, plus a reserve – are fed and tended by the Ravenmaster, one of the Yeoman Warders. Their wings are clipped so they cannot fly, and they strut around like funeral directors. Despite their sinister image as witches' familiars, they are intelligent and playful birds. They are not, however, pets, but 'enlisted' military personnel, and can be dismissed, as Raven George was in 1986 for 'conduct unsatisfactory'.

Another, less beguiling theory about the ravens is that they were a punning gift from the 3rd Earl of Dunraven (1812–71), and the legend may be no more than a Victorian invention. However, tradition prefers the Charles II version, and the ravens are part of the whole solemn picture. They are long-lived and a memorial stone lists all of those buried since 1956.

▶ *EC3N 4AB. Tower of London, on N bank of Thames by Tower Bridge. Tower Hill tube.*

52 Medieval Palace

On the Feast of St George in 1240, the foundations of Henry III's new landward gateway collapsed – and, to the hour, a year later, it happened again. The jumble of towers, ramparts, curtain walls, screen and moat that grew up around the White Tower was mostly created by Henry III and his son, Edward I. Henry ordered the building of the Wakefield and Lanthorn Towers on the waterfront as 'his and hers' royal accommodation for himself and his queen, Eleanor of Provence. The Great Hall was

extended, a new defensive wall with nine towers went up around the landward sides, and a moat was dug. The relationship between sovereign and citizens was, meanwhile, increasingly strained, not just because the 'improvements' cost £5,000, but because the Tower was deemed an insult in stone. It was designed to keep them at bay, so little did their king trust them. The collapse of a tower, 'built not for the defence of the kingdom, but only to oppress harmless citizens', could mean only one thing – the intervention of Londoners' guardian saint, Thomas Becket.

Henry III began the regular use of the Tower as a prison, and imported a menagerie of exotic beasts. From 1275, Edward I further extended the enclosure, filled in the moat and erected a second curtain wall and yet more towers. Interiors of what remains of the medieval palace they created have been restored, including the production of replica furniture, textiles, rugs and wall-hangings, hand-made in traditional ways. Kings continued to live here until Henry VIII moved into Whitehall Palace in 1529.

▶ *EC3N 4AB. Tower of London, on N bank of Thames by Tower Bridge. Tower Hill tube.*

53 Tower Green

Here, on this velvety greensward, three queens of England met their end in 'privileged' fashion, away from the eyes of sensation-seeking crowds. High-ranking individuals, and those who commanded wide support, were spared public execution on Tower Hill, in favour of more private beheading. Henry's VIII's second and fifth wives, Anne Boleyn and Catherine Howard, and Lady Jane Grey were all despatched here by the axe. Around the executioner's block, the ravens in their perpetual mourning – black from beak to toe – keep their vigil.

▶ *EC3N 4AB. Tower of London, on N bank of Thames by Tower Bridge. Tower Hill tube.*

ST EDWARD'S CROWN IS QUITE A PARTY HAT
TOWER OF LONDON

OUTER LONDON

Monarchs of old took their pleasure in the hunting grounds around the capital, while patronage of science, astronomy and horticulture, and the indulgence of charitable instincts, showed a more serious side.

❶ Marble Hill

'I have been a slave 20 years without ever receiving a reason for any one thing I ever was oblig'd to do.' Beautiful and gentle Henrietta Howard was one of six 'women of the bedchamber' to Queen Caroline – and from 1723 mistress to George II. In neither role can she have been very happy, but an inheritance from her former brother-in-law – her wastrel ex-husband's older brother – brought her a fortune and the title of Countess of Suffolk. With the money came undreamed of freedom and leisure, and she began building a grand house for herself. Designed in the manner of a Palladian villa of the time and landscaped to include parkland stretching down to the Thames, Marble Hill House was the height of Georgian fashion. Architect Roger Morris was aided by Henry Herbert, 9th Earl of Pembroke, who had been Lord of the Bedchamber to George II when he was Prince of Wales. Horace Walpole, antiquarian, art historian, Whig politician and a friend of the countess's, said of Pembroke, 'No man has a purer taste in building.'

Six years after Marble Hill's completion, the countess married George Berkeley MP, enjoying 11 years of married life before his death. She lived another 32 years in the house. After various owners, it fell into decay until it was rescued by the Cunard family at the beginning of the 20th century. Inside, everything the visitor sees has been reproduced for English Heritage as meticulously as possible, including hand-painted Chinese wallpaper and a chinoiserie collection as well as paintings and furniture of the period.
▶ *TW1 2NL. SW London. N bank of River Thames, SW of Richmond Bridge, off A305. St Margaret's rail. EH.*

❷ White Lodge

'We return'd home by Richmond Park, & went past both the Lodges, but saw nothing of their Majestys, tho' they are always at the White Lodge on a Sunday.' On July 24, 1768, Lady Mary Coke committed to her diary her disappointment at not glimpsing royalty. White Lodge was built for George II by Roger Morris in 1727 as a hunting lodge. George's wife, Caroline, often stayed there, remote from his infidelities. On Caroline's death in 1737, it passed

to Robert, 1st Baron Walpole, then to Caroline's daughter, Princess Amelia, described as 'one of the oddest princesses that ever was known; she has ears shut to flattery and her heart open to honesty'. She became Ranger of Richmond Park in 1751 and closed it to all but a few friends, her ears shut to public protest, until a court order forced her to reconsider.

The lodge was used as a weekend retreat by George III and Queen Charlotte, whom Mary Coke had hoped to have sight of, before the king granted it to Henry Addington, 1st Viscount Sidmouth, the prime minister, in 1805. Prince Albert Edward, the future Edward VII, kicked his heels here when his father, Prince Albert, chose this secluded location as a kind of educational hothouse for him. Another Prince of Wales was born here, the future Edward VIII, who also hated the seclusion. Edward's brother, Prince Albert, and Elizabeth Bowes-Lyon, the future George VI and Queen Elizabeth, made their home here in 1923, but stayed only a year because they had so little privacy from the Mary Cokes of the day. The beautiful Georgian building is today home to the Royal Ballet Lower School. The Prince of Wales is the school's president.
▶ *TW10 5HR. SW London. Within Richmond Park. Mortlake rail.*

❸ Bushy Park

When Cardinal Wolsey made a gift of Hampton Court to Henry VIII, he threw in this parkland for good measure. At the time it was farmland but predictably the king walled it in and created a deer chase. In 1610, Charles I ordered the creation of the Longford River – a 12-mile canal that carried water from the River Colne to supply the thirsty palace and feed water features in the park. Sir Christopher Wren designed the Chestnut Avenue for William and Mary, to make a formal route through the middle of the park, flanked by horse chestnuts and limes, with a round pond at the end of it. In the centre of the pond is a statue of the nymph Arethusa, commissioned by Charles I for Queen Henrietta Maria. It was brought from Somerset House to Hampton Court by Oliver Cromwell, who took a fancy to the royal art collection.
▶ *SW London. N of Hampton Court on N bank of River Thames. Hampton Wick rail.*

❹ Hampton Court

In the reign of William III, 'Hampton Court put on new clothes, and, being dressed gay and glorious, made the figure we now see it in'. The monarch most associated with the palace is Henry VIII, but Daniel Defoe was writing, in 1724, of the transformation wrought by William and Mary. Henry VIII's self-seeking Lord Chancellor, Cardinal Wolsey, made him a gift of the palace. Having failed to secure a divorce from Catherine of Aragon for his master, the cardinal hoped to curry favour. Henry commissioned new royal suites, laid out hunting grounds, tennis courts, bowling alleys – but still set his face against Wolsey. Among the amenities was a vast dining room, known as the Great Hall, and the Great House of Easement – a lavatory with seating for 28 people. John Evelyn visited Charles I at the palace in 1647, when he 'had the honour to kiss his Majesty's hand' – later lamenting that Hampton Court was 'now in the power of those execrable villains who murdered

him'. Indeed, Oliver Cromwell led a rather kingly existence here, spending restful weekends and sleeping in the Queen's Bedroom.

The gay and glorious new look was the work of Sir Christopher Wren, who planned a Renaissance-style residence to rival the palace at Versailles. Only the Great Hall was to be spared, but a complete rebuild would have demanded too much time and money – and time ran out for Mary in 1694, when she died from smallpox. At this point, work stopped, only resuming in 1697, and more speedily in 1698 when Whitehall Palace burned down. Under Wren and his deputy, William Talman, the east and south façades of the palace were translated from Tudor redbrick to grand baroque. 'I know of no palace in Europe,' wrote Defoe, 'Versailles excepted, which can come up to her, either for beauty and magnificence, or for extent of building, and the ornaments attending it.'

▶ *KT8 9AU. SW London. On N bank of River Thames at junction of A308 Hampton Court Road and A309 Hampton Court Way. Hampton Court rail.*

HAMPTON COURT

GRACEFUL DEER GRAZE UNDISTURBED

RICHMOND PARK

❺ Richmond Park

If Henry VIII could stand today on King Henry's Mound, the distant view of St Paul's would no doubt gratify him no end. Wren's great cathedral – the first to be built after Henry's Reformation of the Church of England – can be seen from the highest point in the park, where it is said that Henry would stand to watch the deer. It was Charles I, however, who introduced the herds of 3,000 red and fallow deer that shaped the park. In true cavalier fashion, he threw off the peasant farmers and built an eight-mile wall to enclose a royal hunting ground. These days, the graceful animals can graze undisturbed. They keep down the grass, browse the leaves up to head height and prevent trees from seeding. The whole park, which encompasses bracken, ponds and woodlands, is graded a Site of Special Scientific Interest and a National Nature Reserve.
▶ *TW10 5IIS (Richmond Park Office, Holly Lodge). SW London. S side of River Thames, access from A305, A306, A307 or A308. Richmond tube and rail.*

❻ Ham House

The state of monarchy was 'the supremest thing upon earth', James I informed Parliament in 1609. 'Kings are not only God's lieutenants upon earth, and sit upon God's throne, but even by God himself they are called Gods.' No wonder the tutors to Charles, the king's son and heir, would hesitate to beat the boy for any misdemeanour. The strange practice of chastising a 'whipping boy' instead is first mentioned at this time. Charles's close friend, William Murray of the bedchamber, took his punishments for him – and in 1637 was rewarded for his pains, with the manors of Ham and Petersham and a title, Earl of Dysart.

Ham House had been built by Sir Thomas Vavasour, Knight Marshal to James I, and William Murray greatly extended it, commissioning the Great Staircase, Hall Gallery, Long Gallery and North Drawing Room. Some of his art collection remains. William's daughter Elizabeth and her second husband, the Earl of Lauderdale, brought the house to a degree of splendour, furnished, according to diarist John Evelyn, 'like a great prince's'. It was said of Elizabeth, by Bishop Burnet, 'she was violent in everything she set about, a violent friend, but a much more violent enemy. She … had a restless ambition, lived at vast expense, and was ravenously covetous.' She 'took little care of the decencies of her sex'. Although she courted Oliver Cromwell, it is said she joined the Sealed Knot, a society dedicated to the restoration of Charles II.

Ham House remained in family hands until the National Trust took it over in 1948 and it is one of the greatest surviving houses from the 17th century.

▶ *TW10 3RS. SW London. Close to S bank of River Thames at end of Ham Street, off A307 Upper Ham Road. Richmond tube and rail. NT.*

❼ Richmond Palace

'Freestone building, three stories high, with fourteen turrets covered with lead ... a very graceful ornament to the whole house, and perspicuous to the country round about.' That was 1649. Charles I was scarcely cold in his grave, when Parliament ordered a detailed survey of the Tudor palace at Richmond, where Elizabeth I had died. It was duly demolished and the raw materials were sold for £13,000.

The palace was built by Henry VII between 1499 and 1501 on the site of two previous royal residences. The second of these, built by Henry V, was destroyed by fire in 1497. Henry VIII took possession of his father's palace but preferred Whitehall and Hampton Court Palaces – both acquired from the arch manipulator Cardinal Wolsey. After the death of Elizabeth, royalty used Richmond less, and all that Cromwell's men left for us to see is the gatehouse and old courtyard.

▶ *TW9 1PQ. SW London. Remains of Richmond Palace close to River Thames, W of centre of Richmond. Richmond tube and rail.*

❽ Syon House

When Henry VIII's coffin was brought here overnight *en route* for burial at Windsor, it burst open and his body was set upon by dogs. This might seem fit retribution for the king's act of snatching the abbey of Mount Zion (Syon) from an order of Bridgettine monks when the monasteries were dissolved.

One of London's last surviving ducal residences and estates, this is the home of Ralph Percy, current and 12th Duke of Northumberland, who otherwise resides at Alnwick in that county. The first private owner of the property post-

Reformation, Edward Seymour, Duke of Somerset, built a Renaissance palace, which passed to the Percy family by marriage in 1594. The 1st Duke of Northumberland employed Robert Adam in the 1760s, and the Scottish architect integrated decoration with furniture, fixtures and fittings in what has become known as the Adam style. Imperial Rome is evoked in the Great Hall, Ante Room and Dining Room, while the Red Drawing Room has silk-hung walls, and 293 medallions painted on the ceiling by Giovanni Battista Cipriani.

Paintings of the Stuart royal family recall the time when Charles I's children were cared for in the house while the king was confined to Hampton Court. The beautiful, book-lined Long Gallery has a view over the Thames' last tidal water meadow. At the same time as Adam was at work on the house, Capability Brown was designing the gardens, including many rare trees and an ornamental lake. The highlight of the park is the conservatory, built in 1826, designed by Charles Fowler, and an inspiration for Joseph Paxton's Crystal Palace 25 years later.

▶ *TW8 8JF. W London. N bank of River Thames, S of A315 London Road. Syon Lane rail.*

❾ Kew Palace

George III spent some of his childhood here, and it was to Kew that he retreated in his madness. The smallest of the royal palaces, Kew was first rented to the monarchy in 1728, in the reign of George II, and George III bought it from the Levett family. After Queen Charlotte died in her bedroom here, her granddaughter, Princess Victoria, ordered that it remain just as she left it.

The redbrick, four-storey Jacobean mansion was built for a Dutch merchant as a private home in 1631, which explains the curving gables and its original name, the Dutch House. The ground and first floors have recently undergone a decade-long programme of restoration to take them back to the palace's glorious Georgian days. The building's history is explained in the People's Library, where cartoons of the much-caricatured king may be seen. Jigsaw maps used by the governess of George's 15 children are on display, together with an elegant doll's house. The queen's garden has been re-created around the palace. On their walks the royal family would stop to take tea at Queen Charlotte's Cottage, an elaborate thatched summer house at the southern end of Kew Gardens, designed by Charlotte herself.

▶ *TW9 3AB. W London. Within Royal Botanic Gardens. Kew Bridge rail.*

LONDON

The perils of power

The history of royalty is littered with intrigue and rebellion. Incarceration and even execution were occupational hazards.

The Tower of London can never have appeared more terrible than on March 18, 1554, a day of drenching rain, when a boat approached it from the river, sending the sullen waters slapping against the steps, and Traitor's Gate groaned open. The female passenger, just 21, was highly educated. She would have read of the Welsh prince Gruffyd, imprisoned here by Henry III, who fell to his death in 1244 while trying to climb from the White Tower; and of Henry VI, twice dethroned by Edward IV, held in the Wakefield Tower, and murdered in 1471. She would have heard the story – true or false – of the uncrowned boy king Edward V, and his brother Richard held here by their uncle, the future Richard III, never to be seen again. She would have known of earls, dukes and duchesses, kings of France and Scotland, who languished within London's grim Bastille.

On a knife edge

For Princess Elizabeth, however, there were more immediate reasons for mortal dread. Here her mother, Anne Boleyn, and her aunt, Catherine Howard, had been beheaded on the orders of her father, Henry VIII. And just the month before, Lady Jane Grey, the tragic 'nine-day queen', had met the same dire fate. Was it now to be her turn, for her alleged involvement in Sir Thomas Wyatt's rebellion against Mary I? To the waiting warders she declared, 'O Lord,I never thought to have come in here as a prisoner, and I pray you all bear me witness that I come in as no traitor but as a true woman to the Queen's Majesty...'.

She was taken to the Bell Tower, where Sir Thomas More had been kept by her father in 1534 before he was dispatched by the axe. Beheading was something of a privilege, reserved for the aristocratic élite – lesser mortals were hanged, drawn and quartered; nor were royal or noble prisoners chained up in rat- infested dungeons. They were treated almost as guests, and were allowed to buy whatever they needed – except their freedom.

Elizabeth brought servants with her. She had a comfortable room and for a while was permitted to take exercise on the castle wall as she contemplated the strong likelihood of her imminent death. She was saved by the intercession of Mary's consort, Philip II of Spain, who persuaded his wife that to execute her popular half-sister would cause public outrage. On May 19, having spent two months on the equivalent of death row, Elizabeth was moved to the palace at Woodstock and placed under house arrest.

It's not easy being queen. When Elizabeth ascended the throne in 1558, the Catholic Mary, Queen of Scots, her cousin, represented a threat to her, as Elizabeth herself had represented a threat to Mary I. The Scottish queen had been forced to abdicate in favour of her infant son, James VI, and imprisoned in Lochleven Castle, but she had escaped to England, where she threw herself upon Elizabeth's mercy. Mary had a claim to the English throne, and she had her champions. She was the focal point of a group of English Catholics, planning in the Uprising of the North to oust Elizabeth in her favour. Elizabeth did not know what to do with her, and for 19 years Mary was held captive, with her attendants. She was kept at various locations – Carlisle Castle, Bolton and the hated Tutbury. She sewed exquisitely, wrote letters, even hunted and hawked. Finally, she was executed, for alleged conspiracy, in the thronged great hall of Fotheringhay Castle, on February 8, 1587. She appeared 'full of grace and majesty, as if she were coming to a ball'. Sustained by her faith, she wore a rosary and crucifix, a black silk gown with crimson velvet trim under a satin mantle, and a white veil. She prayed fervently and went to meet her maker, believing that 'in my end is my beginning'.

Dignified exit

Mary's grandson, Charles I, made a similarly decorous departure outside Whitehall Palace in London, on January 30, 1649, wearing two shirts lest he shivered and appeared fearful. 'Ye manner of his deportment,' recalled one spectator, 'was very resolutely with some smiling countenances, intimating his willingness to be out of his troubles.' He had been imprisoned at Carisbrooke Castle, and escaped, only to be recaptured and confined at Windsor Castle. Charles was escorted through the Banqueting House to the scaffold, where he gave a short speech in which he forgave those who signed his death warrant, concluding, 'I am the martyr of the people.' His head was severed with one blow.

None of that horror haunts Whitehall today, as past horrors hang heavy at the Tower, which still has an extraordinary power to strike a chill and is allegedly haunted by former inmates. But a more cheerful picture can be painted of Sir Walter Raleigh spending 12 years a prisoner with his wife and children, growing tobacco outside his apartment, and writing the first part of his *History of the World* (1614). Unfortunately, his second spell of confinement in the Tower had no happy ending and he was beheaded in 1618.

For royal and noble prisoners, the fearsome and often final destination of the Tower of London provided all contemporary and spiritual comforts.
CHAPEL, ST THOMAS' TOWER

ROYAL BOTANIC GARDENS, KEW

❿ Royal Botanic Gardens, Kew

Princess Augusta of Saxe-Gotha-Altenburg shared her mother-in-law Queen Caroline's passion for plants. Caroline of Ansbach, 'Mrs' George II, is recognised as the patron of naturalistic English landscape gardening. The German Princess Augusta was 16 in 1736 when she arrived to marry Caroline's son Frederick, Prince of Wales. He died in 1751, and the following year, Augusta commanded the head gardener to 'compleat all that part of the Garden at Kew that is not yet finished in the manner proposed by the plan', which had been drawn up by her husband. She was assisted with the project by John Stuart, 3rd Earl of Bute, tutor to her son, the future George III. Rumours of an affair between earl and princess were probably false, but whatever their relationship, it was productive, reflecting Bute's scheme for a garden planted with 'all the plants known on Earth'.

In 1757, the princess engaged William Chambers as tutor in architecture to George, and as architect for Kew. Chambers planned many buildings and follies for the garden, including the gorgeous orangery, the towering pagoda and the temple of Aeolus. Covering 120ha (300 acres) of flower beds, glasshouses and hothouses, the gardens today are a tribute to the early explorers and collectors who brought back such a wealth of specimens. Principal among these was the botanist Joseph Banks, who in 1776 accompanied James Cook on his five-year voyage, returning to begin a plant collection that numbers more than 30,000 species. Despite the large temperate house, and the Princess of Wales conservatory, where ten climatic zones share the same roof, the most thrilling structure in the gardens is still Decimus Burton's Palm House, completed in 1848. In this masterpiece in cast iron and glass, staircases and walkways lead visitors on a steamy stroll through the tropics.
▶ *TW9 3AB, W London. S bank of River Thames, W of A307 Kew Road. Kew Bridge rail*

⓫ Greenwich Park

Tall oaks from little acorns grow – and the acorn from which Queen Elizabeth's Oak grew put down roots in the 12th century. Around this oak, it is said, Henry VIII and Anne Boleyn danced, and Elizabeth I 'oft partook of refreshment' in its shade. By 1902 it was quite dead and hollow but continued to provide shelter from the kind of torrential rain that proved to be its downfall in 1987, when the soil was washed from under it. The fallen tree is marked by a plaque, and beside it is a baby oak – planted by the Duke of Edinburgh in 1992, and good for another 900 years.

This is London's oldest enclosed royal park. It came to Humphrey, Duke of Gloucester, brother of Henry V, with the manor of Greenwich in 1427. After Henry VII built the Palace of Placentia at the bottom of the hill, Greenwich became forever associated with the Tudors. Princesses Mary and Elizabeth were born at the palace, and Edward VI died there. Although the land served Henry VIII for a deer park, it was James I who built the enclosing wall, replacing fencing. Important buildings in Greenwich Park include the Royal Observatory (see page 110) and the Queen's House (see below).

The park was opened to the public in the 18th century. Henry VIII would no doubt have been thrilled to see the Olympic equestrian events on his hunting ground in 2012.
▶ *SE10 8QX (Ranger's House). SE London. S bank of River Thames opposite Isle of Dogs. Cutty Sark DLR.*

⓬ The Queen's House

The eponymous queen was Anne of Denmark, the frivolous wife of James I. He is said to have given her the manor of Greenwich by way of an apology for having publicly sworn at her for shooting one of his hunting dogs. As apologies go, it was handsome. Handsome, too, is this centrepiece of the National Maritime Museum, the house that Inigo Jones designed for Anne in 1616. It was the first major commission for Jones, who had recently returned from three years in Italy, and it was England's first fully classical building, modelled on the Medici villa at Poggia a Caiano near Florence.

Anne did not live to see the building's completion in 1638. After her death, Charles I gave it to his queen, Henrietta Maria. In 1805, George III gave it to the Royal Naval Asylum, for the education of the orphaned children of seamen. Daniel Asher Alexander added colonnades and flanking wings for dormitories. Little survives of Jones's interior, just the ironwork of the 'tulip stairs' – the first geometric self-supporting spiral staircase in Britain – and the painted woodwork and marble floors of the Great Hall. The house is now home to a collection of fine art, which includes portraits of the Tudors and a painting, by an unknown artist, of the lost Tudor Palace of Placentia seen from the park.
▶ *SE10 9NF. SE London. N side of Greenwich Park, part of the National Maritime Museum. Cutty Sark DLR.*

⓭ Greenwich Hospital

Mary II bade Christopher Wren build a retirement home for seamen – but let it not obstruct her view! The home was to be on the site of the old Greenwich Palace, renamed Placentia Palace by Henry VII. For 150 years the 'Palace Pleasaunce' had been a favourite royal residence, but it was left to decay after the Civil War. The building Wren originally designed would have interrupted the 'visto' of the river from the Queen's House, so he did away with the centre and built two distinct wings. Mary did not see its completion. The entire project took 55 years. Wren worked on it with Nicholas Hawksmoor, and they were succeeded by John Vanbrugh. Diarist John Evelyn was a royal advisor on building in Greenwich, and dug deep into his own pockets to keep the underfunded hospital project afloat. Dr Johnson's biographer, James Boswell, recorded: 'I was much pleased to find myself with Johnson in Greenwich … He

remarked that the hospital was too magnificent for a place of charity, and that its parts were too detached to make a great whole.' The pair should have taken the ferry across the river, to see how, with the Queen's House, the two parts of the baroque masterpiece of 'Greenwich Hospital' form a single symmetrical sweep.

The Royal Naval College supplanted the hospital as the buildings' occupant in 1869, and decamped in 1998. The current tenant is the University of Greenwich, but the Painted Hall is open to the public. So spectacular was the work of James Thornhill in the hall that the pensioners, for whom it was intended as a dining room, were not allowed inside. The building served as a backdrop in the films *The Madness of King George* and *The Duchess*.
▶ *SE10 9LW. SE London. On S bank of the River Thames opposite Isle of Dogs. Cutty Sark DLR.*

⓮ Royal Observatory

'We have resolved to build a small observatory within Our Park at Greenwich.' The 'we' was Charles II, announcing that the new observatory would be dedicated 'to the finding out of longitude of places for perfecting navigation and astronomy'. Sir Christopher Wren was commissioned to build the observatory and an apartment for the first Astronomer Royal, John Flamsteed. In 1714, an Act of Parliament offered a prize of £20,000 to anyone who could provide a means of finding longitude (east–west position) at sea within 30 nautical miles. This would entail a study of the night sky and certain knowledge of the time at a fixed terrestrial point. Accurate timekeeping at sea was a challenge – the rolling of ships and changes in temperature and humidity upset clock mechanisms. John Harrison spent more than half a lifetime trying to convince the Board of Longitude that he had the answer, producing ever more sophisticated timekeepers. In the end, he was awarded half of the prize.

Once a successor to Harrison's clocks became standard issue, a 'home port' had to be established for the world's shipping, and Greenwich was chosen as the prime meridian at a conference in Washington DC in 1884. Thus, here it is possible to straddle the line at longitude 0°, planting a foot in both east and west hemispheres. Harrison's seminal timepieces are among the items on show, as are the pendulum clocks (regulators) that generated the famous BBC's six-pip signal. Here in SE10 officially begins every day, every week, every month. Here began the new millennium.
▶ *SE10 8XJ. SE London. Within Greenwich Park. Cutty Sark DLR.*

ROYAL OBSERVATORY

⓯ Blackheath

'Everywhere, flags were flying, bells and music sounding, wine and ale flowing in rivers to the health of him whose return was the return of peace, law and freedom.' Thomas Babington Macaulay, in his *History of England*, was describing how, in May 1660, Charles II came here, on his way from Rochester to London to reclaim his crown, amid scenes of great rejoicing.

More wine and ale flowed at the annual fair, the first of which was attended by John Evelyn, who recorded, on May Day 1683: 'I went to Blackheath to see the new faire, being the first, procured by Lord Dartmouth. This was the first day, pretended for the sale of cattle, but I think, in truth, to enrich the new tavern at the bowling greene, erected by Snape, his Majesty's farrier, a man full of projects. There appeared nothing but an innumerable assembly of drinking people from London, pedlars, &c.; and I suppose it is too neere London to be of any greate use to the country.' The exhilarating, wide-open space with long views over Kent and Surrey no longer has a May fair, but hosts an annual kite and bikes festival.
▶ *SE London. S of Greenwich Park, crossed by A2 Shooter's Hill Road. Blackheath rail.*

⓰ Eltham Palace

'Went to see his Majesty's House at Eltham, both the palace and chapel in miserable ruins, the noble wood and park destroyed by Rich the rebel.' John Evelyn was cast down by his visit here in April 1656 after Cromwell's colonel Nathaniel Rich had done his worst. If that great diarist could see it now, he would think he was dreaming. Eltham had been a royal residence since the time of Edward the Confessor. It was rebuilt by Anthony de Beke and, on his death in 1311, passed to Queen Isabella, wife of Edward II. Successive monarchs celebrated Christmas at the palace, and hosted great feasts, such as that laid on for Leo, King of Armenia, who came to petition Richard II for help against the Turks. Henry VIII kept Christmas 1575 at Eltham, when a theatrical spectacle called a 'masque' took place in the Great Hall. Over time, though, the Tudors fell out of love with the place, especially when the stagnant moat was deemed to be unhealthy. During the Civil War every deer in the park was slaughtered, every tree felled – hence the state in which Evelyn found it.

In 1933, Sir Stephen Courtauld and his wife, Virginia, acquired the lease, and this became once more a place of lavish entertainment. Paul Paget and John Seely were commissioned to create an

Art Deco masterpiece. The Great Hall was restored, with the addition of a minstrels' gallery. Ginnie Courtauld's oval bedroom, the Italianate drawing room, and the dining room with ceilings of aluminium leaf are by the Mayfair decorator and marchese Peter Malacrida. The grounds reflect the Courtaulds' love of horticulture. They left in 1944, taking with them their pet lemur.

Until 1992 the house was home to an army educational unit. English Heritage took it over and began restoration in 1995. The reputed existence of at least three escape tunnels hint at the palace's troubled past. A resident ghost occasionally gives guided tours.
▶ *SE9 5QE. SE London. Court Yard, Court Road, off A20 London–Folkestone Road. Eltham or Mottingham rail. EH.*

⓱ Charlton House

'I went to visit my worthy neighbor, Sir Henry Newton, and consider the prospect one ... of the most noble in the world; so as, had the house running water, it were a princely seat.' Newton had inherited the house in 1630 from his father, Sir Adam Newton, who had been tutor and then secretary to Henry, Prince of Wales, son of James I and Anne of Denmark. His visitor, in June 1653, was the diarist John Evelyn. Newton senior had, said Evelyn, built the house with his royal pupil in mind. It is one of Britain's finest examples of Jacobean domestic architecture, probably designed by John Thorpe, who had served as Clerk of the Works at the Palace of Placentia, Greenwich (see page 109) until 1601. Upon the prince's untimely death in 1612, Sir Adam Newton became treasurer in the household of Prince Charles. He translated into Latin King James's *Discourse against Vorstius*, a treatise denouncing a German-Dutch theologian, Conrad Vorstius, for the heresy of suggesting that no man could exercise authority over another in spiritual matters.

Although the house is not open to the public, its fine redbrick exterior with mullioned windows can be enjoyed from the Peace Garden, while the Mulberry Tea Rooms in the foyer celebrate one of several contenders for the title 'oldest mulberry tree in Britain'. This one was planted, apparently, in 1608, on the orders of the future Charles I, who would have been aged eight. A summerhouse, which now overlooks the road, is attributed to Inigo Jones. It was built in around 1630, and for a few years was used as a public convenience.
▶ *SE7 8RE. SE London. Charlton Road, 1½ miles E of Greenwich Park. Charlton rail.*

East Anglia

From she-wolves to noble saints, tragic pretenders
to captive queens, it is the women of the eastern
counties that have left the greatest mark on
East Anglia's royal landscape.

Hunstanton

A149

3

A149

7 Cromer

6

A148

4

5

2

King's Lynn

A47

Fakenham

8

East
Dereham

A140

The
Broads

Wisbech

A47

A1122

Downham
Market

Swaffham

NORFOLK
122-127

Norwich

A47

Great
Yarmouth

A1

A47

A1101

10

A10

9

A134

A1065

A11

11 12 A146

13

Lowestoft

A141

A10

Peterborough

2

A1(M)

A101

3 Ely

A142

A11

Thetford

14

A1066

A143

Southwold

CAMBRIDGESHIRE
114-115

A10

4

SUFFOLK
128-129

A140

A143

A12

A14

Huntingdon

A14

A14

Newmarket

A14

Bury St Edmunds

2

3 4

1

A1

St Neots

A428

Cambridge

A11

1

A134

Stowmarket

Aldeburgh

A10

A505

Saffron
Walden

1

Sudbury

Ipswich

A14

Felixstowe

ESSEX
116-119

2

A131

A12

Harwich

A120

M11

Braintree

A120

Colchester

A133

Harlow

A120

7 8

Clacton-
on-Sea

Chelmsford

Maldon

A414

3

M25

A12

4

A130

Brentwood

A127

Basildon

6

Southend-
on-Sea

A13

5

KEY

1 Main entry

County boundary

Motorway

Principal A road

CAMBRIDGESHIRE

Among these open flatlands, dominated by two ancient cathedrals, Oliver Cromwell launched his coup, Henry's first queen lies at peace and a saintly Anglo-Saxon princess is remembered still.

❶ Kimbolton Castle

'My Lord and dear husband, I commend me onto you. The hour of my death draweth fast on.' In her final days, Catherine of Aragon wrote a dignified letter to Henry VIII, who had divorced her and consigned her to a damp castle to live as a prisoner in failing health and on a pittance. She implored him to put the good of his soul before the 'care and tendering of his own body' – a forlorn hope, the care and tendering of his body being one of his great preoccupations. It is hard now to imagine the grim medieval castle that this once was, rebuilt as a Tudor manor, by the time Catherine arrived. She was held here from 1534 until her dying day in 1536.

The house was extensively remodelled for Charles Edward Montagu, 4th Earl of Manchester, between 1690 and 1695, by a local builder. After the collapse of the southeast corner, Sir John Vanbrugh and Nicholas Hawksmoor were brought in to give it a classical makeover, although they included battlements to lend 'something of the castle air'. In 1708, Venetian painter Giovanni Antonio Pellegrini was brought over to help decorate the house and he created some of the finest murals in England.

Catherine's lord and husband Henry was moved to tears by her letter, and sent her attendant, Lady Willoughby, to be with her at her end. The building is now a school, open to the public on some afternoons. Vanbrugh's State Bedchamber is the headmaster's study, while Catherine's room became the Boudoir.

▶ *PE28 0EA. Huntingdon, 7 miles NW of St Neots at junction of B645 and B660.*

❷ Peterborough Cathedral

Here is the grave of 'Catherine, Queen of England', accorded in death a title that was taken from her in life. Catherine of Aragon was buried in the cathedral in 1536, and this may have caused Henry VIII some compunction, for the ancient church was not sold off in the Dissolution, but instead was elevated to the status of cathedral of the new diocese of Peterborough. Mary, Queen of Scots was also buried here after being beheaded at Fotheringhay Castle, but her body was later removed to Westminster Abbey on the orders of her son, James I.

A Benedictine abbey, founded on the site in 960–70, was rebuilt between 1118 and 1238. The cathedral church of St Peter, St Paul and St Andrew is sensationally beautiful, distinguished by its unique Early English Gothic west front, which has three great arches. Oliver Cromwell's forces cared nothing for that and in 1643, during the Civil War, they came on a wrecking mission, smashing stained-glass, demolishing the choir stalls, the high altar and reredos, the cloisters and Lady Chapel, damaging and defacing monuments.

Today the atmosphere in the cathedral is serene, and it feels as if Queen Catherine is truly at peace. Visitors to her tomb often leave not just flowers but pomegranates – the symbol she chose for herself on her marriage to Henry in 1509, when it was accepted into English heraldry. The pomegranate is a fruit tough on the outside, soft and sweet within. In Greek mythology, it represents life, regeneration and, ironically, the indissolubility of marriage.

▶ *PE1 1XS. Peterborough, 5 miles E of A1/A1(M).*

❸ Oliver Cromwell's House

'**Ely, this day, October 1643. Dear friend, Hasten with all speed you may, and come on the spur to me at Ely:** we have a great work on hand … I must see you by to-morrow sunset, as we start next day.' Oliver Cromwell was writing from this small city, where he had lived for a decade, in the year that he formed his disciplined Ironsides, early in the Civil War. The 'great work on hand' may have been the Battle of Winceby in Lincolnshire on October 11, where the Parliamentarians were triumphant. Visitors can see inside Cromwell's house and contemplate how much better he did for himself at Hampton Court, when the great Puritan scourge of royalty was king in all but name.

▶ *CB7 4HF. Ely, 5 miles N of Cambridge at junction of A10 and A142.*

❹ Ely Cathedral

The reign of William the Conqueror was a troubled one, and he repeatedly and mercilessly put down uprisings. In East Anglia, the Saxon leader Hereward the Wake engaged the king's forces in long and bloody rebellion. In the uneasy peace that followed, William ordered the building of this cathedral. The Saxon princess St Etheldreda founded the first religious community here in around AD 673, but the present building was begun in 1081 and work continued for more than 100 years. The Norman cathedral would be a striking example of Romanesque architecture in any setting, but seen across the broad, flat countryside, seeming to ride against the big sky, it is particularly impressive, and has acquired the nickname 'Ship of the Fens'. Another sobriquet, 'Cromwell's Castle', recalls the ten years when it was closed by the Lord Protector, Oliver Cromwell, who stabled horses for his cavalry within, although it was spared the wanton destruction suffered by so many other religious buildings. For many years, a shrine here to Etheldreda was a place of pilgrimage. It was destroyed in 1541 during the Dissolution, but a slate marks the spot where it stood, and June 23 and October 17 are still festivals for the saint at Ely.

▶ *CB7 4EW. Ely, 15 miles N of Cambridge at junction of A10 and A142.*

ESSEX

Monarchs and their courtiers have played and schemed in the great houses of Essex, buying, selling and giving them away, and two great women rallied armies to battle, shaping history.

❶ Audley End House

As Lord Treasurer to James I, Thomas Howard, 1st Earl of Suffolk, was well-placed to dip into funds to build a veritable palace.
His grandfather, Sir Thomas Audley, Lord Chancellor, was granted the Benedictine monastery of Walden Abbey by Henry VIII in 1538, and he converted it into a house known as Audley Inn. The 1st Earl, having bigger plans, demolished it and began to rebuild on a grand scale. He wanted a mansion in which to entertain the king and queen – perhaps at the king's own expense. In 1619, the earl and his wife were sent to the Tower for suspected embezzlement, securing their release only on payment of a huge fine, to live out their days in disgrace.

In 1668, Charles II bought the house as a handy residence close to Newmarket races. Catherine of Braganza, his queen, held court here. When William III called in Sir Christopher Wren to make repairs, the great architect warned that the cost would be ruinous, so the king handed the house back to the Suffolks in 1701. During the 18th century it was reduced to half its original size. George II's mistress, Henrietta Howard, lived here with her thuggish husband until an inheritance enabled her to move to Marble Hill (see page 102). Sir John Griffin, 4th Baron Howard de Walden, commissioned Capability Brown to landscape the parkland, and Robert Adam to create new reception rooms. Recent refurbishment of the service wing reveals much about the lives of servants here.
▶ *CB11 4JF. Signposted off B1383, 2 miles SE of Saffron Walden (M11 Junction 9). EH.*

❷ Hedingham Castle

Did he or didn't he? That is the question. Could Elizabeth I's best courtier poet have written works attributed to Shakespeare?
This imposing Norman keep was the stronghold of the de Veres for 550 years. Aubrey de Vere was a knight in the service of William the Conqueror. His son Aubrey II built the castle at Hedingham in around 1140. In her brief reign, Queen Matilda, daughter of Henry I and mother of

AUDLEY END HOUSE

Henry II, made Aubrey III 1st Earl of Oxford in 1141. The Oxfords were crusaders, fighting alongside Richard the Lionheart. Robert, the 3rd Earl, was one of the barons who pressured King John to seal the Magna Carta. John, 15th Earl, accompanied Henry VIII at the Field of the Cloth of Gold. As Great Lord Chamberlain, he bore the crown of Anne Boleyn at her coronation. The 16th Earl accompanied Elizabeth I from Hatfield to London to be crowned; his wife became a maid of honour. When the queen visited Hedingham for a few days in 1561, she took a shine to Edward de Vere, the 17th Earl, who wrote verse under the pen name of Spear-Shaker, in celebration of his talent for jousting. He is one of a number of literary figures proposed as the true author of William Shakespeare's plays. The de Vere line died with Aubrey, the 20th Earl, who had no son. His daughter married Charles, Duke of St Albans, son of Nell Gwyn and Charles II.

The castle, with its magnificent parkland and 18th century landscaped gardens, is now privately owned but is open to the public.

▶ *CO9 3DJ. Castle Hedingham, 8 miles N of Braintree on A1017.*

❸ Palace of Beaulieu (New Hall)

In a nice little twist of history, Henry VIII's Palace of Beaulieu, where he made plans to divorce his first wife, became a Catholic girls' school in the reign of Charles I. This is one of Henry's 'lost palaces'. The king bought New Hall from Thomas Boleyn, Viscount Rochford, father of Anne Boleyn, in 1516, and rebuilt it in brick in a manner to impress. He renamed it Beaulieu to reflect the beauty of it, with its eight courtyards, sweeping façade and gatehouse towers. Catherine of Aragon had given birth to his first child, Mary, and no expense was spared in creating a palace for the infant princess. By the time the king stayed here on his summer progress in 1527, he was desperate for a male heir, and it was here that he began to scheme to have his marriage annulled.

The palace was home to Mary Tudor until 1533, the year Henry married Anne, when it was granted to her brother, George Boleyn. It was later restored to Mary as part of her privy purse. Elizabeth I granted the estate to the Earl of Sussex. Oliver Cromwell 'bought' it for five shillings in 1640 (Henry had paid £1,000 for the hall and spent £17,000 on the rebuilding). New Hall is still a school, retaining some of Beaulieu's grandeur, educating boys and girls in the Catholic faith. Mary Tudor would approve.

▶ *CM3 6RB. Purleigh, 4 miles SW of Maldon, on minor roads, just S of A414.*

❹ Ingatestone Hall

'Sir William hath at his own great costs and charges erected and builded a new house, very fair, large and stately, made of brick and embattl'd.' Sir William Petre's great hall dates from 1541 and has been in the same family for 18 generations.

Sir William was sent by Thomas Cromwell to visit monastic houses in southern England to make inventories, as part of Henry VIII's Dissolution of the Monasteries. The abbey at Barking must have caught his fancy, for when its lands were surrendered to the Crown, he bought them for a little less than £850. For this apparent plunder of Church property, he was exonerated by a papal bull, and absolved from the interdict of excommunication imposed upon the king, on condition that he endowed an almshouse, which he did. Almshouses built by his foundation can still be seen in Ingatestone high street. Finding the old steward's house 'scarce mete for a fermor to dwell on', he knocked it down and built the house much as it is seen today. Mod cons included piped water, and all the main bedrooms had 'little rooms within' with a 'close stool'. Elizabeth I stayed here on her royal progress in the summer of 1561. Despite the addition of a new wing and rebuilding in the 18th century, Ingatestone Hall is emphatically Tudor. It is situated a mile from the village, and although it is a private home, in summer visitors can explore the house and grounds.

▶ *CM4 9NR. Ingatestone, 6 miles SW of Chelmsford.*

❺ Tilbury Fort

'I know I have but the body of a weak and feeble woman; but I have the heart of a king, and a king of England, too; and think foul scorn that Parma or Spain, or any prince of Europe, should dare to invade the borders of my realms.' Elizabeth I's speech to her troops at Tilbury as they prepared to confront the Armada, still stirs the blood and stiffens the sinews.

This fort on the Thames estuary was begun by Henry VIII to protect London's seaward approach against vengeful Catholic invasion after his acrimonious split with Rome. Originally a D-shaped blockhouse known as Thermitage Bulwark, it was built on the site of a dissolved hermitage and was designed for crossfire with a similar fort at Gravesend. It was fortified and refortified, against the Armada, and by Charles II after an abortive Dutch attack on the English

HADLEIGH CASTLE

fleet in the Medway (see page 60). Charles commissioned Sir Bernard de Gomme, who had served as an engineer for the Royalists in the Civil War and had followed him into exile. De Gomme designed a pentagon with projecting bastions and retained Henry VIII's block-house. When Daniel Defoe saw it in 1722, it was armed with 26 cannons. 'Tilbury Fort,' he wrote, 'may justly be looked upon, as the key of the river of Thames, and consequently the key of the city of London … They must be bold fellows who venture in the biggest ships the world has heard of, to pass such a battery, if the men appointed to serve the guns, do their duty like stout fellows, as becomes them.'
▶ *RM18 7NR. 6 miles downstream of Queen Elizabeth II Bridge on N bank of Thames. Signposted off A1089 to Tilbury. EH.*

❻ Hadleigh Castle

'At Hadleigh there is the ruin of a castle, which, from its situation, is vastly fine. It commands a view of the Kent hills, the Nore, and the North Foreland, looking many miles to sea.' This was the judgment of the great English landscape artist John Constable, who made a drawing of the scene in 1814 for his painting *Hadleigh Castle; The Mouth of the Thames Morning after a Stormy Night*. The ruins that so pleased him were the remains of a castle begun in about 1215 by Hubert de Burgh, 1st Earl of Kent. De Burgh wielded great power in the reign of King John, deputising for the king when he was abroad, and, on the king's death, governing for the nine-year-old Henry III. Fearing attack from France, he commissioned the stone and flint castle with views over the Thames. As those fears diminished, the castle fell into disrepair. However, Edward III, being at war with France for most of his reign, ordered rebuilding, and the castle became his preferred home. After his death in 1377, it was variously owned by kings and noblemen. Henry VIII granted it to three of his wives. Its high vantage was its downfall – landslides rendered it unstable. Parts of it were sold off for building materials, and by 1600 it was already the picturesque ruin that would catch Constable's painterly eye.
▶ *SS7 2PP. 5 miles W of Southend-on-Sea. EH.*

❼ Colchester

In this ancient town, the Emperor Claudius accepted the surrender of the Celtic kings and so founded the province of Britannia. This, then, was the capital of Roman Britain, reclaimed by Boudicca's army in around AD 60

when it was left poorly defended, in the hands of veteran centurions. The invader in 1666 was of a different nature. Samuel Pepys recorded in his diary in July that the plague 'rages mightily, particularly in Colchester, where it has long been, and it is believed it will quite depopulate the place'. However, when Daniel Defoe visited this 'antient Corporation' in 1722, he remarked, 'The town is large, very populous; the streets are fair and beautiful; and tho' it may not be said to be finely built, yet there are abundance of very good and well-built houses in it.'

From the Middle Ages, Colchester was famous for its oysters. The future Edward VIII and George VI both attended the annual Oyster Feast when they were Prince of Wales. Today, free of plague and violence, Britain's oldest recorded town offers much to delight the visitor.
▶ *24 miles NE of Chelmsford on A12; 20 miles W of Harwich on A120.*

❽ Colchester Castle

In 1650, during the rule of Oliver Cromwell, a Parliamentary survey of this largely complete Norman castle determined its value as £5 for scrap. An ironmonger, John Wheely, was licensed to demolish the building, but after causing 'great devastations' with gunpowder, he gave up.

The castle was begun in 1076, on the orders of William the Conqueror, by Gandulf, Bishop of Rochester. It was founded on the site of the Roman Temple of Claudius, burnt down by Boudicca and her tribe. Lacking suitable local stone, Gandulf's labourers used materials from Roman Colchester for their keep. Crenellation in the walls suggests either that it was a single-storey structure, or that it was hastily fortified in the course of construction, and fortification continued when the threat had passed.

In 1216, the castle was attacked by King John's men, when it was occupied by the French. In 1648, the Royalist army took shelter in the city, holding out for 11 weeks against the besieging Parliamentarians, under Thomas Fairfax. 'It still mourns, in the ruins of a civil war,' wrote Daniel Defoe, '… in which the garrison and inhabitants also, suffered the utmost extremity of hunger, and were at last obliged to surrender at discretion, when their two chief officers … were shot to death under the castle-wall.' Tradition had it that no grass would grow on the spot where the gallant Sir Charles Lucas and Sir George Lisle fell. The castle is today home to a museum.
▶ *CO1 1TJ. 24 miles NE of Chelmsford on A12; 20 miles W of Harwich on A120.*

EAST ANGLIA

Royal treasure – lost and found

Among East Anglia's golden treasure trove, no trace of a
royal baggage train, or its precious cargo, has ever surfaced.

Was King John history's biggest loser? He lost
a bid to seize the throne from his brother
Richard I. He lost the duchy of Normandy to Philip II
of France. He lost the support of French nobles with
the imprisonment and murder of his nephew, Arthur
of Brittany. He lost the respect of British subjects by
wringing every mark he could out of them to fund
his efforts to recapture his territories. At the Battle
of Bouvines in 1214, he lost the Angevin Empire of
Brittany, Normandy, Maine, Anjou and Touraine. He
lost the dispute with his feudal barons, who, in 1215,
forced him to sign the Magna Carta, limiting his
powers. In the ensuing civil war he lost Winchester
and London to the barons in alliance with Philip II's
son, the Dauphin Louis. And most notoriously, he
'lost the crown jewels in the Wash'.

John's rapacious pursuit of wealth was not driven
solely by greed. With money, he could prey on his
enemies; without it, he would be preyed upon. The
power of kings ebbs and flows according to their
wealth, we are told by Richard FitzNigel, treasurer
to John's father, Henry II. Characteristically, the
Plantagenet kings behaved however they pleased,
'obeying their noble mind' in FitzNigel's words, 'and
spending all to best advantage'. Thus John put his
noble mind to raising revenues by every conceivable
means – through taxes, fines, the sale of land, feudal
dues, scutage (opting out of military service for a fee)
– and spending to his best advantage.

From birth, misfortune had been his lot. He
was nicknamed 'Lackland' because, unlike his older
brothers, he received no right to continental

provinces. He inherited a country bankrupted by Richard's crusades, ransoms and wars with France, and an unsustainable empire abroad. A peripatetic monarch, he was everywhere followed by his baggage train, but it was vulnerable to robbers. He kept stores of cash in treasuries at castles around the country, but where he went, his goods and chattels followed.

October 11, 1216, found an ailing John, menaced by Louis, on the move north from Bishop's Lynn (now King's Lynn) in Norfolk, heading for Lincolnshire. He took a route around the head of the Wash – a broad inlet separating Norfolk and Lincolnshire, fed by four rivers, the Witham, Welland, Nene and Great Ouse – fording the Wellstream (where the Nene now flows). The next day, he ordered the lumbering train to join him at Swineshead by cutting across the Wash. The caravan, some three miles long, comprising some 3,000 soldiers, servants, horses, mules, carts and wagons, ventured forth, probably from Cross Keys towards Sutton Bridge. They carried not just a crown, sceptre and orb of childhood imagination, but the war chest, the precious contents of John's movable chapel, the imperial regalia inherited from his grandmother the Empress of Germany, and a haul of gold, silver and relics stripped from the abbeys and churches of Norfolk in revenge for the barons' revolt. If he watched the approach, John would have seen the unfolding horror as men and beasts, engulfed by rising waters, sank in quicksands, and all that he cherished went with them. Weak with dysentery, he was carried to Swineshead Abbey, and on to Newark Castle, where he ate 'a surfeit of peaches', and died on the night of October 18. His nine-year-old son was crowned Henry III with a gold circlet because the crown was gone in a 'bottomless whirlpool'.

The Benedictine monk Matthew Paris of St Albans had a fine line in character assassination when he commented that 'Foul as it is, Hell itself is defiled by the presence of John'. Roger Wendover, writing ten years after John's death, recorded that the king had ordered Archdeacon Geoffrey to be crushed to death under a cope of lead, threatened to slit the noses and to gouge out the eyes of papal emissaries, and lost Normandy as he 'feasted sumptuously with his queen daily, and prolonged his sleep in the morning'.

Modern historians are more generous to this most maligned monarch. It is certain, though, that John was not universally loved, and one conspiracy theory holds that he was actually murdered – poisoned by the monks at Swineshead – and the spoils were divided. Otherwise, the argument goes, why has not so much as an iron wheel been found? This does not deter modern-day treasure hunters from seeking one of the world's greatest bounties.

Digging deep

East Anglia has yielded some thrilling royal secrets. One incredible find, in 1939, buried in a mound at Sutton Hoo, was the ship of Raedwald, 7th-century king of East Anglia, and a remarkable collection of gold, jewellery, silver, drinking vessels, clothing and weaponry, now in the British Museum.

In 2004, at Southend-on-Sea, archaeologists discovered the grave of an Anglo-Saxon king – perhaps Saebert (d AD 616) or Sigebert II (murdered in AD 653). With him were buried gold foil crosses, pots, bowls, a sword, a lyre, counters of bone, dice made of antler and a silver spoon inscribed with a cross. Of the crown of Edward the Confessor, meanwhile, to this day, there is still no sign.

Not so much as an iron wheel has been found, but modern-day treasure hunters still seek what would be one of the world's greatest bounties.

THE WASH

NORFOLK

Amid lavish halls that once welcomed the highest in the land, ancient towns hid royal fugitives, a shrine drew a succession of rulers and a popular seaside resort lured a king's mistress to the stage.

❶ King's Lynn

Edward IV, Yorkist King of England, made his escape from Lynn, in September 1470, during the War of the Roses. He and his men crammed on to a boat, taking nothing but the clothes on their backs, and fled to France. The king had spent the night in the house of Walter Coney, merchant and mayor, at the south end of the High Street. He returned to England with an invasion force a year later, travelling in Hanseatic ships, to seize the throne.

From the early 13th century, Lynn had become an important market town and seaport. When it received its royal charter of borough freedom from King John in 1204, granting its merchants a degree of self-government, it was one of the largest ports in the kingdom. Upon the Dissolution of the Monasteries, the town and manor of Bishop's Lynn became the property of Henry VIII, a manoeuvre reflected in the change of name to King's Lynn or Lynn Regis. It was Henry who granted the right to hold the King's Lynn Mart, a fair that takes place every February. The Queen Mother was its patron from 1951.

In April 1646, Charles I hoped to slip away abroad from Lynn, as Edward had done, but he was foiled by parliamentary watches on the river. Princess Victoria came here with her mother in 1835 on their way to Holkham Hall. They were much alarmed when the excited townspeople unharnessed the horses and tried to pull the coach themselves.
▶ *A17 from W, A10 from S (Ely), A47 from E (Norwich).*

❷ Castle Rising

To this 12th-century castle, Isabella, the 'she wolf of France', was sent by her son, Edward III, for her part in the murder of her husband, Edward II. The beautiful, intelligent and socially adept daughter of Philip IV and Joan I of Navarre, Isabella was just 12 years old when she arrived in England to be married. She was a supportive helpmate to her husband in his struggles with the baron malcontents, and she tolerated his favourite, Piers Gaveston, 1st Earl of Cornwall (it has been said that king and nobleman were more than just good friends). When Gaveston was murdered by the barons in

1312, however, the king transferred his favour to the power-crazed and venal Earl of Winchester, Hugh Despenser. Isabella could not abide him, and the marriage came under intolerable strain. Although the barons forced the odious Despenser into exile, to become a pirate in the English Channel, the queen could not be reconciled to the king. In 1325, Isabella travelled to France and took a lover, Roger de Mortimer, with whom she led an invasion, deposing Edward, whereat Mortimer allegedly ordered his murder.

Isabella may have been happy enough in her 'banishment' at Castle Rising, where she was free to come and go with her retinue and household of 180, enjoying all the privileges of a dowager queen, although some tales tell of a woman driven mad with loneliness, who haunts the castle still. Edward III and his queen, Philippa, paid several visits, and the castle was subject to much improvement. The stone keep dates from around 1140 and was raised by William d'Albini II, a Norman baron. It is one of the finest, best preserved and lavishly decorated surviving examples of its kind in Britain, surrounded by mighty earthworks. In 1544 the castle passed to the Howard family, and has remained in their hands ever since, although it is now under the guardianship of English Heritage.
▶ *PE31 6AH. 4 miles NE of King's Lynn, just W of A149. EH.*

❸ Holkham Hall

When Queen Mary, queen consort of George V, slept in the Green State Bedroom, a painting of Jupiter caressing Juno was considered too lewd and removed to an attic. This is the foremost bedroom at the hall, and several kings and queens have spent a night there. Two years before she took the throne, Princess Victoria, aged 16, stayed for two days, as her mother, the Duchess of Kent, took her about to show her off to her future subjects. Simon Jenkins includes Holkham Hall in *England's Thousand Best Houses*, stating, 'It is the perfect English house from the Golden Age of the Grand Tour'. The superb Palladian mansion provided a location for the film *The Duchess*, starring Keira Knightley as Georgiana, Duchess of Devonshire.

The building is a modernist's nightmare, so lavishly ornamented, furnished, gilded, marbled

HOLKHAM HALL

and swagged it is like being inside a vast jewel box. Forget 'less is more'; here, more is far, far more. Jupiter and Juno (by Gavin Hamilton, 1730–97) are back in the Green Bedroom with the tapestries, the giant four-poster and antiques. Rubens and Van Dyck hang in the saloon. The 'marble hall' is built of softer, more translucent Derbyshire alabaster. The statue gallery is lined with Roman statuary. The house was designed around the art collection of Thomas Coke, 1st Earl of Leicester, by the earl himself, with Richard Boyle, 3rd Earl of Burlington, and William Kent. It was begun in 1736 and is still in the Coke family.

▶ *NR23 1AB. 1 mile W of Wells-next-the-Sea, on A149.*

4 St Mary Magdalene Church

Christmas wouldn't be Christmas at Sandringham without the Christmas Day service at the parish church. This is where the royal family and estate staff worship when by custom they repair to their Norfolk estate (see page 124) to spend time together. It is a fine carrstone edifice with memorials to royalty from Queen Victoria onwards. Carved angels frame a silver altar. The reredos was presented to Queen Alexandra by American Rodman Wanamaker as a tribute to her husband, Edward VII, and there is stained glass from the 16th century.

▶ *PE35 6EH. Sandringham Estate, by main gate.*

❺ Sandringham

'Dear old Sandringham, the place I love better than anywhere in the world!' George V was not the only sovereign to love this country retreat, where the royal family spend Christmas and indulge in a spot of shooting. It was said of George V by Harold Nicolson that 'for 17 years he did nothing but kill animals and stick in stamps', and, indeed, at one royal shooting party he bagged 1,000 pheasants in six hours.

It was Prince Albert's idea that his eldest son should acquire a house conducive to healthy outdoor pursuits, away from the temptations of the gaming table, his mistresses and general decadence, and Edward chose Sandringham Hall. Queen Victoria bought it for him and his new bride, Alexandra. In 1865, the prince rebuilt it as an extensive country house of red brick with stone dressings in a rare mix of styles, which has been a private home for four generations of monarchs. In 1932, George V overcame his misgivings to make the first Christmas broadcast live by the new medium of radio from Sandringham. Written by Rudyard Kipling, the speech touched on the advances that enabled the king to deliver a message across the world, and urged listeners to aim for 'prosperity without self-seeking'. In 1957, the Queen made the first televised broadcast from the Long Library.

The estate encompasses a mixed landscape of the mudflats of the Wash, woodland, wetlands, farmlands and residences. The gardens were opened to the public by Edward VII in 1908, and in her Silver Jubilee year, 1977, the Queen opened the house to the public. Visitors can see ground-floor rooms used by the royal family, which remain much as they were in Edwardian times. In the museum are vintage vehicles, including a 1900 Daimler Phaeton, and a fire engine once used by Sandringham's own fire brigade.
▶ *E35 6EN. 8 miles NE of King's Lynn, just E of A149.*

❻ The Shrine of Our Lady of Walsingham

'The images of Our Lady of Walsingham and Ipswich were brought up to London with all the jewels that hung around them at the King's commandment … They were burnt at Chelsea by my Lord Privy Seal.' The Tudor chronicler Thomas Wriothesley thus relates the fate of the icon of the Virgin Mary that for centuries brought pilgrims to this village. In 1061, a noblewoman, Richeldis de Faverches, had a vision in which the Virgin Mary appeared to her

and asked her to build a holy house to recreate the house in Nazareth that was the scene of the Annunciation. In 1169, Richeldis's son Geoffrey granted the Chapel of Our Lady to his clerk, Edwy, with instructions to found a priory.

Walsingham was a more realistic pilgrim destination than distant Rome or Santiago de Compostela. Henry III, Edward II, Edward III, Henry IV and Edward IV all visited. Tudor kings Henry VII and Henry VIII came by. The devout Catherine of Aragon was a regular sojourner. In 1538, amid widespread iconoclasm, the priory was suppressed during the Dissolution, and Bishop Latimer wrote of the image that – with two of her 'sister' icons – she would 'make a jolly muster in Smithfield. They would not be all day burning.'

The priory gatehouse, chancel and arch remain, along with 20th-century Catholic and Anglican shrines and shop at 'England's Nazareth'.
▶ *NR22 6EE. On minor roads 4 miles S of Wells-next-the-Sea.*

❼ Sheringham Park Gazebo

'Sheringham possesses more natural beauty and local advantages than any place I have ever seen.' From the great 19th-century landscaper Humphry Repton, this is quite an endorsement. Sheringham Park is known especially for its rhododendrons, and a viewing tower opened by the Prince of Wales in 1988, when he became patron of the National Trust's East Anglia Coast and Countryside appeal. The lovely wild coast, Weybourne's windmill, churches, countryside and steam trains can all be seen from the gazebo's breezy top platform.
▶ *NR26 8TL. 2 miles SW of Sheringham at junction of A148 and B1157. NT.*

❽ Blickling Hall

Anna Bolena hic nata 1507 (Anne Boleyn **was born here 1507) reads the legend beneath her statue** at the National Trust's most haunted historic house. But was she? Strictly, no. This fine Jacobean manor was begun 80 years after her execution, on the site of an older Blickling Hall, once owned by Anne's father, Thomas Boleyn. In that house, Anne's older siblings, Mary and George, were almost certainly born, but by the time of Anne's birth, the family had moved to Hever Castle (see page 58).

The current Blickling Hall was designed by Robert Lyminge for Sir Henry Hobart, who was Lord Chief Justice of the Common Pleas from 1616 to 1625, under James I. Even if its royal connections are tenuous, it richly repays a visit. Anne's name echoes through history, her statue is in a niche above the oak staircase and she is said to be one of the resident ghosts. Especially around May 19, the anniversary of her death, susceptible visitors report seeing Anne sitting with her head in her lap, in a coach driven by a headless coachman. A fellow apparition is Sir John Fastolfe of Caister, Shakespeare's comic Falstaff, who owned the 15th-century hall, and whose coat of arms is displayed in the 'new' house. There have also been sightings of Sir Henry Hobart, killed in a duel in 1698.

▶ *NR11 6NF. 1 mile W of A140, 8 miles S of Cromer. NT.*

❾ Oxburgh Hall

Hangings of embroidery worked by Mary, Queen of Scots are on display in this dreamy 15th-century moated manor house built for Sir Edmund Bedingfeld. Held prisoner for 19 years by her cousin, Elizabeth I, Mary would have had many long hours in which to perfect her craft. For most of those years she languished at Tutbury Castle (see page 152) as the 'guest' of George Talbot, Earl of Shrewsbury. There she sewed companionably with the earl's wife, the

Countess of Shrewsbury, 'Bess of Hardwick'. The earl would report: 'This Queen continueth daily to resort to my wife's chamber, where she useth to sit working with the needle in which she much delighteth and in devising work.'

Mary learnt to sew as a girl growing up in France. The designs, bearing her monograms and ciphers, are touching in their detail. A phoenix rising from the flames symbolises Mary's motto, 'In my End is my Beginning'. A dolphin leaping over a crown is an allusion to her first husband, the dauphin, Francis. A marigold turns its face towards the sun, and the many birds are beautifully wrought.

At Oxburgh, the hangings have found a warmer home than the damp and draughty castle at Tutbury. Although Sir Edmund had obtained a licence to crenellate from Edward IV, the manor's fortifications were more a show of status than effective defences. Henry VII visited in 1487, and Elizabeth I in 1578 – despite having been held in custody at the Tower of London when Sir Henry Bedingfeld was governor. In the 16th and 17th centuries, the Bedingfelds were persecuted for holding to their Catholic faith, yet remained loyal to the Crown.

▶ *PE33 9PS. 10 miles E of Downham Market, off A134. NT.*

OXBURGH HALL

⑩ Downham Market

King John was not all bad. He granted the people of this fenland town the right to hold an annual fair – and to hang wrongdoers on the gallows. It was to Downham that Charles I came in 1646, the year after fleeing the carnage at the Battle of Naseby, when Cromwell's New Model Army crushed the Royalists. The king, disguised as a clergyman, stayed at the Swan Inn (on the site of which now stands the Swan Hotel). His plans to sail out of King's Lynn being foiled, he moved on to Snore Hall at Fordham – today a private home, one of the oldest brick houses in England – where he held council. During his reign, Bridge Street in Downham Market was known as King Charles Way.

▶ *PE38 9HF (Swan Hotel). 10 miles S of King's Lynn at junction of A10 and A1122.*

⑪ Norwich City

When a mob ran riot here in 1272, Henry III himself travelled to the city to impose order. The unrest was provoked by the monks of Norwich, who tried to raise tolls on the annual fair held in the marketplace. Angry townsfolk ran amok, damaging the monastery and cathedral cloisters, and starting fires in protest. At least 13 people died in three days of violent disorder. The king fined the city 3,000 marks and condemned 30 men to death. Norwich had been the scene of earlier trouble when the castle was captured in Eleanor of Aquitaine's rebellion of 1173, but by 1194 it was stable enough to be granted a royal charter by Richard I.

In 1578, Elizabeth I visited this prosperous wool town as part of her East Anglia progress, staying for five days, possibly at the Maid's Head in Tombland (the word 'tomb' implying nothing more chilling than an open space). The hotel, which has its origins in the 1280s or before, had previously played host to Edward, the Black Prince, son of Edward III, and to Catherine of

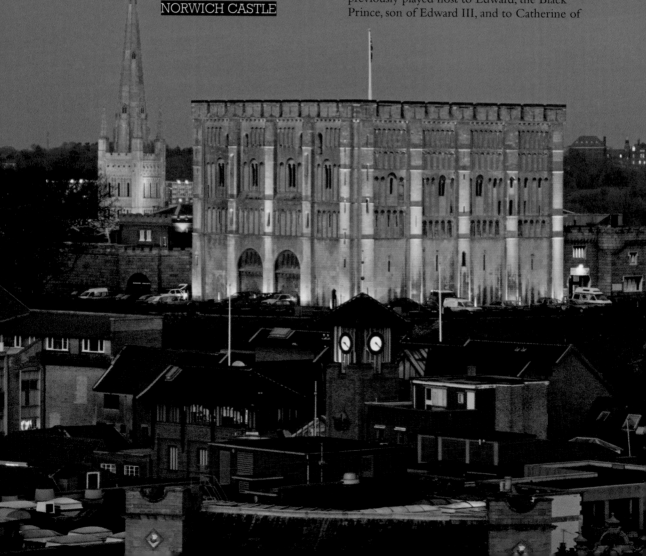

NORWICH CASTLE

Aragon, first wife of Henry VIII. George VI opened City Hall in 1938, watched by a huge crowd and recorded by Pathé News. On the same day, he became the first monarch to attend a Football League match – at Norwich City FC.
▶ *45 miles N of Ipswich and 22 miles W of Great Yarmouth.*

⑫ Norwich Cathedral

Three years after being summoned from Normandy by William Rufus in 1087, Herbert de Losinga committed the grave sin of simony. He was Abbot of Ramsey when the see of Thetford became vacant in 1090. De Losinga so coveted it that he offered Rufus £1,000 to secure it for himself, plus the abbacy of Winchester for his father. He was subsequently consecrated Bishop of Thetford and moved the diocese to Norwich in 1094. He had what he wanted, but he had bought it. His conscience drove him to Rome to confess, and he returned to lay the foundation stone of a new church 'for the redemption of my soul and the remission of all my sins'.

This graceful Norman cathedral survived the Dissolution, but in the reign of Charles I, in 1643, the Puritans stormed the building, destroying all Catholic symbols. Norwich's Bishop, Joseph Hall, known as 'the English Seneca' for the clarity and purity of his meditations, described a litany of vandalism. 'It is tragical to relate the furious sacrilege … what clattering of glasses, what beating down of walls, what tearing down of monuments and wresting out of irons and brass … The singing-books and service-books were carried to the fire in the public market-place; a lewd wretch walking before the train in his cope trailing in the dirt … The cathedral was filled with musketeers, drinking and tobacconing as freely as if it had turned ale-house.' Such ugliness is easily forgotten when contemplating this remarkable survivor, raised between 1096 and 1145, faced with cream Caen limestone and so serene, so little changed by centuries of wear – not to say tear.
▶ *NR1 4EH. 45 miles N of Ipswich and 22 miles W of Great Yarmouth.*

⑬ Great Yarmouth

Edward I had a taste for the salted herrings produced at Great Yarmouth, which he bought by the barrel-load. At Christmas in 1300 he ordered 18,500 for his household at Stirling Castle. His father, Henry III, had granted a charter under which the town was bound to send to the sheriffs of Norwich every year, 100 herrings baked in four pasties, to be delivered onward to the lord of the manor of East Carlton and thence to the king.

The sea has shaped the history and fortunes of this fishing town and port, granted its first royal charter by King John in 1207. In 1588, with the looming threat of the Spanish Armada, a boom was thrown across the harbour, mounds were raised, and a warship fitted out to harry the enemy at sea. Charles II visited in 1671, and was presented with four golden herrings and a chain. In 1722, Daniel Defoe wrote admiringly that 'the town facing to the west also, and open to the river, makes the finest key in England, if not in Europe, not inferior even to that of Marseilles itself'. By 1760, Great Yarmouth had become a popular resort. In the 19th century, Lily Langtry appeared at the Royal Aquarium and the Hippodrome, and the Prince of Wales, Edward VII long in waiting, would come to see his mistress perform. They stayed at the Royal Hotel, which bears his crest.
▶ *NR30 3AE (Royal Hotel). 22 miles E of Norwich at junction of A12, A47 and A149.*

⑭ Euston Hall

When Charles II paid his first visit to his Secretary of State here in 1671, among his court was John Evelyn, who found the hall 'magnificent and commodious'. Evelyn, best known for his diaries, was also a passionate gardener and noted landscaper. He designed the walk through the pleasure grounds here that visitors enjoy today. The wider park, laid out by William Kent and finished by Capability Brown, is considered among Kent's masterworks.

The *Domesday Book* records a manor on this site in 1087, belonging to Bury St Edmunds Abbey. Elizabeth I stayed there on her way to Norwich, but when Henry Bennet, Earl of Arlington, bought it in 1666, it was a ruin, and he set out to create a grand house in the French style, around a courtyard with pavilions on each corner. The property passed to Arlington's daughter and son-in-law, the Duke and Duchess of Grafton, who had it remodelled by Matthew Brettingham. The 10th Duke found the property unmanageable, and the south and most of the west wing were demolished in 1952.

In his travel writings, Daniel Defoe said of the hall, 'It lies in the open country towards the side of Norfolk, not far from Thetford, a place capable of all that is pleasant and delightful in Nature, and improved by art to every extreme that Nature is able to produce.'
▶ *IP24 2QP. 4 miles S of Thetford on A1088.*

SUFFOLK

Intrigue once reigned in these peaceful surroundings. A saint's shrine and a ruined Norman castle mark where a coterie of barons ganged up on King John, and Mary Tudor refused to be pushed aside.

❶ Newmarket Races

The first race to be run here under written rules was decreed by Charles II in 1665. It became an annual event and in 1671 he rode his own horse to victory. Charles's grandfather, James I, had discovered the joys of the heathland around the 'poor little village' of Newmarket when hunting hares in 1605. He built a palace, with a brewery, stables and kennels, and made many 'sporting journeys' to what became a royal town. The first record of a race here is in March 1622 when Lord Salisbury pitted a horse against one owned by the Marquis of Buckingham. The race won Buckingham £100.

Charles I found Newmarket entirely salubrious. The heath, said his servant Sir Thomas Herbert, 'for good air and pleasure gives place to no other in this great island'. After Cromwell came to power, the palace was sold to a consortium of his men, who systematically wrecked it. Charles II built Palace House, of which the southwest pavilion survives, and began to visit twice a year, regularly riding the July Course, the stand area of which has been redeveloped and now stages Newmarket's summer Music Nights. Charles was also responsible for adapting another stretch of turf for racing, now known as the Rowley Mile, apparently using this when he was blinded by the sun on the July Course. His favourite horse was Old Rowley, a nickname that attached to he king himself. Samuel Pepys makes several mentions of the king's jaunts to the races, including one on May 22, 1668, when the king romped to victory in the Town Plate. The race is still run today – the world's oldest horse race.
▶ *Newmarket Rowley Mile CB8 0TF; July Course CB8 0XE. 12 miles E of Cambridge, just off A14.*

❷ Bury St Edmunds

'Shrine of the King and Cradle of the Law' stands as the motto of a town where 25 barons met in secret and swore a solemn oath. The barons congregated in the Abbey of St Edmund in November 1214, and vowed that they would force King John to put his seal to a new charter, the Magna Carta. The town of 'St Edmund's Bury' recalls St Edmund, king of East Anglia, who was hounded and killed by Vikings in AD 869. His remains were brought to the monastery in the 10th century, whereupon the place became a shrine. In the 11th century, the Danish King Cnut (Canute) replaced the monastery with an abbey. It burnt down in 1465, but was rebuilt. Less than a century later, antiquarian John Leland was commissioned by Henry VIII to visit the libraries of the abbeys that the king would suppress, to rescue books and manuscripts of special value and interest. No doubt Leland did his best, but thousands were destroyed in the wholesale vandalism of the Dissolution. When Leland visited St Edmund's abbey in 1538, he remarked that any man who saw it 'would say it was a city, so many gates, so many towers and a most stately church'. The king closed the abbey the following year, and the townspeople – having a long history of resentment towards the controlling abbots – plundered it for its raw materials. Nonetheless, the rugged remains of the richest and most powerful Benedictine monastery in England, and the shrine of St Edmund, can still be seen in a peaceful park setting, including a 14th-century great gate, a Norman tower and the altered west front of Leland's 'most stately church', all now in the care of English Heritage.
▶ *IP33 1XL (Bury St Edmunds Abbey). 30 miles E of Cambridge on A14. EH.*

❸ Framlingham Castle

There is a price to pay for challenging the might of a monarch, and when Hugh Bigod incurred the wrath of Henry II, it cost him his castle. Hugh's father, the Norman knight Roger de Bigod fought alongside William the Conqueror at Hastings. It may be that he or Hugh himself built a ringwork or motte and bailey castle on this site. When Henry I lay dying in distant Normandy of a 'surfeit of Lampreys', the strange-looking, eel-like fish of which he was too fond, Hugh was at his bedside. He was able to testify on oath before the Archbishop of Canterbury that Henry had willed his kingdom to his nephew, Stephen of Blois, and not to his daughter, Matilda. He thus won the gratitude of Stephen, but they also had many differences before Hugh was created Earl of Norfolk in 1140.

A volatile character, Hugh's relations with royalty were fractious. Henry II first confiscated the castle and then partially destroyed it after the earl took part in the abortive rebellion of 1173-4,

when Henry's wife, Eleanor of Aquitaine, and three of his sons tried to depose him. Hugh's son Roger, 2nd Earl of Norfolk, began a new castle in 1189. It comprised a series of 13 towers, of which 12 remain, joined by a curtain wall, and, unusually, with no fortified keep, perhaps drawing inspiration from Byzantine strongholds seen on the crusades. Crowning a small mound, it is a magnificent ruin, offering a great insight into 12th-century engineering. A poorhouse within the sheltering flint walls, built in 1729, houses a visitor centre.

The castle's most famous occupant was Mary Tudor, who was given the castle by her brother, Edward VI, shortly before his death. She retired here in July 1553, after Lady Jane Grey was proclaimed queen by the Northumberland faction, to orchestrate her campaign for the crown. Just nine days later the news reached her – Queen Jane's nominal rule was over. The throne was hers.

▶ *Framlingham IP13 9BP. 22 miles NE of Ipswich.*

❹ St Michael's Church

The name of Howard echoes through history, and seems especially resonant in this church, which has some extraordinary monuments to the family. The Howards were Dukes of Norfolk in the fifth creation of that title, for whom Framlingham was an important

seat. Since 1300 all the Dukes of Norfolk have been descendants of Edward I, to whom the Norman Bigods forfeited their castle after one of that family's serial fall-outs with the Crown.

The 3rd Duke, Thomas Howard, began rebuilding this church, which dates originally from 1350. He pulled down the old chancel, which had two aisles, and had partly built another one, with the aim of creating a grand religious house for the Howard tombs after they lost their mausoleum at Thetford Priory in the Dissolution, when he suffered a disastrous fall from grace. Uncle to both Anne Boleyn and Catherine Howard, Thomas had engineered his nieces' doomed marriages to Henry VIII, and was subsequently imprisoned in the Tower. He kept his head only by outliving the king, who died in 1547. The new king, Edward VI, ordered the completion of the church.

Thomas Howard's is the most outstanding of the tombs here, situated just south of the altar, and featuring figures of apostles and saints around the four sides. A tomb of coloured alabaster commemorates his son, Henry, Earl of Surrey, and his son's wife, Frances de Vere. Known as 'the Poet Earl', as a young man Henry found favour with Henry VIII, but he was eventually executed for treason – so many memorials, so many tales to tell, of a family that was close, often too close, to monarchy.

▶ *Framlingham IP13 9BP. 22 miles NE of Ipswich.*

EAST ANGLIA

The Wolds

A180
Grimsby●
A46
A16
A158

7

Skegness ●

LINCOLNSHIRE
142-145

A52

Boston ●

A52
A15
A16
A17
A151
●Spalding

amford

Central England

The Heart of England has seen many historic
battles, and many an English heart broke
when the future Charles II was vanquished at
Worcester. Across the land, grand houses and
castles recall the fate and fortune of other
monarchs, from King John to George III.

DERBYSHIRE

Long before royal marriages were commemorated in delicate Derby porcelain, the hand of one charismatic woman was bestowed four times, and her influence is reflected in the county's foremost stately homes.

❶ Royal Crown Derby

What started life as Derby Porcelain in 1747 acquired its 'Crown' from a king, and the 'Royal' appellation from a queen. Characterised by its vibrant colours and intricate gilding, Derby porcelain has graced many high tables. The company was begun by André Planché, a Huguenot, who was soon joined by the renowned porcelain painter William Duesbury. In 1775, George III bestowed upon the factory the right to incorporate a crown symbol into its backstamp, and in 1795 dozens of pieces were ordered for the dismal marriage of the Prince of Wales and Caroline of Brunswick. The prince arrived at the wedding drunk, setting the tone for what was to come. In 1973, a Derby Panel Green dinner service was the choice of Princess Anne for her wedding to Captain Mark Phillips – an altogether more promising match, although by 1992 it had run its course.

The Queen Mother was another Derby devotee. In 1965 she commissioned a dinner service based on an 18th-century plate she had in her collection. When she visited the factory in 1971, she commissioned a new tableware shape, and in 1978 she granted a new royal warrant.

The company has maintained its distinctive style. It is a prolific producer of collectibles and memorabilia, issuing mugs, plates, thimbles and figurines among many other items. The wedding of Prince William and Catherine Middleton inspired a limited-edition range that included Wedding Bell, Posie Loving Cup and paperweights. In 1956 the Emir of Qatar ordered a 3,000-piece service, which included 12 bowls each large enough to hold a sheep.
▶ *DE23 8JZ. 7 miles W of Junction 25 of M1. Visitor Centre and Museum in Osmaston Road, just S of Derby city centre.*

❷ Chatsworth

From time to time Mary, Queen of Scots was held at 'the palace of the Peaks', although she would not know the English baroque masterpiece of today. Sir William Cavendish began to build a splendid Elizabethan house at Chatsworth in 1552. The situation was idyllic, beside the River Derwent, with a view of gentle hills and a theatrical backdrop of rocky uplands. Cavendish was the second of Bess of Harwick's four husbands, and in the fullness of time their son, William, was created Earl of Devonshire by James I. Together with her fourth husband, the Earl of Shrewsbury, Bess had the unlooked-for task of guarding the Scottish queen. Mary was brought to Chatsworth occasionally from Tutbury Castle (see page 152). Her rooms, on the top floor above the Great Hall, although changed beyond recognition, are still known as the Queen of Scots Apartments.

The 4th Earl of Devonshire ordered some remodelling of the house in 1686. He intended to rebuild just the south wing while retaining the Elizabethan courtyard plan, but over the next 20 years he rebuilt the house completely. The south and east wings were designed by William Talman, who found the earl an impossible employer. The design of the west front was the work of another architect, probably Thomas Archer. The lavish interiors contain an important art collection, with works by Leonardo da Vinci, Rembrandt and Van Dyck. The exterior, with its gold detail, is grand indeed. Architectural historian Nikolaus Pevsner tells us: 'Only with Chatsworth does Derbyshire appear on the truly national stage. The work of Talman then of Archer is among the essential document of the English style of c. 1700.' The 4th Earl was created Duke of Devonshire in 1694 for his role in helping William of Orange and Mary to take the throne. This spectacular house, brimming with treasures, is still the seat of the Duke of Devonshire today.
▶ *DE45 1PP. 8 miles N of Matlock, off A6 Bakewell Road.*

❸ Hardwick Hall

Bess of Hardwick may have been 'first lady of Chatsworth', but it is here that her personality finds its greatest expression. She was born at the now-ruined Hardwick Old Hall, a modest Tudor manor, and went on to make four strategic marriages to wealthy men. Her relationship with husband number four, the Earl of Shrewsbury, was so stormy that Elizabeth I intervened to separate them. The burden of being warders to Mary, Queen of Scots had placed great pressure on the couple, who used to harangue each other publicly, Bess calling her husband a 'knave, fool and beast'.

HARDWICK HALL

When the foundations were laid for a new Hardwick Hall, in 1591, Bess was around 70 years old. Upon the earl's death a year earlier, she had become the second richest woman in the kingdom, after the queen. This house is one of the most extraordinary survivors from the Tudor period, scarcely altered over centuries. In describing it, architectural historian Nikolaus Pevsner seems to conflate the style of the house with the received wisdom about Bess. He put it thus: 'There is nothing of surrounding nature either that could compete with its uncompromising, unnatural, graceless, and indomitable self-assertiveness. It is an admirable piece of architectural expression: no fussing, no fumbling, nor indeed any flights of fancy.'

In fact, this is a very special building. It is true that there is ego in the 'niggly strapwork frills on the tower balustrades which frame Bess's proud and ostentatious initials', but its windows are so many and so beautiful that it is often said the hall is 'more glass than wall'. The atmospheric interiors are hung with tapestries and embroideries. Portraits of the châtelaine show that Bess was no great beauty, but she seems to have a gravitas or majesty. Her garden with its 'madly crenellated walls' and banqueting hall with 'crazy headgear' are idiosyncratic delights. A country park surrounds the house and gardens, and there is a café and shop.

▶ *S44 5QJ. Chesterfield, 15 miles N of Nottingham, Junction 28 off M1. NT.*

GLOUCESTERSHIRE

Kings murdered, rivals locked in battle, overweening ambition exposed – the pursuit of power lies behind the bloody history of castles and abbey. Happily, modern-day rivalry is confined to the equestrian world.

❶ Berkeley Castle

Home of the Berkeley family for 850 years, this is one of the March Castles, designed to keep the Welsh at bay. It comes complete with arrow slits, murder holes, bolts and bars to keep out attackers and trip-steps to wrong-foot them. One of the finest examples in Britain of medieval domestic architecture, the castle was begun in 1067 by William FitzOsbern, a relative and counsellor of William the Conqueror. In 1215 the West Country barons gathered here on their way to the showdown with King John at Runnymede. Its far more infamous role, however, was as Edward II's prison after he was deposed by his wife, Isabella, and her lover, Roger Mortimer, in 1327. The hope was that, consigned to a damp dungeon over a noxious pit of waste, Edward would succumb to illness and die, but after five months he was dispatched in a more certain way. He had been a bad king, indulging court favourites, ruling with contempt for law, allowing the ruthless Hugh Despenser effectively to govern the country. All the same, his symbolic ritual disembowelling with a red-hot poker was hideous. If his screams are still heard at the dead of night, it is not to be wondered at. The Berkeleys were away when the deed was done, and for the 24th generation of the family, who now live here, this is a 'fairytale' castle of which they are justly proud. Among their treasures are Francis Drake's cabin chest from the *Golden Hind* and a bedspread that belonged to Elizabeth I.
▶ *GL13 9PJ. 1 mile W of A38, 16 miles SW of Gloucester.*

❷ Tewkesbury

'Where Severn with Avon waters joins,/The sacred resting place of nobles shine;/Here lodg'd the mould'ring bones and ashes are/ Of men renown'd for glorious feats of war.' The verse recalls the events of May 4, 1471, when the Yorkists (White) and Lancastrians (Red) fought one of the decisive battles of the Wars of the Roses. This historic town, with its wealth of Tudor architecture, crooked timber buildings and narrow alleys, stands at the site of a massacre. Margaret of Anjou had arrived from France with her son Edward, Prince of Wales, to claim the throne from Edward of York, who had deposed her husband, Henry VI. It was a misadventure that resulted in many deaths, not least in Bloody Meadow, south of the town. Margaret's son was among the dead and he lies buried in Tewkesbury Abbey. A plaque marks his grave below a ceiling boss of the Yorkist badge, the Sun in Splendour.

The abbey, which has the largest surviving Norman central tower in the world, is the town's great glory. It was first consecrated in 1121, but had to be re-consecrated after the battle, when blood was spilled in the nave as desperate Lancastrians sought sanctuary.
▶ *10 miles N of Gloucester on A38.*

❸ Sudeley Castle

'This day died a man with much wit and very little judgement.' Thus, with chill incisiveness, Princess Elizabeth dismissed Sir Thomas Seymour of Sudeley, executed in 1549 for 'Treason and other Misdemeanours' against Edward VI. He died somewhat as he had lived, 'dangerously, irksomely and horribly'. Among his crimes were bribery, blackmail, an attempt to kidnap the king, and the persistent wooing of Elizabeth. Sudeley had been a royal castle since the reign of Edward IV. Henry VIII stayed here with Anne Boleyn in 1535. As cracks appeared in their marriage, the Seymour brothers pushed their sister Jane, one of Anne's ladies in waiting, towards the king. Days after Anne was beheaded, Henry married Jane and she bore him a son, Edward, but she died shortly afterwards. On his accession, Edward granted Sudeley to Thomas, his uncle, who lived here with his wife, Catherine Parr, Henry's widow. In 1548 Catherine died, and Seymour planned his coup.

Elizabeth came here on her summer progress in 1592 to celebrate the defeat of the Spanish Armada. During the Civil War these stone walls sheltered Charles I, and the castle was slighted on Cromwell's orders. For 200 years it remained a picturesque ruin. George III came sightseeing in 1788, and tripped on the stairs of the Octagon Tower. Mrs Cox, the housekeeper, broke his fall. Today the castle appears intact in its 16th-century majesty thanks to rescue by the Worcester glove-makers John and William Dent, who began restoration in 1837.
▶ *GL54 5JD. Winchcombe, 7 miles NE of Cheltenham on B4632.*

TEWKESBURY ABBEY

❹ Chavenage House

Christmas 1648 was a merry occasion at this Elizabethan hall, until one of the guests ruined the fun. The host was Nathaniel Stephens, lord of the manor. He was a colonel for Parliament against Charles I, but a moderate man who would have urged a treaty on the king. Among the visitors, however, was Henry Ireton, a general and son-in-law of Oliver Cromwell. In true Puritan spirit, he pressed Stephens to leave the revelry and come to Parliament to support a vote for Charles's execution. Nathaniel's daughter Abigail, on learning after New Year that he had done so, cursed her father for the deed. The legend of Chavenage has it that, soon afterwards, Stephens fell sick and died. Mourners were gathered around his deathbed when a hearse drew up at the door, drawn by plumed black horses and driven by a headless man. Before their eyes the colonel rose, paid his deepest respects to the coachman and entered the hearse, which bore him away. Until the family line became extinct, upon the death of each lord of the manor the same phantom would appear to carry him away.

Almost unchanged in 400 years, Chavenage remains extremely atmospheric. In rooms where Cromwell and Ireton slept, Civil War relics are on display – a hat, horse tackle, swords and pikes.

In an earlier incarnation, the manor was granted to Thomas Seymour by Henry VIII, and upon Seymour's execution (see page 134) it became forfeit to the Crown. Edward Stephens bought and rebuilt it, incorporating ecclesiastical glass from dissolved churches and monasteries, and timbers from galleons broken up on the Severn.
▶ *GL8 8XP. 1 mile NW of Tetbury on minor roads, off B4014.*

❺ Badminton Horse Trials

Zara Phillips, 12th in line to the throne, is one of the great attractions at this grand three-day event. Badminton Horse Trials have been held at the Duke of Beaufort's estate since 1949. Princess Anne used to compete – never too grand to pitch in with the grooms – and now attends to cheer her daughter Zara (pictured below) along. Anne's former husband, Captain Mark Phillips, was champion in 1971 and 1972 on Great Ovation, in 1974 on the Queen's horse, Columbus, and in 1981 on Lincoln. Royal watchers may spot Prince Harry and Mike Tindall, Zara's rugby-player husband, among the spectators. As a single girl, Kate Middleton often attended the event.
▶ *GL9 1DF. On minor roads 5 miles NE of Junction 18 of M4.*

BADMINTON HORSE TRIALS

HEREFORDSHIRE

Amid the unrest and bitter feuding of centuries, one mighty border castle was passed from hand to powerful hand, but a church with a magical well has been left alone for the waters to work their miracles.

❶ Goodrich Castle

The impressive red sandstone ruins of this medieval castle loom up on a wooded rock outcrop above the River Wye. The castle was established in 1095 by Godric Marplestone. A small Norman keep was built in the 1130s by Gilbert de Clare, amid the unrest in Stephen's reign known as the Anarchy. Stephen's cousin, Matilda, had been named heir to the throne by her father Henry I, and she was bent on taking the Crown.

For his support for King John, William Marshal, 1st Earl of Pembroke, was granted the castle in 1204, and his fourth son, Walter, the 5th Earl, added the surrounding outer wall and turrets in 1220–45. On Walter's death, Goodrich passed to the Crown and, by marriage, to Henry III's half-brother, William de Valence, who added the entrance barbican.

In Edward I's reign, the castle was a vital link in the chain of fortifications that surrounded Wales, and then, briefly, it fell into the clutches of Hugh Despenser, Edward II's rapacious, power-crazy favourite, who once lamented that he could not control the wind. Following the king's hideous murder at Berkeley Castle (see page 134), Despenser was brought to trial and publicly executed in sickening fashion. The castle was returned to Richard Talbot, the de Valence heir, and the Talbots owned and improved Goodrich over the following centuries. As a result of their support for the Lancastrian cause, the family were temporarily dispossessed, and although Goodrich was returned to them, they moved away and it fell into neglect.

In the Civil War, the castle was held first for Parliament, then for the Crown. Its formidable strength was tested by a four-and-a-half-month siege and its walls were finally breached by the mortar 'Roaring Meg', designed to fire 90kg (200lb) projectiles. Goodrich nonetheless still possesses one of the most complete surviving sets of English domestic castle buildings.
▶ *HR9 6HY. Just E of A40, 4 miles S of Ross-on-Wye. EH.*

❷ St Ethelbert's Well

Ethelbert, king of East Anglia, was to marry Alfthrytha, daughter of Offa, king of Mercia, who held sway over most of Britain. Offa is remembered most of all for the dyke that he built on the border with Wales as a defence against invading Welsh tribes. His invitation to Ethelbert to marry into such a family was enticing, but Offa's wife, Cynethryth, fearing that Ethelbert represented a threat, urged that he should be killed. In AD 794, the pagan Offa duly demanded the head of the Christian Ethelbert. The young Ethelbert was assassinated and his body hidden, but there were rumours of his ghost being seen around Marden. This affected Offa and, full of remorse, he begged the pope for absolution. He was ordered to build a church where Ethelbert had been buried, and to dedicate it to the Virgin Mary. When Ethelbert's body was exhumed to be taken to Hereford Cathedral (dedicated to Our Lady and St Ethelbert), a well appeared where his body had rested in the earth. The water of the well allegedly displayed miraculous healing powers, and a church was built around it. The 13th-century Church of St. Mary the Virgin now stands on the site, replacing the original church, but the well can still be seen in a special room inside.
▶ *HR1 3EN. Marden, 5 miles N of Hereford just E of A49.*

THE CASTLE FELL INTO THE CLUTCHES OF EDWARD II'S RAPACIOUS FAVOURITE

Tudor transformation

Henry's resolve to produce a male heir led to upheaval on a grand scale – continued by his more than capable daughter.

The mighty Tudor dynasty ruled Britain for more than a century, and changed the face of the land. Most intensively under Henry VIII (1509–47), and in the Elizabethan era (1558–1603), the country was transfigured. The years from the accession of Henry VII in 1485, to the death of Elizabeth I in 1603, were a time of huge political, economic, social and cultural change, architectural and military advances and religious turmoil. Palaces, mansions and castles were built, parks and estates laid out.

Henry VIII's divorce from Catholic Catherine of Aragon was to have an extraordinary impact upon the landscape. Declaring himself Supreme Head of the Church of England, the king ordered the Dissolution of the Monasteries, an exercise in wholesale vandalism

that, in five years from 1536, left many great religious houses in ruins. Monks and nuns were expelled, treasures seized, bells silenced. The land was strewn with hundreds of broken monasteries, friaries, priories and nunneries. Ancient manuscripts 'flew like butterflies'. Roofs were stripped, windows smashed.

Here and there a nave was saved to serve as a parish church. Domestic buildings were plundered, so that Gothic windows, arches and carved stone fragments turned up built improbably into farmhouse, cottage and barn. Lands and ecclesiastical properties were granted to royal favourites, rented out, sold off, sold on. Former abbeys were turned into ostentatious mansions. Henry made Reading a royal residence, staying often. Not since the Norman Conquest had

there been so massive a transfer of lands; an estimated third of the country changed hands. By the 18th century, the ruins had acquired a peculiar beauty, an aura of dreamy melancholy, but at the time, such wanton destruction must have been deeply shocking, especially to those who remained Catholic in their hearts. How appalling to see not just beautiful Romanesque edifices but a way of life swept away!

Embattled isle

In some ways, with its fabulous wealth and abuses of privilege, the Church had courted disaster. In the 1700s, William Gilpin, exponent of the picturesque, described 'great nurseries of superstition, bigotry and ignorance ... stews of sloth, stupidity', which, reduced to fragments, could be viewed with 'moral and religious satisfaction'. This justification for Henry's Reformation was, however, pure cant. The king's avarice, his desire for Anne Boleyn and his longing for a legitimate son drove the Reformation. A further consequence of the split with Rome was the threat

of attack from Catholic France and Spain. Against this eventuality, Henry commissioned a chain of more than 30 stout castles and towers, built to defend the south coast from Tilbury in Essex to Cornwall.

To wrath, greed, lust and gluttony can be added pride and envy – of the seven deadly sins, Henry was innocent only of sloth. He envied Cardinal Thomas Wolsey's Italianate Palace of Hampton Court, which the cardinal had built for himself. Henry 'acquired' it in 1529 and rebuilt it in the hand-made red brick characteristic of Tudor architecture. Henry also gratified his pride by splashing out on Nonsuch Palace, which was to be the envy, in turn, of his rival François I of France.

In the Tudor period the formidable power bases of the Middle Ages gave way to palatial Renaissance-inspired residences for the moneyed, many on an 'H' or 'E' plan (for Henry or Elizabeth), with no defensive purpose. At Hardwick Hall in Derbyshire the number of windows, when glass came at such a cost, declared the immense wealth of its owner, Bess of Hardwick. Several noblemen poured money into 'prodigy' houses, worthy of a visit by the queen. Elizabeth's beloved Robert Dudley made over Kenilworth Castle in fine style for her. Longleat in Wiltshire was partly built when she stayed there on her summer progress in 1575 as the guest of Sir John Thynne.

At a humbler level, the Tudors left a legacy of vernacular black-and-white half-timbered houses, so cosy, so amenable to use as pubs. In 1558 the 'Great Rebuilding' of homes for the lower orders began, with more warmth, light, space, ventilation and privacy, dwellings with unlimited lifespan. Indeed, beautiful timber-frame houses can still be seen, holding up against the centuries, in such towns as Stratford-upon-Avon, where William Shakespeare was born. He enjoyed the patronage of the queen, and during Elizabeth's reign, such legendary theatres as the Globe in London were built, designed to reflect ancient Rome and Greece, and to elevate the status of the actor from reprobate to classical player.

No expense was spared by Sir William Cecil who, in 1555, began building a magnificent mansion in which to receive and entertain Elizabeth I.
BURGHLEY HOUSE

LEICESTERSHIRE & RUTLAND

The gardens of a stately home reveal where the country's longest serving monarch once strolled while her ladies enjoyed afternoon tea. Elsewhere, in sharp contrast, lie vivid reminders of reigns curtailed.

❶ Bradgate House and Deer Park

The birthplace of Lady Jane Grey, tragic 'nine-day queen', is now a beautiful ruin set in a peaceful deer park. The house was begun by Thomas Grey, 1st Marquis of Dorset, in around 1499, and completed by his son in 1520. One of the earliest unfortified mansions in England, it had two wings joined by a Great Hall and parlour. The west wing housed an industrial-scale kitchen, bakery and servants' quarters. The chapel and family apartments were in the east wing. Lady Jane Grey was beheaded in 1554, aged just 17.

Charles I and Henrietta Maria were received here in 1634 by Henry Grey, Lord Grey of Groby, and his wife, Ann Windsor. Their son, Thomas, aged 10 or 11 at the time, grew up to repudiate the monarchy, raising and training forces for Parliament in Leicestershire. For this, Bradgate was attacked by Prince Rupert (nephew of Charles I) and a gang of Cavaliers, who beat up the servants and seized arms and goods. A fire in the northwest tower did more damage, but repairs were effected in time for a visit from William III in 1696. The house fell victim not to violence but to neglect. It was left unoccupied from 1719. The only part that remains complete is the chapel, in which can be seen the alabaster tomb of Sir Henry Grey and Ann.

▶ *LE6 0HE. Newton Linford, 6 miles NW of Leicester.*

❷ The Battle of Bosworth Field

'A horse, a horse! My kingdom for a horse!' One of the best-known lines of Shakespeare recalls the Battle of Bosworth, August 22, 1485, in which Richard III was killed and Henry Tudor took the throne. Recent finds by archaeologists working for the Battlefields Trust include round shot, fragments of armour and, most excitingly, in 2010, a silver-gilt badge of a boar. This was Richard's emblem, almost certainly worn by one of the knights who rode with him in his last frantic cavalry charge. Richard led the charge but was driven back on to marshy ground where his men were picked off with halberds and daggers. Ambion Hill, where there is a heritage centre, was previously thought to be the most likely site for the thick of battle, but now it seems

the fighting centred on a spot more than a mile to the southwest. In the Civil War the battle location must have been common knowledge, since it was said that there was fighting 'on the very field in which King Richard was slain' – but that information has not been handed down.

▶ *Battlefield 6 miles N of Nuneaton on minor roads. Bosworth Battlefield Heritage Centre, near Market Bosworth, CV13 0AD.*

❸ Melton Mowbray

For 200 years royalty would come here to ride to hounds with the famous Belvoir, Cottesmore and Quorn hunts. Edward, Prince of Wales, the future Edward VIII, attended meets with the Quorn, staying at Newport and Craven hunting lodges. Private quarters were built for him at Craven Lodge Club, and from 1924 to 1929 became his 'second home'. He was a darling of society. Fashion columnist Diana Vreeland dubbed him 'The Golden Prince' and declared that all women of her generation were in love with him. It was in Melton, on January 10, 1931, at the country house of his mistress Thelma Furness, that he was introduced to Wallis Simpson, a married woman. His chat-up line was prosaic: did she, an American, miss central heating when she was in England? Mockingly, she told him, 'I'm sorry, Sir, but you have disappointed me … I had hoped for something more original from the Prince of Wales.' Her refreshing honesty disarmed him. He was smitten. To marry her he gave up the throne in 1936, after less than a year.

A business centre now stands on the site of Thelma Furness's house, Burrough Court. All that remains of the original are the stable yard, chauffeur and groom quarters – and a giraffe house from the 1920s.

▶ *18 miles NE of Leicester on A607.*

❹ Oakham Castle

Here is a real curiosity, a Great Hall hung with a collection of some 240 weird and wonderful horseshoes, given as gifts by visiting peers and monarchs. The hall is one of the finest examples of late 12th-century domestic architecture in the country, with superb carvings of animals and musicians. The remains of other parts of the castle complex lie beneath the grass

of the inner bailey. It was built between 1180 and 1190 in the reign of Henry II, for Walchelin de Ferrière, Norman lord of the manor of Oakham. According to custom, every king, queen or peer of the realm who was entertained here had to bring a gift of a horseshoe. At first, guests brought the real thing, but over the centuries the horseshoes became more ornate and of all sizes. The one given by Edward IV in about 1470 is huge and highly wrought, bearing a shield. Several of the horseshoes are topped with crowns. The Queen paid her due in 1967, Prince Charles in 2003. One, dated 1699, is said to be from Elizabeth I. The largest, presented by the Prince Regent, the future George IV, is made of bronze and stands 2m (7ft) high. It cost £50, and it is said he left his host to pick up the bill.

▶ *LE15 6DX. On A606, 9 miles SE of Melton Mowbray and 10 miles W of Stamford. Castle in town centre.*

❺ Belvoir Castle

Prince Albert greatly enriched British life and culture, but in the early days of his marriage to Queen Victoria, the public did not take him to their hearts. A visit to Belvoir in 1843 was conceived partly as a public relations exercise. Albert would cut a dash riding with the Belvoir hunt and gain in stature. The royal couple arrived at the castle with an entourage

that included the Duke of Wellington and the prime minister, Sir John Peel – namesake of the great Cumbrian huntsman.

The home of the Dukes of Rutland stands on high ground on the site of a Norman castle, with sweeping views over the Vale of Belvoir. This is the castle's fourth incarnation. It was rebuilt in Gothic style by James Wyatt for the 5th Duke and his wife, Elizabeth Howard, starting in 1799 and taking 30 years. Victoria was 24, not quite four years married and the mother of three children, when she came to stay. Belvoir provided a backdrop for the 2009 film *The Young Victoria*, in which a bed slept in by Victoria and Albert was used. It can be seen in a room ornately decorated with hand-painted Chinese wallpaper.

As well as the extravagance of house and furnishings, and a fabulous art collection, Belvoir has two other great claims to fame. The gardens designed by Elizabeth Howard are glorious, and the castle was famously the birthplace of that very British tradition, afternoon tea. Anna Maria Stanhope, Duchess of Bedford, a lady in waiting to Victoria, finding that she suffered 'a sinking feeling' at around 4pm, would have her servants bring her a pot of tea and a little something to tide her over until supper. Friends began to join her in her room for tea, sandwiches and fancies, and the practice soon became all the rage with society hostesses.

▶ *NG32 1PE. 8 miles W of Grantham.*

CENTRAL ENGLAND

LINCOLNSHIRE

Generosity and ruthlessness, pleasure and sorrow, birth and death – the lives of monarchs and their consorts are encapsulated in the castles, houses and cathedrals of this green and pleasant land.

① Belton House

Enriched by an inheritance from his uncle, Sir John Brownlow, High Sheriff of Lincolnshire, set about building a fine country house and enclosing a deer park. The identity of the architect of this serene, honey-coloured stately home, which is one of the most complete examples of an English country house still standing, is a matter of debate. Sir Christopher Wren, no less, is cited, although Belton is more probably the work of William Winde and William Stanton. It incorporated the latest innovations, sash windows on its principle floors and a rooftop cupola with a viewing platform and surrounding balustrade.

Sir John and Lady Brownlow took up residence in November 1688, not four years after building began, and became known for their lavish entertaining, playing host to William III. A later royal visitor to the house was George III. The Queen's Room was redecorated in 1841 when William IV's widow, Queen Adelaide, came to stay. The rococo-style canopied bed in which she slept, embroidered with her monogram, is still here. The Windsor Bedroom was used by Edward VIII and his mistress Wallis Simpson. The 6th Baron Brownlow, as the king's lord in waiting, must have been caught up in the abdication crisis. Prince Charles also used the room during his time as a cadet at RAF Cranwell. The interiors were refurbished by Sir Jeffrey

BELTON HOUSE

Wyatville in the early 1800s. There are more than 200 pictures on display, many from the late 1600s, as well as porcelain, silver and Regency furniture. Very little survives of the original garden, but Wyatville's grand plans included the Italian Garden, Fountain and Orangery.

▶ *NG32 2LS. 2 miles NW of Grantham on A607. NT.*

❷ Burghley House

'Next Burleigh-house ... worthily reckoned among the noblest seates in England, situate on the brow of a hill, built a la moderne, near a Parke Waled in, & a fine Wood at the descent.' Diarist John Evelyn, on his way to Belvoir Castle, was deeply impressed by this superb early Elizabethan house, as the visitor is today. It was built for William Cecil, Lord Burghley, mostly to his own design. Cecil was for 40 years the most trusted servant of Elizabeth I – although he would find himself for a time in bad odour for expediting the execution of Mary, Queen of Scots, over which the queen had been torn and tormented. During his career he held almost every high office, including Lord High Treasurer, and this very grand house befits his status as one of the most powerful figures of his day. There are 35 major rooms on the ground and first floors, and more than 80 more modest rooms, halls and corridors, all under 0.3 hectares (¾ acre) of lead roof. Cecil brought to bear a considerable talent for art and architecture at his stately home. He was a bibliophile, an antiquary and was fascinated by heraldry and genealogy.

The limestone exterior is little changed since the 16th century, but the interiors have been altered by successive generations. The state rooms were transformed in the 17th and 18th centuries, from Tudor mansion to treasure house for the spectacular art collection. Landscaping is largely by Capability Brown. In accordance with the will of the 6th Marquis, access to the park is free.

▶ *PE9 3JY. 1 mile SE of Stamford.*

❸ Grimsthorpe Castle

Katherine Willoughby, the young châtelaine of this castle, was 14 in 1533, when she was married to her guardian, Charles Brandon, Duke of Suffolk, a friend of Henry VIII's. Grimsthorpe was begun in the late 13th century for Gilbert de Gaunt, but it had been remodelled by the time John Leland wrote thus of it in his *Itineraries of England* (1535–43): 'The place of Grimsthorpe was no great thing, before the building of the second court. Yet was all the old

work of stone and the gatehouse was fair and strong, and the walls on each side of it embattled.'

Henry VIII gave the castle as a wedding gift to Maria de Salinas, closest friend of Catherine of Aragon, and William, 11th Baron Willoughby de Eresby, master of the royal hart hounds. In 1520, Maria gave birth to a daughter, Katherine, who was six when her father died and she became 12th Baroness. She was made a ward of the Crown until 1528, when the king sold the wardship to Brandon for £2,666 (£1,039,300). Five years later, Brandon, then 47, married his ward. When he set about rebuilding the castle for a visit by the king, he had plentiful supplies of stone from the Abbey of Vaudey, which stood south of the lake and was laid waste in the Dissolution.

On the death of Brandon in 1545, Katherine married Richard Bertie ('Barty'), her handsome usher. Staunch Protestants, the couple went into exile in the reign of Mary I, returning to a house suffering from neglect. By 1611, however, it was fit for a visit from James I. The 15th Baron rebuilt the north front in the classical style, and the 17th employed John Vanbrugh to replace it with its baroque façade. In the state rooms, the visitor can see thrones and furnishings from the House of Lords, reflecting the Willoughby de Eresbys' hereditary office as Lord Great Chamberlains to the Palace of Westminster.

▶ *PE10 0LY. 5 miles NW of Bourne on A151.*

❹ Lincoln Castle

This Norman castle, built on the site of a Roman fortress by William the Conqueror, is one of two in the country to have two mottes, or mounds. (The other is at Lewes, see page 71.) For 900 years it was used as a prison and courthouse, and remains remarkably intact. It is still possible to walk around the walls, enjoying the views. On one motte stands the Observatory Tower, built in 1150 towards the end of the Anarchy, the battle for the crown between Stephen and his cousin Matilda. On the other motte is the Lucy Tower, built in the 1100s by the Countess Lucy, castle constable.

In Norman times, Lincoln was the third city in the realm in wealth and importance, and even had its own mint. The Crown Court still sits here, and there is a museum. The castle's greatest possession is housed within the Charters of Liberty exhibition – one of the four surviving original copies of the Magna Carta, the charter that King John so sullenly added his seal under duress from his feudal barons in 1215.

▶ *LN1 3AA. A46 from SW, A15 from N and S. Castle just N of city centre.*

GAINSBOROUGH OLD HALL

❺ Lincoln Cathedral

The love stories of two great women are commemorated in this glorious cathedral. It was begun by William the Conqueror and rebuilt from 1186, in the Early English Gothic style, after an earthquake caused structural damage. The work was commissioned by Hugh of Avalon, Bishop of Lincoln, who lived to see just the choir completed. During his life, he was a critic of, as well as a friend to, three kings, Henry II, Richard I and John. In 1290 Edward I and Eleanor of Castile were on their way to visit Hugh's tomb when the queen died and the grieving Edward honoured her with a grand funeral procession (see Charing Cross, page 92). Her body was prepared for embalming and the viscera were buried here in Lincoln. A replica of her tomb in Westminster was installed, but although the stone chest survives, her memorial is 19th-century and also a replica. It would be pleasing to think that the two prominent statues on the cathedral exterior were Edward and Eleanor, but this is open to queston.

John of Gaunt, Duke of Lancaster, was the third surviving son of Edward III. In 1398, he and his mistress and future third wife, Katherine Swynford, founded a chantry in the cathedral to pray for their souls. When the couple married here, their four children were legitimised. Their descendant Lady Margaret Beaufort was the mother of Henry VII. Katherine died in 1403; her tomb is near the high altar. This did not deter her great-great-great grandson, Henry VIII, from sending his agents in 1540 to destroy the cathedral shrines, stripping gold and silver from them, and to carrying off precious vestments, plates and jewel-encrusted statues.

▶ *LN2 1PX. A46 from SW, A15 from N and S. Cathedral just N of city centre*

❻ Gainsborough Old Hall

Visitors will look in vain for the bed slept in here by Henry VIII. He brought his own, especially built to take his great weight. This almost unchanged medieval hall was built of red brick with some half-timbering for Sir Thomas Burgh, a senior courtier to Edward V, Richard III and Henry VII, in 1460. The Burghs were a prominent local family, and the hall was both a home and a declaration of status. In October 1483, Richard III visited on his progress through the realm after his coronation, and was entertained in the magnificent Great Hall. He brought his whole court, and each new dish at the banquet was heralded with a fanfare, from

pottage of stewed broth and calves' feet pies, through baked cranes and bustards to cream of almond and marchpaynes. In 1510, Sir Thomas's son, Edward Burgh, 2nd Baron, was declared insane and locked up at the hall. His son, also Edward, was married to Catherine Parr, who was destined to become Henry VIII's sixth wife, and to survive the king. Henry visited twice, in 1509 and 1541, with his fifth wife, Catherine Howard, when they stayed for four days. She was accused of indiscretions with her cousin Thomas Culpeper while at Gainsborough, for which she was beheaded. Catherine Parr, by now a widow, was free to become the obese king's last queen.

The kitchens where royal feasts were prepared are something to seen, with two huge open fireplaces, each large enough to roast an ox. Visitors prepared to climb 59 steps to the top of the tower gain a great view of the town. The house is managed by English Heritage and is said to be haunted by the 'Grey Lady', who died of a broken heart. She is allegedly the daughter of a former lord of the manor.

▶ *DN21 2NB. Junction of A156 and A631, 15 miles NW of Lincoln. EH.*

❼ Bolingbroke Castle

'Uneasy lies the head that wears a crown.' Henry IV had a lot on his conscience, having almost certainly ordered the murder of his cousin, Richard II. Where better to learn the story of his reign (1399–1413) than at what remains of his birthplace, a ruined hexagonal castle, a national monument, which in summertime hosts the plays of Shakespeare? The present castle was founded by Ranulf, Earl of Chester, in 1220, on his return from the Fifth Crusade. When he died without male heir in 1232, it passed to John of Gaunt and the House of Lancaster, and here, in 1366, John's son Henry was born. Before he ascended the throne as Henry IV, he was known as Henry of Bolingbroke, in the same way as his father was named for his birthplace, Ghent.

By the 15th and 16th centuries, the castle was falling into ruins. A survey in Tudor times revealed that the towers were beyond repair. Nonetheless, in the Civil War, Bolingbroke was used as a Royalist garrison. It was damaged in 1643 in a siege and captured for Parliament. In 1644 it was recaptured, then relinquished, and in 1652 it was slighted by Cromwell's men to prevent further use. The towers were dismantled and dumped in the moat. Although little remains today, the outline of the lower walls is still visible.

▶ *15 miles north of Boston, off A16. EH.*

ALTHORP

NORTHAMPTONSHIRE

A Tudor house stands where great councils of state were once held. Other momentous events are marked with monuments and plaques, and a stately home pays homage to the life of the people's princess.

❶ Althorp

The ancestral home of the Spencers since the 16th century will be forever associated with the late Diana, Princess of Wales.
Diana was born at Sandringham and brought up on the estate. She was eight when her parents divorced, and she spent her teenage years at Althorp (pronounced 'All-trup') with her father when she was not at boarding school. Here she met her future husband, Prince Charles, when he came to shoot in November 1977 – and it was to Althorp that 'England's rose' was brought from Westminster Abbey on September 6, 1997, for burial on an island in the lake. An exhibition in the Italianate stables celebrates her life and work.

Although she outshines all former residents in the popular imagination, Diana cannot entirely eclipse the family personalities who went before

her. Henry Spencer, son of the 2nd Lord Spencer, fought for Charles I at Edghill and later lent the king £10,000. Georgiana, Duchess of Devonshire, sister of the 2nd Earl Spencer, was an 18th-century feminist and socialite who cultivated a salon of literary and political figures. The greatest tribute to her beauty came not from some society beau but an Irish dustman, who exclaimed, 'Love and bless you, my lady, let me light my pipe in your eyes!' In April 1992, Diana's brother, Charles, Viscount Althorp, became the 9th Earl.

The first house at Althorp was a moated medieval manor, built of local orange stone. It was rebuilt in Tudor redbrick, added to over generations, and refaced and embellished by Henry Holland in 1790. The visitor can see an impressive art collection. Every summer Althorp hosts a literary festival. Georgiana would have approved.
▶ *NN7 4HQ. 5 miles NW of Northampton on A428.*

❷ The Battle of Northampton

Across the ancient battlefield a warning shout rings out: 'Fore!' A golf course covers much of the terrain where Yorkists defeated Lancastrians in the Wars of the Roses in 1460. The battle was short and casualties relatively light due to the perfidy of Sir Ralph Grey, who switched his allegiance from Lancaster to York and assured an important victory for the White Rose. Soon afterwards, the Duke of York returned from Ireland, and in October Henry VI signed an Act of Settlement granting him the right of succession. Anyone who thought that the matter was decided, however, had reckoned without Henry's queen, Margaret of Anjou, and her disinherited son, Edward.

The Hardingstone Cross, one of Edward I's memorials to Queen Eleanor (see pages 92-93), survives here at the edge of Delapré Abbey. It was begun in 1291 by John of Battle, who worked with William of Ireland to carve the statues; William was paid £3 6s 8d (£3.33) for each figure.

▶ *Access Northampton from Junctions 15, 15A and 16 of M1.*

❸ Naseby

'I could not riding out alone about my business, but smile out to God in praises, in assurance of victory because God would, by things that are not, bring to naught things that are.' Who knows if Oliver Cromwell had God on his side at the battle of Naseby, but it was to be a crushing defeat for the Royalists and a pivotal point in the Civil War, assuring Charles I's doom. The battle was fought on June 14, 1645, and the king's men were no match for Cromwell's nascent New Model Army under the command of Sir Thomas Fairfax. The 'self-denying ordnance' barred Cromwell himself from military service, but a special temporary commission enabled him to assume the title of Lieutenant-General of Horse. An eyewitness at the battle related that at Naseby, 'he did laugh so excessively as if he had been drunk; his eyes sparkled with spirits' in anticipation of the imminent fighting.

The Parliamentarian army was ranged along a ridge overlooking Naseby, but Cromwell ordered them down, reasoning that it was too good a vantage point, and Charles would not be induced to attack. The Royalists had around 12,000 men and lost some 1,000; Parliament had 15,000 – and lost fewer than 150.

A monument marks the spot where Cromwell's cavalry began the engagement.

▶ *12 miles W of Kettering. Battlefield just N of A14.*

❹ Fotheringhay Castle

The story that James I destroyed this once great castle in revenge for the execution of his mother may be appealing, but is untrue. The castle was the birthplace of Richard III in 1452, and it was here that Mary, Queen of Scots was tried and sentenced to death – the verdict a foregone conclusion. She was beheaded on February 8, 1587, and buried in Peterborough Cathedral, but was moved by her son James to Westminster Abbey.

What is amazing is that so little trace should remain of a place where so much history took place. The sad reality is that the castle was allowed to fall into disrepair and was broken up to supply the locals with building material. A mound of rubble enclosed by railings with a plaque is all there is for walkers to see.

▶ *8 miles W of Peterborough.*

❺ Rockingham Castle

Were the crown jewels really lost in the Wash – or did cunning King John bury them here? The castle at Rockingham stands on an escarpment with commanding views over the Welland Valley and five counties. From the battlements, a look-out could have seen an advancing army 20 miles distant. The castle was founded by William the Conqueror, who hunted in the grounds, and it became an important seat of government. The Great Council of Rockingham was held here in 1095, in the reign of William Rufus. At the time there were two popes, Urban II and Clement III, and 'bishops, abbots and princes or principal men' in vain exhorted Anselm, Archbishop of Canterbury, to conform to the king's will and accept Clement.

Richard the Lionheart entertained William of Scotland here. William was nicknamed Garbh, 'the Rough', and after his lifetime, 'the Lion'. King John came to hunt, and left the treasure chest that gives rise to the implausible suggestion that he stashed the royal treasures at Rockingham, and only pretended to have lost them.

Little remains of the original Norman castle. Behind a medieval gatehouse is essentially a Tudor house, built for Edmund Watson, who was granted the castle by Henry VIII. A Royalist stronghold in the Civil War, Rockingham was surrendered under threat of cannon fire, and later successfully besieged by the king's men. It remains the home of James Saunders Watson and his family, who welcome the public on 50 days of the year.

▶ *LE16 8TH. Market Harborough, 1 mile N of Corby just W of A6003.*

NOTTINGHAMSHIRE

One king started a civil war where, centuries earlier, another had lingered before confronting his date with destiny, and a ruined Royalist stronghold was the scene of an even earlier monarch's demise.

❶ Nottingham

On the wall of the general hospital on Standard Hill, an insignificant-looking plaque tells of a momentous event.
The inscription reads: 'On a mound about 60 yards to the rear of this tablet Charles I raised his standard, August 25th, 1642'. Traditionally, this marked the start of the Civil War, which tore the kingdom in two. The standard was raised on Derry Mound, just north of the gateway of Nottingham Castle. Sir Edmund Verney, Knight Mareshal and Standard-bearer of England, stepped up to declare, 'They who would take the Standard from him must first wrest his soul from his body' – which, of course, in the end, they did. There followed a rousing roll of drums, fanfares of trumpets and shouts of 'God save the King!'

Charles had chosen Nottingham because of its central position, and in the belief that the people would rally round. They did not. The castle came under the command of Colonel John Hutchinson, a Puritan and stalwart of the Parliamentary cause, who held the fort against several Royalist attacks. He was one of the 'regicides', the signatories of Charles I's death warrant. After the king's execution, the castle was razed to prevent further use. The gatehouse, outer walls and caves beneath give some idea of how it appeared. Today, the 17th-century Ducal Mansion stands on the site, and the remnants of the castle walls are in its grounds. The first provincial Museum of Fine Art opened here in 1878. The labyrinth of man-made caves and tunnels is fascinating to explore.
▶ *NG1 6EL (castle). 6 miles E of Junctions 25 and 26 of M1.*

❷ Bestwood Country Park

Henry I granted to the Priory of Lenton 'the right of having two carts to fetch deadwood and heath daily out of the Royal Forest of Bestwood'. This may not sound such a big deal, but royalty was possessive of its hunting forests, and punishments for poaching or taking timber were draconian. A hunting lodge was built and the park enclosed for Edward III. When Edward IV stayed at Nottingham Castle in October 1469, he came here to ride to hounds. Richard III was fond of his 'Castle of Care' in the city, and he, too, would come to Bestwood when he was in residence. His last visit was on August 16, 1485, six days before he met his end at Bosworth Field (see page 140).

Charles II gave Bestwood Lodge to his mistress, Nell Gwyn, and their illegitimate son, Charles Beauclerk, 1st Duke of St Albans. The story is that Charles and his fellows would tease Nell for sleeping in and missing a morning's sport. He offered her 'all the land she could ride around before breakfast', and was astonished to find her up first the next day. She had ridden out at cockcrow, dropping handkerchiefs on her way, and the encircled area became Bestwood Park.

The first lodge was demolished in 1863 and a new one built for the 10th Duke. It is in the domestic Gothic style and since the mid-1970s has been a Best Western Hotel. The park covers 260ha (650 acres) of wildlife habitats, meadows, mill lakes and oak woodland.
▶ *NG5 8NE (Bestwood Lodge Hotel).*
5 miles N of Nottingham.

❸ Newark Castle

On the night of October 18, 1216, Sherwood Forest was rocked by a terrible storm – the devil had come to claim the soul of King John.
It is popular belief that John died at this castle after losing the crown jewels in the Wash. Already ill, he consumed 'a surfeit of peaches' and passed away in agony. According to legend, however, John, pantomime villain to heroic Robin Hood, was poisoned by Friar Tuck for the murder of Maid Marian.

The castle was begun in 1123 and rebuilt in the 13th century, but the Norman gatehouse, crypt and a rectangular tower survive. This would have been a ruin if Cromwell had had his way. In the Civil War, Newark declared for the king and 400 men were garrisoned here to command the passage over the River Trent. As a 'key to the north', it endured three sieges before being surrendered in 1646 on the king's own orders. The command to demolish it was issued, but an outbreak of the plague made Newark too dangerous. Over time, materials from the partial ruins were plundered, and many houses in Newark have castle stone built into their walls. What remains still has the power to impress.
▶ *NG24 1BG.*
Close to junction of A1 and A46.

SHROPSHIRE

Where a queen and her lover plotted her husband's downfall, two young princes were hidden away, their fate still a mystery, while a more modest house played a vital role in an uncrowned king's escape.

❶ Ludlow Castle

When Daniel Defoe came here in 1722, he observed that 'A small expense would make this castle a habitable and beautiful place, lying high and looking over fine country.' It was left alone, though, in a state of dignified decay. The castle served as a base for Roger Mortimer, who was complicit, with Queen Isabella, in the hideous murder of Edward II. In 1425, it came to Richard Plantagenet, Duke of York, and was sacked by Lancastrians in 1459 in the Wars of the Roses. In 1473, Edward IV sent his son Edward, Prince of Wales, to Ludlow, remote from the intrigues of court – but intrigue has a long reach. Edward V was declared king, aged 12, in 1483, and on his journey back to London he was captured by his uncle, Richard of Gloucester, who sent him and his brother Richard to the Tower. They were never seen again outside its walls.

The heart of Arthur, elder son of Henry Tudor, is buried at Ludlow. He died at the castle on April 2, 1502, on honeymoon with Catherine of Aragon, and history took one of those swerves – his brother married his widow and ascended the throne as Henry VIII. Among the substantial remains of a Norman castle much improved in Tudor times, is Arthur's Tower, and, in the inner bailey, the chapel of Mary Magdelene, the only round church in an English castle.
▶ *SY8 1AY. 24 miles N of Hereford off A49. Castle in town centre.*

❷ Boscobel House

In 2001, Prince Charles planted an oak tree by this 17th-century timber-framed house, in memory of the deliverance of another Charles. After the execution of Charles I, his son made a doomed attempt to take back the crown. When all hopes were dashed by his defeat at Worcester (see page 150 and 156), the uncrowned king was escorted from the battlefield by Charles Giffard, and taken first to White Ladies Priory and then to his home, Boscobel House. Giffard was aided by the loyal Penderell family. To disguise the royal fugitive, Richard Penderell dressed him in 'a Country-Fellowes habbit with a pair of ordinary Cloath Britches, a Leathern Dublett and greene Jerkin'; and he cut off those flowing locks. Charles and Penderell were met at

Boscobel by Colonel Carlos, one of the last Royalists to escape from the battle. By dawn, Cromwell's men were searching the surrounding woods, and the king and Carlos spent a long, nerve-racking day perched high in an oak tree, sustained by 'Bread, Cheese, Small Beere, and nothing elce'. At times, Cromwell's men came very close. According to the king's account: 'We see soldiers goeing up and down in the thickest of the Wood, searching for persons escaped, we seeing them now and then peeping out of the Wood.' Only at nightfall did they descend, to hide in a priest hole, and Charles embarked on a long and tortuous journey to France.

The sapling planted by Prince Charles is a descendant of that great 'Royal Oak'. Although it will be a long time before anyone can hide in it, visitors can see it, along with the dairy, farmyard, smithy and gardens of the farm.
▶ *ST19 9AR. Stafford, 9 miles E of Telford close to Junction 3 of M54. EH.*

❸ Shrewsbury Castle

'Among the infinite number of party skirmishes and fights this winter, one was the surprise of the town and castle of Shrewsbury.' In his fictitious *Memoirs of a Cavalier*, Daniel Defoe sets the scene for the events of February 22, 1645, when Colonel Thomas Mytton and his troops took this castle for Parliament in the Civil War, springing their surprise early on a Sunday morning. Only with the Restoration and the accession of Charles II was Shrewsbury Castle returned to the Crown.

It began as an Anglo-Saxon timber fortification, replaced by a red sandstone Norman castle. In the summer of 1138 it suffered its first onslaught when Stephen laid siege and captured the castle from supporters of his rival, Matilda. The castle was substantially strengthened in around 1300 by Edward I, but subsequently fell into disrepair. Elizabeth I granted it to the bailiffs and burgesses of Shrewsbury in 1586, but little was done to maintain it until the Civil War. The corporation of Shrewsbury did better by it when it came into their hands in 1924, restoring it as far as possible to its 14th-century grandeur. It now passes muster as home to the Shropshire Regimental Museum.
▶ *SY1 2AT. 15 miles W of Telford on A5. Castle in town centre.*

Flight of the uncrowned king

Undaunted by defeat, determined to live to fight another day, young Charles Stuart wended his hazardous way to France.

BOSCOBEL HOUSE AND A DESCENDANT OF THE ORIGINAL ROYAL OAK

October 29, 1651: 'Came news and letters to the Queen and Sir Richard Browne ... of his Majesty's miraculous escape, which exceedingly rejoiced us.' More than five weeks had passed since diarist John Evelyn had learned of the Royalist defeat at Worcester (see page 156) by Oliver Cromwell's New Model Army. In that time, Charles II had embarked on a journey fraught with perils, and full of narrow escapes. With a bounty of £1,000 on his head, he was the quarry in quite a manhunt. The longest inland trail in England, 650 miles, takes in Stratford-upon-Avon, the Cotswolds, the Mendips and the South Coast from Charmouth to Shoreham,

tracing Charles' route to safety. From the 'Faithful City' of Worcester, the king made his way to Boscobel House, the hunting lodge of his comrade John Giffard (see page 149), with Lord Wilmot and others of his officers. There he famously evaded capture by hiding in an oak tree. Nothing could disguise the king's 6ft 2in (1.9m) stature, but his hair was cut, and he passed a wretched day in the rain, disguised as a woodsman.

Thirty years later Charles would dictate to diarist Samuel Pepys an account of his miserable adventure. His first thought had been to head for London, to arrive there, if possible, ahead of the news that 'the battle was so absolutely lost'. But that day in the

150

out. In 90 years of persecution, however, Catholics had learned to keep secrets and were practised at concealing people.

From here it was on to Bentley Hall near Walsall, home of John Lane, whose sister Jane, by good fortune, had obtained a permit to travel with a servant to Somerset to visit a friend who was about to give birth. (Catholics were forbidden, without such a licence, to travel more than five miles from their homes.) So it was that the king now posed as the son of a tenant farmer, and, mounted upon the same mare as Jane, continued his odyssey.

At Bromsgrove they found that the mare had cast a shoe, and Charles took her to a blacksmith. 'What news?' he asked the smith, as he held the mare's foot. 'No news, said the smith, 'since the good news of beating the rogues of the Scots.' No, he did not know if 'that rogue, Charles Stuart, were taken'. Playing his part, Charles told him that, if he had been, he deserved to hang, and they parted on good terms.

At Bristol, failing to find a ship to sail to France, he and his entourage decided to make for the south coast. Charles spent several days at Trent House near Sherborne, Dorset, the home of Colonel Francis Wyndham, a Royalist officer, while Wyndham and Wilmot made enquiries in Lyme Regis and Weymouth.

Mission accomplished

Finally, after many reverses, a Captain Nicholas Tattersell agreed to carry passengers from Shoreham in Sussex aboard a coal boat named *Surprise*, on payment of £80. They were negotiating this sum in the George Inn in Brighton when the innkeeper, although drunk, recognised the tall, dark guest and fell on his knees, at which Tattersell, realising whom he would be carrying, demanded a further £200 for the risk he would be taking. The rest of the crew must be kept in ignorance.

As in all the best suspense movies, only hours after the *Surprise* sailed out of Shoreham, a troop of cavalry came clattering into town to arrest Charles. The royal party landed in Fécamp near Le Havre, and travelled onwards to Rouen. He had made it, but his travails had taken their toll. No one would have known him for a king. 'At Rouen he looked so poorly, that the people went into the rooms before he went away to see whether he had not stole something or other.' From Rouen, Charles continued to Paris to join his mother, Queen Henrietta Maria. Nine years later, in 1660, he would return to England to scenes of wild rejoicing, to ascend the throne.

Long-distance walkers can follow in his footsteps today, retracing his route. Waymarks show depictions of the *Surprise*, the Prince of Wales crown and the site of the original Royal Oak at Boscobel.

woods he 'resolved of another way of making my escape, which was, to get over the Severn into Wales and so get either to Swansea or some other sea town that I knew had commerce with France'.

Cromwell's men were ahead of him. With every crossing guarded, the mighty River Severn thwarted Plan B. The royal party moved on and at Moseley Old Hall in Cheadle (see page 152), Charles found a refuge, the luxury of a bed and solicitude from the Catholic Whitgreaves and the family's priest, John Huddleston, who bandaged his sore feet. These kind and loyal souls showed tremendous courage, for they would surely have been executed had they been found

STAFFORDSHIRE

A welcome haven for a fleeing king survives but the castle where Mary, Queen of Scots was detained for years – destroyed by Act of Parliament but never totally abandoned – is now a striking ruin.

❶ Moseley Old Hall

September 22, 1651: 'Arrived the news of the fatal battle at Worcester, which exceedingly mortified our expectations.'
Diarist John Evelyn had been abroad when the Royalists were routed at the Battle of Worcester. Now, back in London 18 days after the event, he heard the crushing news. But what of Charles II? If he had not been killed or taken prisoner, where was he? It must have seemed that he had disappeared off the face of the earth. After hiding at Boscobel House (see page 149) he was brought by the Penderell brothers to the home of the Whitegreave family, travelling under cloak of darkness, and arriving in the early hours of September 8. Thomas Whitegreave gave Charles II dry clothes and food, and for the first time since the battle he could rest on a bed. For two days he was hidden in a priest hole, along with the family's priest, John Huddleston, who bathed and bandaged his sore feet, while plans were advanced for his escape. These brave Catholic families took a terrible risk in rescuing the king, and played a significant role in history.

The house dates from around 1600, and remained the property of the Whitegreaves until 1925, during which time they made a very few structural alterations. It seems that the family moved away after the 1820s, preferring the Regency-style Moseley Court. Old Hall was in a state of neglect when it was acquired by the National Trust in 1962. It has been fully restored, with heavy oak panelling, and the four-poster where Charles II rested is still in the King's Room. Other period furniture is on display, too, and there are a number of paintings of Charles II.
▶ *WV10 7HY. Wolverhampton, just SW of Junction 1 of M54. NT.*

❷ Staffordshire Potteries

The official commemorative china for the wedding of Prince William and Catherine Middleton was made here in 2011, and the choice of these famous potteries for the task was a crowning achievement. They have been a centre of ceramic production since the 17th century. The term 'Staffordshire Potteries' describes an area of six towns – Turnstall, Burslem, Hanley, Stoke, Fenton and Longton – united as Stoke-on-Trent.

Each piece of fine bone china made for the Royal Collection bears the couple's entwined initials, 'C' and 'W', in gold and silver, surmounted by Prince William's coronet and the wedding date. The range is decorated with doves, white ribbons and hearts in silver, gold and grey, against a pale-grey striped background.
▶ *ST1 3DW. Museum and Art Gallery in Stoke-on-Trent. Access from Junctions 15 and 16 of M6.*

❸ Tutbury Castle

Mary, Queen of Scots was brought to this damp and draughty edifice from Bolton Castle. She fell ill on the journey, and on arrival must have felt, for the first time, that she was truly a prisoner. The castle, which was built for John of Gaunt, had been a powerhouse in the 15th century, under the Lancastrian kings, but by the time Mary arrived, in February 1569, it was in decline. She described her prison as 'sitting squarely on top of a mountain in the middle of a plain'. Here she was to live for many years in the custody of a reluctant George Talbot, Earl of Shrewsbury, spending her days reading, writing and sewing with Shrewsbury's wife, Bess of Hardwick. She made gifts to send to powerful figures, including her cousin Elizabeth I, who had ordered her detention. She sewed a dress and night coiffes (bonnets) for Bess, and reins for her son, James VI of Scotland, the future James I of England. When Nicholas White stopped off at Tutbury, he reported to his master, William Cecil, Elizabeth's chief minister, 'All the day she wrought with her needle and that the diversity of colours made the time less tedious.' Mary must have worked with numbed fingers, as the 'injures of heaven' howled through the cracks. White further related that 'she hath withal an alluring grace … and a searching wit clouded with mildness'. Her darkest days began in April 1585 when Puritan jailer Sir Amyas Paulet denied Mary even her walk in the garden. Almost two years later she would meet her end at Fotheringhay (see page 147). Tutbury Castle met its end in 1647, when under an Act of Parliament it was partially destroyed for support given to Charles I in the Civil War, resulting in the dramatic ruins that remain today.
▶ *DE13 9JF. 5 miles N of Burton on Trent.*

WARWICKSHIRE

The shades of Elizabeth and Leicester drift across this landscape, in and out of castles and churches, echoing the footsteps of kings, queens princes and kingmakers, forever preserving their mutual affinity.

❶ The Battle of Edgehill

'So now was that bloody difference between the King and Parliament broken out, which ended in the fatal tragedy so many years after … This day was fought that signal battle of Edgehill.' Diarist John Evelyn was writing in hindsight about the first battle of the Civil War. On October 23, 1642, the army of the Earl of Essex clashed with the king's army at Edgehill, near Kineton. It was supposed to be one great battle that would decide the issue. It broke out at nightfall, and ended when Essex and his men retreated to the garrison at Warwick, leaving the Royalists in control of the road to London. The opposing forces were evenly matched, each some 15,000 strong. The terrain is much changed and public access limited, but visitors can reflect upon a day that left 1,000 dead and nothing resolved.
▶ *8 miles NW of Banbury, off B4086.*

❷ Charlecote Park

The Lucy family came to England with William the Conqueror and have owned the land here since 1247. Deer have roamed the park that surrounds their grand country home, on the banks of the Avon, for slightly less time.

Charlecote was built by Sir Thomas Lucy in 1558. Elizabeth I spent a night here in 1572, sleeping in what is today the drawing room. Her arms are displayed over the porch. In outline, the house is Tudor. It was modified over generations, but in 1823 George Hammond Lucy set about returning it to its original style. Allegedly, the fallow deer 'have been here since Tudor times'. There is even a story that William Shakespeare was caught poaching rabbit and deer in the park in his youth, and that Sir Thomas 'had him oft whipt' for his crime. However, the antiquary John Leland, passing by in Tudor times, made no mention of a park, only noting, 'Here Mr Lucy hath an ancient Mannour Place on the left Ripe of Avon.' Not until 1618, in the reign of James I, did the third Sir Thomas Lucy take out a licence from the Crown to maintain a deer park.

There is a fine collection of family portraits in the Great Hall, which has a barrel-vaulted ceiling. In the dining room is 'the Warwickshire Sideboard', a masterpiece of craftsmanship, shown with pride to Queen Victoria when she visited. The landscape of the park today was inspired by the work of Capability Brown and laid out in around 1760.
▶ *CV35 9ER. 6 miles S of Warwick just W of A429. NT.*

CHARLECOTE PARK

❸ Kenilworth Castle

'... the sweetness of savour on all sides, made so respirant from the redolent plants and fragrant herbs and flowers, in form, colour, and quantity so deliciously variant; and fruit-trees bedecked with apples, pears, and ripe cherries ...' When Elizabeth I granted Kenilworth Castle to her favourite, Robert Dudley, Earl of Leicester, he set about transforming it into a splendid palace in which to receive his queen. He commissioned the garden described by Robert Langham, keeper of the council door, who was allowed to see this private Eden by a gardener one day when the queen was out hunting. In his letter extolling 'The Magnificent Pageants presented before Queen Elizabeth at Keinilworth in 1575' Langham writes of 'obelisks, and spheres, and white bears, all of stone upon their curious bases', of 'lively Birds, English, French, Spanish, Canarian, and I am deceived if I saw not some African'. He tells of a 'very fair fountain', of arbours and every imaginable delight. Elizabeth visited four times on her summer progresses – the last time in July 1575, when she stayed for 19 days. She never spent longer at a courtier's house. In her honour, Dudley, who had long hoped to marry her, built lavish apartments, richly decorated, hung with tapestries, and with great windows affording captivating views.

Although Langham's account of the garden seems fanciful, archaeological study confirms the existence of an eight-sided fountain as he describes. Lost for more than 400 years, the garden was reconstructed in 2009. The castle was built over several centuries and was the scene of the enforced abdication of Edward II in 1326. Kenilworth was a Lancastrian base in the Wars of the Roses, and was partly destroyed by Parliamentary forces in 1649. Two of its buildings remain habitable; the rest are noble ruins.
▶ *CV8 1NE. 5 miles SW of Coventry at junction of A429 and A452. EH.*

❹ St Nicholas' Church

Here, Elizabeth I and Robert Dudley came to pray more than once when the queen visited Kenilworth during her summer progress of 1575. Apparently, on one occasion they heard a 'most fruitful sermon'. On a pinnacle on the south side of the church there is a weathered sundial, which, when viewed from a distance, can be seen to bear the badge of Dudley, Earl of Leicester, the 'Bear and Ragged Staff'.
▶ *CV8 1BP. Church in Kenilworth town centre.*

❺ Warwick Castle

Despite a violent history, Warwick survives as everyone's ideal of the quintessential English castle. If Rapunzel were to let down her hair from one of the towers, it should hardly be surprising. The castle's origins can be traced back to Saxon times when a fortification was built for Ethelfreda, daughter of Alfred the Great. A timber motte-and-bailey castle was constructed in 1068, on the orders of William the Conqueror. By the early 13th century it had been replaced by a stone castle with a shell keep, crenellated walls and fighting platforms within a curtain wall. Substantial rebuilding took place in the 14th and 15th centuries. The addition of the irregular quatrefoil Caesar's Tower and the 12-sided, five-storey Guy's Tower transformed the castle.

Among the castle's many formidable inhabitants was Richard Neville, 16th Earl of Warwick. Known as 'Kingmaker', Warwick was one of the main protagonists in the Wars of the Roses, responsible for the deposition of two kings. In the 1480s, the castle was held by the Duke of Gloucester, the future Richard III, who commissioned an additional tower. Elizabeth I visited on her progress of 1566, returning in 1572, when she spent four nights in a timber building erected especially for her. On a Sunday, from her window she watched country folk dancing in the courtyard, firework displays and a mock battle. In the Civil War, the castle fought off besieging Royalists, and in the 17th and 18th centuries considerable extravagant refurbishment took place. When Victoria and Albert came to lunch in 1858, they were entertained in the State Dining Room before making a tour of the ramparts and planting trees in the garden.
▶ *CV34 4QU. Off A46, 2 miles from M40 (Junction 15). Castle in town centre.*

❻ St Mary's Church

'I continue still your medicine and find that [it] amends much better than with any other thing that hath been given me. Thus hoping to find perfect cure at the bath ...' Robert Dudley was aged 56 and in failing health. On August 29, 1588, he was on his way to the spa at Buxton, a well-established curative centre, which was often visited by members of the court, when he wrote his last letter to his beloved Elizabeth. He did not make it to Buxton, and when news reached the queen of the death of her 'Sweet Robin', her 'Eyes', she descended into the deepest grief. She kept the letter in a box at her bedside for the rest of her life.

ST MARY'S CHURCH

Dudley's wife, Lettice Knolly, spent £4,000 on his funeral, and he was buried in the Beauchamp Chapel of the Collegiate Church of St Mary's, alongside his son, Robert Dudley, Lord Denbigh. Little Robert, who had died in 1584, aged three, was affectionately nicknamed 'the noble Impe', suggesting that even the most ambitious and power-hungry in those times took delight in their chidren. In 1634, Lettice joined her husband and son. Their tombs are appropriately fine.

▶ *CV34 4RA. Church in Warwick town centre.*

❼ Royal Leamington Spa

'Where but a few years before Cattle grazed undisturbedly and yellow Corn waved, and the plough Boy whistled carelessly over the lea, we now behold … extensive Mansions, arising as if by magic, fit for Royalty, and these arrive on Friday Sep 9th, 1819, his Royal Highness the Prince Regent, accompanied by the Earl and Countess of Warwick.' Sarah Medley, in *The Beauties of Leamington Spa*, describes the impact of a royal visit on a resort in the golden age of spa bathing. The fashion for taking the waters resulted in the population of the village of Leamington Priors growing from 543 in 1811 to 12,600 by 1841, and in that time some fine Regency buildings had sprung up to accommodate them. The Pump Room opened five years before the future George IV came strolling through, declaring himself 'highly gratified with the varied beauties of the excursion'.

Among the diseases for which the waters famously proved salubrious were liver and bilious complaints, visceral obstruction, obstinate costive habits, hypochondriasis, cutaneous eruptions, scrophulous tumours, white swelling of the knee, and of course rheumatism and gout. It was visits from Victoria, however, both as princess in 1830, and as queen in 1838, that brought the town the ultimate seal of approval, with the granting of the 'Royal' prefix as a special mark of her favour. Victoria's statue, made of Sicilian marble, was moved an inch on its plinth in World War II when a German bomb fell close by.

Today, the Pump Room is home to Leamington's art gallery, museum and library, and there is also a café.

▶ *CV32 4AA (Pump Rooms on the Parade). 10 miles S of Coventry.*

CENTRAL ENGLAND

155

WORCESTERSHIRE

Two parliamentarians brought carnage to this fertile terrain. One, a medieval baron ahead of his time, was killed and monarchy restored; the other, a puritanical republican, put a young king to flight.

❶ The Battle of Evesham

'Let us commend our souls to God, because our bodies are theirs.' Simon de Monfort, Earl of Leicester, surely knew that his forces were no match for the army of Prince Edward (later Edward I) at their final showdown. The king's son had been taken prisoner at the Battle of Lewes (see page 72), but in May 1265 he escaped, meeting in June with Gilbert the Red in Ludlow, raising an army and capturing Gloucester. There had, meanwhile, been discontent among Leicester's confederacy of barons, who had overthrown the Crown only to find the earl behaving like a despotic king. Many of them rallied to the prince's banner.

On the morning of May 26, 1265, bringing along Henry III as a captive, de Montfort led out his cavalry to confront a force that outnumbered his men by three to one. On the summit of Greenhill or thereabouts, de Montfort headed an attack on three divisions of royal forces, putting some of them to flight. But he had rightly judged the hopelessness of his cause, and his troops were swiftly surrounded and scythed down – de Montfort was killed and dismembered. Fugitives were pursued back to the town, where blood ran in the streets. An eyewitness called it, 'the murder at Evesham, for battle it was none'. Henry was restored to the throne, and was succeeded by his far more able son, Edward I, in 1272.

Despite some 20th-century development, the character of the land is not much changed. Although he perhaps let power go to his head, Simon de Montfort is today regarded as the man who called the first true Parliament. He invited each county to send two elected representatives. Three memorials to him stand near the battle site, including an impressive obelisk.
▶ *15 miles SE of Worcester at junction of A44 and A46.*

❷ The Battle of Worcester

'On September 3, 1651 – nine years after the first battle of the Civil War was fought scarcely two miles away – the army of the uncrowned king, Charles II, lost a final bid to regain the throne. In the first engagement, Prince Rupert's Royalist cavalry had been triumphant. Now the Royalists faced a more deadly enemy, a mean fighting machine, Oliver Cromwell's New Model Army. The king's troops numbered some 12,000; Cromwell's 28,000. Around 3,000 Royalists were killed and 7,000 captured. Just 200 or so died for Parliament.

The carnage happened south of Worcester, and the best sense of it can be had between Powick Bridge and the confluence of the Rivers Severn and Teme. Powick church bears scars from shot. At the heart of the city, in the Commandery, is a Civil War visitors' centre, where the story is told. It is possible to climb to the top of the cathedral tower to scan the terrain, as Charles did as the fateful hour approached. Footpaths lead across the battlefield, north of the Teme and on both sides of the Severn, the great river that thwarted Charles's hope of escape to Wales.

On his triumphant return from exile in 1660, he 'fell into discourse of his escape at Worcester' with diarist Samuel Pepys, who wrote: 'It made me ready to weep to hear the stories that he told of his difficulties that he had passed through, as his travelling four days and three nights on foot, every step up to his knees in dirt, with nothing but a green coat and a pair of country breeches on, and a pair of country shoes that made him so sore all over his feet, that he could scarce stir.' But he had lived to tell the tale.
▶ *Battlefield 2 miles S of Worcester city centre. WR1 2HU for Commandery, WR1 2LA for Cathedral.*

❸ Royal Worcester Porcelain Museum

'The visit of King George III and Queen Charlotte to the Porcelain Works commenced a new era in the history of the manufactory.' In his *Guide through the Royal Porcelain Works*, the then managing director, E.P. Evans, conveys something of the value of royal patronage to such a business. Until the 18th century, porcelain came from the Far East (hence 'China'). British potters were much preoccupied with discovering the formula. In 1751 a medical doctor, John Wall, and an apothecary, William Davis, developed a method of porcelain production and convinced a group of businessmen to invest in a factory at Worcester on the banks of the Severn.

The factory made its first royal dinner service for the Duke of Gloucester, George III's brother. 'The Worcester Tonquin Manufactory' was sold to

THE KING GRANTED A WARRANT
ROYAL WORCESTER MUSEUM

Thomas Flight in 1783, and in 1788 the king granted a royal warrant to what could now call itself the 'Royal Porcelain Works'. With this came the right to use the royal coat of arms and the words 'Manufacturers to their Majesties'

Mr Evans tells us that, 'having recommended that an establishment should be opened in London, the Royal family and the Nobility generally speedily availed themselves of the facilities thus offered'. In 1830, William IV chose Royal Worcester to make the Coronation Service. In 1860, Prince Albert admired the Worcester enamels and ordered a dessert service for Queen Victoria.

The first Royal Worcester factory museum was opened in November 1879. The present museum was opened by Princess Elizabeth in 1951, and Royal Worcester still produces porcelain by appointment to Her Majesty Elizabeth II.

▶ *WR1 2ND. Museum in Worcester city centre.*

❹ The Monarch's Way

The uncrowned king Charles II fled defeat at Worcester, and set off on a harrowing journey, in fear for his life. The modern rambler can follow his route in a more relaxed frame of mind, visiting places where he found shelter. The fugitive Charles's flight to France is described on page 150-151. Walkers setting off from Worcester on a trail of 650 miles are guided by waymarks on a snaking journey that leads across the Mendips, to the Dorset coast, across the Downs, and at length to Shoreham-by-Sea – where fair stood the wind for France.
▶ *Footpath starts at the Old Powick Bridge in Worcester and is waymarked along its length with a symbol of a ship and oak tree.*

❺ Witley Court

Here is a mirage, a dream, a vast shell of a palatial home once loaned to Queen Adelaide, widow of William IV. A Jacobean brick manor house was built on this site for the Russell family, and sold to Thomas Foley in 1655. He added towers on the north side, and his grandson, Thomas, 1st Lord Foley, added wings that enclose the entrance courtyard. A new parish church was constructed in the west courtyard in 1735, and James Gibb was engaged to create a fantastic baroque interior in 1747, using paintings and furnishings bought at auction from the Middlesex home of the Duke of Chandos. In the latter 18th century, the entire village of Great Witley was relocated to clear the way for a landscaped park, and in 1805 the 3rd Lord Foley commissioned John Nash to carry out ambitious rebuilding, including the addition of vast Ionic porticoes to the north and south fronts (probably the largest of any country house in England). So it was a very splendid country house that Queen Adelaide borrowed from the Dudley family in 1843. Courtiers were entertained with music from pianos tuned for her by a local man, William Elgar. His son, the composer Edward Elgar, Master of the King's Musick, would later play for the Dudleys in the ornate music room. When fire tore through the building in 1937, it spared the church but left the house a spectacular ruin, open to the skies. In recent times, under the care of English Heritage, the park created by William Andrews Nesfield (his 'monster work') has been restored – and the massive Perseus and Andromeda fountain in the south parterre garden once again roars like an express train.
▶ *WR6 6JT. Great Witley, 10 miles NW of Worcester on A443. EH.*

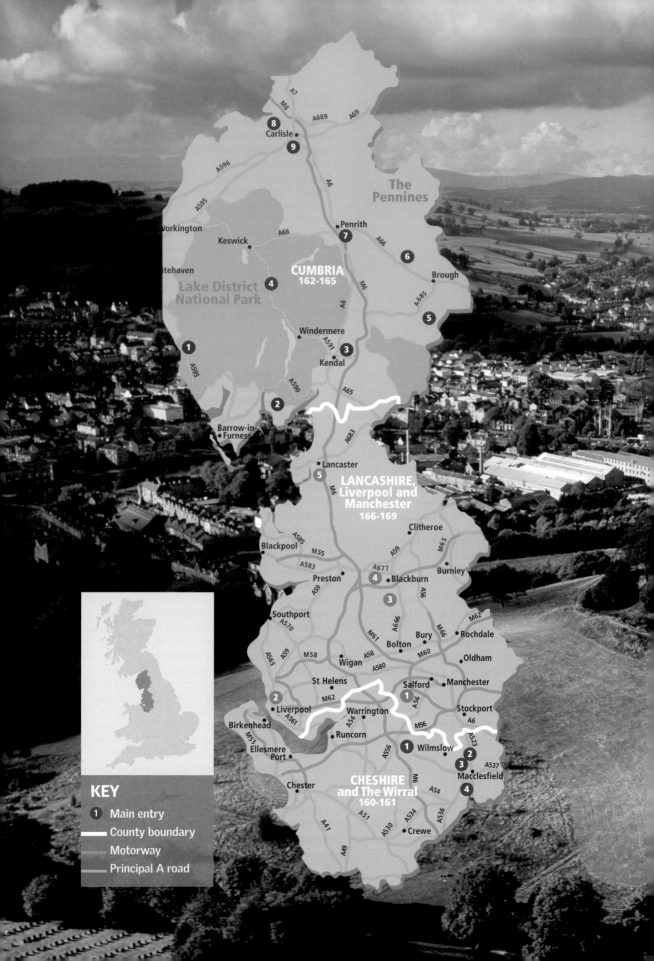

KEY

1 Main entry

— County boundary

Motorway

Principal A road

CUMBRIA
162–165

The Pennines

Lake District
National Park

Carlisle

Workington

Keswick

Whitehaven

Penrith

Brough

Windermere

Kendal

Barrow-in-Furness

**LANCASHIRE,
Liverpool and
Manchester**
166–169

Lancaster

Clitheroe

Blackpool

Preston

Blackburn

Burnley

Southport

Bolton

Bury

Rochdale

Wigan

Oldham

St Helens

Salford

Manchester

Liverpool

Warrington

Stockport

Birkenhead

Runcorn

Wilmslow

Ellesmere
Port

Macclesfield

Chester

**CHESHIRE
and The Wirral**
160–161

Crewe

A7

M6

A689

A69

A596

A595

A6

A66

A66

M6

A685

A6

A591

A65

A590

A683

M6

A585

M55

A59

A677

A583

A59

A570

A666

M61

M66

M62

A565

A59

M58

A58

A580

M60

A56

A56

M62

A561

A56

M56

A6

M53

A56

A523

A537

M6

A54

A51

A530

A534

A536

A41

A49

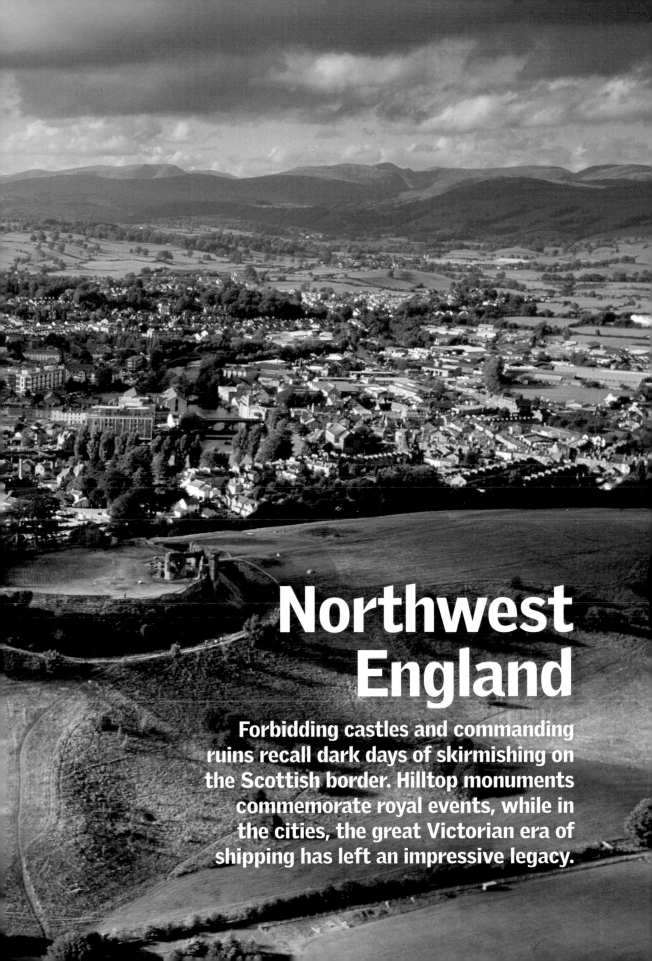

Northwest England

Forbidding castles and commanding ruins recall dark days of skirmishing on the Scottish border. Hilltop monuments commemorate royal events, while in the cities, the great Victorian era of shipping has left an impressive legacy.

CHESHIRE & THE WIRRAL

Tales of Tudor misbehaviour that outraged the queen vie for attention with Arthurian legend. A gift from William the Conqueror survives as a Georgian mansion, and sand in the streets amused the young Victoria.

❶ Knutsford

'We arrived at Knutsford, where we were most civilly received, the streets being sanded in shapes, which is particular to the town.' Victoria was writing, in 1832, of the peculiar May Day tradition of using coloured sand to create patterns and pictures on the street. These reflect the legend that King Cnut, while fording the River Lily in 1017, threw sand into the path of a wedding party, to wish the happy couple as many children as there were grains of sand. It is an appealing but improbable notion that Knutsford derives from Cnut's Ford.

▶ *15 miles SW of Manchester, close to Junction 19 of M6.*

❷ Adlington Hall

Earl Edwin of Mercia was relieved of his manor and hunting lodge by William the Conqueror, who gave the land to Hugh d'Avranche, Earl of Chester. Hugh can't have done much hunting. He became so obese that he could hardly walk. He was known also as Hugh Lupus (wolf), and Hugh the Fat. The lodge remained the property of the Norman earls until the reign of Henry III, who took it for the Crown, then gave it to Hugh de Corona.

In the reign of Edward II it became the ancestral home of the Legh family, since which time it has changed beyond recognition. Of the original hunting lodge just two oaks remain, around which the lodge was constructed. They stand at the east end of the Great Hall, which was built of timber between 1480 and 1505, and later

GAWSWORTH HALL

refaced with brick and stone. In the Civil War this was a Royalist garrison, held for the king by Colonel Thomas Legh. The moat provided a useful defence, although the hall was taken by Parliament first in 1642 and again in 1644. It was confiscated from Colonel Thomas Legh the Younger after the war, but he recovered it in 1656, when it was suffering from damage and neglect. Charles Legh, who inherited Adlington in 1739, was responsible for the transformation of a fairly modest Tudor dwelling into a fine Georgian manor with a ballroom running the length of the first floor. Further changes were made in 1928 to designs by the architect Sir Hubert Worthington.

▶ *SK10 4LF. 4 miles E of Wilmslow, just W of A523.*

❸ Alderley Edge

Legend has it that King Arthur's knights sleep in a cave beneath the 'Edge', and will ride out again in England's hour of need. (However, see also Sewingfield Crags, page 173; as with all things Arthurian, there is more mystery than history.) Close to Castle Rock is a natural spring known as the Wizard's Well. A wizard's face was carved into the rock some 200 years ago, and an inscription reads: 'Drink of this and take thy fill, for the water falls by the wizard's will.' Fanciful though this may seem, visitors to this dramatic, red-sandstone, oak-clad escarpment will find it magical.

▶ *Just N of B5087, 2 miles S of Wilmslow. NT.*

❹ Gawsworth Hall

'Thine eyes I love, and they as pitying me,/Knowing thy heart torment me with disdain.' Who was the 'Dark Lady' of Shakespeare's sonnets? Among the names proposed is that of Mary Fitton, younger daughter of Sir Edward and Lady Alice Fitton, whose home this was. Mary became a maid of honour to Elizabeth I, her father trusting Sir William Knollys to chaperone her. Having promised to be 'as careful of her well doing as if I were her own true father', Knollys, aged 50 and married, became besotted with her – and was mocked at court for his passion. For a time she was compelled to leave, suffering from a form of hysteria known by Elizabethans as 'the mother' (King Lear bewails it: 'O, how the mother swells up towards my heart! Hysterica passio, down, those climbing sorrows.') Upon her recovery and return she gave Knollys the brush-off, and in her turn pursued William Herbert, Earl of Pembroke, by whom she became pregnant, earning both their dismissals by the indignant queen.

The original Norman house at Gawsworth was rebuilt in 1480 and further remodelled in 1701. It was the scene of an infamous duel in 1712 between Lord Mohun and the Duke of Hamilton, fought over the estate. The duel ended in a draw – both were killed. A tiltyard forms part of a large Elizabethan pleasure garden that lies within acres of parkland. A brick tomb in Maggoty Johnson's Wood at Gawsworth commemorates another former resident, Samuel Johnson – not the lexicographer, but the last professional jester, also known as Lord Flame, who died in 1773. The half-timbered house is beautiful and fascinating.

▶ *SK11 9RN. Just E of A536, 3 miles SW of Macclesfield.*

CUMBRIA

Amid myths and ghostly tales, royal intentions focused on war and defence with the building of border fortresses, while one determined lady battled on until she had regained her rightful inheritance.

❶ Muncaster Castle

Henry VI, lost and wandering after the Battle of Hexham in 1464, was given shelter here by Sir John Pennington. This castle, overlooking the River Esk, was founded in 1258 and enlarged in the 1300s, gaining a pele tower, and in 1783, John Pennington, Lord Muncaster, built the tower known as Chapels to mark the rescue of the king. Henry VI was a military liability, and was kept away from the action at Hexham. But he was a king for all that, and upon leaving, had bestowed upon the family his drinking bowl – the 'Luck of Muncaster' – with the promise that as long as it remained unbroken, Penningtons would live and thrive here.

The 1st Baron Muncaster ordered extensive renovations in the late 1700s, and the castle was further updated in 1862 on the orders of the 4th Lord Muncaster, when Anthony Salvin covered the courtyard with a barrel-vaulted ceiling to create the Drawing Room. Upon the death of the 5th Lord Muncaster in 1917, the Pennington male line died out and the estate reverted to his mother's family, the Ramsdens. In 1983 the castle, 'with all its beauties and liabilities', was handed

HENRY VI, LOST AND WANDERING, WAS GIVEN SHELTER HERE
MUNCASTER CASTLE

over by Sir William Pennington-Ramsden to his daughter Phyllida as her family home. The 'liabilities' include a number of ghosts. Chilling are the tales of Tom Skelton, nicknamed Tom Fool, castle jester in the 16th century, who still indulges his sadistic sense of humour. A child is sometimes heard crying, a woman sings to comfort a sick infant, door handles turn and doors open inexplicably.

▶ *CA18 1RQ. On A595, 1 mile E of Ravenglass.*

❷ Holker Hall

The bedroom where Queen Mary slept in 1937 appears just as she would have seen it, with William Morris fabrics, George I gilded armchairs, a Minton washstand, Venetian glass candlesticks (adapted for electricity) and a 19th-century armoire from Normandy. Such attention to detail continues throughout the home of Lord and Lady Cavendish. Since the earliest record of a house here, Holker has been in the ownership of the Preston, Lowther and Cavendish families, never bought or sold, passing down through inheritance, subject to alteration, refurbishment, ornamentation – and, in the wake of a fire in 1871, partially rebuilt. Along with the west wing, paintings, statues, rare books and antiques were lost. The 7th Duke of Devonshire, rising to the challenge, employed the Lancashire pioneer architects Edward Graham Paley and Hubert Austin to refurbish it on a grand scale. This wing is open to the public. Architectural historian Nikolaus Pevsner deemed the work 'the grandest of its date in Lancashire [as it then was] by the best architects living in the county … It is their outstanding work, red sandstone in the Elizabethan style.' In the silk-lined Drawing Room, on a Chippendale silver table, is the book on Buckingham Palace that was a gift from Queen Mary on her stay. The gardens and parkland are ravishing.

▶ *LA11 7PL. 4 miles W of Grange-over-Sands.*

❸ Kendal Castle

By the time Catherine Parr married Henry VIII in 1543, this castle was already a ruin. At one time, it was thought that Henry's sixth queen was born here, but by Tudor times it was derelict. The stone castle was founded by William de Lancaster in the early 13th century on the site of a 12th-century fortress, which de Lancaster enclosed within a curtain wall. Richard II granted it to a prominent local family, the Parrs, who can't have valued it greatly since it was abandoned. All the same, it is worth climbing Castle Hill – bought by Kendal Corporation for 'public enjoyment' in 1897 to celebrate Queen Victoria's Diamond Jubilee – to see what remains, and to enjoy spectacular views. Catherine's prayer book is kept at the town hall. An exhibition at Kendal Museum tells the story of the castle and the life of the town famous for its mint cake and as the original home of K Shoes.
▶ *6 miles W of Junction 37 of M6. Castle just E of Kendal town centre.*

❹ Dunmail Raise and Grisedale Tarn

A large cairn on a hilltop in the Lake District National Park is reputed to be the burial mound of Dunmail, the last king of Cumbria. According to legend, this was the scene of a battle between Dunmail and the combined forces of Malcolm, King of Scotland, and a Saxon king, Edmund. Dunmail was slain. His sons were mutilated and his men were forced to build the cairn where he fell. His golden crown was thrown into Grisedale Tarn, and has never been recovered. His lands went to Malcolm.
▶ *Dunmail Raise on A591, 3 miles N of Grasmere. Grisedale Tarn 1 mile E.*

❺ Pendragon Castle

Legend has it that a castle was founded here by Uther Pendragon, father of King Arthur. According to the tale, a hundred of Pendragon's men died here when Saxon invaders poisoned the well. What the curious can see are the remains of a Norman castle beside the River Eden. It was built in around 1160 by Hugh de Morville, Lord of Westmorland, who served Henry II and was one of the assassins of Thomas Becket. The castle was owned by the Clifford family when it was torched by Scottish raiders in 1341. In 1360 it was rebuilt as one of the largest keeps in northern England, and was occupied until another fire, in 1541, left it in ruins. Despite this, George Clifford, 3rd Earl of Cumberland, a courtier, admiral and accomplished jouster, chose to style himself 'Knight of Pendragon Castle'. He was a witness to the execution of Mary, Queen of Scots, and commanded the *Bonaventure* against the Spanish Armada. A favourite of Elizabeth's, he wore one of her gloves in his jewel-encrusted hat.

In defiance of an entail dating from the reign of Edward II, George disinherited his daughter Anne, and on his death in 1605, the Clifford barony passed to his brother Francis. Lady Anne, aged 15, embarked upon a marathon legal battle to claim what was rightfully hers, and the estate finally reverted to her in 1644. As a child she had dreamed of restoring Pendragon Castle, and she spent Christmas 1663 within its walls, noting that this was the first time for more than a century that her family had stayed there. After her death in 1676 the castle fell into ruin once more.
▶ *4 miles S of Kirkby Stephen on B6259.*

❻ Appleby Castle

'I have been bullied by a usurper. I have been neglected by a Court, but I will not be dictated to by a subject. Your man shan't stand. Anne Dorset, Pembroke and Montgomery.' Lady Anne Clifford had made it her life's mission to claim the Clifford estates. Only on the death of her nephew, the 5th Earl of Cumberland, in 1643, did vast tracts of Westmorland revert to her, including this fine castle. Even then, she would have to wait until after the Civil War had ended to begin an ambitious rebuilding programme. Having been so tenacious in pursuit of her rights, she was taking no nonsense from Sir John Williamson, Secretary of State to Charles II, who had written to name a candidate for the borough of Appleby. His man would not stand!

This castle, at the heart of the Eden Valley, was begun when William Rufus won most of Westmorland from the Scots in 1092. The keep, Caesar's Tower, is the oldest surviving part. Appleby Castle was owned by kings of England but seized by the Scottish King William in 1174. It became the fortress of the Clifford barons, and finally home to Lady Anne. The round tower and parts of the walls date from the 13th century. The eastern segment was built in 1454. The castle was partially demolished in 1648 and restored by her ladyship. On her death in 1676 it passed to the Earls of Thanet, and the hall block was converted into a classical mansion. Further restoration and modernisation was carried out in the 19th century.
▶ *CA16 6XH. Appleby-in-Westmorland on A66, 13 miles SE of Penrith. Castle in town centre.*

❼ Penrith Castle

'Penrith is agreeably situated on the slope of a hill with a southern aspect. It is a neat and clean, and well-built town; its castle is a noble ruin.' William Cobbett, in *A Tour Through England Described in a Series of Letters from a Young Man*, written in 1806, could be describing Penrith Castle today. It remains a noble ruin, a square of red sandstone, some walls standing to full height, in a public green space.

It was built in the late 1300s, probably by Ralph Neville, 1st Earl of Westmorland, who, as warden of the West March, had the task of defending the Scottish border. Other accounts attribute it to William Strickland, later Bishop of Carlisle and Archbishop of Canterbury, and suggest that Ralph's son Richard, 1st Earl of Salisbury, made it his headquarters, adding the Red Tower and strengthening the defences. In July 1471, the castle passed to Richard, Duke of Gloucester, Lord Warden of the Marches toward Scotland, the future Richard III, courtesy of his older brother, Edward IV. Richard ordered improvements, including the addition of a banqueting hall.

The ruination probably began with damage inflicted during the Civil War, when it was a base for the Parliamentary general John Lambert. The castle remained part of the Crown Estate until the reign of William III, who gave it to Hans Willem Bentick, 1st Earl of Portland. The castle eventually, and more prosaically, passed to the Carlisle Railway Company, and then to Penrith Urban District Council, who converted the grounds to a park in 1920.

▶ *CA11 7JQ. Penrith close to Junction 40 of M6. Castle just S of town centre. EH.*

❽ St Michael's Church

A stained-glass window depicts Edward I, whose body lay in state in this humble 12th-century church, a world away from Westminster Abbey where he is buried. 'The Hammer of the Scots' was on his way to fight Robert the Bruce when he died in 1307. On the death of Alexander III of Scotland, Edward had claimed the right to nominate his successor, favouring John Balliol over Robert the Bruce. The Scots, unhappy at this turn of events, formed an alliance with Philip IV of France, and in 1296 Edward led an army north, forcing a Scottish surrender and seizing the Stone of Scone, a sacred symbol of Scottish nationhood (see page 204). Over the years, fighting continued. Edward suffered setbacks at the hands of William Wallace,

but even with Wallace's capture and execution in 1305, the situation was not resolved. Hence Edward's final journey in 1307.

The church was built within a Roman fort on Hadrian's Wall in the late 1100s. In July 2007 the Duke of Kent unveiled a bronze statue on the village green to mark the 700th anniversary of Edward's death. There is a monument to him nearby on Solway Plain, and a Latin inscription proclaims him 'the greatest English king'. This must depend on whether or not it can be considered an achievement to have initiated the Hundred Years War with France and ushered in 300 years of warfare with Scotland. Daniel Defoe was unequivocal: 'No English man, that has any honour for the glorious memory and truest hero of all our kings of the English or Saxon race, can go to Carlisle, and not step aside to see the monument of King Edward I, at Burgh upon the Sands … where the victorious prince dy'd.'

▶ *CA5 6AP. Burgh by Sands, 6 miles NW of Carlisle.*

❾ Carlisle Castle

'The castle is a very large, lofty pile, now used for the purpose of one of those great modern improvements commonly known as barracks. Upon the top has been recently erected a sort of shed for the purpose of placing musket, in a situation to shoot up the streets if necessary.' This forbidding red-stone castle was built to repel the Scots, although by the time William Cobbett saw it in 1832, its fighting days were over.

In 1122, Henry I ordered the building of a stone castle on the site of a timber one. The Scots, who then owned Cumberland, were not easily driven out. Carlisle city and castle were captured by the Scottish King David, and held for several years in the reign of Stephen. Henry VIII had the stronghold converted for artillery, employing the Moravian armourer and architect Stefan von Haschenperg as surveyor of the works, but after two years Haschenperg was sacked for having 'lewdlye behaved himself' and overspent. For a few months in 1568, the castle was a prison for Mary, Queen of Scots, but her quarters have been pulled down. In the Civil War the castle held out for eight months for the king. In 1745 it was caught up in the second Jacobite rising when Charles Edward Stuart, 'Bonnie Prince Charlie', attempted to reclaim the throne. In the next century it was partly demolished. It served as a depot for the Border Regiment until 1959, and today is home to the regiment's museum.

▶ *CA3 8UR. Access Carlisle from Junctions 42, 43 or 44 of M6. Castle in city centre. EH.*

LANCASHIRE, LIVERPOOL & MANCHESTER

John of Gaunt's grim castle and a haunted house may still cause a few shivers, but these are dispelled by the sight of Victorian innovation at its best, and a monument to the queen's sixty years in the top job.

❶ Manchester Ship Canal

'A strain of purely joyous sentiment suggestive of youth and high hopes and bright anticipation' animated the crowds, the *Manchester Guardian* recorded on May 21, 1894. The occasion was the arrival in the city of Queen Victoria, and the official opening of this historic waterway, which would assure 'more direct friendly commerce … with the uttermost parts of the world'. For the queen's visit, the city council pulled out the stops. It had set aside £10,000 for decorations, and men from the fire brigade had been up ladders creating an archway on Deansgate. People had decked their houses, putting out the flags. The royal train drew in to

what is now Piccadilly station and the royal party were taken on a tour by carriage before arriving at a special pavilion on the Stretford side of the canal. The queen took her seat on the royal yacht *Enchantress*. The Lord Mayor of Manchester and the Mayor of Salford were knighted, and a 21-gun salute from the nearby racecourse marked the moment when the queen pulled a cord, the lock gates opened, and the *Norseman* glided out.

In 1994, the Princess Royal attended centenary celebrations for the canal, and the Queen opened Centenary Bridge, linking Trafford Park with the motorway system and uttermost parts of the realm for friendly commerce.

▶ *Canal runs for 36 miles from Manchester to the River Mersey.*

❷ Liverpool, Albert Dock

'All gaiety and splendour' attended the first royal state visit to Liverpool, when Prince Albert opened the docks named after him, in July 1846. According to the *Pictorial Times*, 'balconies were erected along the line of procession, and these and the windows of houses were filled with gay and animated parties. There was a most brilliant display of flags, banners & c. All business is suspended. There are 200,000 strangers in town, and all the inhabitants are in the streets.' The river was thronged with boats. Cheering and the deafening roar of artillery filled the air. Albert sailed from the Cheshire side of the Mersey aboard the *Fairy*, which performed a lap of honour, to the delight of onlookers. Dock engineer Jesse Hartley had used Scottish granite, red sandstone, brick and limestone for the impressive buildings, and his design was considered radical. However, the dock was conceived for sailing ships and was too small for the steamers that would replace them; as early as the 1860s trade was in decline.

On the opening day, Albert's wife was very present in his thoughts. He sent Victoria a loving letter: 'As I write you will be making your evening toilette, and not be ready in time for dinner. I must set about the same task and not, let me hope, with the same result. I cannot get it into my head that there are two hundred and fifty miles between us. I must conclude and enclose, by way of close, two touching objects – a flower and a programme of the procession.'

Today the dock is a World Heritage site and represents the largest concentration of Grade I listed buildings in the country. It was reopened by Prince Charles in May 1988, and is home to Tate Liverpool, the Merseyside Maritime Museum, the International Slavery Museum, waterfront bars, restaurants and cafés.

▶ *Access Liverpool from E by M62.*

BUILT IN 1897, THE DIAMOND JUBILEE OF QUEEN VICTORIA

JUBILEE TOWER

❸ Jubilee Tower

The 'Battle of the Moors' had nothing to do with Morocco but was the hard-won right of local people to cross Darwen Moors without hindrance from landowners. The Jubilee or Darwen Tower, built in 1897, thus represents a double celebration – the Diamond Jubilee of Queen Victoria in that year, and victory for campaigners for the right to roam. The 26.5m (87ft) high octagonal tower was designed by David Ellison and built by R.J. Whalley. The visitor, mounting a stone spiral staircase, arrives at viewing platforms affording wonderful prospects in all directions. A smaller iron spiral staircase leads upwards to the highest point, from where on a clear day views of Blackpool Tower, North Wales and the Isle of Man are splendid. The new stainless steel dome is the third to top the tower. The first, made of wood, blew off in high winds in 1947. The second, made from fibreglass, suffered the same fate in 2010.

▶ *BB3 1DF. Darwen on A666, 4 miles S of Blackburn. Tower W of Darwen town centre.*

❹ Hoghton Tower

In 1617 Sir Richard Hoghton rolled out the red carpet for James I – down the three-quarter mile driveway. This fortified hilltop Elizabethan manor has been home to the de Hoghton family since it was rebuilt in 1565. At the banquet laid on for him, the king was so impressed by the loin of beef that he took a sword and knighted it Sir Loin ('sirloin'). Sir Richard was anxious to gain royal favour because he wanted to sell his loss-making alum mines to the king, which he succeeded in doing. Despite this, he was still dispatched to Fleet Prison for debt a few years later. In the Civil War, Sir Richard's son, Sir Gilbert, fought for Charles I, while Gilbert's son, another Richard, made cause with Parliament. For its Royalist stance, Hoghton Tower came under siege in 1643.

As well as James I, the royal guests allegedly entertained here include William III, George V and Queen Mary, and the Duke of Edinburgh. Writers and artists who visited include William Shakespeare, J.M.W. Turner and Charles Dickens. There is, at any rate, some written evidence that a 'William Shakeshafte' had connections with the family or house. When Dickens came in 1854, the building was in a woeful state of disrepair. He wrote of it in his story *George Silverman's Explanation*: 'A house centuries old, deserted and falling to pieces … the ancient rooms … with their floors and ceilings falling, and beams and rafters hanging dangerously down … the oaken panels stripped away, the windows half walled-up …'

Restoration began in 1870 after a century of neglect and today Hoghton is Grade I listed. House and gardens are open to the public. A tour of the house includes state rooms, the banqueting hall with minstrels' gallery and a collection of dolls' houses. Ghost tours explore 'the third most haunted house in Britain'. From the ramparts the views of Lancashire, the Lake District and North Wales are spectacular. Beneath are dungeons and a Tudor well house.

▶ *PR5 0SH. 7 miles E of Preston on A675.*

❺ Lancaster Castle

'John of Gaunt's Castle' dominates the historic town of Lancaster, looking down from its vantage above the River Lune. Its most striking feature is the octagonal twin-towered gatehouse built by John of Gaunt's son, Henry IV. The four-storey keep, known as the Lungess Tower, is older but less spectacular. Many kings and queens have visited or held court here. The castle is protected for the sovereign by the Duchy of Lancaster, which dates from 1265, when Henry III gave his son, Edmund Crouchback, lands that had been forfeited by Simon de Montfort, Earl of Leicester, after his failed rebellion. In 1267, Edmund was formally granted the county of Lancashire, this castle and the title of 1st Earl of Lancaster. The inheritance was temporarily lost by Edmund's son Thomas, who was executed for his part in a rebellion against Edward II in 1322, but it reverted to Edmund's grandson, Henry, who was awarded the title 1st Duke of Lancaster in 1351. John of Gaunt, whom Shakespeare referred to as 'time-honoured Lancaster', came into the dukedom in 1362 through his first wife, Blanche, the 1st Duke's daughter.

He added to the duchy's possessions and Lancaster became a County Palatine, affording the duke privileges within the county that would otherwise belong to the king. The law courts of Lancashire were in the duke's control. He appointed the sheriff, judges and justices of the peace. The Crown Court within the castle as it is today dates from 1796, but its history is much longer, and chilling. For centuries, miscreants were sent to Lancaster from around the country to stand trial at the twice-yearly sessions. Until 1800 convicts were hanged on Gallows Hill. The statue of John of Gaunt in the gatehouse was added in 1822.

▶ *LA1 1YJ. 2 miles SW of Junction 34 of M6.*

Northeast England

The royal castles of the northeast have withstood centuries of turbulence, as they were possessed or besieged by one warring noble after another, while the city of York both thrived and suffered under successive kings and their enemies.

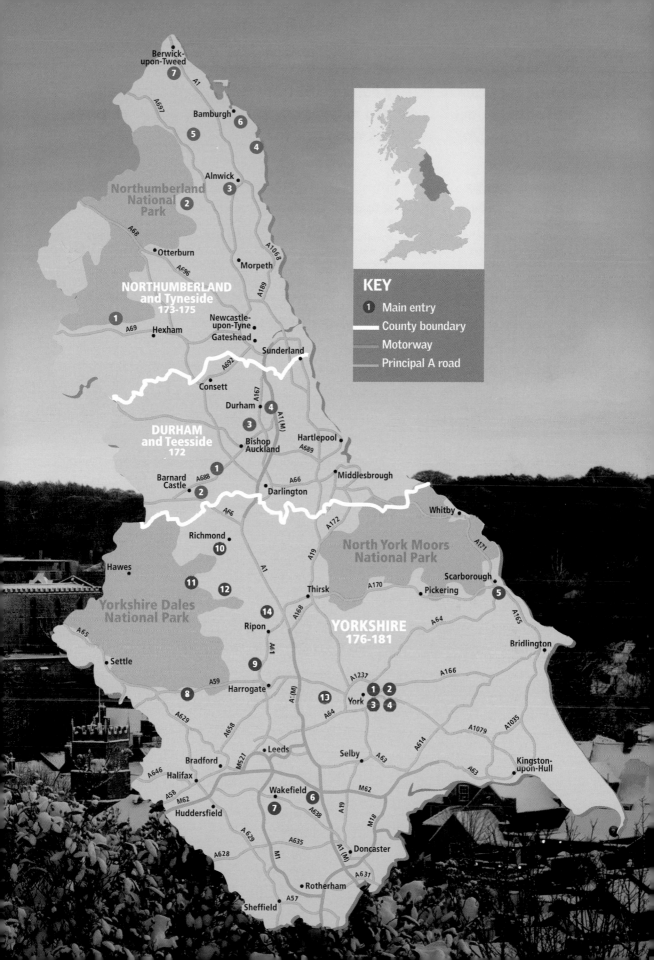

DURHAM & TEESSIDE

Within castles and stately homes, and even in the ancient cathedral, influential families conspired in favour of the deposed Scottish queen, but such passionate support was not enough to gain her the throne.

❶ Raby Castle

This was the birthplace, in 1415, of Cecily Neville, 'the rose of Raby', mother of Edward IV and Richard III. Her nephew, Richard Neville, 16th Earl of Warwick, was known as 'Kingmaker' for his role in making, and breaking, two kings in the Wars of the Roses, Henry VI and Edward IV. So it is not difficult to picture the Great Hall of their medieval castle on November 13, 1569, where the nobility of the north were gathered. With Charles Neville, 6th Earl of Westmorland, they planned insurrection against Elizabeth I and the rescue of Mary, Queen of Scots. When the coup, dubbed by history the Rising of the North, failed, the castle was forfeit to the Crown. Sir Henry Vane, an MP and member of Charles I's retinue, bought it in 1626. His son, also Henry, fought for Parliament in the Civil War but opposed the king's execution. Nevertheless, he was beheaded in 1662 on the orders of Charles II as he was 'too dangerous a man to let live'. One of the largest occupied castles in the country, Raby was renovated in the 18th and 19th centuries, although its towers and turrets date from the 11th. Interiors are a mix of medieval, Regency and Victorian.

▶ *DL2 3AH. Staindrop, 8 miles SW of Bishop Auckland on A688.*

❷ Barnard Castle

Built in around 1095, Barnard Castle was occupied in the Wars of the Roses by the future Richard III. Over the centuries it had endured many insults – besieged by Alexander II of Scotland, captured by barons supporting Simon de Montfort against Henry III, occupied by the Bishop of Durham, neglected by the Earls of Warwick. In the Rising of the North, the castle was held by Sir George Bowes for 11 days against 5,000 insurgents. Underfunded and demoralised, the rebels fell apart. Damage done then was made much worse by its later owner, Sir Henry Vane, who stripped Barnard of its roof and much of its masonry for maintenance of his favoured residence, Raby (see above). Now the spectacular ruins of the castle overlook the Tees and the town with which it shares its name.

▶ *DL12 8PR. 15 miles SE of Bishop Auckland on A688. EH.*

❸ Brancepeth Castle

Here is a third castle confiscated from the Nevilles in retribution for their part in the Rising of the North. Within these walls, Charles Neville and Thomas Percy established their common banner under which they would march in the rebellion of 1569.

James I gave it to Robert Carr, 1st Earl of Somerset. In the late 1700s it was acquired by the Russells, and in the 1820s, William Russell, a Whig politician and future High Sheriff of Durham, commissioned Anthony Salvin to restore it. Salvin was known for his expertise in medieval building. This, then, is largely a 19th-century castle – good as old.

▶ *DH7 8EA. 5 miles SE of Durham on A690.*

❹ Durham Cathedral

'Going to see the Church of Durham, they showed me the old Popish Vestments of the Clergy before the Reformation ... They are so rich with embroidery and embols'd work of Silver, that indeed it was a kind of Load to stand under them.' By the time Daniel Defoe saw this Romanesque masterpiece in 1734, on one of his 'curious and diverting journeys', the cathedral had survived the convulsions of history and was once more a peaceful place of worship. The priory and monastic community had been disbanded in 1540 under the Reformation, but in 1541 the cathedral was refounded, the prior became its first dean, and 12 of the monks became canons. While the fanatical destruction of furnishings and treasures had been going on during the Dissolution, evidently some fine threads were tucked away in the vestry. In November 1569, Charles Neville, 6th Earl of Westmorland, and Thomas Percy, 7th Earl of Northumberland, with their rebel army, occupied Durham Cathedral and symbolically celebrated Mass – a Catholic rite outlawed by the Protestant Elizabeth I – before leading the doomed Rising of the North against Elizabeth's forces. In the Civil War and under the Commonwealth, Cromwell used the building as a prison for 3,000 Scots. After the Restoration, the new bishop, John Cosin, began refurbishing 'the greatest Norman building in England'.

▶ *DH1 3EH. 2 miles SW of Junction 62 of A1(M).*

NORTHUMBERLAND & TYNESIDE

Castles once centres of intrigue, a town refortified at vast expense by successive Tudor monarchs, and a wonder of the Victorian age stand alongside a cavern where Arthur sleeps, awaiting a final summons.

❶ Sewingshield Crags

Among competing claims for the final resting place of King Arthur, a case is made for this site at Sewingshield, including an 'eyewitness account'. A farmer once sat knitting at the site of Sewingshields Castle, the long-lost domain of Sir Robert Ogle, who died in 1437. When his ball of wool rolled through a crevice in the rock, he managed to squeeze through to retrieve it, and found Arthur and his knights sleeping soundly. On a table beside them lay a horn, a sheathed sword and a garter. In England's hour of greatest need, we have only to unsheathe the sword, cut the garter and blow the horn for Arthur and his court to rise up and come to our aid – if, that is, we can find that same crevice.
▶ *12 miles NW of Hexham, close to Housesteads Roman Fort.*

❷ Cragside

When the Prince of Wales brought his family here in 1884, he found a house that outshone Buckingham Palace. This was the home of William George Armstrong, a Tyneside industrialist and engineer, ennobled as Baron Armstrong of Cragside. The future Edward VII invited himself, with Princess Alexandra and their children, for a visit from August 19 to 22, to see the achievements of a 'modern magician'.

The house Armstrong created with architect Norman Shaw is often described as 'Wagnerian' and 'fairytale'. Architectural historian Nikolaus Pevsner was impressed by its picturesque aspect, but it was not for aesthetic qualities that this Victorian wonder was most admired. It was the first house in the world to be lit by hydroelectric power. Among other mod cons were a tiled hot tub; a double-height kitchen with hydraulically powered spit and a lift to help staff carry food and coal; hot and cold running water; central heating; and the first filament light bulbs. The grounds are intended to evoke the Himalayas and include one of the largest rock gardens in Europe. They are best seen when the azaleas are in bloom.
▶ *NE65 7PX. Rothbury 12 miles SW of Alnwick. NT.*

CRAGSIDE

③ Alnwick Castle

'Earle Percy is into his garden gone,/And after him walkes his faire ladie;/I heard a bird sing in mine eare,/That I might either fight, or flee'. It was a little bird, then, according to the ballad, that told Thomas Percy, 7th Earl of Northumberland, that the queen's men were on the march against him. He must throw himself upon her mercies or join the uprising of northern nobles to free Mary, Queen of Scots, and depose Elizabeth I. Fatally, he chose the latter. Fleeing the battle at Clifford Moor, he was captured in Scotland and held prisoner, before being sold to the English and beheaded in York. This was not the first time since William de Percy came to England with William the Conqueror that the Percys had written themselves into the gory chapters of history. Henry, 1st Baron Percy, bought Alnwick Castle in 1309 from the Bishop of Durham, and began rebuilding his palace-fortress in a style at once practical, theatrical and opulent. The most renowned of his descendants, Sir Henry Percy ('Harry Hotspur'), sits astride his warhorse in a courtyard. Hotspur took up arms against the Scots when he was a teenager. In 1403 he led a rebellion against Henry IV, met his death at Shrewsbury, was respectfully buried, then disrespectfully exhumed and cut in quarters. His head was displayed on a pole at York's gates, as the head of the hapless Thomas would be in 1572.

The castle was abandoned, but in the later 1700s, Robert Adam made many alterations. In the 19th century the 4th Duke engaged Anthony Salvin to remove Gothic additions and create new, palatial accommodation. 'The Windsor of the North' is today home to Ralph Percy, 12th Duke of Northumberland, and his family.
▶ *NE66 1NQ. Alnwick town centre.*

④ Dunstanburgh Castle

Thomas Plantagenet, Earl of Lancaster, had reason to build himself a mighty fortress. Not only did he fear invading Scots, but there was the matter of his cousin, Edward I!. Lancaster had served at Edward's coronation in 1308, carrying 'Curtana' – the symbolically broken 'Sword of Mercy' of Edward the Confessor – but he eventually took up the sword against the king. When Queen Isabella and her lover, Roger Mortimer, raised an army to overthrow Edward, Lancaster weighed in, was taken prisoner at the Battle of Boroughbridge and beheaded for treason.

John of Gaunt, Duke of Lancaster, made improvements to Dunstanburgh in the late 1300s. It was twice held for Lancaster in the Wars of the Roses, but damage from cannon fire was not repaired and it fell into decline. By 1550 it was in 'wonderfull great decaye'. Wonderful indeed!

ALNWICK CASTLE

It rises up in splendid isolation on a windswept crag, overlooking the roiling North Sea. Its massive twin-towered gatehouse and turreted watchtower, known as the Lilburn Tower, stand stark against the sky, and the ghost of Thomas Plantagenet has allegedly been seen, carrying his mangled head and wearing an expression of horror and agony (see Pontefract Castle, page 178).
▶ *NE66 3TT. Craster, 7 miles NE of Alnwick. NT/EH.*

❺ Chillingham Castle

Edward I's base for the attack on William Wallace at the Battle of Falkirk in 1298 is as immaculate as Dunstanburgh is worn.
In 1297, Wallace had led a raid over the border, torching the local abbey, burning folk alive. Sir Walter Scott tells us: 'What Edward prized more than the surrender of the last fortress which resisted his arms in Scotland was the captivity of her last patriot.' He got his man! Wallace, betrayed by one of his countrymen, was captured and tried in London 'with as much apparatus of infamy as the ingenuity of his enemies could devise.'

The Elizabethans added the Long Galleries. In 1752, Capability Brown laid out the park, and in the 19th century Sir Jeffrey Wyatville designed the Italian Garden. In the Edward I Room, where the Gothic window was installed especially for the king, a secret compartment was discovered during renovations, containing documents relating to the Spanish Armada and the succession of James VI of Scotland. James himself came to visit, Charles I stayed for three nights before his imprisonment, and Edward VIII came to hunt. The present royal family continue to visit. This is the home of Sir Humphry Wakefield. The visitor can hope to catch a glimpse of roe and fallow deer, hare and red squirrel, and the only wild cattle in the world.
▶ *NE66 5NJ. 5 miles SE of Wooler, off A697 or B6348.*

❻ Bamburgh Castle

'Henry Duke of Somerset Delyverid Bamburgh to King Edward by Apoyntment, and so he cam yn to King Edwardes Grace, which graunted him a M. Markes by yere, where of he was not payde.' In 1462, the castles of Northumberland were holding out for Henry VI and the house of York. On Christmas Eve, the defenders of Bamburgh and Dunstanburgh agreed to surrender them on condition that Sir Ralph Percy would have both castles after he had renounced Henry's cause. Henry Beaufort, Duke of Somerset, and Ralph Percy were taken

to Durham, where Edward IV was laid up with measles, and both swore allegiance. Beaufort went with the king to London. Sir Ralph returned to Bamburgh. Three months later, he surrendered it to the Yorkists, declaring once more for Henry VI. Somerset, as the antiquary John Leland tells us, was not 'payde' money promised him by Edward, and he, too, declared again for Henry.

This truly dramatic seaside castle, perched high on a basalt rock outcrop, appears invincible thanks to rebuilding and restoration in the 18th and 19th centuries. After the battering it took in the Wars of the Roses – it was the first castle to succumb to cannon fire – it fell into decay. The great edifice, built on the site of a stronghold of the ancient kings of Northumbria, was by 1704 a ruin. Yet by 1799 it was not merely habitable but housed a public library.
▶ *NE69 7DF. Bamburgh, 4 miles E from A1, 14 miles SE of Berwick-upon-Tweed.*

❼ Berwick-upon-Tweed

'Not willing to omit seeing Berwick upon Tweed, we turn'd to the east, and visited that old frontier, where indeed there is one thing very fine … That is the bridge over the Tweed, built by Queen Elizabeth, a noble, stately work consisting of 16 arches, and joining, as may be said, the two kingdoms.' By the time Daniel Defoe made his *Tour thro' the Whole Island of Great Britain* in the 1720s, the border wars between England and Scotland were history. Over centuries, however, control of Berwick was 13 times won and lost, and this became one of the most important fortified towns in Europe.

When Edward I passed through in 1292, Berwick had been part of Scotland for three centuries. In 1296, he captured it for England, and in 1318 it was recaptured by Robert Bruce. Its medieval, high, flanking walls were defence against siege engines, but would not withstand 16th-century gunpowder artillery. So in 1539, a massive circular fortification was begun at the northeast corner of town. Defences were improved under Henry VIII, and in 1558, with the French urging the Scots to invade, Mary I commissioned Sir Richard Lee to replace the medieval walls with bastions. Elizabeth I continued with the project – the most expensive of her reign, costing £128,000, more than was spent to defend the realm against the Spanish Armada. The bridge that Defoe saw cannot have been the timber structure over which James VI of Scotland crossed in 1603 on his way to London – that was so rickety that a new one had to be built.
▶ *65 miles N of Newcastle upon Tyne on A1.*

YORKSHIRE

Schemers plotted, uprisings took off, battles raged and retribution inevitably followed, stalking fields and moors, prisons and castles, but through it all York and its wonderful cathedral escaped destruction.

❶ York

'Fires, sieges, plunderings and devastations, have often been the fate of York; so that one should wonder there should be anything of a city left.' The visitor acquainted with York's many misadventures will share the wonderment of Daniel Defoe in the 1720s. Its history is, said George VI, the history of England. York suffered in William the Conqueror's 'harrying of the north'. With the Dissolution, it lost its abbey, priories and friaries – although not without resistance. In 1536, the city was at the centre of the Pilgrimage of Grace, a Catholic uprising against Henry VIII's split with Rome. Robert Aske led thousands of followers into the city, driving out the king's new tenants and supervising the return of the monks and nuns. Negotiations with the king's emissaries, and promises of pardons, proved hollow. Aske was hanged in chains at Clifford's Tower. The ruins of the once wealthy Benedictine Abbey of St Mary serve as a reminder of those turbulent times.

The abbot's house survives as handsome King's Manor, which was granted by Henry VIII to the Council of the North. Guy Fawkes was born on Petergate at 1570. Charles I stayed at the manor, and set up a Royal Mint in the city, but left in 1642 as the Civil War loomed. Proudly Royalist, York was twice besieged by Parliament – briefly rescued by Prince Rupert – before it was surrendered to Sir Thomas Fairfax.

Mercifully, Fairfax ordered that nothing be destroyed, and the beautiful city within its medieval walls repays endless exploration. When Prince William visited in 2008, he enjoyed an £8 chicken curry, a dish named the 'Royal Delight', at a restaurant on Micklegate.
▶ *12 miles E of Junction 47 of A1(M). St Mary's Abbey, Museum Gardens YO1 7FR.*

❷ King's Square, York

'Jorvik' in the kingdom of Northumbria was a power base for Scandinavian warrior-kings, who had, it is said, a palace on this site. The city was founded as a Roman fortress, and was operating as an Anglo-Saxon trading port when it was captured in AD 866 by the 'Great Heathen Army' of the Viking Ivar the Boneless. A 'berserker', he fought with trance-like fury, although some speculate that he could not walk

and had to be carried into battle on a shield. The Danes had landed in East Anglia and travelled northwards. An uprising in AD 872 temporarily drove the Norsemen out of the city, and archbishop Wilfhere was expelled for collaborating with the enemy. In AD 895, King Guthred was entombed in 'the chief church' of York, now the Minster. Viking coinage from a mint at York attests to the status of the region.
▶ *York city centre.*

❸ Richard III Museum, York

'King Richard, late mercifully reigning over us, was through the great treason of the Duke of Norfolk piteously slain and murdered, to the great heaviness of this City.' Although history has heaped odium upon 'Richard Crouchback', the people of York have a different perspective. The king was popular in the north, defending England against the Scots, pioneering reforms, improving the lot of the common people. Among his many alleged crimes the most foul was the murder of his nephews, Prince Edward of Wales (the uncrowned Edward V) and Richard, Duke of York. But did he do it, or was he the victim of Tudor character assassination, the calumny of Sir Thomas More and a diverting work of fiction by Shakespeare?

Sir George Buck, James I's Master of the Revels, challenged the received view in *The History of King Richard III*. 'Because he hath been accused of great crimes and slanderously (as I verily believe) I shall make endeavour to answer for him and to clear and redeem him from those improbable imputations and strange and spiteful scandals.' In 1768, Horace Walpole weighed in, writing of More's account of the fate of the princes in the Tower: 'It is difficult to crowd more improbabilities and lies together than are comprehended in this short narrative.'

This museum was the brainchild of a former York tour guide, who took over the lease of the medieval gatehouse in 1992, having learnt that the topmost room had been added on the orders of Richard III in 1484, under his supervision and at his expense. An exhibition explores the controversy around him. A king who reigned for just 26 months (1483–85) still presents an enigma.
▶ *YO1 7LQ. Museum in Monk Bar gatehouse in city walls.*

CHOIR SCREEN, YORK MINSTER

❹ York Minster

Like York itself, the glorious Minster has survived 'fires, sieges, plunderings and devastations' from its beginnings in AD 637.
The first church on the site was built of timber, and in haste for the baptism of Edwin, King of Northumbria. It was replaced in stone in 637, destroyed by fire in 741, rebuilt, damaged by William the Conqueror's 'harrying of the north' and by another fire in 1137, and remodelled in 1154. The second-largest Gothic cathedral in northern Europe, the Minster of today was begun in 1220, and work continued into the 15th century. The chapter was used for parliamentary sittings by Edward I and II. Edward III married Philippa of Hainault in the Minster in 1328. The only royal tomb is that of their son, Prince William of Hatfield, who died as a baby. In 1541, with the Dissolution almost complete, the Minster lost valuable silver, vestments and altar frontals. When Royalist York was under siege from Parliament in the Civil War, cannon balls crashed through the windows, but on the city's surrender, agreement was reached to spare the beautiful medieval stained-glass windows. Diarist John Evelyn, visiting in the dour days of the Commonwealth, noted: 'Most remarkable and worth seeing is St Peter's Cathedral, which of all the great churches in England has been best preserved from the fury of the sacrilegious … It is a most entire magnificent piece of Gothic.' Fires in 1829, 1840 and 1984 caused more devastation. Lightning was blamed for the most recent conflagration, and some £2.5 million was spent on restoration. The Queen visited in 1988, and again in 2000. The magnificent 15th-century choir screen shows 15 kings of England, from William I to Henry VII.
▶ *YO1 7HH. York city centre.*

❺ Scarborough Castle

When Edward II's favourite Piers Gaveston took refuge from rebellious barons in this stupendous castle, he counted on its impregnable defences. The remains of the stronghold, which was begun in the reign of Stephen, dominate a rocky headland between two bays, with sheer drops to the North Sea and a narrow approach from land. A towering keep was added in the 12th century by Henry II. ▶

The fortress continued to grow over centuries in response to repeated ferocious onslaughts. The future Edward I held court at the castle in 1275 and 1280. Edward II used it as a prison for Scots. He appointed the malign Gaveston as castle governor in April 1312, and as king and barons squared up for war, Gaveston began to improve fortifications. By May, the Earls of Pembroke and Warenne, with Henry de Percy, had laid siege, and although the castle fabric did not fail him, Gaveston was starved out.

The castle came under siege again in 1536, this time by Robert Aske in the Pilgrimage of Grace (see York, page 176), but was not breached. Seven times it changed hands between Royalists and Parliament during the Civil War. Sir Hugh Cholmondeley held it valiantly for 12 months for the king, surrendering, like Gaveston, only when all the stores were gone. Of the original 500 defenders, half staggered out 'like a procession of spectres'. During the Commonwealth, the castle served as a prison, and was restored to the Crown in the reign of Charles II. What Cromwell's men had begun with their cannons was continued in 1914 by German battle cruisers, but the ruins still stand tall to tell their own heroic tale.

▶ *YO11 1HY. Scarborough, 40 miles NE of York. Castle in town centre. EH.*

❻ Pontefract Castle

'Pomfret, Pomfret! O thou bloody prison,/ Fatal and ominous to noble peers!/Within the guilty closure of thy walls/Richard the second here was hack'd to death.' In *Richard III*, Shakespeare records as fact the suspicion that a king was murdered here. The castle was begun in 1070 on land granted by William the Conqueror to a Norman noble, Ilbert de Lacy. In the 12th century it was confiscated from Robert de Lacy by Henry I for his failure to support him in his power struggle with his brothers. However, it reverted to the de Lacy family, who lived in it until the early 14th century and built the multi-lobed donjon, or heavily fortified central keep, that is the wonder of this castle's remnants. In 1311 Pontefract passed by marriage to the House of Lancaster. Six days after his defeat at Boroughbridge in 1322 (see Dunstanburgh Castle, page 174), Thomas, Earl of Lancaster was sentenced to death by his cousin, Edward II, in the Great Hall. The execution was a hideous botch – it took 11 blows of the axe to hack off Thomas's head.

John of Gaunt, Duke of Lancaster, son of Edward III, made Pontefract Castle his principal residence and lavished money on it. In 1536 it

was handed to the leaders of the Pilgrimage of Grace, a northern Catholic rebellion against the rule of Henry VIII. For the act of 'surrendering it', the castle's guardian, Thomas Darcy, 1st Baron Darcy de Darcy, was executed.

Here, on a royal tour in 1541, it was alleged, Henry's fifth wife, Catherine Howard committed adultery with Sir Thomas Culpeper – for which 'crime' she, too, was beheaded without trial. Pontefract was a Royalist stronghold in the Civil War, besieged three times or more by Parliament, and under the Commonwealth was reduced to the state of ruin that the visitor sees today. Pontefract Castle is no longer 'the strongest castle in the North'.

▶ *WF8 1QH. Pontefract, 12 miles SE of Leeds. Castle in town centre.*

❼ The Battle of Wakefield

Richard of York had been forced to flee to Ireland, but in September 1460 he returned, and that October, in a dramatic scene in Parliament, he walked up to the throne and placed his hand upon it. The gesture of usurpation shocked the assembly. Parliament would not accept regime change, and the Act of Accord of October 31 proclaimed that Henry VI would keep the throne for his lifetime, but his son Edward, Prince of Wales, would be disinherited in favour of York as Henry's successor. 'Accord' it was not. The arrangement suited nobody, and in the afternoon of December 30, at Sandal Magna, was fought the fifth battle of the Wars of the Roses, where Richard met his death. His son, as Edward IV, took turns with Henry VI for the throne, the latter reigning from 1422–61 and 1470–71, the former from 1461–70 and 1471–83.

When Daniel Defoe visited Wakefield in the 1720s, he related how, at Sandal, 'they shewed us a little square piece of ground, which was fenced off by itself; and on which, before the late war, stood a large stone cross, in memory of that fatal battle; just upon that spot, the Duke of York fighting desperately, and refusing to yield, tho' surrounded by his enemies, was kill'd.' Indeed, a memorial to his father, erected by Edward IV, had been destroyed in the Civil War along with Sandal Castle.

In 1897 residents built a new stone monument inscribed with the words: 'Richard Plantagenet, Duke of York, fighting for the cause of the white rose, fell on the spot in the Battle of Wakefield December 30th 1460'. It can be seen within the boundary of a Victorian school on Manygates Lane (formerly Cock 'n' Bottle Lane).

▶ *WF2 7DQ. 10 miles S of Leeds.*

SKIPTON CASTLE

8 Skipton Castle

'Glad were the Vales, and every cottage hearth;/The Shepherd Lord was honour'd more and more:/And, ages after he was laid in earth,/"The Good Lord Clifford" was the name he bore.' Wordsworth tells the extraordinary tale of Henry, 10th Lord de Clifford, who, in the reign of Henry VIII, came down from the fells of Cumberland to claim his castle and title. His father, John, was known as 'Butcher Clifford' for the mayhem he caused at Wakefield under the banner of Henry VI. 'Upon his character, also,' wrote one Baroness de Clifford in her 19th-century memoir, 'rests the imputation of having stabbed to the heart, in, or after, the battle, young Edmund Plantagenet … fourth son of Richard, Duke of York; an incident of which the bard of Avon has powerfully availed himself.' Fearful that her son would suffer retribution at the hands of Yorkists, his mother sent Henry, aged seven, to live as a shepherd boy, and he remained on the fells for 25 years.

This castle was begun by Robert de Romille in 1090 on a rocky bluff, backing on to a sheer drop to the Eller Beck. Edward I took it for the Crown, and Edward II granted it, first to his favourite Piers Gaveston, then, in 1311, to Robert, 1st Lord de Clifford. An inscription tells us: 'This Skipton Castle was repayred by the Lady Anne Clifford … It had layne ruinous ever since December 1648, and the January following, when it was then pull'd down and demolisht.' The castle was held for the king through a three-year siege in the Civil War, and afterwards paid the price. That it appears today perfectly complete is thanks to the redoubtable Anne Clifford, whose story is linked to Pendragon Castle (see page 164).
▶ *BD23 1AW. Skipton, 22 miles W of Harrogate on A59. Castle in town centre.*

9 Ripley Castle

'Trooper' Jane Ingleby was not faint-hearted. She fought hard alongside her brother, Sir William Ingleby, for Charles I at Marston Moor. When the king's northern armies were crushed, the siblings escaped back to Ripley, where they were followed by Oliver Cromwell. While William hid, Jane at first refused Cromwell admission, and upon letting him in, held him at gunpoint all night.

Everywhere in the rich tapestry of English history since the Middle Ages, Inglebys seem to have been caught up in the warp and weft. This castle came to Sir Thomas Ingleby by marriage in around 1308. His son Thomas was a courtier of Edward III's, and on a hunting trip in Knaresborough Forest, saved the king's life by spearing a wild boar. This won him a knighthood. He was allowed to use the boar's head emblem on the family crest, and to hold a weekly market and annual horse fair in Ripley, a tradition that continued until the early 1900s. Another Sir William Ingleby joined the Pilgrimage of Grace, the Catholic protest against Henry VIII's suppression of the monasteries. Although 200 'pilgrims' were put to death, Sir William was rewarded by Mary I, who appointed him Treasurer of Berwick. His sons David and Francis were part of the failed Rising of the North against Elizabeth I. A priest hole in which they hid was discovered by chance in 1964. James VI of Scotland, on his way to London to be crowned James I of England, stayed at Ripley in 1603 as the guest of yet another Sir William. Within two years, this Sir William was implicated in the Gunpowder Plot, although he and his son were acquitted at their trial.

Ripley village is as astonishing as the castle. It was rebuilt in the 19th century by Sir William Amcotts Ingleby, on the model of a village in Alsace Lorraine – complete with Hôtel de Ville. Dying without issue, he left the Ripley estates to his cousin, because 'I don't believe that you are any longer the canting hypocrite I took you for'.
▶ *HG3 3AY. 4 miles N of Harrogate on A61.*

⑩ Richmond Castle

'The town of Richmond is wall'd, and had a strong castle; but as those things are now all slighted, so really the account of them is of small consequence, and needless.' This prestigious ruin failed to charm Daniel Defoe, who saw the castle before 19th-century repairs had revived it. Only the castles of Colchester and Durham are of as venerable an age as Richmond, one of the greatest Norman fortresses in Britain.

After William the Conqueror put down the rebellion at York in 1069, he parcelled out North Yorkshire to his followers. Alain Le Roux de Ponthièvre was given Richmond and he set about building a fortress power base. The 12th-century sandstone keep was begun by Duke Conan the Little, and probably completed by Henry II, who added defensive towers and a barbican. Today, the views from the keep are glorious. Edward I made improvements to the interior, but the castle had fallen out of use by the end of the 1300s. J.M.W. Turner was aged 22 when he first visited Richmond in 1797, and was beguiled by the sight of the ruin on its rocky promontory above the River Swale.

▶ *DL10 4QW. Richmond, 12 miles SW of Darlington at junction of A6108 and A6136. Castle in town centre. EH.*

⑪ Bolton Castle

'The Queen of Scots had been sitting at the window side knitting at a work ... She rose and went to the fireside. Making haste to have the work finished, she would not lay it down, but worked of it at the time she was warming herself. She looked for one of her servants, which indeed were all gone to fetch up her meat, and, seeing none ... called me to hold her work, who was looking at my Lord Scrope and Sir Francis Knollys playing chess.' In giving this account of events at Bolton, Christopher Norton was answering a charge of involvement in the Rising of the North, the aim of which was to have Mary enthroned as Queen of England. He was not spared execution, but provided a picture of the Scottish queen's relatively comfortable time here in the charge of Sir Henry Scrope and Sir Francis Knollys.

Mary had arrived in England with nothing, after fleeing Scotland in April 1568, and was installed at Bolton on July 16. Sir George Bowes sent her rugs and tapestries. Scrope wrote for her belongings to be sent on from Loch Leven Castle. On January 26, 1569, in the midst of a snowstorm, she was moved 'further into the realm, unto Tutburie', where she felt at last truly and wretchedly a prisoner (see page 152).

One of Britain's best-preserved medieval castles, Bolton was completed in 1399 by Richard le Scrope, Chancellor to Richard II. Although it was partially slighted in the Civil War, it remains in good condition as the property of Lord Bolton, a direct Scrope descendant. As well as the Scottish queen's bedroom, the visitor can see the castle's kitchens, dungeon, armoury – and marvel at the superb views over Wensleydale.

▶ *DL8 4ET. 5 miles W of Leyburn on minor roads off A684.*

⑫ Middleham Castle

This Norman castle begun by Alain le Roux became home to Richard Neville, Earl of Warwick, the 'Kingmaker'. In the course of the Wars of the Roses, Warwick held both Edward IV and Henry VI prisoner at Middleham. In 1462 he brought the young Richard, Duke of Gloucester here to finish his education, instilling in him the skills of war. Richard married Warwick's daughter, Anne Neville, in 1472. He was given charge of the north by his brother, Edward IV, and enjoyed great local popularity while building his power base. By the age of 17 he was a leading figure in the struggles between the houses of York and Lancaster, distinguishing himself in the fighting at Barnet and Tewkesbury, with decisive victories against the Lancastrians.

He aquired the throne in 1483, but any fond memories he had of Middleham must surely have died there with his only son, Edward, aged 11, in April 1484, followed in May 1485 by the death of Anne, aged 28. Richard would not be long a widower; he was killed that year at Bosworth Field (see page 140). A requiem Mass is still said at Middleham Church for the last reigning English monarch to die in battle. In 1485 the castle passed to the new king, Henry VII. It fell into decay under the Tudors. In the Civil War it was used as a prison, and in 1646 the east range wall and most of the wall walks were destroyed on the orders of Parliament, leaving the impressive shell that the visitor sees today.

▶ *DL8 4QG. 2 miles S of Leyburn on A6108. EH.*

⑬ The Battle of Marston Moor

'Truly England and the Church of God hath had a great favour from the Lord, in this great victory given unto us, such as the like never was since the war began.' Oliver Cromwell, in a letter to his brother-in-law, Colonel Valentine Walton, expresses his belief that God had assured his success at Marston Moor. The largest battle ever fought on English soil raged here on the evening of July 2, 1644. Within two hours the Royalists' northern army was destroyed. Prince Rupert had 18,000 men at his command. They faced the 28,000-strong alliance of Scottish Covenanters, under the Earl of Leven, and Parliament, under Lord Fairfax. Some 4,000 Royalists were killed and 1,500 captured.

Cromwell's account continues: 'We never charged but we routed the enemy. The Left Wing, which I commanded, being our own horse, saving a few Scots in our rear, beat all the Prince's horse. God made them as stubble to our swords …' Then comes a devastating blow: 'Sir, God hath taken away your eldest son by a cannon-shot. It brake his leg. We were necessitated to have it cut off, whereof he died.' The site of the battleground is today open fields and moorland. A monument with interpretation panels stands on the road that runs through it, midway between Long Marston and Tockwith.

▶ *6 miles W of York, off B1224.*

⑭ Norton Conyers

'Thee, Norton, wi' thine eight good sonnes,/ They doom'd to dye, alas! For ruth!/They reverend lockes thee could not save,/Nor them their faire and blooming youthe.' The ballad celebrates Richard Norton and his sons, executed for their part in the Rising of the North of 1569, the aim of which was to depose Elizabeth I in favour of Mary, Queen of Scots. Their estate at Norton Conyers was seized and given to the Musgraves, from whom it passed in 1624 to the Grahams, who have occupied the manor almost continuously since then.

Sir Richard Graham was master of the horse to the Duke of Buckingham, and fought gallantly for Charles I at Marston Moor. Wounded 26 times, he managed to return home to die. It has been said that Cromwell felt particular animus towards Graham, and personally followed him with a troop of horse from the field. Charles I himself had visited Norton Conyers in 1633, as did James II and his wife in 1679. Visitors can see the room and bed where that couple slept.

This late-medieval manor with Stuart and Georgian additions and Dutch gables has another claim to fame. It was here, in 1839, that Charlotte Brontë heard the tale of a mad woman confined to the attic a century before. Here was her model for Thornfield Hall which inspired the idea of Mrs Rochester and *Jane Eyre*. In 2004 a blocked staircase was discovered, connecting the first floor to the attics, lending intriguing substance to the legend.

▶ *HG4 5EQ. 3 miles N of Ripon.*

Wales

From the time of the Norman conquest, England's kings strove to subdue the Welsh, raising great castles from which their lords could exert power and wage war. But the Welsh princes never surrendered and today those castles – ruined, restored or rebuilt – recall those days of strife.

KEY

1. Main entry
County boundary
Motorway
Principal A road

Holyhead

Anglesey

12

13

Bangor

8

10

9 Caernarfon

11

Llandudno

Rhyl

A55

Mold

7

A470

Betws-y-Coed

A5

A494

Wrexham

Llangollen

6

A499

A487

14 Porthmadog

5

Snowdonia National Park

Bala

Dolgellau

A494

A458

Welshpool

3

Machynlleth

NORTH and MID WALES
184-191

A483

Newtown

Aberystwyth

A44

LLangurig

2

A470

Cambrian Mountains

1

Llandrindod Wells

A44

4 Builth Wells

A483

A487

A485

Cardigan

A470

A438

Fishguard

Llandovery

Brecon

Black Mountains

Pembrokeshire Coast National Park

SOUTH WALES
192-195

Carmarthen

Llandeilo

2

Brecon Beacons National Park

A479

Abergavenny

Monmouth

Haverfordwest

A40

7

8

A4076

A477

A48

A465

Merthyr Tydfil

A449

6

Milford Haven

1

Tenby

A470

4 Chepstow

M48

Llanelli

Neath

3

Newport

Swansea

Port Talbot

M4

Bridgend

Cardiff

5

NORTH & MID WALES

Attempts by Lancastrian monarchs to subdue a rebel of Welsh princely descent are stamped across the region. The ceremonial investiture of the current Prince of Wales was an altogether more peaceful affair.

❶ Strata Florida Abbey, Ceredigion

'1201. On the eve of Whitsunday, the monks at Strata Florida came to the new church, which had been erected of splendid workmanship.' *The Chronicle of the Princes of Wales* (*Brut y Tywysogion*) contains repeated references to the abbey of the 'Valley of Flowers', a community of Cistercian monks founded in 1164 by an Anglo-Norman knight, and richly endowed by the Lord Rhys of Deheubarth. The abbey was known for a library that included works of the bards, and, it is believed, an important chronicle of Welsh princes and prominent families. The annals were begun – if Geoffrey of Monmouth can be believed – by Caradog of Llancarfan in the 12th century, and continued at Strata Florida. The chronicle brims with tales of wars, feuds, fratricide, duplicity, castles seized, surrendered, torched … What a relief it is to read: 'One thousand one hundred and sixty was the year of Christ when nothing happened.'

Edward I captured and burned the abbey, but it was rebuilt in 1294. Eleven Welsh princes were buried here and are commemorated in the Chapter House. Henry IV and his son, the future Henry V, set up base at Strata Florida (Latin for 'island of flowers') in 1401, during the rebellion of Owain Glyndwr, and their forces plundered the abbey. It was dissolved in the Reformation. The imposing great west door to the abbey church remains, fragments of wall, and a tiny church built with materials from this once renowned religious house.
▶ *SY25 6BJ. On minor road 1 mile E of B4343, 6 miles NE of Tregaron. CADW.*

❷ Clochfaen House, Powys

Guests at this holiday home can sleep in the room where Prince Albert, the future George VI, spent three weeks recuperating. In 1913, Harry Lloyd-Verney inherited the Clochfaen estate. Old Clochfaen, built in 1810, had been left standing empty and was ripe for demolition. In the shadow of war, architect William Arthur Smith Benson, a genius of the Arts and Crafts movement, was called in to advise on rebuilding, and local materials from the old house were kept for use in the new. Lloyd-Verney, Groom in Waiting to George V, was seconded to the Foreign Office. In November 1914, his cousin Ralph's wife Nita wrote: 'Joan [Harry's wife] hears so much about the War from people in the know. French's secretary came over the other day and had a talk with the King. Harry saw him too and was told that "everything was going simply splendidly for us at the front".' But the war would take a terrible toll and even the royal family was affected. On May 31, 1917, Prince Albert, Duke of York, aged 21, served at the Battle of Jutland aboard HMS *Collingwood*, and was mentioned in despatches. He was, however, suffering from a duodenal ulcer, and was sent to the new Clochfaen, where even 'the quietest of lives … the simplest of foods' did nothing to relieve his condition. For the locals, the great novelty was the sight of a sentry box at 'Mr Benson's liveable and charming' black-and-white house overlooking the Wye.
▶ *SY18 6RP. On minor road just S of Llangurig at junction of A44 and A470.*

❸ Powis Castle, Powys

Prince Charles has lodged at 'The Red Castle' when visiting the Royal Welsh Show, and is reported to hold it as the most beautiful castle in Britain. The original castle of 'Pole' was a stronghold of a dynasty of Welsh princes. Owain ap Gruffydd ap Gwenwynwyn renounced his royal claim in 1266 and was granted the title of Baron de la Pole. In the Civil War, Piercy, Lord Powys, declared for the king and fortified the castle, which came under siege. An order to demolish it was overturned, 'with the exception only of the outworks, and the making of some breaches in the wall, in order to render it indefensible in case of any future insurrection'.

Later, the castle received a visit from Charles II, who slept in the State Bedroom. Princess Victoria slept here in 1832. Window latches in the shape of Prince of Wales' feathers mark a royal visit by the future Edward VII, with his son and daughter-in-law, later George V and Queen Mary, in 1909.

The red sandstone edifice that has grown up around a medieval stone keep has been preserved by continuous occupation over centuries. The Clive Museum exhibits artefacts collected in the 18th century by Edward Clive, eldest son of Clive of India, who married Lord Powys's daughter in 1784. Edward commissioned Sir Robert Smirke

HARLECH CASTLE

to make improvements. This grand mansion dominates a rocky ridge, surrounded by terraces, world-renowned baroque gardens and a deer park.
▶ *SY21 8RF. 1 mile S of Welshpool close to junction of A458 and A483. NT.*

❹ Royal Welsh Showground, Powys

Britain's best-known organic farmer, Prince Charles, and the Queen attended the largest show of its kind in Europe in its centenary year. The first show was held in 1904 under the presidency of the Earl of Powys. Horse shows, sheepdog trials, sheep shearing, falconry, four-in-hand and carriage driving are among the attractions for four days each July. The coveted George, Prince of Wales Cup is the ultimate accolade for the prize-winning Welsh Cob. The first winner was Pride of the Hills in 1908, when the award was presented by the future George V.
▶ *LD2 2SY. 1 mile N of Builth Wells.*

❺ Harlech Castle, Gwynedd

'Three times hath Henry Bolingbroke made head/Against my power: thrice from the banks of Wye,/And sandy-bottom'd Severn, have I sent him,/Bootless home, and weather-beaten back.' In 1400, Henry IV faced a Welsh uprising led by Owain Glyndwr (quoted in Shakespeare's *Henry IV Part I*). Glyndwr declared himself Prince of Wales and waged the kind of guerrilla war at which his people excelled. He was a descendant of the Princes of Powys through his father, and of Deheubarth through his mother. He studied law at the Inns of Court in London and entered Richard II's military service. When he was treated with gross injustice by Parliament under Henry, over a quarrel with Lord Grey of Ruthyn, he took up arms against Grey and the king. This was no peasants' revolt. The Welsh flocked from all over England, even from their studies at Oxford, to fight for an independent Wales. What a coup it must have been when he took this castle in 1404, making it his residence and holding parliaments.

This is one of the castles built for Edward I by his military architect, Master James of St George. Begun in 1282, it exploited rock and cliff face. In 1408 it was retaken from Glyndwr by the future Henry V. Sixty years later it survived the longest known siege in the history of the British Isles, holding out from 1461 to 1468, under Constable Dafydd ap Ieuan, before being taken by Lord Herbert of Raglan for York. The rousing anthem *Men of Harlech* recalls this historic episode.

Although it was slighted after the Civil War, it remains well preserved. Waves no longer crash on the rocks below, but the 'way from the sea', a fortified stairway plunging almost 60m (200ft), once gave access to vital supplies brought by boat.
▶ *LL46 2YH. 15 miles S of Porthmadog and 20 miles NW of Dolgellau on A496. Castle in town centre. CADW.*

WALES

Kingdom of castles

Stirring tales of intimidation and defiance lie behind the grim citadels and scenic ruins of this once unruly Celtic land.

The great medieval chronicler and clergyman Gerald of Wales attributes to a sage old Welshman this advice to Henry II, a century after William I sent his noblemen to subdue a dissident people. 'This nation, O king, may now ... be harassed and in great measure weakened and destroyed by your and other powers ... but it can never be totally subdued through the wrath of man, unless the wrath of God shall concur.'

At the time of the Norman Conquest, the 'kingdom of castles' was neither a kingdom nor had it castles. Today it has around 400, some ruins, some mere mounds and footings, others in splendid entirety, upstaged only by the breathtaking landscape.

In the 11th century, Wales had no central government, but was made up of the 'kingdoms' of Gwynned, Powys, Deheubarth and Gwent. Being little engaged with agriculture, the Welsh were free to

devote themselves to the raids, ambushes and skirmishes at which they excelled. They were fleet, bold, ingenious, but divided among themselves, and not geared for pitched battle or all-out war. Of their fearless nature Gerald tells us, 'Though defeated and put to flight on one day, they are ready to resume the combat on the next ... and although, perhaps, they do not display great fortitude in open engagements and regular conflicts, yet they harass the enemy by ambuscades and nightly sallies.'

Iron grip

Wales had long experience of resisting Viking infiltration of their northern shores, but after 1066 they faced a new kind of foe. The 'Marcher Lords' were Norman barons loyal to William I, who built an intricate series of defensive strongholds on the English-Welsh borders, or 'Marches', from Chester down to Chepstow. This was indeed a wild frontier, and densely wooded. Deep rivers and high mountains favoured the natives, but the Normans clamped down with a mailed fist. Their legacy is the largest concentration of motte and bailey castles anywhere in England and Wales, and the magnificent stone edifices that replaced them.

The Lords of the Marches had the rare freedom to crenellate their castles and to raise their own militia. Hugh d'Avranches, Earl of Chester, Roger de Montgomery, Earl of Shrewsbury, and William FitzOsbern. Earl of Hereford, the most important of the land-grabbing Normans, set up administrative centres in their earldoms. Chepstow, Ludlow, Monmouth, Hay-on-Wye and Powys were other fortified Marcher towns.

FitzOsbern was one of the masterminds of the Norman invasion, and he set the pattern, in turn, for the conquest and administration of the Welsh borderlands. His castle at Chepstow, the first Marcher castle, is a formidable ruin, looming over the Wye. Of his castle at Monmouth, only a fragment remains, but an impressive one, overlooking the River Monnow. The remains of William de Braose's Abergavenny Castle are still evident, although it was burnt down in 1182 by Hywel ap Iorwrth, Lord of Caerleon. The low-lying fortress at nearby Skinfrith is also a ruin, which appears to have landed, Tardis-like, at the centre of the village.

Another great wave of castle-building in Wales came with Edward I's invasion and efforts to eradicate Welsh identity. What his father Henry III had begun, Edward took forward according to his own vision. He rebuilt a number of Henry's castles, and created a 'ring of iron' made up of daunting fortresses, including the great castle of Conwy, with its eight massive towers, and spectacular Harlech, which stands on a cliff edge, at one time overlooking the sea. Most impressive is Caernarfon, designed by the great military architect Master James of St George and inspired by the walls of Constantinople. Last, and most technically perfect of Edward's castles, is Beaumaris, on the Isle of Anglesey, another James of St George triumph, although it was never finished for want of funds. Its perfect symmetry, its four lines of fortifications – walls within walls within walls – was a work of the late 1200s.

Struggle for liberty

The Welsh themselves had not been castle-builders; their defences were those of nature – woodland and marsh. But to answer the invader and oppressor, the native rulers began to raise castles of their own to protect themselves and their people. These castles are not world-renowned, they were not so structurally perfect or long-lived as the Norman and English castles, but they had their own kind of poetry, occupying the most stunning situations, and seem to have grown out of the natural landscape.

The views from the ruined keep of Dinas Bran are stunning. The remains of Llywelyn ap Iorwerth's Castell-y-Bere sit on Cadair Idris, the Chair of Idris, surrounded by glorious mountain scenery. The slate and rubble round tower of Dolbadarn stands an atmospheric shell in the heavenly landscape of Snowdonia National Park.

Gerald of Wales commented: 'The English fight for power, the Welsh for liberty; the one to procure gain, the other to avoid loss; the English hirelings for money, the Welsh patriots for their country.' The visitor who explores what survives of the native Welsh castles, keeping these words in mind, will find them truly touching and heroic. Tourists seeing only the magnificent edifices of Harlech, Beaumaris and Caernarfon will be missing half of the picture. Visitors to Wales will also find that, as Edward I was to discover, Welsh identity runs in the veins; it is profound and ineradicable.

Towering over the estuary of the River Conwy, the dark stone walls still exude an aura of power and authority, unaffected by modern surroundings.
CONWY CASTLE

❻ Chirk Castle, Wrexham

'On a smaul hille there is a mighty large
and strong castel with dyvers towers, as
late repayred by Syr Wylliam, the yerls of
Darby's brother.' When antiquarian John Leland
saw Chirk Castle in the 16th century, it was in
mid-evolution from formidable Marcher fortress
to magnificent stately home. The place was built
on the estuary of the Ceiriog in around 1295 by
Roger Mortimer, who was granted the lordship
of Chirkland by Edward I. In 1595 it was sold
to Sir Thomas Myddelton for £5,000. His
Parliamentarian son Thomas was a Sergeant-
Major-General in the Civil War, and in 1643
Chirk was seized by Royalists in his absence.
Thus, on December 21, 1644, Thomas found
himself attacking his own castle. His heart cannot
have been in it, for on Christmas Day Prince
Rupert wrote that he had beaten Myddelton
off. In 1659 the now-Royalist Thomas joined
Charles Booth's 'Cheshire Rising' against Oliver
Cromwell's son Richard, and his castle was slighted.
Upon the Restoration, the castle's curtain wall
and five semi-circular towers were rebuilt, and
a new stone range was added, including the
first-floor Long Gallery, with an arcaded walkway
overlooking the courtyard.

The gardens, landscaped by William Emes
from 1764, are Chirk's great glory, with sculpted
yews, herbaceous borders, shrub and rock gardens,
and long views from the terrace. The parkland is
approached through ornate wrought-iron gates
made in 1719 to present a grand entrance to the
castle forecourt. They are by the Davies brothers,
Robert and John, of Wrexham – whose work
architectural historian Nikolaus Pevsner described
as 'miraculous' – and incorporate the Myddelton
coat of arms, complete with 'bloody hand'.

▶ *LL14 5AF. 8 miles S of Wrexham on A5. NT.*

❼ Ruthin Castle, Denbighshire

'At my nativity,/The front of heaven was
full of fiery shapes,/Of burning cressets, and
at my birth/The frame and huge foundation
of the earth/Shaked like a coward.' In 1400 it
was the frame and huge foundation of this castle
that 'shaked' – but although the town of Ruthin
was captured and burned by the rebel Owain
Glyndwr, the stronghold stood firm.

Glyndwr was heir to two Welsh princedoms.
He fought for Richard II against the Scots,
sporting a scarlet flamingo feather and driving the
foe before him with the hilt of his broken lance.
But when Reginald, Baron Grey de Ruthyn stole
land from him, the proud Welshman, being

CHIRK CASTLE

denied justice by Henry IV, declared himself Prince of Wales and called his countrymen to arms. In 1402, his followers took the sighting of a comet as an omen of victory and captured de Grey, releasing him for a ransom of £6,666.

Ruthin was first granted by Edward I to Dafydd, brother of Prince Llywelyn ap Gruffudd, in 1277. In 1282, it was bestowed upon Reginald de Grey, who had a wall built around the small town. The castle was further strengthened and extended under the supervision of Edward's military architect Master James of St George. By the time Sir Thomas Myddelton of Chirk bought it in 1632, however, it was valued at just £5. It was repaired in the Civil War and garrisoned by the Crown against Myddelton – its owner. It came under bombardment in 1646, and was surrendered after 11 weeks. Two years later it was torn down. The castellated edifice seen today was built in 1826 and has been a luxury hotel since 1963. Substantial 13th-century remnants survive in the grounds.
▶ *LL15 2NZ. 18 miles NW of Wrexham at junction of A494 and A525. Castle in town centre.*

❽ Penrhyn Castle, Gwynedd

'August 15, 1847. We stopped in a most beautiful spot, with almost Swiss scenery, opposite Penrhyn Castle, Colonel Douglas Pennant's (which I saw in the late possessor's time, unfinished).' Queen Victoria records in her journal that Albert went ashore to visit this fantasy 'Norman' castle between Snowdonia and the Menai Strait. It began life as a fortified manor for Ednyfed Fychan. Ioan ap Gruffued obtained a licence to crenellate in 1438, founded a stone castle and added a tower house. The 16th-century antiquarian John Leland noted, 'Grifith hath a faire house at Penryne, a ii. Myle this side Bangor'.

The property was rebuilt in the 1780s by Samuel Wyatt, in Gothic style, and again between 1820 and 1840, when the young queen saw it, to designs by Thomas Hopper for the wealthy Pennant family. Although it was changed beyond recognition, it incorporated an original spiral staircase and vaulted basement. The term 'mock castle' does not do justice to what has been described as an 'outstanding instance of Norman revival', with the appearance of a medieval fortress. The interiors reflect the Norman style, and among specially designed pieces of furniture is a one-tonne slate bed built for Queen Victoria when she visited in 1859. The stable block houses a museum of industrial and model railways and dolls. The surrounding grounds include exotic trees and shrubs and a Victorian walled garden.
▶ *LL57 4HN. 1 mile E of Bangor off A5. NT.*

WALES

9 Caernarfon Castle, Gwynedd

'I, Charles, Prince of Wales, do become your liege man of life and limb and of earthly worship and faith and truth I will bear unto you to live and die against all manner of folks.' On July 1, 1969, Prince Charles received at his Investiture the Insignia of the Prince of Wales, with the earldom of Chester, a sword, coronet, mantle, gold ring and gold rod. In the 1720s Daniel Defoe wrote of the first ever such investiture: 'Edward I kept his Court often here, and honour'd it with his presence very much, and here his eldest son and successor, tho' unhappy, (Ed. II.) was born … This Edward was the first Prince of Wales; that is to say, the first of the kings of England's sons, who was vested with the title.' It was surely by the king's design that his heir was born in Wales – and with what a heavy-handed gesture did he create him 'Prince of Wales'!

One of the most impressive of Edward's Welsh castles (see page 186), Caernarfon stands at the southern end of the Menai Strait as an emphatic statement of English supremacy after the defeat of Llywelyn the Last in 1282. In rebuilding Hugh Avranche's Norman motte and bailey castle, Master of the Royal Works James of St George integrated a bastide, a fortified township, as part of one grand design. This was to be the capital of a new dominion, seat of a new dynasty. By the mid-1300s, however, the castle was used mostly to stockpile armaments. It held out against the rebel Owain Glyndwr in 1403 and 1404, but was surrendered to Parliament in the Civil War, and left to decay. Repairs in the late 1800s fitted it for the Investiture, in 1911, of the future Edward VIII in a fanciful ceremony devised by David Lloyd George, Chancellor of the Exchequer and Constable of the Castle. Unhappy Edward VIII would reign for not quite 11 months.
▶ *LL55 2AY. 7 miles SW of Menai Bridge on A487. CADW.*

10 Pen y Bryn, Gwynedd

Could this be the site of the lost palace of the Welsh princes Llywelyn the Great and his grandson Llywelyn the Last? When Kathryn and Brian Pritchard bought an Elizabethan manor in 1988, with a 14.5ha (36-acre) chicken farm, they had no notion of the local tradition that surrounded it. Only when they moved in did they start to hear from neighbours that on this spot once stood Garth Celyn, Prince Llywelyn's stronghold. The stone manor sits, against the backdrop of a wooded hillside, above the village of Abergwyngregyn,

'the mouth of the white shell river'. Time out of mind ago a four-storey circular tower to one side of the house became known as 'Twr Llywelyn' – 'Llywelyn's Tower'. The site of the royal palace was believed to have been beside a motte, known as Pen y Mwd, across the river from the house, but recently the manor's tower has been reassessed as medieval, predating the rest of the house, and it is an intriguing possibility that the palace was moved at some point from the motte to this location. The Pritchards have told how, under floorboards, they found secret stairways, hidden rooms and tunnels, lending substance to the folk tale of a chamber below the tower, and a tunnel running under the Menai Strait to Anglesey, where Prince Llywelyn's horse waited to bear him to safety if the English king attacked. The manor house is open to the public by arrangement.
▶ *LL33 0LA. 6 miles E of Bangor on A55.*

11 Plas Dinas, Gwynedd

In January 2010, this country-house hotel had a royal visitor when Prince William dropped by for lunch. Plas Dinas became the home of the Armstrong-Jones family in the 19th century but it has its origins in the mid-1600s, when a house was built around a large stone fireplace, which can be seen in the gun room. The house was greatly extended in the Victorian age. Prince William took time off from his RAF duties to join friends for a lunchtime aperitif in the drawing room, where his great aunt, Princess Margaret, used to entertain after her 1961 marriage to Antony Armstrong-Jones, Lord Snowdon. Snowdon was appointed Constable of Caernarfon Castle in 1963, and organised the investiture of the Prince of Wales in July 1969. The house, owned by Peregrine Armstrong-Jones, has been a hotel since the mid-1990s. A 'mini museum' of photographs and memoirs has been created in the upper corridor leading to the Snowdon bedroom. 'Plas Dinas' means 'large house', and so it is.
▶ *LL54 7YF. 2 miles S of Caernarfon on A487.*

12 Anglesey

'There is nothing to be seen in the Isle of Anglesea but the town, and the castle of Baumaris … for here the country is very level and plain, and the land is fruitful and pleasant.' Nothing to be seen? If Daniel Defoe could visit 'the garden of Wales' today, he might catch a glimpse of Prince William and his wife, Catherine, who are based in a rented farm cottage on the island until the prince fulfils his commitments as an RAF search and rescue pilot. Meanwhile, they have been spotted riding the back roads on a red-and-white Ducati superbike, and shopping in Tesco at Holyhead. On Anglesey they can enjoy something like a normal married life, before they move to Kensington Palace. When they were courting, the prince and Kate would often pop into the White Eagle pub at Rhoscolyn, like any other couple – except with bodyguards.

Traditionally, Anglesey was known as 'Mam Cymru' (Mother of Wales), as its 'fruitful and pleasant' land provided food for north Wales. Edward I defeated Llywelyn ap Gruffudd, the last of the Welsh princes, partly by blocking grain supplies from Anglesey to the Welsh army. Daniel Defoe tells us the king had planned a giant stone bridge – 'it would indeed have been a work fit for so great a king … But the bottom being so doubtful, and the sea in that place sometimes very raging and strong, the workmen thought it impracticable, and tho' … the king was very positive in his design for a great while, yet he was prevail'd with at last to decline it.' The island is today connected to the mainland by Thomas Telford's Menai Bridge, one of the world's first modern suspension bridges, opened in 1826, and by Robert Stephenson's 1850 Britannia Bridge, guarded by 80-tonne lions sculpted by John Thomas of Gloucestershire.

▶ *LL65 2NJ (the White Eagle). Rhoscolyn 4 miles S of Holyhead off B4545.*

⓭ Beaumaris Castle, Anglesey

'In case you should wonder where so much money could go in a week, we would have you know that we have needed 400 masons … 2,000 less skilled workmen, 100 carts … 60 wagons and 30 boats bringing sea coal; 200 quarrymen; 30 smiths; carpenters … The men's pay has been and still is very much in arrears, and we are having the greatest difficulty in keeping them.' Edward I's military architect Master James of St George's letter to the exchequer provides an insight into why the last and greatest of his ring-of-iron castles was left unfinished. Money ran out before he could complete his masterpiece, yet many people regard this vast castle as the most beautiful in Wales.

It was begun in the spring of 1295, on a virgin site with no footings of an earlier stronghold to dictate the design. A tidal dock allowed supply ships to sail to the south side. Its wall-within-wall layout represents the acme of medieval concentric castle design. Invaders would be thwarted by numerous obstacles – a wide moat, barbican,

portcullises, murder holes and arrow slits. The octagonal outer wall with 12 towers and a landward and seaward gate enclosed a rectangular inner wall with a round tower at each corner, two gatehouses and two D-shaped towers. The first-floor Great Hall suggests just how lavish the planned royal apartments would have been if the building had been completed. Even in its partially realised state it inspires awe. In the event, with Welsh opposition crushed, it was scarcely needed. As Defoe put it in the 1720s, 'The castle … built by King Edward I and call'd Beau-Marsh, or the Fine Plain … was very large, as may be seen by its remains, and that it was strong … but 'tis now of no use.'

▶ *LL85 8AP. 4 miles NE of Menai Bridge on A545. CADW.*

⓮ Criccieth Castle, Gwynedd

'In 1239 a son was born to king Henry, called Edward. And Dafydd, son of Llewellyn, seized his brother Gruffud and imprisoned him and his son at Criccaeith.' *The Chronicle of the Princes of Wales* tells of the conflict between Dafydd, legitimate son of Llywelyn the Great, and his elder half-brother, the illegitimate Gruffud, whom he would ultimately betray to Henry III.

This was a rare native Welsh castle, built by Llywelyn the Great on a rocky headland jutting out into Tremadog Bay. It was begun in the 1230s to a design copied from one of the Marcher castles, with an inner ward protected by a twin-towered gateway. In around the 1260s Llywelyn ap Gruffudd, last Prince of Wales, added an outer curtain wall, a new gateway and a two-storey tower. The castle was captured for Edward I in 1283, and it was probably his military architect James of St George who oversaw the building of the now ruined 'Engine Tower' to house a siege engine, with the addition of another storey to the gatehouse and an outer barbican. In 1292 the English occupants held out against a siege by Welsh rebels led by Madog ap Llywelyn, sustained by supplies from Ireland. When, in 1404, the rebel Owain Glyndwr, laid siege to Criccieth, he had the support of a French navy blockade to prevent Irish ships from docking. The defenders of the castle were forced to surrender, and Glyndwr's men tore down the walls and burned the castle. Visitors mounting a steep path feels dwarfed by the monumental remains, which stand in forlorn defiance, bearing up under the weight of history.

▶ *LL52 0DP. 4 miles W of Porthmadog on A497. Castle in town centre. CADW.*

SOUTH WALES

A great warrior king and a Tudor who brought an end to war both have their roots in this dramatic land where, some years earlier, another Welsh-born monarch took refuge from his determined wife.

❶ Pembroke Castle, Pembrokeshire

'The greatest knight who ever lived', William Marshal acquired this castle, together with the earldom of Pembroke, after his marriage to 17-year-old Isabel de Clare in 1189. Bride and estates had been vouchsafed to him by Henry II. Aged 42, William was transformed from a landless knight to one of the richest men of his day. As well as Henry, he served Richard I, John and Henry III. After Henry II appointed him head of his son Prince Henry's military household, he became the prince's mentor and hero, infecting him with his passion for deadly tourneying. William led teams in all the important tournaments of the day. When, at the age of 15, the prince was crowned Henry the Young King, to reign with his father, William acted as his regent, but the young king predeceased his father.

Although the castle was begun by the Marcher Lord Roger de Montgomery in 1093 (see page 186), it was largely Marshal's creation. In 1245 it came into the hands of William de Valence, half-brother of Henry III. In 1454 Edmund, Earl of Richmond sent his pregnant wife, Lady Margaret Beaufort, here, entrusting her to the care of his younger brother, Jasper Tudor. In the Henry VII Tower the future first Tudor king was born. The Lancastrian Richmond did not live to see his son and heir. He was captured by Yorkists and died of the plague at Carmarthen Castle.

Pembroke Castle withstood Cromwell's onslaught in 1648. Afterwards, parts were demolished in retribution, but the castle underwent major restoration in the early 1900s and remains a prodigious edifice, with a fine round keep and Great Gatehouse. A spiral staircase leads down to a natural cave, giving access to the River Cleddau.
▶ *SA71 4LA. 2 miles SE of Pembroke Dock at junction of A4139 and A4075. Castle in town centre.*

❷ Carreg Cennen Castle, Carmarthenshire

The Welsh prince of Deheubarth, Lord Rhys, built a stronghold on this vertiginous limestone crag, but it was replaced in Edward I's great castle-building enterprise. The king gave the earlier fortress to John Gifford, who, together with his son, built the new one. In the 14th century it passed to John of Gaunt, third surviving son of Edward III, and in turn to John's son, Henry Bolingbroke. The castle became Crown property in 1399 when Henry became Henry IV. It fell to Owain Glyndwr's rebels in 1403 (see Ruthin Castle, page 188), and in the Wars of the Roses harboured maverick Lancastrians, who terrorised the surrounding countryside. The 'robbers' den' was captured by Yorkists in 1462, under Edward IV, and the work of a 13th-century baron was undone by 500 men. Yet here it stands in its spectacular setting, 'Carreg Cennen, King of Time', as the Reverend Eli Jenkins describes it in Dylan Thomas's *Under Milk Wood*.
▶ *SA19 6UA. 3 miles SE of Llandeilo, signposted from A483 near Ffairfach. CADW.*

❸ Caerphilly Castle

The southeast tower of this gigantic castle leans at a tipsy angle – damaged, some say, by the troops of Queen Isabella. Gilbert de Clare, one of Henry III's barons, built the castle against the incursions of Prince Llywelyn ap Gruffudd, 'Llywelyn the Last', who had control of most of mid and north Wales. When a castle was begun at Caerphilly in 1268, Llywelyn wrecked it with siege engines, but building resumed and by 1280 the daunting edifice was complete. Its concentric layout includes the curtain wall of a central ward surrounded by an outer curtain wall, lapped by vast water defences. The castle's revolutionary design was made possible by the use of a virgin site.

In the 1320s, the Great Hall and domestic buildings were remodelled for Hugh le Despenser, who inherited the lordship of Glamorgan and parts of the de Clares' estates through his marriage to Eleanor de Clare. His malign influence over the weak-willed Edward II set the Marcher barons against the king, and Despenser and Edward were forced to seek refuge at Caerphilly in September 1326. From that December to March, Queen Isabella laid siege, but the fugitives had moved on. The castle fell into ruin, and its existence today as one of the most splendid castles in all of Europe is thanks to restoration ordered by the 3rd Marquess of Bute in around 1870, and continued by the 4th Marquess in the early 1900s.

▶ *CF83 1JD. 8 miles N of Cardiff close to junction of A469 and A468. CADW.*

❹ Chepstow Castle, Monmouthshire

The earliest of the castles built to defend the badlands of the Welsh–English borders was begun by William FitzOsbern just a year after the Battle of Hastings. A close friend of William I and an architect of the Norman invasion, FitzOsbern, later created Earl of Hereford, led by example in the barons' management of the Welsh frontier, wielding power along the southernmost regions of the Marches.

Chepstow is, at its heart, the oldest stone castle of its kind in Britain, and FitzOsbern's greatest legacy. The original stone Great Hall still inspires awe. Occupying a clifftop overlooking the River Wye, the castle grew over centuries, spreading along a narrow ridge, and evolving with advances in military architecture. In 1175 Henry II granted the castle to the de Clare family, and like Pembroke (see opposite) it came by marriage to the great knight William Marshal, who fortified it extensively, rebuilding the eastern wall and adding round towers with arrow slits for his bowmen to pick off native raiders. Marshal's son added a twin-towered gatehouse and a barbican with a round tower, and he updated the keep.

In 1270–1300 the castle was further developed by Roger Bigod III, Earl of Norfolk. One of his additions was a commodious round tower that, centuries later, became known as Marten's Tower. In the Civil War the castle was garrisoned by Royalists and damaged in a forced surrender to Cromwell. Henry Marten was one of the signatories of Charles I's death warrant and upon the Restoration, he and his wife were imprisoned here by Charles II.

▶ *NP16 5EY. 1 mile N of Junction 2 of M48. Castle in town centre. CADW.*

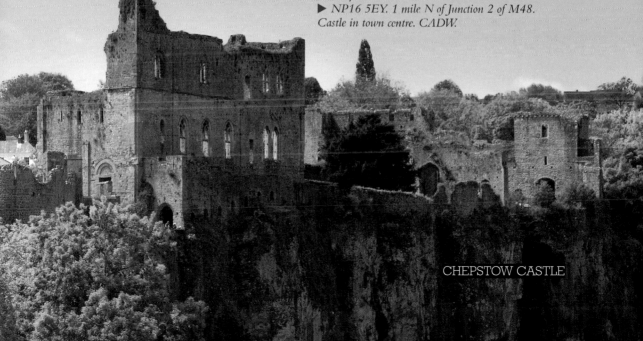

CHEPSTOW CASTLE

OMNIA VINCIT AMOR ET NOS CEDAMVS AMORI

CARDIFF CASTLE

❺ Cardiff Castle

'John, Marquess of Bute built this in 1881. William Burges designed it.' A Latin inscription on a marble overmantel in the Arab Room tells succinctly how a Norman stronghold came to be transformed into a Victorian extravaganza of eye-watering opulence.

The Marcher Lord Robert Fitzhamon (see page 187) first built a motte and bailey castle here in 1061 on the site of a Roman fort. The keep still stands on its mound, flying the red dragon for Wales. Over the centuries the castle has had many famous and infamous owners, including two arch villains of history, Hugh le Despenser, the monstrous favourite of Edward II, and the possibly maligned Richard III. Henry VII granted the castle to his uncle, Jasper Tudor. William Herbert, brother of Henry VIII's surviving wife, Catherine Parr, took it over in 1550. The family, staunch Royalists, offered Charles I refuge in 1645. Although the castle was taken by Cromwell's men in the Civil War, it was spared the slighting that was the fate of so many strongholds.

In 1766 it passed by marriage to the Bute family, who had helped to transform Cardiff into 'the coal metropolis of the world'. John Patrick Crichton-Stuart, 3rd Marquess of Bute, was a keen medievalist. In 1865 he unleashed William Burges upon the castle. This stately home of unimaginable lavishness was Burges's most important work; he was still engaged upon it at his death in 1881. Never have the words 'no expense spared' rung more true.

▶ *CF10 3RB. Access Cardiff from Junctions 29, 30, 32 or 33 of M4. Castle in city centre.*

❻ Tintern Abbey, Monmouthshire

'When we stood at one end of this awful piece of ruin, and surveyed the whole in one view, the elements of air and earth, its only covering and pavement; and the grand and venerable remains which terminated both … the eye was above measure delighted with the beauty, the greatness and the novelty of the scene.' William Gilpin was actually not entirely pleased by this ruined abbey; he wished he might take a mallet to it, to fracture the gable ends and leave it more distressed. It was Gilpin who introduced the 'picturesque' aesthetic in 1782 with his *Observations on the River Wye*, which instructed the leisured traveller to examine 'the face of the country by the rules of picturesque beauty'.

Today's leisured traveller will want to look deeper, to explore the history of a Cistercian abbey built by Walter de Clare in 1131 and endowed by Roger Bigod III with a new church in the late 13th century, the remains of which dominate the site today. Edward II took refuge here when he was fleeing Queen Isabella and her lover, Roger Mortimer. In 1536, Abbot Richard Wyche surrendered the abbey to Henry VIII. It was dissolved and granted to Henry Somerset, Earl of Worcester, who stripped the roofs of lead for Raglan Castle and left the buildings to decay. In the latter 1700s, 'Romantic' tourists flocked to see Tintern, 'jewel and highlight of the tour'. Wordsworth extolled it, Turner painted it, the Duke of Beaufort preserved it. It was sold to the Crown in 1901, and by 1928 had been restored to the state of perfect Gothic ruin.

▶ *NP16 6SE. 5 miles N of Chepstow on A466.* *CADW.*

❼ Raglan Castle, Monmouthshire

'The stately Tower, that lookes ore Pond and Poole:/The fountaine trim, that runs both day and night./Doth yield in showe, a rare and noble sight.' Thomas Churchyard, in *The Worthines[s] of Wales* (1537), extols this grand late medieval castle. Raglan was begun in the 1430s by Sir William ap Thomas, who had fought in France in the 100 Years War. His son, William, took the English name of Herbert, and lavished the fortune made from Gascon wines upon remodelling a building without peer in all of Wales. Grounds included a deer park, a 'Great Poole' and fountain court, and orchards 'full of every fruit that is sweet and delicious'. William supported York in the Wars of the Roses, though,

and for him, bitter were the fruits of his Yorkist adventures. He was executed in 1469 after the Battle of Edgecote Moor. His son, also William, took over the rebuilding, and in 1492 the castle passed to his daughter, Elizabeth, and her husband, Sir Charles Somerset, created Earl of Worcester by Henry VIII. His son Henry used lead reclaimed from Tintern Abbey in the Dissolution for further rebuilding. Henry's son William added the Long Gallery and a Renaissance garden.

Charles I visited twice in the Civil War, and played bowls on the castle green. After an epic siege by Parliament the castle was surrendered and slighted to prevent further use. It is a ruin, but an awe-inspiring one. For the visitor it is not too difficult to imagine how it was in the days of wine and roses, when Dafydd Llwyd proclaimed – with some poetic licence – its 'hundred rooms filled with festive fare, its hundred towers, parlours and doors, its hundred heaped-up fires of long-dried fuel, its hundred chimneys for men of high degree'.

▶ *NP15 2BT. 7 miles W of Monmouth on A40.* *CADW.*

❽ Monmouth Castle, Monmouthshire

'The King here borne, did prove a peereles Prince,/He conquerd Fraunce, and raign'd nine yeeres in hap:/There was not here, so great a Victor since/That had such chaunce, and Fortune in his lap.' Poet Thomas Churchyard was writing in 1537, lauding that great warrior Henry V, who was born at this castle in around 1386. The castle was begun within five years of the Norman Conquest by William FitzOsbern, and slighted by Parliament in the Civil War. A local man recorded in his diary that on March 30, 1647, the soldiers and townsmen began pulling down the round tower, and that on December 22, 'about 12 o'clock the Tower of the Castle of Monmouth fell down, upon its side, whilst we were at sermon'. In its place, Henry Somerset built Great Castle House, in 1673, for a family home to replace Raglan Castle. In 1875 the Monmouthshire Royal Engineers set up headquarters at the house. One of the oldest regiments in the country, it traces its origins back to the 1530s. There is a regimental museum, and the castle can be viewed from the parade ground. The curtain wall, gatehouse and round keep have all been swept away, but substantial parts of the Great Tower and Hall remain.

▶ *NP25 3BS. 10 miles SW of Ross-on-Wye and 17 miles E of Abergavenny on A40.* *Castle in town centre.*

WALES

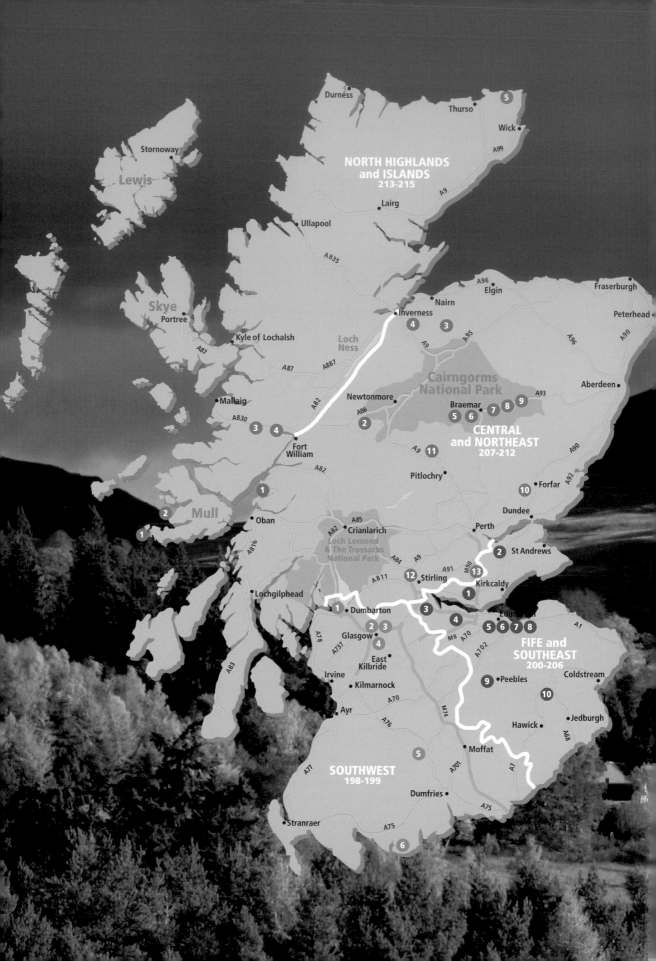

Scotland

From the wild beauty of the Highlands beloved of Queen Victoria to the Old Town of Edinburgh, Scotland provides many vivid backdrops to royal history. Across the land, historic battlefields and ancient castles evoke the spirits of William Wallace, Mary, Queen of Scots and Bonnie Prince Charlie.

KEY

① Main entry
County boundary
Motorway
Principal A road

SOUTHWEST SCOTLAND

Victoria and her beloved Albert are ever present in Glasgow, but events of the distant past are inescapable. The area is redolent of the doomed Scottish queen's last defiant bid to regain her throne.

❶ Dumbarton Castle, West Dunbartonshire

'August 17, 1847. The castle's situation is very fine, the rock rising straight out of the river, the mountains all around, the town behind it, making it very picturesque.' Victoria and Albert did not just admire this stronghold from afar, but climbed the many steps to reach the battery. The castle stands upon the 73m (240ft) volcanic Dumbarton Rock, lapped by the Rivers Clyde and Leven. 'Dun Breatann' (Fortress of the Britons) has the longest recorded history of any fortress in Britain, dating from AD 450. In 1222 Alexander II began a new defensive castle on the site. William 'Braveheart' Wallace was held here in 1305 by governor Sir John Stewart Montieth, before being taken to London and his execution. The infant Mary, Queen of Scots was brought here for safety in 1548 before being sent to France. She was on her way to Dumbarton in 1568 when her forces were defeated at Langside. The governor, Lord Fleming, held the castle in her name until 1571, when Captain Thomas Crawford led his men up the 'impregnable' rocks and ramparts on the northern side to take it.

After the castle was surrendered to Cromwell in 1652 it was demolished and rebuilt, although the Portcullis Arch survives from the 14th century, and the Guard House beneath from around 1580. The Clyde side is dominated by the Governor's House, built in 1735. The Duke of York's Battery replaced the North Gate in 1795. On her visit, Queen Victoria enjoyed extensive views of the Clyde, but Ben Lomond was shrouded in mist.
▶ *G82 1JJ. 14 miles W of Glasgow off A82. HS.*

❷ Glasgow City Chambers

When Queen Victoria visited Glasgow in 1849, she declared the town 'a handsome one with fine streets built in stone, and many fine buildings and churches'. What it did not have was a building for civic government to reflect Glasgow's stature as 'second city of the Empire'. In the early 1880s, Paisley-born architect William Young submitted a prize-winning design, and his City Chambers were formally opened by Victoria in August 1888. The imposing, highly ornate building draws on Renaissance Classicism with extensive embellishment. The pediment was redesigned to celebrate Victoria's Golden Jubilee, and depicts her surrounded by figures emblematic of Scotland, England, Ireland, Wales and the colonies. Visitors will see in the Loggia a vaulted ceiling with more than 1.5 million pieces of Venetian mosaic, and a marble staircase rising three storeys. The Banqueting Hall is hung with paintings representing the history of Glasgow. Members of the royal family are among those to have signed the visitors' book.
▶ *G2 1DU. Access Glasgow from M8. City Chambers on George Square.*

❸ George Square, Glasgow

Queen Victoria's reaction to the equestrian statue of the Duke of Wellington on Royal Exchange Square in 1848, was that it was 'very like and beautifully executed'. Somewhat like, and beautifully executed, are the statues of Victoria and Albert, both on horseback, by the same sculptor, Baron Carlo Marochetti, which stand in George Square. The statue of Victoria was hailed in 1854 by the *Illustrated London News* as 'by far the finest statue of [the Queen] yet produced'. Victoria herself so admired the statue of Albert that she ordered a copy to be made and erected at Windsor.
▶ *Glasgow city centre.*

❹ Langside Battle Memorial, Glasgow

At the top of an ornate column, a lion rests a paw on a cannonball. It looks down on a busy road junction, once the scene of defeat for Mary, Queen of Scots. This was the village of Langside, where James Stewart, Earl of Moray, lay in wait with his army to ambush the forces of his sister-in-law, the deposed Scottish queen. Upon her escape from Lochleven Castle (see page 212), Mary raised a force of 6,000 and headed for Dumbarton, where she planned to take refuge and await reinforcements from the north. A plaque on the 18m (58ft) column by Alexander Skirving commemorates May 13, 1568, and the engagement that marked the queen's final defeat in Scotland. She must have watched in despair from Cathcart Hill (Court Knowe) as her forces were routed and she was put to flight.
▶ *G41 3DJ. 2 miles S of Glasgow city centre.*

5 Drumlanrig Castle, Dumfries & Galloway

'The gallery may well be call'd a gallery of beauties, itself a beauty. And being fill'd from end to end ... with the family-pieces of the duke's ancestors ...' Daniel Defoe was bowled over by the palatial country seat built by William, 3rd Earl of Queensberry upon being created 1st Duke by Charles II in 1684. The family's associations with royalty had not always been so felicitous. James Douglas, 4th Earl of Morton, was one of those responsible for coercing Mary, Queen of Scots to abdicate and for routing her troops at Langside. Her son, James VI, ordered his execution in 1581 for being party to the conspiracy to kill his father, Lord Darnley.

Throughout the splendiferous pink sandstone palace can be seen the motif of a winged heart. According to the tale, in 1329, as Robert Bruce lay dying, he asked that his embalmed heart should be carried on a crusade. James Douglas travelled to Spain wearing about his neck Bruce's heart in a silver and enamel casket. Alfonso XI of Castile entrusted Douglas with command of a division of men against the Moors of Granada, but he was lured into a trap and, facing death, took Bruce's heart and flung it into the enemy's midst, crying, 'Forward, brave heart, as ever thou were wont to do, and Douglas will follow thee and die!' The family motto remains to this day 'Forward'. The Jacobite army stopped here on its march north in 1745. The room in which Bonnie Prince Charlie slept, the Buccleuch Art Collection, the gardens and a bicycle museum are among Drumlanrig's considerable charms.

▶ *DG3 4AG. 15 miles N of Dumfries on A76.*

6 Dundrennan Abbey, Dumfries & Galloway

Mary, Queen of Scots spent her last night in Scotland at this Cistercian abbey, in 1568, after her defeat at the Battle of Langside (see opposite). The abbey was founded in 1142 by Fergus, Lord of Galloway, with assistance from King David of Scotland. The white-robed monks came from Rievaulx Abbey in Yorkshire. In 1587, during the Scottish Reformation, the abbey passed to the Crown and fell into ruin. The north and south transepts survive as singularly fine examples of late 12th-century Cistercian architecture, along with the remains of the chapter house. These grey sandstone fragments symbolise the chaste purity of the Cistercian ideal. The grave slabs of four abbots are set into the floor, while a blue marble slab is mounted with a brass depicting a knight and lady.

DG6 4QH. 6 miles E of Kirkcudbright on A711. HS.

DRUMLANRIG CASTLE

FIFE & SOUTHEAST SCOTLAND

Palaces, castles and abbeys all bear witness to the turbulent history of an area where rebellion, reprisals and plunder were once rife. More cultural pursuits are offered under the aegis of the House of Windsor.

❶ Dunfermline Abbey and Palace, Fife

Here is the final resting place of Robert the Bruce – and the birthplace of Charles I, the last British monarch born in Scotland.
A church stands on the site of the chancel and transepts of the medieval Benedictine Abbey of the Holy Trinity and St Margaret. The abbey was founded by David I, but there was a monastic community here in the reign of Malcolm III, whose second wife was created St Margaret of Scotland. She was interred here in 1093, and upon her beatification was disinterred and moved to a reliquary at the high altar. Malcolm was also disinterred and buried next to her. In 1303, Edward I of England held his court at the abbey – and burned it the following year. Although the heart of Robert the Bruce lies at Melrose (see page 206), his body was buried here in 1329. A monumental brass marks the royal vault.

During the Scottish Reformation in 1560 the abbey church was sacked. Surviving parts of the building include the refectory, the gatehouse and rooms above (part of the former city wall), and the nave, now the church vestibule. The present church opened for worship in 1821. Next to the abbey, and connected to it via the gatehouse, is a palace built by James VI (James I of England) as a gift for his wife, Anne of Denmark. Here she gave birth to three of their children, including the sickly Charles, future king of England. The kitchen, cellars and south wall remain.
▶ *KY12 7PE. Dunfermline town centre. HS.*

❷ Falkland Palace, Fife

James IV and James V transformed this former castle into a beautiful Renaissance palace with glorious gardens. In 1401, Robert Stewart, 1st Duke of Albany, imprisoned his nephew, the Duke of Rothesay, eldest son of Robert III, here and, it was said, let him die of starvation. Parliament exonerated him, but suspicion remained. John Debrett, in 1805, had no doubt: 'This Robert, Duke of Albany, having obtained the entire government from his brother, King Robert, he caused the Duke of Rothesay to be murdered.'

James IV, a cultured, educated patron of the arts, engaged a new keeper of the castle to tame the overgrown garden and park, and ordered the building of a new palace complex. James V, in his turn, had it remodelled, employing craftsmen from France and Italy. He also installed a court for real tennis – Scotland's oldest, which can be seen today. The Stewarts used Falkland as a retreat, where they hunted native deer and wild boar imported from France. Here, James V died in December 1542, having heard that at Linlithgow his wife, Mary of Guise, had given birth to a daughter. So it was that, at the age of seven days, the baby Mary became Queen of Scots. Following her return from exile in France in 1561, already a widow, Mary was a frequent visitor to the palace. After the Union of the Crowns, her son James VI (James I of England), Charles I and Charles II all visited Falkland. In the Civil War, Cromwell's men set the palace on fire and it fell into ruin. John Crichton-Stuart, 3rd Marquess of Bute, began restoration in 1887, and in the 1950s the 5th Marquess gave palace and gardens over to the care of the National Trust for Scotland.
▶ *KY15 7BU. 10 miles SW of Cupar. NTS.*

❸ Callendar House, Falkirk

Here was signed the agreement that little Mary, Queen of Scots should marry Francis, Dauphin of France. At six months old she had been betrothed to Edward, son of Henry VIII, but the Scottish Parliament repudiated the match, provoking an invasion of Scotland in 1547, known as 'the Rough Wooing'. The Callendar lands were granted by David II to Sir William Livingston in 1345. Alexander, 5th Lord Livingston was Queen Mary's guardian; his daughter Mary was her maid of honour. The Scottish queen's son, James VI (James I of England) entrusted the upbringing of his daughter Elizabeth to Alexander, 7th Lord Livingston, at Callendar.

In the 18th century the Livingstons fell foul of royalty. James, 4th Earl of Callendar, was forced into exile for supporting the 'Old Pretender', James Stuart, Prince of Wales, son of the exiled James II of England, in the First Jacobite Rising of 1715. The Callendar estates were forfeit, but

SPERAT · IN · DOMINO · ET · MISERICORDIA · ALTISSIMI · NON · COMMOVEBITVR

FALKLAND PALACE

the house was leased back by the earl's daughter, Lady Anne, from 1724. Bonnie Prince Charlie stayed here in 1746 before the Battle of Falkirk, and Lady Anne's husband, the Earl of Kilmarnock, was beheaded for treason after the prince's defeat at Culloden.

None of them would recognise Callendar House today – although the Scottish queen might feel a pang for her beloved France. Later in the 18th century it was extensively altered by the Forbes family, so that it appears for all the world like a Renaissance château. These days, the house is a heritage centre, where all the staff wear period costume and visitors may admire two grand reception rooms, a working Georgian kitchen and exhibition galleries.

▶ *FK1 1YR. 1 mile SE of Falkirk town centre.*

❹ Linlithgow Palace, West Lothian

'Please your most Sacred Majestie; this sext of September, betuixt thre and four in the morning, the north quarter of your Majesties Palice of Linlithgw is fallin, rufe and all, within the wallis, to the ground.' The Earl of Linlithgow's letter of September 6, 1607 to James VI (James I of England) tells of a royal pleasure palace in sorry decline, although it was rebuilt between 1618 and 1624 for James's visit.

In 1425, James I of Scotland ordered the rebuilding of a palace begun by David I and fortified for Edward I of England. The palace was extended by James III, IV and V to comprise four wings around a central courtyard garden. In the castle's northwest tower, the English queen, Margaret Tudor, daughter of Henry VII, waited vainly, in 1513, for her husband James IV to return from battle at Flodden Field. Mary, Queen of Scots was born at Linlithgow in December 1542. After the Union of the Crowns in 1603, the royal court was based in England, and Linlithgow dwindled in importance. In September 1745, Bonnie Prince Charlie looked in on his way south, but did not spend the night, although it is claimed that the courtyard fountain was adjusted to flow with wine in his honour. In January 1746, the Duke of Cumberland, son of George II, stayed here with a contingent of his army and they caused a fire that gutted the building.

A glorious ruin, it stands by a loch, its roofless Great Hall still inspiring awe. The restored tiered fountain, a masterpiece of Renaissance stonemasonry, flows again on summer Sundays – and it is said that Margaret Tudor still watches at the window of Queen Margaret's Bower, high up in the northwest tower, for the husband who will never return.

▶ *EH49 7AL. 2 miles from Junctions 3 and 4 of M9. Palace in town centre. HS.*

SCOTLAND

The Palace of Holyroodhouse

Weddings, murder and all kinds of chicanery have been enacted within the walls of The Queen's official residence.

The wedding of Margaret Tudor, daughter of Henry VII, and James IV of Scotland took place at Holyrood Abbey in August 1503. She was 13; he was 30. The Palace of Holyroodhouse was completed for the couple two years later. Designed to a quadrangle plan, it was grand in its way, comprising royal apartments, a chapel, gallery and great hall, although to a princess raised in style at Eltham it must have seemed somewhat chilly and spartan.

This palace, to the west of the cloister of Holyrood Abbey, is today the Queen's official Scottish residence, and has been rebuilt more than once.

It was completely remodelled after the Restoration of the Monarchy in 1660 as a showpiece of Louis XIV baroque architecture, although a massive tower commissioned by James V was retained. The palace looks so serene in its parkland setting. Lofty Arthur's Seat, described by Robert Louis Stevenson as 'a hill for magnitude, a mountain in virtue of its bold design', provides an impressive backdrop. When Her Majesty visits, she visibly warms to the good manner and nature of Scotland, and it is hard to imagine the episodes of violence and intrigue that played out at Holyroodhouse in the 16th century.

The palace was completely remodelled after the Restoration of the Monarchy in 1660 as a showpiece of Louis XIV baroque architecture.
HOLYROODHOUSE

lords. At Holyroodhouse she made two disastrous marriages. The first was to Henry Stuart, Lord Darnley, whom she wed in the chapel in 1565; the second was to James Hepburn, 4th Earl of Bothwell, solemnised in the great hall in 1567.

Poor judgement

Darnley was her cousin and had a claim to both the Scottish and English thrones, so he would bolster her own claim. Three years her junior, he was immature, mean, petulant and a violent drunk. When she conceived his child, he was persuaded that her secretary, David Rizzio, was the father. He and his accomplices dragged the Italian from her apartments and stabbed him 56 times, on a spot now marked by a plaque. Distraught, Mary wrote to Bothwell of the husband she now hated, 'Cursed be this poxy fellow that troubleth me this much.' A year later, Darnley was assassinated. Were Mary and Bothwell behind this? Her detractors believed so. Bothwell was exiled. Mary was forced to abdicate in favour of her son, James VI, aged 13 months, and eventually fled to England (see Tutbury Castle, page 100).

With the Union of the Crowns in 1603, James VI became James I of England, and his court transferred to London. He promised to return every three years, but failed to do so. The palace sunk into decline before Charles II's rebuilding. In 1745, Charles Edward Stuart (Bonnie Prince Charlie) occupied it as he made his bid for the English throne. After George IV visited in 1822, he ordered repairs, and some remodelling, but instructed that Mary's bedchamber should not be further changed. In 1854 the palace was opened to the public. Only after Prince Albert's death did it become a residence for Queen Victoria.

Zara Phillips, the Queen's granddaughter, chose Holyroodhouse for the celebration of her wedding to Mike Tindall in July 2011. Visitors will see why. Here are magnificently furnished Royal Apartments, and, in the Great Gallery, Jacob de Wet's 17th-century portraits of 110 monarchs of Scotland, real and legendary.

Poor Mary, Queen of Scots! She should have stayed in France. Clever, vivacious, beautiful, Catholic, she was more in her element at the dazzling, sophisticated French Court than she would ever be in the dour, puritan Edinburgh of the day. From the first it seems that fate had marked her out for tragedy. She was seven days old when she became queen on the death of her father, James V. As granddaughter of Margaret Tudor, the infant Mary was, in Henry VIII's eyes, an ideal bride for his son, Edward, and when his plan for a match was thwarted, he instigated the vengeful 'Rough Wooing'. Edinburgh was sacked, and the palace and abbey looted and burned.

Mary grew up in France, and married the dauphin, Francis. When, as a widow, aged 18, she returned to claim her throne (with an eye also to succeeding Elizabeth I as queen of England), she was viewed with resentment and suspicion by her Protestant

SCOTLAND

203

❺ Edinburgh Castle

'The castle is strong by situation ... and far from being impregnable, as has been prov'd more than once. It is not of little use, unless for salutes, and firing guns upon festivals … and to receive prisoners of State.' David I built a castle here in the 1120s. In its long history it has been captured, occupied, recaptured and reoccupied by English invaders, Scottish heroes, rebels and zealots. Its iconic image, towering above the city, is familiar from shortbread tins. It appears rugged and formidable, yet as Daniel Defoe wrote in the 18th century, it proved all too vulnerable. Perhaps most famously, this is where Mary, Queen of Scots gave birth to her son, the future James VI of Scotland and James I of England, in 1566. When she was forced to abdicate in James's favour a year later, the impact upon Edinburgh was catastrophic. During the following intermittent civil war both castle and town were subject to bombardment, fire-setting and siege. Few of the surviving buildings predate the 'Lang Siege', when Sir William Kirkaldy of Grange, as keeper, held the castle for the queen, and the medieval fortifications were destroyed. Exceptions are the 12th-century St Margaret's Chapel, the Royal Palace and early 16th-century Great Hall. The castle also houses the National War Museum of Scotland. In 1953, the newly crowned Elizabeth II visited Edinburgh and was presented by the governor with the keys to the castle. And in November 1996 the Stone of Scone, the sacred coronation stone taken by Edward I from Scone Abbey to Westminster, was returned to remain here with the crown jewels of Scotland.
▶ *EH1 2NG. Edinburgh city centre.*

❻ The Queen's Gallery, Edinburgh

Scotland's first permanent exhibition space for the Royal Collection was opened by the Queen in November 2002. When the devout and philanthropic Elisabeth, last Duchess of Gordon founded and funded a school and church in Edinburgh, she could not have dreamt of the purpose to which they would eventually be put. In 1844, two years after Queen Victoria's visit to the city, Archibald Simpson designed the Duchess of Gordon's School in the Scots Renaissance style, and in 1848 John Henderson was engaged to build Holyrood Free Church on an adjacent site. They stand between the Palace of Holyroodhouse and the Scottish Parliament building, but by the turn of the century, both church and school were disused. As part of the Queen's Golden Jubilee celebrations, they were converted by architects Benjamin Tindall for the display of precious works of art and artefacts. Old Masters, drawings, sculpture, furniture, ceramics, clocks, exquisite jewellery, manuscripts, prints and maps, armour, fans and textiles are all on show here in changing exhibitions. The duchess did not believe in storing up treasures on earth, and once persuaded the duke to allow her to sell jewellery worth £600 – 'Or, rather, what brought that, for they cost more than double' – to endow a chapel, 'for he agreed that the stones were much prettier in a chapel wall than around my neck'. For the less pious visitor it is fascinating to see what royalty has acquired over 500 years.
▶ *EH8 8DX (Palace of Holyroodhouse). Canongate.*

❼ Holyrood Abbey, Edinburgh

The abbey where James II of Scotland and Charles I of England were crowned has stood in ruins since the 18th century.
Founded in 1128 for the Augustinian Canons Regular by David I, the abbey hosted the Scottish Parliament several times until 1410. Robert the Bruce used the building as a palace and here signed the treaty that ended the First War of Scottish Independence. Henry VIII, no respecter of abbeys, did not spare this one in the 'Rough Wooing' (see Callendar House, page 200). Roofs were stripped, bells taken, the abbey plundered. During the Scottish Reformation, in 1559, a mob came on a looting spree and destroyed the altar. John Knox, the leader of the Reformation, made Edinburgh his home. William Lithgow, despite sharing his hatred of 'the calumnious and vituperious Papists', denounced Knox for wrecking 'our glorious Churches of Abbacies and Monasteries (which were the greatest beauty of the kingdome), knocking all downe to desolation; leaving naught to be scene of admirable Edifices, but … lumpes of Walls and heapes of stones'. In 1570 the choir and transept were demolished, retaining only the nave to serve as the parish church for Canongate. The abbey was remodelled for the coronation of Charles I in 1633, and in 1689, under James VII of Scotland, James II of England, it became a Catholic chapel royal. Come the Glorious Revolution in 1688 and the overthrow of the king, the mob descended once again to wreak havoc. Then in 1768, during a storm, the roof fell in. Now time has cast its spell over the ruined abbey. The 'lumpes of Walls and heapes of stones' are beautiful today, imposing upon the visitor 'a weight of awe'.
▶ *EH8 8DX (Palace of Holyroodhouse). Canongate. HS.*

EDINBURGH CASTLE

NEMO ME IMPUNE LACESSIT

SCOTLAND

❽ The Royal Yacht *Britannia*, Edinburgh

For 44 years one of the world's most famous ships plied the oceans, calling at more than 600 ports in 135 countries. The Royal Yacht was the 83rd in a succession stretching back to the reign of Charles II. She rolled down the slipway at John Brown's Shipyard, Clydebank in 1953 and was commissioned for service the next January. In January 1997 she set off on her last and longest voyage, to Hong Kong – and that December the Queen, with tears clearly visible, Prince Philip and members of the royal family were present to see her decommissioned.

Britannia was begun for George VI to replace *Victoria and Albert III*, but the king died in 1952 before it was complete. The Queen and the Duke of Edinburgh were consulted upon the design, approving plans prepared by architect Sir Hugh Casson, with bespoke furniture, fabrics and artworks. Each room reflected the Queen's tastes. Family photographs and possessions lent touches of home. The ship took the Queen around the world. Monarchs and statesmen were entertained on board. The royal party travelled with 5 tonnes of luggage and 45 members of the household. Four royal couples used *Britannia* on their honeymoons. Princess Margaret and Antony Armstrong-Jones made a voyage to the Caribbean in 1960. Princess Anne and Captain Mark Phillips took a cruise in 1973. The Prince and Princess of Wales sailed the Med in 1981, and in 1986 the Duke and Duchess of York spent five days in the Azores. This luxury yacht has greater longevity than any of those marriages, and visitors can go aboard to see what life was like on this floating royal residence.
▶ *EH6 6JJ. Ocean Terminal, Leith. 2 miles N of Edinburgh city centre.*

❾ Neidpath Castle, Borders

'Disease had been in Mary's bower,/And slow decay from mourning./Though now she sits from Neipath's tower/to watch her love returning.' Sir Walter Scott tells the tale of the 'the Maid of Neidpath', whose ghost is said to appear in a brown dress with white collar. The daughter of William Douglas, Earl of March, she wasted to a shadow when her lover was banished, and died of heartbreak when, on his return, he could not recognise her. It is a story readily imagined when the passer-by on the Tweed Walk from Peebles to Lyne Water has sight of this L-shaped, almost windowless, rubble-built tower house overlooking the Tweed. The castle dates from the late 14th century. Mary, Queen of Scots visited on her summer progress in July 1563. In the Civil War, Neidpath was garrisoned for the Crown. In one version of history, the castle was surrendered without a fight, in 1650, on Cromwell's invasion of Scotland. Other versions tell of it standing defiant against the longest assault on any stronghold south of the Forth. In the 1660s, the 2nd Earl of Tweeddale remodelled the castle, which was sold to William Douglas, 1st Duke of Queensberry, in 1686. In 1693 the duke gave it to his second son, William Douglas, later Earl of March. Over the years it suffered neglect, and by 1790 had partly collapsed. Only the main block and south range remain roofed. Nonetheless, it has appeared in the films *The Bruce, Merlin* and *Joan of Arc*.
▶ *EH45 8NW. 1 mile W of Peebles on A72.*

❿ Melrose Abbey, Borders

It is said that the heart of Robert the Bruce was buried here at one of the most beautiful religious houses in the realm, where a community of Cistercian monks was founded in 1136 at the behest of David I. It was a remote and wild place until the town grew up around it. Over the centuries the abbey was attacked by Edward II, torched by Richard II, damaged by Henry VIII and finally bombarded by Oliver Cromwell. After that first assault, it was rebuilt on the orders of Robert the Bruce. When the body of Lord Douglas (see Drumlanrig Castle, page 199) was brought home from a fateful crusade in 1330, the Bruce's embalmed heart, which Douglas had carried with him, was buried in the abbey church. After Henry VIII's army passed through, the abbey was never again fully repaired and fell into a decline. The last abbot, James Stuart, illegitimate son of James V of Scotland, died in 1559 – and the forlorn last monk in 1590. Even so, Melrose suffered the cannon fire of Parliamentarians in the Civil War.

In *The Pleasure of Ruins* Rose Macaulay evokes the abbey's 'rich and pictorial elaboration of beauty … haunted romantic gloom'. Statues and carved work are extremely fine. Medieval artefacts found in the cloister are displayed in the Commendator's House Museum. Excavation in 1996 unearthed a conical lead container and a plaque inscribed: 'The enclosed leaden casket containing a heart was found beneath the Chapter House floor, March 1921, by His Majesty's Office of Works'. It was reburied on June 22, 1998, and a plinth covering the site was unveiled on June 24. On Sir Walter Scott's advice, 'If thou would'st view fair Melrose aright,/Go visit it by the pale moonlight.'
▶ *TD6 9LG. 35 miles S of Edinburgh. HS.*

CENTRAL & NORTHEAST SCOTLAND

After the tumult of previous centuries, Victoria and Albert gave their clear seal of approval to all things Scottish, buying property, relaxing and spending time here, a tradition maintained by today's royal family.

❶ Castle Stalker, Argyll & Bute

James IV of Scotland was a cousin of the Stewarts of Appin and would often stay at their four-storey castle, situated on a tiny tidal islet on Loch Liach. 'Stalker' derives from 'stalcaire', Gaelic for 'hunter', and apparently the king loved to hunt here.

This is the best-preserved medieval tower house in western Scotland. Entirely surrounded by water, it is almost too picturesque to be true. The house was begun in around 1320 by the MacDougalls, formerly Lords of Lorn. The family had allied themselves with Edward I against Robert the Bruce, and lost their title when the Scottish king defeated them at the Battle of Brander Pass in around 1308. The lordship of Lorn, with accompanying land, was given to the Stewarts in 1388, and the castle in its present form was built by John Stewart in the 1440s. In 1513 the Stewarts fought for James IV at the Battle of Flodden, where the king, their cousin, met his end.

In around 1620 Duncan, 7th Stewart chief, lost the castle to the Campbells of Airds in a drunken bet, but the Stewarts regained it in 1689 when they declared for James VII (James II of England) against William and Mary. After the

THE KING LOVED TO HUNT HERE
CASTLE STALKER

Battle of Dunkeld it was again forfeit to the Campbells, who laid siege for months when the Stewarts refused to surrender it. In the Second Jacobite Rising, in 1745, the castle was garrisoned by the Campbells with government troops, its walls shrugging off the cannon balls fired by Stewarts in the cause of Bonnie Prince Charlie. In about 1800 the Campbells departed for the mainland, and by 1840 the roof of the abandoned castle had caved in. Charles Stewart bought it back for his family in 1908. After a do-it-yourself restoration by Lt Col Stewart Allward, family and friends, from 1965 to 1975, the building was habitable once more. Tours are available, and anyone can admire it from afar.

▶ *PA38 4BL. 26 miles S of Fort William on A828.*

SCOTLAND

❷ Ardverikie Castle, Highland

This Scottish baronial house situated in the Highlands played a starring role in the BBC television series *Monarch of the Glen*. A Victorian fantasy castle, it stands on a promontory overlooking the ancient ruins of King Fergus's Island and is approached by a three-mile private drive. The lands around the estate have long associations with Clan Macpherson, who paid a high financial penalty when they were persuaded to shift their allegiance in the Second Jacobite Rising, in 1745, to declare for Bonnie Prince Charlie. In the mid-19th century the impoverished Macphersons let the estate of Ardverikie to the Duke of Abercorn. He was Groom of Stool to Prince Albert, and through this connection, Victoria and Albert came to stay at Ardverikie for a month, on August 21, 1847. They were greeted by the duke in full Highland dress, and driven to a house bristling with stag horns. The drawing room was hung about with paintings of stags by Sir Edwin Landseer. The royal family loved the house, but the weather wasn't kind. The queen wrote in her journal: 'It is quite near to the lake, and the view from the window … though obscured by rain, is very beautiful and extremely wild … The house is a very comfortable shooting lodge with lots of nice rooms in it.'

In 1871 that house burnt down and was replaced to a design by John Rhind of Inverness, using local granite. It was barely complete when, in October 1873, it burnt down again, and was rebuilt once more, incorporating an oak library bought from the Duke of Sussex at Kensington Palace, and a set of carved panels to replace the Landseer paintings that had been destroyed. The term 'fairytale castle' is impossible to resist. Self-catering accommodation, walking, stalking and climbing are among the attractions on offer.
▶ *PH20 1BX. 16 miles SW of Newtonmore. On private road on S side of Loch Laggan, off A86.*

❸ Lochindorb Castle, Highland

The remains of the 14th-century castle of Sir John ('the Black') Comyn stand on a partially man-made island in the middle of a freshwater loch. The stronghold of the Comyns, Lords of Badenoch, was captured by Edward I in 1303, and again by Edward II, who refortified it. From 1372 it was the lair of Alexander Stewart, 'the Wolf of Badenoch', son of Robert II and one of the most damnable figures in Scottish history. It was his habit to burn the homes of those who crossed him. When his deserted wife, Countess of Ross, appealed to the Bishop of Moray, who gave judgment in her favour, Alexander ransacked and torched Forres and Elgin, the ecclesiastical centre of the Bishopric of Moray. The terrified people of Elgin fled as the college, the canon's houses and Hospital of the Maison Dieu went up in flames. In 1390 it was the turn of Elgin Cathedral. Legend holds that Alexander died in 1406 after being beaten at chess by the devil.

By 1455 the castle was the property of Archibald Douglas, Earl of Moray, who fortified it against the Scottish king, James II. With Moray's defeat and death at Arkinholm in 1456, the castle was once more forfeit to the Crown, and the Thane of Cawdor was sent to slight it, leaving substantial ruins. The Gaelic *Loch nan Doirb* is variously translated as 'Loch of Tadpoles', 'Loch of Minnows', and, most appositely, 'Loch of Trouble'.
▶ *10 miles N of Grantown-on-Spey on minor road, off A939.*

❹ Culloden, Highland

The last pitched battle fought on these shores resulted in the moorlands running with Jacobite blood. In scarcely an hour, on April 16, 1746, the forces of Charles Edward Stuart were routed by the troops of William 'Butcher' Augustus, Duke of Cumberland, younger son of George II, for the British government. The Jacobites were bent on overthrowing the House of Hanover and restoring the Stuarts to the throne, but this was the final stand that Bonnie Prince Charlie would take for the cause.

From the outset, the Jacobites were at a severe disadvantage, low on food, low on finance, and exhausted. At 1pm, amid swirling smoke and skirling bagpipes, they advanced, walking into cannon shot, mortar bombs, gunfire and grapeshot, firing their muskets, brandishing their broadswords. Not much later they were in disorderly retreat. What hubris made 'the Young Pretender' choose to fight? From dawn his senior commanders had been urging that they make for high ground or withdraw to Inverness. The French envoy went down on bended knee, but the prince would not be dissuaded. The day, and the manner of his escape to Skye, secured his place in history as a romantic hero, but he died in exile in Rome in 1788, a broken alcoholic. Visitors to the battle scene can pause at a memorial cairn, built by Duncan Forbes in 1881, to reflect on the battle – the name still sounds like a death knell – then 'purchase a Culloden branded memento from the enhanced range of gifts available at the shop' in the visitors' centre.
▶ *IV2 5EU (visitor centre). The battlefield is just S of the B9006, 5 miles E of Inverness.*

❺ Braemar Castle, Aberdeenshire

'Ereskines, Earls of Marr, have their country seat in the county of Marr, where the late unhappy earl first set up his standard of the Pretender.' In the 1720s, when Daniel Defoe was writing his extraordinary 'Itinerary', the Hanoverian George I was on the throne, and the Jacobites were still avid for the return of the Stuarts. Defoe was, then, very close to the events he relates. In 1707 John Erskine, 6th Earl of Mar, had been Secretary of State for Scotland. He was one of the politicians responsible for negotiating the treaty that brought together the parliaments of England and Scotland, but on George's succession in 1714, after the death of the Stuart Queen Anne, Erskine was dismissed. He returned to Braemar, changed sides (earning the nickname 'Bobbin Jock') and recruited an army of clansmen, raising the standard for the House of Stuart. So began the 1715 Jacobite Rebellion. After his defeat in battle that September, the 'unhappy earl' was forced to flee to France, his lands forfeit, his title extinguished. By 1730 most of the estates, including Braemar, were returned to his son Thomas, but not until 1824 was the ancient and noble Mar title restored to Thomas's grandson, John Francis Erskine.

Meanwhile, in the aftermath of the Jacobites' defeat at Culloden, this castle was leased to the government and remodelled as a military headquarters by John Adam, brother of the famous Robert, with a star-shaped curtain wall. It was garrisoned until 1831, when it was refurbished as a family home by James Farquharson, 10th Laird, and its turrets and curtain wall were crenellated. Victoria and Albert took tea with the Farquharsons in their drawing room. Since February 2007 the castle has been managed by the charity Braemar Community Ltd and maintained by volunteers.
▶ *AB35 5XR. On A93 16 miles W of Ballater.*

❻ Braemar Gathering, Aberdeenshire

'September 12, 1850. We lunched early, and then went at half-past two o'clock ... to the Gathering at the Castle of Braemar ... There were the usual games of "putting the stone", "throwing the hammer" and "caber", and racing up the hill of Craig Cheunnich, which was accomplished in six minutes and a half; and we were all much pleased to see our gillie Duncan, who is an active, good-looking young man, win.' There have been Gatherings at Braemar since the reign of Malcolm Canmore, 900 years ago.

The Queen is patron of the Gatherings and is said to enjoy them greatly. They are organised by the Braemar Royal Highland Society, which began life as the Braemar Wright Society in July 1815. Queen Victoria first came in 1848, and granted the 'Royal' prefix.

After the Battle of Culloden in 1746, the British government sent its army and navy across Scotland to punish suspected Jacobite sympathisers, and to 'pacify' the Highlands, to suppress further uprisings and dismantle the clan system. Highland garb was prohibited by the Dress Act, 1746. There must be no more wearing of the kilt and tartan, no more playing of the bagpipes. Of course, the Gathering was banned, but by 1800 it had resumed, amid a resurgence of romantic interest in all things Highland, and since Victoria first came, it has been attended by the reigning monarch. The Gathering, held on the first Saturday in September, is a riot of Highland dress and display. As well as the events that so entertained Victoria, there are massed pipe bands, Highland dancing, sprinting, the long leap, relay and tug-of-war – a proud display of Scottish culture to make the Duke of Cumberland turn in his grave.
▶ *AB35. The Princess Royal and Duke of Fife Memorial Park, Braemar.*

❼ Royal Deeside, Aberdeenshire

'All seemed to breathe freedom and peace, and to make one forget the world and its sad turmoils ... We walked beside the Dee, a beautiful rapid stream, which is close behind the house.' Queen Victoria's marriage to her cousin, Albert of Saxe-Coburg, in 1840, was arranged for her, but she fell for him at first sight, noting that he had 'the most pleasing and delightful exterior and appearance'. Theirs was one of the greatest royal love stories. Her *Leaves from the Journal of our Life in the Highlands* is a testament not just to their mutual devotion, but to the other love affair they had – with Scotland, and particularly Royal Deeside around Balmoral. The River Dee rises high in the Cairngorms and runs east to Aberdeen, flowing through some of the most breathtaking scenery Scotland has to show. Here Victoria and Albert would walk, ride their ponies, sketch, stalk deer, sharing their pleasure with each other – and with a wider public, through the journal she kept. The decision of the queen and her consort to buy a Scottish estate made an important contribution to the revival of Highland culture and the assertion of Celtic identity.
▶ *The Dee runs close to the A93 from Braemar to Aberdeen.*

⑧ Balmoral, Aberdeenshire

'October 13, 1856. Every year my heart becomes more fixed in this dear Paradise, and so much more so now that all has become my dear Albert's own creation … his great taste, and the impress of his dear hand, have been stamped everywhere.' Soon after Victoria and Albert bought 'a pretty little castle in the old Scottish style' at Balmoral, they commissioned William Smith of Aberdeen to build a larger one. Albert then amended Smith's designs, taking a close interest in such details as windows and turrets. The new house was somewhat dated for its time, being very similar to the demolished castle, which had been remodelled in the 1830s. It has been described as too ordered, pedantic and 'Germanic', but it is pure Scottish baronial, built from granite quarried on the estate, and sits contentedly in its surroundings. The Scottish idyll ended with Albert's death on December 14, 1861. On October 16, 1861, Victoria wrote of a blissful day, concluding: 'The moon rose and shone most beautifully, and we returned … much pleased with this delightful expedition. Alas! I fear our last great one!' A poignant footnote reads: 'IT WAS OUR LAST ONE! 1867.'

The bond that the widowed queen forged with John Brown, her ghillie at Balmoral, has been a source of great intrigue. In a letter to Viscount Cranbrook upon Brown's death at Windsor in 1883 she confessed: 'Perhaps never in history was there so strong and true an attachment … between the sovereign and servant … The Queen feels that life for the second time is become more trying and sad to bear … the blow has fallen too heavily not to be very heavily felt.'

The royal family continue to make August visits to Balmoral. The estate is within the Cairngorms National Park, and the grounds and gardens and are open from April 1 until July 31.
▶ *AB35 5TB. 8 miles W of Ballater on A93.*

⑨ Ballater, Aberdeenshire

A pretty timber railway station at the centre of this town was once the terminus serving Balmoral, bringing backpackers, cyclists, sightseers and VIPS. For passengers, the Deeside–Ballater line offered not just enthralling scenery, but the thrill of seeing royalty and heads of government. But Dr Beeching knocked that on the head. The line closed in 1966.

Since Victoria and Albert first came to Balmoral, about eight miles to the west, Ballater has been shaped by the patronage of royalty. In 1770 it was a spa resort, but the number of Victorian buildings attest to its development in that era. The arrival of the railway in 1866 was a tremendous boon. The original station comprised a booking office and a single platform. Then in 1886 the royal waiting room was built to a design approved by Queen Victoria.

After the line closed, the station fell into disuse but was later refurbished for use by the local council. On its centenary, the waiting room received a visit from the Queen. Afterwards, she inspected the Royal Guard in front of the station, as had been the tradition with the arrival of the

royal train, which clattered out of here at 7.15pm on October 15, 1965, never to return. Enthusiasts have plans to operate a train once more, over a short stretch between Crathes Castle and Banchory.

The station now houses a tourist information centre and a café/restaurant. Local sadness over the death of the Queen Mother in 2002 was compounded five years later when the royal warrants that she had liberally bestowed on the town's shopkeepers all lapsed, but Ballater still revels in its royal connections, and every August holds Victoria Week, with Highland Games, parades, guided walks, history and ghost tours and musical events.

▶ *AB35 5RB. 40 miles W of Aberdeen on A93.*

⑩ Glamis Castle, Angus

The ninth of Lord and Lady Glamis's ten children, Elizabeth Bowes-Lyon spent happy childhood days here – and grew up to marry Albert, Duke of York, the future George VI. In 1904 her father inherited the earldom of Strathmore and Kinghorne, and this castle. It has been in the family since 1372, when Robert II granted it to his son-in-law, Sir John Lyon. In the reign of James V, John Lyon, 6th Lord Glamis, married Janet Douglas. Her father, Master of Angus, was engaged in a feud with the king, and in December 1528 she was burnt as a witch. The king seized the castle to use for a hunting lodge,

holding court here between 1538 and 1542. In 1543 it was returned to John Lyon, 7th Lord Glamis, who played host to Mary, Queen of Scots when she visited in 1562. She was apparently very gracious – as well she might be after what her father did to Janet Douglas.

During the Commonwealth the castle was garrisoned for Parliament, and when Patrick Lyon, 3rd Earl, recovered it, he found it wrecked. Thorough restoration, completed in 1689, included the creation of a baroque garden. The 9th Earl and his wife, Mary Eleanor Bowes, made the grounds over in the Picturesque style after 1735. It was at a castle more reminiscent of a sublime French château than a medieval fortress that in 1930 the Duchess of York, 'the little Scots lass from Glamis', soon to be queen consort, gave birth to a second daughter, Princess Margaret Rose.

▶ *DD8 1RJ. On A928, 12 miles N of Dundee.*

BALMORAL

⑪ Blair Castle, Perth & Kinross

Prince Albert chose the home of the earls and dukes of Atholl as the ideal place for Queen Victoria to recuperate after the birth of their fourth child, Alfred, in 1844. The couple stayed from September 11 to October 1. In her journal, Victoria described 'a large plain white building, surrounded by high hills'. The Georgian stately home had been built around a 13th-century edifice, the Cumming's Tower. From the 1860s the castle was remodelled for the 7th Duke of Atholl in the Scottish baronial style, complete with turrets, crenellations and a ballroom.

The original castle and earldom of Atholl were granted to John Stewart by his half-brother, James II of Scotland, in 1457. Mary, Queen of Scots stayed in 1564 and joined a hunt at Glen Tilt during which 360 deer and five wolves were slaughtered. Prince Albert had less success on his stay. As Victoria sat sketching, a herd of deer were driven down, but 'most provokingly two men were walking on the road ... and then the herd all ran back up again and the sport was spoilt ... My poor Albert had not fired one shot.' More than a few shots were fired in 1652 when the castle was besieged by Cromwell's forces, and in 1689, when it was occupied by Jacobites in support of the exiled James VII (James II of England).

The stuffed stag and displays of weaponry that greet the visitor on entering set the tone for the interiors, which include tapestries that belonged to Charles I. Every May bank holiday, a gathering of the Atholl Highlanders, Blair Castle's private army, includes a parade and Highland Games.
▶ *PH18 5TL. 8 miles NW of Pitlochry on A9.*

⑫ Stirling Castle, Stirling

More than just a castle, this magnificent edifice stands as a symbol of Scottish fortitude and fierce independence.
A monumental survivor of centuries of siege and attack, it looms above the plain, dominating its surroundings. The principal buildings date from the 15th and 16th centuries, but its history as a royal stronghold stretches back to the 1100s. It was occupied by Edward I on his invasion in 1296 – and bore witness to his son Edward II's defeat by Robert the Bruce at Bannockburn. Between 1490 and 1600, Stirling took shape under the Stewart kings. James IV spent a fortune remodelling it for himself and Margaret Tudor, including the forework gatehouse and the largest medieval banqueting hall ever built in Scotland. James V was crowned at Stirling; he and Mary of Guise created the centrepiece Renaissance palace.

In 1542, his daughter succeeded him at just seven days old. She was crowned Mary, Queen of Scots at this castle on September 9, 1543. After her return from France in 1561 she would often visit Stirling, where she nursed her cousin and future second husband, Henry Stewart, Lord Darnley, through an illness in 1565. Their son James, the only child of their hopeless marriage, was baptised here in 1566, and brought up as James VI after Mary's forced abdication in 1567, closely guarded against her supporters. In 1594 he built the Chapel Royal for the baptism of his son, Prince Henry. With the Union of the Crowns he departed for London as James I of England. Elaborate preparations were made for the crowning here of Charles I – who deigned to stay for two days. After he was beheaded in 1649, the Scots acknowledged his son Charles as king, crowning him at Scone in 1651. In between, Charles II became the last reigning monarch to stay at Stirling Castle, in 1650.
▶ *FK8 1EJ. Access Stirling from Junction 10 of M9. Castle in city centre. HS.*

⑬ Lochleven Castle, Perth & Kinross

'We passed Loch Leven, and saw the castle on the lake from which poor Queen Mary escaped.' Queen Victoria had its history very much in mind when she saw this castle in 1842. Here in 1567–8 Mary, Queen of Scots was imprisoned and forced by her Protestant lords to abdicate in favour of her infant son. It has, even now, an intractable air, standing on its island, a sullen ruin, although the tower house where Mary was confined is still almost entire.

Robert the Bruce came to Lochleven by choice in 1313 and 1323. Robert, the High Steward (heir apparent), was brought in chains in 1389, two years before he was crowned Robert II. On Mary's first visit in 1561 she was the guest of Sir William Douglas. The second time she was his prisoner. Soon after she arrived, she miscarried the twins she had conceived with the rugged Earl of Bothwell. In a pitiful state, then, in July 1567, she signed away her throne. However, her beauty, charm and intelligence worked their magic on Sir William's brother, George. On the night of May 2, 1568, a young orphaned relative, Willie Douglas, stole the keys and allowed Mary, dressed as a servant, to slip out. She was rowed across the loch to be met by George Douglas and others, and sent on her way to England – out of the frying pan into hellfire.
▶ *KY13 8AS. 1 mile E of Kinross, close to Junction 6 of M90. HS.*

NORTH HIGHLANDS & ISLANDS

An early royal burial spot and a magical cave were bypassed by the bonnie prince, *en route* to legendary status. Meanwhile, a retreat of a different kind stands on the windswept coast at Mey.

❶ Iona, Argyll & Bute

'That man is little to be envied ... whose piety would not grow warmer amid the ruins of Iona.' Samuel Johnson, the famed lexicographer and essayist, was stirred by his visit here in 1775. This was for four centuries a centre of Irish monasticism after the exiled monk Columba founded a monastery here in AD 563. The abbey, a place of pilgrimage, is a medieval gem, not large but rich in architectural detail and historical interest. Duncan I was interred here, as was his nemesis, Macbeth. A 16th-century inventory listed 48 Scottish, eight Norwegian and four Irish monarchs' burials, but even when Johnson saw them, the graves were not identifiable and he expressed scepticism. 'Iona has long enjoyed, without any very credible attestation, the honour of being reputed the cemetery of the Scottish Kings ... But by whom the subterraneous vaults are peopled is now utterly unknown. The graves are very numerous, and some of them undoubtedly contain the remains of men, who did not expect to be so soon forgotten.' Visitors can see the site of St Columba's writing cell, his shrine and the abbey church and cloisters.

▶ *PA76 6SQ. By ferry from Fionnphort, Isle of Mull.*

❷ Staffa and Fingal's Cave, Argyll & Bute

For Sir Walter Scott, this cave 'baffled all description'. He wrote that it was 'one of the most extraordinary places I ever beheld. It exceeded, in my mind, every description I had heard of it ... composed entirely of basaltic pillars as high as the roof of a cathedral, and running deep into the rock, eternally swept by a deep and swelling sea, and paved, as it were, with ruddy marble.' A cave on the uninhabited island of Staffa, it is part of a National Nature Reserve owned by the National Trust for Scotland.

Queen Victoria came with her family in 1847, and noted 'the effect was splendid, like a great entrance into a vaulted hall: it looked almost awful as we entered, and the barge heaved up and down on the swell of the sea. The rocks, under water, were all colours – pink, blue and green – which had a most beautiful and varied effect. It was the first time the British standard with a Queen of Great Britain, and her husband and children, had ever entered Fingal's Cave, and the men gave three cheers, which sounded very impressive there.'

▶ *8 miles N of SW tip of Isle of Mull. NTS.*

FINGAL'S CAVE

SCOTLAND

❸ Glenfinnan, Highland

Early in the afternoon of August 19, 1745, a small rowing boat was moored at the north end of Loch Shiel, and Charles Edward Stuart, 'The Young Pretender', came ashore. An escort of 50 MacDonalds met him and accompanied him to a barn where he waited in hope for a response to his appeal for the support of the Highlanders. A further 150 MacDonalds presented themselves, but would anybody else? Time passed. The prince waited. One can only imagine how his heart swelled when in the distance was heard the sound of bagpipes, and perhaps 1,000 members of Clan Cameron approached from Achnacarry and Loch Arkaig. Next to arrive were 300 Macdonnells, who had been intercepted by government troops near Spean Bridge. With some ceremony, then, the prince climbed the hill and raised his father's standard. So began 'the 45', the Second Jacobite Rebellion that would be brutally put down at Culloden the next year (see page 208), ushering in a period of appalling oppression of the Highland way of life by the English.

The visitor cannot fail to be moved by the monument that stands by the loch against a beautiful mountainous backdrop. Designed by James Gillespie Graham, it was erected by Alexander MacDonald of Glenaladale in 1815. A tower is surmounted by the figure of an unknown Highlander, the embodiment of the Jacobite spirit.

▶ *PH37 4LT. 16 miles W of Fort William on A830. NTS.*

❹ *Jacobite* Steam Train, Fort William to Mallaig

The wild beauty of the Highlands, the nostalgia of steam travel and the romance of Bonnie Prince Charlie's story combine in one breathtaking journey. In summer, a steam train named *Jacobite* takes the visitor on a spectacular journey through time and place. The starting point is Fort William, named after William of Orange. Here, in 1690, on the site of a stronghold built by Oliver Cromwell, the Williamite commander Major-General Hugh Mackay of Scourie erected a fort to suppress Jacobite sympathisers. The train follows the legendary 'Road to the Isles', travelling along the shores of Loch Eil. It stops at Glenfinnan, where Bonnie Prince Charlie raised his banner (see above), so passengers can alight to admire the monument and look in at the visitors' centre. A concrete viaduct at Glenfinnan, built by Robert McAlpine ('Concrete Bob') spans 300m

(1,000ft) 30m (100ft) above the ground. The onward journey offers views of the beautiful villages of Lochailort, Arisaig and Morar, before arrival at the fishing village of Mallaig. On this stretch of coast, Bonnie Prince Charlie's big adventure began in 1745 – and from here he fled in 1746. Motorists may prefer to drive the scenic A830, and take a ferry 'over the sea to Skye'.

▶ *West Coast Railway Company* Jacobite *Steam Train. 0845 129 0977.*

❺ Castle of Mey, Highland

Elizabeth, the Queen Mother, bought this castle in 1952 while in deep mourning for George VI. She had heard that it was to be abandoned, and resolved to rescue it. It is Britain's most northerly mainland castle, and its isolated situation allowed the widowed queen to 'get away from everything'.

The castle stands on the rugged Caithness coast overlooking the Pentland Firth. It was built by George Sinclair, 4th Earl of Caithness, for his second son, William. The Sinclairs were evidently a dysfunctional family. William was murdered in 1573 at their seat, Girnigoe Castle, by his elder brother, John, who had been disinherited by his father and locked up there for seven years. William, learning that John planned to escape, had reported this to the earl and, the escape thwarted, the brothers quarrelled violently. Subsequently, John was murdered by his two jailers, both relatives of his, and the Castle of Mey went to the third son, George.

Its evolution over centuries has resulted in a certain architectural dissonance. In the 1800s it gained height, a grand entrance, a new west wing and crenellation. The Queen Mother engaged Sinclair Macdonald of Thurso to carry out further remodelling. The Great Wall of Mey, 3.7m (12ft) high, protects the garden and parkland from gales and salt spray. Elizabeth outlived her husband by 50 years. Was her secret to eat, drink and be merry? *A Taste of Mey: Recipes and Memories Inspired by the Castle of Mey* contains such favourites as brandy-laced Tipsy Tart, Bloody Bull (Bloody Mary with beef consommé) and After Eight Ice Cream (double cream, more brandy). Prince Charles, Duke of Rothesay, contributed a foreword and the recipe for Oeufs Drumkilbo, but the greatest interest in the book, as in the castle, lies with its associations with the fondly remembered 'Queen Mum'. The castle and gardens are run by a charitable trust and are open to the public in the summer months.

▶ *KW14 8XH. Just N of A836, 12 miles E of Thurso.*

THE EMBODIMENT OF THE JACOBITE SPIRIT
GLENFINNAN

SCOTLAND

Index

Page numbers in **bold** refer to main entries. Page numbers in *italic* refer to pictures.

A

abbeys
Bath Abbey *32*, **33**
Battle Abbey **72**
Dundrennan Abbey **199**
Dunfermline Abbey and Palace **200**
Glastonbury Abbey **29**
Hartland Abbey **22**
Holyrood Abbey **204**
Melrose Abbey **206**
Reading Abbey **43**
Romsey Abbey **48**
Shaftesbury Abbey **26**
Strata Florida Abbey **184**
Tewkesbury Abbey 134, *135*
Tintern Abbey **195**
Westminster Abbey 8, **89**, *96*, **97**, 114
Woburn Abbey **38**, *38*
see also cathedrals, churches and chapels
Abdication Crisis 66, 142
Abergavenny Castle 187
Abingdon **64**
Adam, John 209
Adam, Robert 105, 116, 174
Addington, Henry 102
Adelaide, Queen 20, 87, 142, 157
Adlington Hall **160-1**
Aethelred I 27
Agincourt, Battle of 71
Albert, Prince Consort 14, 15, 17, 19, 23, 34, 35, 38, 40, 45, 53, 65, 69, 79, 80, 81, 98, 124, 141, 154, 157, 167, 198, 203, 208, 209, 210, 212
Albert Bridge **99**
Albert Dock, Liverpool *166-7*, **167**
Albert Memorial 78
The Albert Rock 15
Albertopolis **79**
Alderley Edge **161**
Alderney **35**
Alexander II of Scotland 172, 198
Alexander III of Scotland 165
Alexander, Daniel Asher 109
Alexandra, Queen 85, 123, 124, 173
Alfred, King (Alfred the Great) **8**, 25, 26, 28, 54, 64, 71, 99

Alfred's Statue, Winchester **47**, *47*
Alnwick Castle **174**, *174*
Althorp **146**, *146*
Amelia, Princess 102
the Anarchy 137, 143
Andarida 72
Anglesey **190-1**
Ankerwycke Yew **43**
Anne, Queen 15, 33, 43, 65, 78, 89
Anne, Princess 33, 132, 136, 166, 206
Anne of Bohemia 59
Anne of Cleves 39, 58, 63, 71, 87
Anne of Denmark 66, 109, 200
Antony *20-1*, **21**
Appleby Castle **164**
Archer, Thomas 89, 132
Ardverikie Castle **208**
Armoury House **98**
Armstrong, William George 173
Arthur, King 14, 19, 20, 27, 29, **30-1**, 31, 161, 173
Arthur, Prince 30, 47, 149
Arthur of Brittany 120
Arundel, Sir John 16
Arundel Castle **69**, *69*
Ashdown House **39**
Aske, Robert 176, 178
Astor, William Waldorf 58
Atholl Highlanders 212
Atkinson, Robert 71
Attlee, Clement 99
Aubrey, John 24
Audley End House **116**, *116-17*
Augusta, Princess 109
Austin, Hubert 163
Avington Park **47**
Aylesbury **44-5**

B

Badbury Rings **27**
Badminton Horse Trials **136**, *136*
Ballater **210-11**
Balliol, John 165
Balmoral **210**, *210-11*
Bamburgh Castle **175**
Bankes, Dame Mary 26
Banks, Joseph 109
Banqueting House **88**
Barnard Castle **172**
Barrie, J.M. 40
Barry, Sir Charles 27
Barry, Sir Edward Middleton 94
Bath *33*
Bath Abbey *32*, **33**
Bath Pump Rooms **33**
Battle Abbey **72**
battlefields
Bosworth Field **140**
Culloden **208**
Edgehill **153**

Evesham **156**
Langside **198**
Lewes **72**
Marston Moor 179, **181**
Naseby 126, **147**
Northampton **147**
Sedgemoor 24, *28-9*, **29**
Wakefield **178**
Worcester **156**
Bazalgette, Sir Joseph 99
Beacon Hill 45
Bear Hotel **39**
Beaton, Cecil 66, 81
Beatrice, Princess 50, 53
Beaufort, Lady Margaret 27, 145, 192
Beaumaris Castle 187, **191**
Becket, Thomas 43, 61, 63, 101, 164
Bedfordshire 38
Belton House **142-3**, *142*
Belvoir Castle **141**
Benson, William Arthur Smith 184
Bentley Hall 151
Berkeley Castle **134**
Berkshire 39-43
Bernhardt, Sarah 94
Bernini, Charlotte 181
Berwick-upon-Tweed **175**
Bess of Hardwick *see* Shrewsbury, Countess of ('Bess of Hardwick')
Bestwood Country Park **148**
Biddle, Professor Martin 66
Bigod, Hugh 128
Bishop's Palace **74**
Black Death 9, 72
Blackheath **111**
Blair Castle **212**
Blanche of Lancaster 39, 43, 169
Blenheim, Battle of **65**
Blenheim Palace **65**
Blickling Hall **124-5**
Blomfeld, Sir Arthur 79
Blore, Edward 84
Bognor Regis 68
Boleyn, Anne 43, 44-5, 46, 48, 58, 69, 94, 98, 100, 101, 106, 109, 117, 124, 125, 129, 134
Boleyn, George 117, 124
Boleyn, Mary 58, 124
Bolingbroke Castle **145**
Bolton Castle **180-1**
Bonnie Prince Charlie *see* Stuart, Prince Charles Edward
Boscobel House **149**, 150, *150-1*
Boswell, James 110
Bosworth Field, Battle of **140**
Bothwell, Earl of 203, 212
Boudicca 119
Bradgate House and Deer Park **140**

Braemar Castle **209**
Braemar Gathering **209**
Brancepeth Castle **172**
Brandard, John 81
Brettingham, Matthew 127
Bridgeman, Charles 78
Brighton Royal Pavilion *70*, **71**
Britannia Bridge 191
Broadlands **48-9**
Brontë, Charlotte 181
Brown, John 210
Brown, Lancelot 'Capability' 39, 49, 105, 116, 127, 143, 153, 175
Buck, Sir George 176
Buckingham **44**
Buckingham Palace **84**, *84-5*
Buckinghamshire 44-5
Bucklebury **39**
Bulwer-Lytton, Edward 56
Burges, William 194
Burghley House *138-9*, **143**
Burlington House 92
Burne-Jones, Sir Edward 30
Burney, Fanny 25
Burton, Decimus 109
Bury St Edmunds **128**
Bushy Park **102**
Bute, Marquess of 194

C

Cadbury Castle **29**
Caernarfon Castle 187, **190**
Caerphilly Castle **193**
Callendar House **200-1**
Calshot Castle **49**, *49*
Camber Castle **72-3**
Cambridge, Catherine, Duchess of 39, 78, 89, 92, 94, 132, 136, 152, 190-1
Cambridge, Prince William, Duke of 22, 39, 55, 68, 81, 89, 92, 132, 152, 176, 190-1
Cambridge, Richard, Earl of 48
Cambridgeshire 114-15
Camden, William 60
Cameron, David 43
Canterbury Castle **62**
Canterbury Cathedral **61**
Cardiff Castle **194**, *194*
Carême, Marie-Antoine 71
Carew, John 21
Carew, Richard 19
Carisbrooke Castle **50**
Carlisle Castle **165**
Carlyle, Thomas 93
Caroline of Ansbach 78, 102, 109

Caroline of Brunswick
62, 94, 132
Carreg Cennen Castle **192**
Casson, Sir Hugh 89, 206
Castell-y-Bere 187
Castle of Mey **214**
Castle Rising **122**
Castle Stalker **207**, *207*
castles
  Abergavenny Castle 187
  Alnwick Castle **174**,
  174
  Appleby Castle **164**
  Ardverikie Castle **208**
  Arundel Castle 69, *69*
  Bamburgh Castle **175**
  Barnard Castle **172**
  Beaumaris Castle 187,
  191
  Belvoir Castle **141**
  Berkeley Castle **134**
  Blair Castle **212**
  Bolingbroke Castle **145**
  Bolton Castle **180-1**
  Bracmar Castle **209**
  Brancepeth Castle **172**
  Caernarfon Castle 187,
  190
  Caerphilly Castle **193**
  Calshot Castle 49, *49*
  Camber Castle **72-3**
  Canterbury Castle **62**
  Cardiff Castle **194**, *194*
  Carisbrooke Castle **50**
  Carlisle Castle **165**
  Carreg Cennen Castle
  192
  Castell-y-Bere 187
  Castle of Mey **214**
  Castle Rising **122**
  Castle Stalker **207**, *207*
  Chepstow Castle 187,
  192-3, **193**
  Chillingham Castle **175**
  Chirk Castle **188**, *188-9*
  Colchester Castle **119**
  Conwy Castle *186*, *187*
  Corfe Castle **26**, *26-7*
  Criccieth Castle **191**
  Deal Castle 54, *62*
  Dinas Bran 187
  Dolbadarn Castle 187
  Dover Castle **63**
  Drumlanrig Castle **199**,
  199
  Dumbarton Castle **198**
  Dunstanburgh Castle
  174-5
  Dunster Castle **28**
  Edinburgh Castle **204**,
  205
  Elizabeth Castle **34**,
  34-5
  Fotheringhay Castle
  147
  Framlingham Castle
  128-9, *129*
  Glamis Castle **211**
  Goodrich Castle **137**
  Grimsthorpe Castle
  143

  Hadleigh Castle *118*,
  119
  Harlech Castle *184-5*
  185
  Hedingham Castle
  116-17
  Hever Castle **58**
  Hurst Castle **49**
  Kendal Castle **164**
  Kenilworth Castle 139,
  154
  Kimbolton Castle **114**
  Lancaster Castle **169**
  Launceston Castle **20**
  Leeds Castle **59**
  Lewes Castle **71**
  Lincoln Castle **143**
  Lochindorb Castle **208**
  Lochleven Castle **212**
  Ludlow Castle **149**
  Middleham Castle **181**
  Monmouth Castle 187,
  195
  Mont Orgueil Castle **34**
  Muncaster Castle **162**,
  162-3
  Neidpath Castle **206**
  Newark Castle **148**
  Norris Castle **53**
  Norwich Castle *126*
  Oakham Castle **140-1**,
  141
  Oxford Castle **65**
  Pembroke Castle **192**
  Pendennis Castle **16**
  Pendragon Castle **164**
  Penrhyn Castle **189**
  Penrith Castle **165**
  Pevensey Castle **72**, *73*
  Pontefract Castle **178**
  Portchester Castle **48**
  Portland Castle **25**
  Powis Castle **184-5**
  Raby Castle **172**
  Raglan Castle **195**
  Restormel Castle *18*, **19**
  Richmond Castle *68*,
  180, *180*
  Ripley Castle **179**
  Rochester Castle **61**
  Rockingham Castle **147**
  Ruthin Castle **188-9**
  St Mawes Castle **16**
  Scarborough Castle
  177-8
  Sherborne Castle **24**
  Shrewsbury Castle **149**
  Skipton Castle **179**, *179*
  Southsea Castle **48**
  Stirling Castle **212**
  Sudeley Castle **134**
  Tintagel Castle **19**
  Tiverton Castle **22**
  Trematon Castle **21**
  Tutbury Castle **152**
  Upnor Castle **60**, *60-1*
  Walmer Castle **62-3**
  Warwick Castle **154**
  Westenhanger Castle **63**
  Winchester Castle 30,
  46

Windsor Castle **40**
see also historic houses
cathedrals, churches and
  chapels
  Canterbury Cathedral
  61
  Durham Cathedral **172**
  Ely Cathedral *114-15*,
  115
  Lincoln Cathedral **145**
  Newport Minster, Isle
  of Wight **53**
  Norwich Cathedral **127**
  Peterborough Cathedral
  114-15
  Queen's Chapel,
  London **85**
  St Albans Cathedral **56**
  St Andrew's Church,
  Trent **24**
  St George's Chapel,
  Windsor **40**, *41*
  St John's, Smith Square
  89
  St Mary Magdalene
  Church, Sandringham
  123
  St Mary's Church, Isle
  of Wight **50**
  St Mary's Church,
  Warwick **154-5**, *155*
  St Mawgan in Pydar
  Church **19**
  St Michael's Church,
  Burgh-by-Sands **165**
  St Michael's Church,
  Framlingham **129**
  St Mildred's Church,
  Isle of Wight **50**
  St Nicholas' Church,
  Kenilworth **154**
  St Paul's Cathedral **95**
  St Saviour's Church,
  Jersey **35**
  St Thomas' Tower **107**
  Salisbury Cathedral **74**,
  75
  Wimborne Minster
  Church **27**
  Winchester Cathedral **47**
  York Minster **177**, *177*
  see also abbeys
Catherine of Aragon 44,
  46, 59, 64, 94, 114, 115,
  117, 124, 126-7, 149
Catherine of Braganza 58,
  116
Catherine of Valois 59
Catherine the Great,
  Empress 66
Cavendish, Sir William 132
Cecil, Sir William 139, 143
Celts 30
Cenotaph, London **91**
Central and Northeast
  Scotland 207-12
Chadwick, William 99
Chained Library 27
Chambercombe Manor **22**
Chambers, Sir William 94,
  95, 109

Changing of the Guard
  84
Channel Islands 34-5
Charing Cross **92-3**, *93*
Charlecote Park **153**, *153*
Charles I 19, 21, 26, 39,
  40, 48, 49, 50, 65, 74, 82,
  87, 88, 90, 91, 94, 97,
  102, 103, 104, 106, 111,
  122, 126, 128, 134, 140,
  146, 147, 148, 175, 176,
  181, 195, 200, 204, 212
Charles I statue **92**
Charles II **10**, 15, 16, 20,
  24, 28, 39, 40, 43, 44,
  45, 46, 47, 55, 58, 65,
  66, 68, 74, 81, 82, 87,
  88, 92, 94, 97, 100, 110,
  111, 116, 117, 118-19,
  127, 128, 148, 149,
  150-1, 152, 156, 157,
  172, 184, 200, 212
Charles, Prince of Wales
  14, 17, 20, 21, 24, 33,
  40, *41*, 48, 55, 68, 79,
  81, 87, 94, 95, 102, 124,
  141, 142, 146, 149, 167,
  184, 185, 190, 206, 214
Charlotte, Queen 33, 40,
  84, 102, 105, 156
Charlton House **111**
Chatham Dockyards **60**
Chatsworth **132**
Chavenage House **136**
Chenies Manor **45**
Chepstow Castle 187,
  192-3, **193**
Cheshire and The Wirral
  160-1
Chillingham Castle **175**
Chirk Castle **188**, *188-9*
Cholmondeley, Sir Hugh
  178
Christ Church, Oxford
  65
Christian, Ewan 93
Christmas broadcasts 124
Churchill, Winston 49, 65
Churchyard, Thomas 195
Cinque Ports 54, 63, 73
Cipriani, Giovanni
  Battista 105
Civil War 14, 16, 19, 20,
  22, 24, 25, 26, 28, 31,
  39, 40, 44, 45, 46, 47,
  48, 61, 62, 65, 69, 81,
  93, 97, 111, 114, 115,
  119, 126, 134, 137, 140,
  145, 147, 148, 150-1,
  152, 153, 156, 161, 165,
  169, 172, 176, 177, 178,
  179, 181, 184, 188, 189,
  190, 192, 193, 194, 206
Clarence House **87**
Cleveland, Barbara,
  Duchess of 66
Clifford, Lady Anne 164,
  179
Clifford, Henry, 10th
  Lord de 179
Clifford, Rosamund de 63

Clive, Robert (Clive of India) 184
Clochfaen House **184**
Cnut 26, 47, 128, 160
Cobbett, William 165
Colchester **119**
Colchester Castle **119**
Cole, Henry 80
Colt, Maximilian 56
Constable, John 119
Conwy Castle *186*, 187
Cook, James 109
Corfe Castle **26**, *26-7*
Corn Market and Dome, Brighton **71**
Cornwall 14-21
Cornwall, Camilla, Duchess of 14, 33, 40, *41*, 66, 87
Courtauld Sir Stephen 111
Cowdray Park **68**
Cowes **53**
Crace, John G. 56
Cragside **173**, *173*
Creevey, Thomas 84
Criccieth Castle **191**
Cromwell, Oliver 28, 90, 94, 97, 100, 102, 103, 105, **115**, 117, 136, 147, 179, 181, 206
Cromwell, Richard 188
Cromwell, Thomas 62, 118
Crouchback, Edmund 50, 169
Cubitt, Thomas 53, 66
Culloden **208**
Culpeper, Sir Thomas 145, 178
Cumberland, William Augustus, Duke of 201, 208
Cumbria 162-5
Curtis, Sir William 62
Cymbeline 45

D

Darnley, Lord 199, 203, 212
Dartmouth **23**
Darwen Moors 169
Darwin, Charles 81
David I of Scotland 200, 201, 204, 206
Davies, Robert and John 188
Davis, Arthur 66
De Gomme, Sir Bernard 119
Deal Castle 54, **62**
Debrett, John 200
Defoe, Daniel 24, 74, 103, 119, 127, 149, 165, 172, 175, 176, 178, 180, 190, 191, 199, 204, 209
Deheubarth 185, 192
Denham, Sir John 92
Dent, John and William 134

Derbyshire 132-3
Despenser, Hugh le 122, 134, 137, 193, 194
Devon 22-3
Devonshire, Dukes of 132
Devonshire, Georgiana, Duchess of 146
Diana, Princess of Wales 48, 68, 78, 85, 89, 95, 146, 206
Dickens, Charles 95, 169
Dickens, Charles, Jnr 87
Dinas Bran 187
Disraeli, Benjamin 45, 53, 79, 81
Dissolution of the Monasteries 26, 29, 33, 38, 43, 47, 61, 72, 98, 115, 118, 122, 124, 128, **138-9**, 176, 177, 195
Dolbadarn Castle 187
Doniert 14, 20
Dorset 24-7
Douglas, George 212
Douglas, Lord James 199, 206
Douglas, Janet 211
Dover 54
Dover Castle **63**
Downham Market **126**
Doyle, Sir Arthur Conan 40
Dozmary Pool **20**
Drake, Sir Francis 17, 21, 54-5, 69, 134
Drumlanrig Castle **199**, *199*
Duesbury, William 132
Dumbarton Castle **198**
Duncan I of Scotland 213
Dundrennan Abbey **199**
Dunfermline Abbey and Palace **200**
Dunmail Raise **164**
Dunstanburgh Castle **174-5**
Dunster Castle **28**
Durham and Teeside 172
Durham Cathedral **172**
Dyce, William 91

E

Eden Project **17**
Edgar I (the Peaceable) 33
Edgehill, Battle of **153**
Edinburgh 204-6
Edinburgh, Philip, Duke of 17, 35, 48, 53, 55, 68, 87, *90*, 109, 169
Edinburgh Castle **204**, 205
Edward the Confessor **8**, 89, 97, 100
Edward the Martyr 26
Edward I **9**, 24, 29, 50, 59, 62, 92, 93, 97, 101, 127, 145, 149, 156, 165, 175, 177, 179, 180, 184, 185, 187, 189, 190, 191, 192, 200, 207, 208, 212

Edward II 26, 27, 48, 122, 124, 134, 154, 174, 177, 178, 179, 190, 193, 195, 206, 208, 212
Edward III 20, 27, 40, 45, 119, 122, 124, 148, 177, 179
Edward IV 14, 40, 43, 106, 122, 124, 141, 148, 149, 172, 175, 178, 181
Edward V 73, 100, 106, 149
Edward VI 43, 44, 54, 58, 66, 74, 109, 129, 134
Edward VII 14, 27, 50, 53, 58, 66, 68, 79, 81, 83, 94, 102, 124, 127, 173, 184
Edward VIII 45, 66, 81, 102, 119, 140, 142, 175, 190
Edward, the Black Prince 19, 20, 61, 126
Edwin, King of Northumbria 177
Eleanor of Aquitaine 30, 91, 126, 129
Eleanor of Castile 46, 59, 92-3, 97, 145
Eleanor of Provence 46, 101
Eleanor Crosses 93
Elgar, Sir Edward 79, 157
Elizabeth I 17, 24, 33, 38, 39, 40, 46, 54, 56, 58, 60, 63, 67, 74, 79, 87, 89, 98, 100, 105, 106, 109, 117, 118, 125, 126, 127, 132, 134, 139, 141, 143, 149, 152, 153, 154
Elizabeth II 17, 21, 33, 34, 35, 48, 68, 85, 87, 88, *90-1*, 97, 98, 99, 124, 141, 157, 166, 177, 185, 202, 204, 206, 209, 210-11
Elizabeth of Bohemia (Winter Queen) 39, 200
Elizabeth Castle **34**, *34-5*
Elizabeth, The Queen Mother 46, 63, 66, 81, 85, 87, 89, 99, 100, 102, 122, 132, 211, 214
Elizabeth of York 89, *96*
Elizabeth, Princess (daughter of Charles I) 53
Ellison, David 169
Eltham Palace **111**
Ely Cathedral *114-15*, 115
Emes, William 188
Essex 116-19
Ethelbert of Kent **62**
Eton College *42*, **43**
Euston Hall **127**
Evelyn, John 39, 59, 66, 78, 82, 87, 97, 103, 105, 110, 111, 127, 143, 150, 152, 153, 177
Evesham, Battle of **156**
Excalibur 14, 20

F

Fairfax, Sir Thomas 119, 147, 176
Falkland Palace **200**, *201*
Farringdon, Hugh Cook 43
Fastolfe, Sir John 125
Fawkes, Guy 176
Festival of Britain (1951) 99
Fiennes, Celia 33
Fife and Southeast Scotland 200-6
film and TV locations
  Antony 21
  Ardverikie Castle 208
  Belvoir Castle 141
  Eton College *42*, **43**
  Greenwich Hospital **110**
  Holkham Hall **122-3**
  Neidpath Castle **206**
  St Mawgan **19**
  Wilton House **74**
Fingal's Cave **213**, *213*
Fitton, Mary 161
Fitzherbert, Maria 47
FitzNigel, Richard 120
FitzOsbern, William 134, 187, 193, 195
Flamsteed, John 100, 110
Fletching **71**
Flitcroft, Henry 38
Flodden Field 201, 207
Forbes, Duncan 208
Fort Belvedere **66**
Fotheringhay Castle **147**
Fowey *16-17*, **17**
Fowke, Captain Francis 80, 81
Fowler, Charles 105
Framlingham Castle **128-9**, *129*
Frederick, Empress 53
Frederick V, Elector Palatine 39
Frogmore House and Mausoleum **40**
Furness, Thelma 140

G

Gainsborough Old Hall *144*, **145**
Gandulf, Bishop of Rochester 119
Garth Celyn 190
Gaveston, Piers 122, 177, 178, 179
Gawsworth Hall *160-1*, **161**
Geoffrey of Monmouth 19, 30, 184
George II 78, 81, 82, 94, 102
George III 25, 40, 55, 71, 78, 84, 92, 94, 102, 105, 109, 132, 134, 142, 156
George IV 40, 47, 53, 62,

66, 67, 68, 71, 83, 84, 87, 94, 97, 141, 155, 203
George V 17, 20, 34, 40, 66, 68, 81, 124, 169, 184, 185
George VI 11, 20, 40, 55, 66, 99, 102, 119, 127, 184, 206
George Square, Glasgow **198**
Gerald of Wales 186, 187
Gibb, James 157
Gibbons, Grinling 95
Gilbert, Alfred 85
Gildas 30
Gilpin, William 139, 195
Glamis Castle 211
Glasgow City Chambers **198**
Glastonbury Abbey **29**
Gleichen, Count 64
Glenfinnan **214**, *215*
Glorious Revolution 23, 204
Gloucester, Humphrey, Duke of 109
Gloucestershire 134-6
Glyndwr, Owain 184, 185, 188-9, 190, 191, 192
Godolphin **15**
Goodrich Castle **137**
Goodwood House **68**
Goodwood Racecourse **68**
Gordon, Elisabeth, Duchess of 204
Gough, Piers 94
Graham, James Gillespie 214
Graham, Sir Richard 181
Great Exhibition (1851) 79, 82
Great Fire of London (1666) 95, 98
Great Kimble **45**
Great Yarmouth **127**
Green Park **82-3**
Greene, Graham 94
Greenwich Hospital **110**
Greenwich Park **109**
Greville, Margaret 66
Grey, Lady Jane 22, 100, 101, 106, 129, 140
Grey, Sir Ralph 147
Grey, Sir Thomas 48
Grimsthorpe Castle **143**
Grisedale Tarn **164**
Guernsey 35
Guildford, Sir Edward 73
Guinevere 29
gun salutes 98
Gundulf, Bishop 61
Gunpowder Plot 179
Guthred, King 176
Gwyn, Nell 47, 94, 117, 148

H

Hadleigh Castle *118*, **119**
Haile Selassie, Emperor 22
Hall, Joseph 127
Ham House **104-5**
Hamilton, Duke of 161
Hamilton, Gavin 123
Hampden, John 45
Hampshire 46-51
Hampton Court **103**, *103*, 139
Handel, George Frideric 82, 94
Hardingstone Cross 147
Hardwick Hall **132-3**, *133*, 139
Hardy, Thomas 25, 26, 40
Harlech Castle *184-5*, **185**
Harold II (Harold Godwinson) 72
Harold Hardrada 72
Harrison, John 110
Harry, Prince 68, 136
Hartland Abbey **22**
Hartley, Jesse 167
Haschenperg, Stephen von 54, 62, 73, 165
Hastings 54
Hastings, Battle of 71, 72
Hatfield House **56**, *57*
Hawkins, John 54-5
Hawksmoor, Nicholas 65, 89, 110, 114
Hayter, Sir George 94
Hedingham Castle **116-17**
Henderson, John 204
Henley Royal Regatta 65
Henrietta Maria 58, 63, 85, 92, 109, 140, 151
Henry I 26, 43, 48, 56, 61, 62, 63, 128, 165
Henry II 30, 43, 48, 54, 61, 63, 91, 128, 177, 180, 186, 192, 193
Henry III 46, 47, **50**, 59, 71, 72, 89, 97, 100, 101, 106, 119, 121, 124, 126, 127, 156, 160, 169, 191, 192
Henry IV 27, 59, 61, 124, 145, 169, 174, 184, 185, 192
Henry V 27, 48, 59, 71, 105, 185, 195
Henry VI 43, 100, 106, 134, 147, 162, 172, 178, 181
Henry VII 30, 89, 96, 105, 110, 124, 125, 181, 192, 194
Henry VIII 10, *10*, 16, 17, 22, 25, 30, 33, 39, 40, 43, 44, 46, 47, 48, 49, 54, 56, 58, 59, 62, 63, 64, 65, 66, 67, 69, 74, 82, 87, 94, 98, *98*, 99, 102, 103, 104, 105, 109, 111, 114, 117, 118, 119, 122, 124,

129, 134, **138-9**, 143, 145, 165, 176, 203
Herefordshire 137
Hereward the Wake 115
Hertfordshire 56-7
Hever Castle **58**
hillforts
  Badbury Rings **27**
  Cadbury Castle **29**
historic houses
  Adlington Hall **160-1**
  Althorp **146**, *146*
  Antony *20-1*, **21**
  Ashdown House **39**
  Audley End House **116**, *116-17*
  Avington Park **47**
  Balmoral **210**, *210-11*
  Belton House **142-3**, *142*
  Bentley Hall 151
  Blenheim Palace **65**
  Blickling Hall **124-5**
  Bradgate House and Deer Park **140**
  Brighton Royal Pavilion *70*, **71**
  Broadlands **48-9**
  Burghley House *138-9*, **143**
  Callendar House **200-1**
  Chambercombe Manor **22**
  Charlecote Park **153**, *153*
  Charlton House **111**
  Chatsworth **132**
  Chavenage House **136**
  Chenies Manor **45**
  Clarence House **87**
  Clochfaen House **184**
  Cowdray Park **68**
  Cragside **173**, *173*
  Euston Hall **127**
  Fort Belvedere **66**
  Gawsworth Hall *160-1*, **161**
  Godolphin **15**
  Goodwood House **68**
  Hampton Court **103**, *103*, 139
  Ham House **104-5**
  Hardwick Hall **132-3**, *133*, 139
  Hatfield House **56**, *57*
  Holker Hall **163**
  Holkham Hall **122-3**, *123*
  Hughenden Manor *44-5*, **45**
  Ingatestone Hall **118**
  Knebworth House **56**
  Knole **58-9**, *69*
  Longleat **74**, 139
  Loseley Estate **66-7**
  Marble Hill **102**
  Moseley Old Hall 151, **152**
  Mount Edgcumbe House and Country Park **20-1**

Norton Conyers **181**
Osborne House *52*, **53**
Oxburgh Hall **125**, *125*
Pen y Bryn **190**
Penshurst Place **58**
Place House **17**
Plas Dinas **190**
Polesden Lacey **66**
The Queen's House **109**
The Red House **27**
Sandringham **124**
Spencer House **85**
Stratfield Saye **46**
Syon House **105**
The Vyne **46**
Wilton House **74**
Witley Court **157**
Woburn Abbey **38**, *38*
see also castles; palaces
Hobbes, Robert 38
Hobhouse, Penelope 63
Hoghton Tower **169**
Holbein, Hans 67, 87, 94, 98
Holker Hall **163**
Holkham Hall **122-3**, *123*
Holland, Henry 49, 71, 85
Holm Island **45**
Holst, Gustav 79
Holyrood Abbey **204**
Holyroodhouse **202-3**, *202-3*
Honourable Artillery Company 98
Hopper, Thomas 189
Horse Guards **92**
horse-racing
  Goodwood Racecourse **68**
  Newmarket Races **128**
  Royal Ascot **43**
Household Cavalry 82, 90, 92
Houses of Parliament **90-1**, *90-1*
Howard, Catherine 69, 101, 106, 129, 145, 178
Howard, Elizabeth 141
Huddleston, John 151, 152
Hughenden Manor *44-5*, **45**
Hughes, Arthur 30
Humbert, Albert Jenkins 50
Hungerford **39**
Hunt, William Holman 95
Hurst Castle **49**
Hutchinson, Colonel John 148
Hyde Park **82**, *82-3*
Hythe 54

I

Ina, King of West Saxons 27
Ingatestone Hall **118**
Ingleby, Jane 179
Inner London 78-101

Iona **213**
Ireton, Henry 136
Isabella, Queen 111, 122, 134, 149, 174, 193
Isle of Athelney **28**
Isle of Wight 50-3
Ivar the Boneless 176

J

Jacobite Steam Train **214**
Jacobitism 165, 199, 200-1, 207, 208, 209, 212, 214
James I (James VI of Scotland) 24, 56, 66, 74, 82, 85, 88, 89, 95, 104, 109, 111, 114, 128, 152, 169, 172, 175, 179, 200, 203, 204, 212
James II (James VII of Scotland) 24, 29, 39, 74, 94, 181, 204, 207
James II of Scotland 204
James IV of Scotland 200, 201, 202, 207, 212
James V of Scotland 200, 212
Jenkins, Simon 122
Jersey 34-5
Jewel House, Tower of London **100**
Joan of Navarre 59, 61
John, King 26, 34, 43, 48, 61, 67, 72, 74, 117, 119, **120-1**, 122, 126, 127, 128, 134, 147, 148, 192
John of Gaunt 27, 39, 43, 145, 152, 169, 174, 178, 192
Johnson, Lionel 92
Johnson, Dr Samuel 92, 110, 213
Johnson, Samuel (jester) 161
Jones, Inigo 46, 56, 85, 88, 109, 111
Jonson, Ben 88
Josephine, Empress 66
Jubilee Tower *168*, **169**
Jurassic Coast 24

K

Kendal Castle **164**
Kendall, H.E. Jnr 56
Kenilworth Castle 139, **154**
Kensington Gardens **78**
Kensington Palace **78**
Kent 58-63
Kent, Edward, Duke of 78
Kent, Hugh de Burgh, 1st Earl of 119
Kent, William 92, 123, 127
Keppel, Alice 66
Kew Palace **105**

Kimbolton Castle **114**
King Arthur's Stone 19, 30
King Doniert's Stone **20**
King Ricatus's Cross **14**
King's Lynn **122**
King's Square, York **176**
The King's Way **22**
Kingston Lacy **27**
Kipling, John Lockwood 53
Kipling, Rudyard 40, 124
Knebworth House **56**
Knole **58-9**
Knollys, Sir William 161
Knox, John 204
Knutsford **160**
Koh-i-Noor diamond 100
Kynance Cove **15**

L

Lancashire 166-9
Lancaster Castle **169**
Landseer, Sir Edwin 208
Langham, Robert 154
Langside Battle Memorial **198**
Langtry, Lily 27, 35, 94, 127
Launceston Castle **20**
Lawrence, Thomas 94
Layton, Richard 72
Le Sueur, Hubert 92
Leeds Castle **59**
Leicester, Robert Dudley, Earl of 58, 154-5
Leicestershire and Rutland 140-1
Leland, John 17, 45, 89, 128, 143, 153, 175, 188, 189
Lely, Sir Peter 94
Leo, King of Armenia 111
Lewes **71**
Lewes, Battle of 71, **72**
Lewes Castle 71
Lincoln Castle **143**
Lincoln Cathedral **145**
Lincolnshire 142-5
Linlithgow Palace **201**
Lithgow, William 204
Liverpool 167
Lloyd George, David 190
Lloyd-Verney, Harry 184
Llywelyn the Great 190, 191
Llywelyn the Last 190, 191, 193
Lochindorb Castle **208**
Lochleven Castle **212**
Loe Pool **14**
Longleat **74**, 139
Lord Mayor's show 98
Loseley Estate **66-7**
Loudon, George 78
Loyd-Lindsay, Colonel Robert 64
Ludlow Castle **149**

Lutyens, Sir Edwin 40, 67, 91
Lyme Regis **24**
Lyminge, Robert 56, 124

M

McAlpine, Robert 214
Macaulay, Thomas Babington 93, 111
Macbeth 213
Macdonald, Sinclair 214
Maggie Jones **78**, *79*
Magna Carta 43, 67, 74, 117, 120, 143
Malacrida, Peter 111
Malcolm III of Scotland 200
The Mall **88**, *88-9*
Malory, Thomas 30
Manchester Ship Canal **166**
Mar, John Erskine, 6th Earl of 209
Marble Hill **102**
Marcher Lords 187, 192, 193, 194
Margaret, Princess 78, 190, 206, 211
Margaret of Anjou 134, 147
Margaret Tudor 201, 202
Marie Antoinette 66
Marie, Queen of Romania 53
Marlborough, John Churchill, Duke of 65
Marlborough, Sarah, Duchess of 15, 65
Marochetti, Carlo 40, 91, 198
Marryat, Captain Frederick 49
Marshal, William 137, 192, 193
Marshall, Joshua 92
Marston Moor, Battle of 179, **181**
Marten, Henry 193
Martyrs Memorial 71
Mary I (Mary Tudor) 24, 44, 47, 54, 56, 62, 71, 87, 89, 106, 109, 117, 129, 175, 179
Mary II 23, 78, 97, 103, 110, 132
Mary, Queen of Scots 46, 69, 98, 106, 114, 125, 132, 143, 147, 152, 164, 165, 172, 174, 180, 198, 199, 200, 201, **203**, 204, 206, 211, 212
Mary Queen of Scots House **95**
Mary of Guise 200, 212
Mary of Teck (Queen Mary) 17, 40, 66, 68, 81, 122, 163, 169, 184
Mary Rose 48, 54
Master James of St

George 185, 187, 189, 190, 191
Matilda (consort of Henry I) 48
Matilda (daughter of Henry I) 9, 65, 116-17, 137, 143, 149
Maufe, Sir Edward 67
Maurice, Prince 24
Maurice the Engineer 63
May, Hugh 40
Meadows, John 22
Medieval Palace, Tower of London **101**
Melrose Abbey **206**
Melton Mowbray **140**
Melton, Steve 62
Menai Bridge 191
Merlin's Cave 19
Mewes, Charles 66
Michael of Kent, Princess 62
Middleham Castle **181**
Middleton, Catherine see Cambridge, Catherine, Duchess of
Mohun, Lord 161
Monarch's Way **157**
Monmouth, James, Duke of 24, 29
Monmouth Castle 187, **195**
Monmouthshire Royal Engineers 195
Mont Orgueil Castle **34**
Montfort, Simon de 50, 59, 61, 71, 72, 156, 169, 172
More, Sir Thomas 106, 176
Morris, Roger 102
Morris, William 71
Mortimer, Roger 122, 134, 149, 174, 188
Moseley Old Hall 151,**152**
Mount Badon 27
Mount Edgcumbe House and Country Park **20-1**
Mountbatten, Lord 48, 68
Muncaster Castle **162**, *162-3*
Murray, William 104
museums and galleries
National Portrait Gallery **93-4**
Natural History Museum 79, **81**
Queen's Gallery, Edinburgh **204**
Queen's Gallery, London **85**
Richard III Museum **176**
Royal Academy of Arts **92**
Royal Worcester Porcelain Museum **156-7**, *157*
Victoria and Albert Museum 79, **81**

Myddelton, Sir Thomas 188, 189
Myten, Daniel 94

N

Napoleonic Wars 62, 82
Naseby, Battle of 126, **147**
Nash, Beau 33
Nash, John 71, 83, 84, 85, 87, 99, 157
National Portrait Gallery **93-4**
Natural History Museum 79, **81**
Navy **54-5**, 60
Neidpath Castle **206**
Nelson, Lord 55
Nennius 30
Nesfield, William Andrews 157
Neville, Cecily 172
New Forest **49**, 50
New Romney 54
Newark Castle **148**
Newmarket Races **128**
Newport Minster, Isle of Wight **53**
Newton, Sir Adam 111
Nicolson, Harold 124
Nonsuch **66**, 67, 139
Norfolk 122-7
Norfolk, Dukes of 69, 129
Norman Conquest 30, 72
Norris Castle **53**
North and Mid Wales 184-91
North Highlands and Islands 213-15
Northampton, Battle of **147**
Northamptonshire 146-7
Northumberland and Tyneside 173-5
Northumberland, Dukes of 105, 174
Norton, Christopher 180
Norton Conyers **181**
Norwich Cathedral **127**
Norwich City **126-7**, *126*
Nottingham **148**
Nottinghamshire 148

O

Oak Apple Day 81
Oakham Castle **140-1**, *141*
Offa, King of Mercia 137
Oliver Cromwell's House **115**
Order of the Garter 40
Ordish, Rowland Mason 99
Osborne House *52*, **53**
Oswald, Sir James 56
Outer London 102-11
Owen, Sir Richard 81

Oxburgh Hall **125**, *125*
Oxford, Earls of 117
Oxford Castle **65**
Oxfordshire 64-5
Oyster Feast 119

P

Paget, Paul 111
Palace of Beaulieu (New Hall) **117**
palaces
  Bishop's Palace **74**
  Blenheim Palace **65**
  Buckingham Palace **84**, *84-5*
  Dunfermline Palace 200
  Eltham Palace **111**
  Falkland Palace **200**, *201*
  Hampton Court **103**, *103*, 139
  Holyroodhouse **202-3**, *202-3*
  Kensington Palace **78**
  Kew Palace **105**
  Linlithgow Palace **201**
  Medieval Palace, Tower of London **101**
  Nonsuch **66**, 67, 139
  Palace of Beaulieu (New Hall) **117**
  Placentia Palace 109, 110, 111
  Richmond Palace **105**
  St James's Palace **86**, *87*
  see also castles; historic houses
Paley, Edward Graham 163
parks and gardens
  Bestwood Country Park **148**
  Bradgate House and Deer Park 140
  Bushy Park **102**
  Green Park **82-3**
  Greenwich Park **109**
  Hyde Park **82**, *82-3*
  Kensington Gardens 78
  Queen Eleanor's Garden 46
  Regent's Park **99**
  Richmond Park **104**, *104*
  Royal Botanic Gardens, Kew *108*, **109**
  St James's Park **87**
  Sheringham Park **124**
  Windsor Great Park **40**
  Woburn Deer Park **38**, *38*
Parliament Square **91**
Parr, Catherine 39, 94, 134, 145, 164
Paulet, Sir Amyas 152
Pearson, Harold 68
Peel, Sir John 141
Pellegrini, Giovanni Antonio 114

Pembroke, Henry Herbert, 9th Earl of 102
Pembroke Castle **192**
Pen y Bryn **190**
Pendennis Castle **16**
Pendragon Castle **164**
Penrhyn Castle **189**
Penrith Castle **165**
Penshurst Place **58**
Pepys, Samuel 55, 58, 60, 97, 100, 119, 128, 150, 156
Percy, Sir Henry (Harry Hotspur) 174
Peterborough Cathedral **114-15**
Petre, Sir Wiliam 118
Pevensey Castle **72**, *73*
Pevsner, Nikolaus 39, 45, 132, 133, 163, 173, 188
Philip II of France 120
Philip II of Spain 47, 55, 106
Philip IV of France 165
Philippa of Hainault 122, 177
Philips, Captain Mark 132, 136, 206
Phillips, Zara 53, 136, 136, 203
Pilgrimage of Grace 176, 178, 179
Pitt, William 63
Place House **17**
Placentia Palace 109, 110, 111
Planché, André 132
Plantagenet, Katherine 22
Plas Dinas **190**
Polesden Lacey **66**
polo 68
Pontefract Castle **178**
Porden, William 71
Portchester Castle **48**
Portland Castle **25**
Portsmouth, Louise de Keroualle, Duchess of 68
Portsmouth Dockyard **48**
Poundbury 24
Powis Castle **184-5**
Princes in the Tower 73, 100, 106, 149, 176
Pugin, Augustus 90

Q

Qatar, Emir of 132
Queen Adelaide's Grotto 20
Queen Charlotte's Cottage 105
Queen Eleanor's Garden **46**
Queen Elizabeth's Oak 109
Queen Mary's Dolls' House 40
Queen Victoria Memorial 88

Queen's Chapel, London **85**
Queen's Gallery, Edinburgh **204**
Queen's Gallery, London **85**
The Queen's House **109**

R

Raby Castle **172**
Raedwald, King of East Anglia 121
Raglan Castle **195**
Rahere 98
Raleigh, Sir Walter 17, 24, 34, 46, 100, 106
Ramsgate Royal Harbour **62**
ravens in the Tower 100-1
Reading Abbey **43**
The Red House **27**
Redvers, Countess Isabella de 50
Reformation 62, 139
see also Dissolution of the Monasteries; Scottish Reformation
regattas
  Cowes 53
  Fowey 17
  Henley Royal Regatta **65**
Regent's Park **99**
Remembrance Sunday 91
Repton, Humphrey 38, 124
Restoration of the Monarchy 19, 82, 90, 92, 97, 100, 111, 193
Restormel Castle *18*, **19**
Reynolds, Sir Joshua 92
Rhind, John 208
Rich, John 94
Rich, Nathaniel 62, 111
Richard I (Lionheart) 23, 91, 117, 126, 147, 192
Richard II 48, 59, 111, 145, 188, 206
Richard III 73, 100, 106, 140, 145, 147, 148, 154, 165, 172, 181, 194
Richard III Museum **176**
Richmond, Charles, Duke of 68
Richmond Castle 68, **180**, *180*
Richmond Palace **105**
Richmond Park **104**, *104*
Ripley Castle **179**
Rising of the North 106, 172, 174, 179, 180, 181
Rivett, John 92
Rizzio, David 203
Robert the Bruce 26, 165, 175, 199, 200, 206, 207, 212
Robert II of Scotland 208, 211, 212
Rochester Castle **61**

Rockingham Castle **147**
Romsey Abbey **48**
Rossetti, Dante Gabriel 30
Rotten Row **82**
Rough Wooing, the 200, 203, 204
Round Table 30, 46
Rowlandson, Thomas 33
Royal Academy of Arts **92**
Royal Albert Hall **80**, *80*
Royal Ascot **43**
Royal Ballet 102
Royal Botanic Gardens, Kew *108*, **109**
Royal College of Music **79**
Royal Courts of Justice **95**
Royal Crown Derby **132**
Royal Deeside **209**
royal dynasties 8–11
Royal Festival Hall **99**
Royal Hospital, Chelsea **81**
Royal Leamington Spa **155**
Royal Mews **83**
Royal Naval College 110
Royal Observatory **110**, *110*
Royal Opera House **94**
Royal Tunbridge Wells **58**
royal warrants 87, 211
Royal Welsh Showground **185**
Royal Worcester Porcelain Museum **156–7**, *157*
Royal Yacht Britannia **206**
Royal Yacht Squadron 53
Rubens, Peter Paul 88
Rufus Stone **50**, *51*
Rules (restaurant) **94**
Runnymede **67**
Rupert, Prince 140, 156, 176, 181, 188
Ruthin Castle **188–9**
Ruthven-Taggar, Ben 66
Rutland, Dukes of 141

S

Sackville-West, Vita 58, 59
Saebert 121
St Albans, Charles, Duke of 117, 148
St Albans Cathedral **56**
St Andrew's Church, Trent **24**
St Aubyn family 14
St Augustine 62
St Austell **17**
St Bartholomew's Hospital **98**, *98*
St Columba 213
St Cuthburga 27
St Dunstan's-in-the-West **98**

St Edmund 128
St Edward's Crown 100, *101*
St Ethelbert's Well **137**
St Etheldreda 115
St George's Chapel, Windsor **40**, *41*
St Helier **34**
St James's, London **86**
St James's Palace **86**, *87*
St James's Park **86**
St John's, Smith Square **89**
St Margaret of Scotland 200
St Mary Magdalene Church, Sandringham **123**
St Mary's Church, Isle of Wight **50**
St Mary's Church, Warwick **154–5**, *155*
St Mawes Castle **16**
St Mawgan in Pydar Church **19**
St Michael's Church, Burgh by Sands **165**
St Michael's Church, Framlingham **129**
St Michael's Mount **14**, *14-15*
St Mildred's Church, Isle of Wight **50**
St Nicholas' Church, Kenilworth **154**
St Paul's Cathedral **95**
St Saviour's Church, Jersey **35**
Salisbury Cathedral **74**, *75*
Salvin, Anthony 162, 172, 174
Sandringham **124**
Sandwich 54
Sark **35**
Scarborough Castle **177–8**
Science Museum 79
Scott, Sir George Gilbert 22, 33, 43, 56
Scott, Lt Col Henry Darracott 80
Scott, Sir Walter 175, 206, 213
Scottish Reformation 199, 200, 204
Scroop, Henry, Lord 48
Scrope, Sir Henry 180
Sealed Knot 105
Sedgemoor, Battle of 24, *28-9*, **29**
Seely, John 111
Servan, Jean-Nicolas 82
Sewingshield Crags **173**
Seymour, Jane 40, 43, 134
Seymour, Sir Thomas 134, 136
Shaftesbury **25**
Shaftesbury, Anthony Ashley, 7th Earl of 49
Shaftesbury Abbey **26**

Shakespeare, William 117, 139, 153, 169
As You Like It 74
Henry IV Part I 185
Henry V 48
Richard II 54
Richard III 176, 178
sonnets 161
Shaw, Norman 173
Sherborne Castle **24**
Sheringham Park Gazebo **124**
Shrewsbury, Countess of (Bess of Hardwick) 125, 132–3, 152
Shrewsbury Castle **149**
Shrine of Our Lady of Walsingham **124**
Shropshire 149
Sidney, Sir Philip 58, 74
Sigebert II 121
Silent Pool **67**, *67*
Simpson, Archibald 204
Simpson, Wallis (Duchess of Windsor) 45, 66, 81, 140, 142
Singh, Bhai Ram 53
Sitwell, Osbert 66
Skipton Castle **179**, *179*
Skirving, Alexander 198
Slaughterbridge **19**, 30
Sloane, Sir Hans 81
Smirke, Sir Robert 184–5
Smith, Sydney 71
Smith, William 210
Snore Hall 126
Snowdon, Lord 78, 190, 206
Soane, Sir John 99
Somerset 28–9, 32–3
Somerset House **94–5**
South Wales 192–5
Southbank Centre 99
Southend-on-Sea 121
Southsea Castle **48**
Southwest Scotland 198–9
Spanish Armada 55, 63, 69, 87, 118, 127, 164, 175
Spencer House **85**
Staffa **213**
Staffordshire **152**
Staffordshire Potteries 152
Stanhope, Philip Henry 93
Stanton, William 142
Stephen 65, 128, 137, 143, 149
Stephens, Nathaniel 136
Stephenson, Robert 191
Stewart, Alexander (Wolf of Badenoch) 208
Stirling Castle **212**
Stone of Scone 97, 165, 204
Strata Florida Abbey **184**
Stratfield Saye **46**
Stuart, Prince Charles

Edward (Bonnie Prince Charlie) 165, 199, 201, 203, 208, 214
Stuart, Prince James Francis Edward (Old Pretender) 200
Stuart, James 85
Sudeley Castle **134**
Suffolk 128–9
Suffolk, Henrietta Howard, Countess of 102, 116
Suffolk, Thomas Howard, 1st Earl of 116
Summer Exhibition 92
Surrey 66–7
Surrey, Henry, Earl of 129
Sussex 68–73
Sutton Hoo 121
swan upping 64, *64*
Swiss Cottage, Osborne House **53**
Swynford, Katherine 145
Syon House **105**

T

Talman, William 103, 132
Tattersall, Captain Nicholas 151
Telford, Thomas 191
Tennyson, Alfred, Lord 14, 15, 19, 30
Tewkesbury **134**
Tewkesbury Abbey 134, *135*
Theed, William 83
Thomas, John 191
Thornball, John 95
Thornhill, Sir James 65, 110
Thornycroft, Hamo 47, 90
Thorpe, John 111
Thynne, Sir John 74, 139
Tilbury Fort **118–19**
Timbs, John 82
Tindall, Mike 136, 203
Tintagel Castle **19**
Tintern Abbey **195**
Tissot, Jean 95
Tiverton Castle **22**
Torbay **23**, *23*
Tower Green **101**
Tower of London **100–1**, *101*, **106**, *107*
Trafalgar, Battle of 55
Trematon Castle **21**
Trent House 151
Trinity Church Square **99**
Trooping the Colour 83, 87, 92
Troyes, Chrétienne de 30
Turner, J.M.W. 169, 180, 195
Tutbury Castle **152**
Tyrell, Sir Walter 50

U

Upnor Castle 60, *60-1*
Uther Pendragon 19, 30, 164

V

Vanbrugh, Sir John 65, 110, 114, 143
Vane, Sir Henry 172
Vardy, John 85
Vavasour, Sir Thomas 104
Verderers' Court 49
Verney, Sir Edmund 148
Vicary, Thomas 98
Victoria and Albert Museum 79, **81**
Victoria, Queen **11**, 14, 17, 19, 20, 21, 23, 33, 34, 35, 38, 40, 45, 46, 50, 53, 56, 58, 69, 78, 80, 81, 87, 88, 93, 95, 100, 105, 122, 124, 141, 153, 154, 155, 160, 166, 169, 184, 189, 198, 203, 208, 209, 210, 212, 213
Victoria Tower, Guernsey **35**
HMS *Victory* 60
Vikings 25, 27, 28, 54, 128, 176
Virginia Water 40
Vreeland, Diana 140
The Vyne **46**

W

Wakefield, Battle of **178**
Wakefield Tower, Tower of London **100-1**
Walden Abbey 116
Walker, Robert 94
Wallace, William 165, 175, 198
Walmer Castle **62-3**
Walpole, Horace 59, 78, 102, 176
Wanamaker, Rodman 123
Wantage **64**
War of Austrian Succession 82
Warenne, William de 71
Wars of the Roses 14, 28, 43, 122, 134, 147, 149, 154, 174, 175, 178, 181, 192, 195
Warwick Castle **154**
Warwick, Richard Neville, Earl of 154, 172, 181
Warwickshire 153-5
the Wash **120-1**, *120-1*
Waterhouse, Alfred 81
wayside crosses 20, 22
Webb, Sir Aston 84, 88
Webb, John 46, 74
Wellington, Duke of 46, 63, *63*, 141, 198
Welsh castles **186-7**
Wendover, Roger 121
Westenhanger Castle **63**
Westminster Abbey 8, **89**, *96*, **97**, 114
Westminster Hall **90**, 99
Weymouth **25**, *25*
Whispering Gallery 95
White Lodge **102**
White Tower, Tower of London 61, **100**
William I, the Conqueror 40, 46, 47, 49, 59, 62, 63, 72, 97, 100, 115, 119, 128, 143, 145, 147, 154, 160, 177, 178, 180
William II (Will Rufus) 50, 62, 90, 127, 147, 164
William III (William of Orange) 23, 24, 39, 78, 94, 97, 103, 116, 132, 140, 142, 169
William IV 33, 87, 97, 99, 157
William of Orange *see* William III
William, Prince see Cambridge, Prince William, Duke of
William Augustus, Prince 40, 66
Wilton House **74**
Wiltshire 74-5
Wimborne Minster Church 27
Winceby, Battle of 115
Winchester Castle 30, **46**
Winchester Cathedral 47
Winde, William 39, 142
Windsor Castle **40**
Windsor Great Park **40**
Wise, Henry 78
Witley Court **157**

Woburn Abbey **38**, *38*
Woburn Deer Park **38**, *38*
Wolsey, Cardinal 56, 65, 102, 103, 105
Worcester, Battle of **156**
Worcestershire 156-7
World War I 55, 91, 178, 184
World War II 20, 89, 91, 99
Worthington, Sir Hubert 161
Wren, Sir Christopher 46, 65, 81, 89, 95, 102, 103, 110, 116, 142
Wriothesley, Thomas 124
Wyatt, James 53, 68, 74, 78, 141
Wyatt, Samuel 189
Wyatt, Sir Thomas 106
Wyattville, Sir Jeffrey 66, 142-3, 175
Wyndham, Colonel Francis 24, 151

Y

Yeomen of the Guard 83, 91
Yevele, Henry 90
York **176-7**
York Minster **177**, *177*
York, Prince Andrew, Duke of 55
York, Richard, Duke of 178
Yorkshire 176-81
Young, William 198

Acknowledgements

Front Cover Richard Bryant/Arcaid/Corbis; **Back Cover** Suzanne and Nick Geary/Getty Images; **1** VisitBritain/ Britain on View/Getty Images (The Union flag flying at the Tower of London); **2-3** Derek Croucher/Travel Pictures Ltd

(Glenfinnan Monument and Loch Sheil). **6/7** Pool/Tim Graham Picture Library/Getty Images (Queen Elizabeth II in a carriage procession to Windsor Castle); **8** Courtesy Nicholas Fry/Chester Cathedral; **9** Dave Willis/Alamy; **10** Liquid Light/Alamy; **11** Antony Nettle/Alamy; **12/13** David Noton Photography/Alamy (Cadbury Castle, Somerset); **14/15** Peter Adams/AWL Images Ltd; **16/17** Andrew Holt/Getty Images; **18** Paul Bradforth/ Alamy; **20/21** NTPL/John Bethell; **23** Lee Pengelly/Loop Images/Corbis; **25** geogphotos/Alamy; **26/27** Guy Edwardes/Robert Harding World Images; **28/29** Duncan Shaw/Getty Images; **30/31** English Heritage Photo Library; **32** Photoshot/TIPS; **34/35** A1 Images/Travel Pictures Ltd; **36/37** VisitBritain/Pawel Libera/Getty Images (The Long Walk towards Windsor Castle); **38** Doug Blane/City Of Milton Keynes/Alamy; **41** Chris Young/AFP/Getty Images; **42** Steve Vidler/Photoshot; **44** NTPL/Andreas von Einsiedel; **47** John Goulter/Alamy; **49** English Heritage Photo Library; **51** Irek/4Corners; **52** English Heritage Photo Library; **54/55** Kos/Kos Picture Source; **57** Kim Sayer/Getty Images; **59** NTPL/Andreas von Einsiedel; **60/61** English Heritage Photo Library; **63** Heritage Images/Corbis; **64** Homer Sykes/Corbis; **67** Javier Carcamo Photography; **69** His Grace The Duke of Norfolk, Arundel Castle/The Bridgeman Art Library; **70** Charles Bowman/age fotostock; **73** Adrian Warren /www.lastrefuge.co.uk; **75** Maurizio Rellini/4Corners; **76/77** Bill Bertram/Pixel8 (Old Royal Naval College, Greenwich); **79** Courtesy of amadeodesign.co.uk; **80** Eric Nathan/ Travel Pictures Ltd; **82/83t** Kristel Richard/naturepl.com; **84/85** VisitBritain/Pawel Libera/Getty Images; **87** Toby Melville/Reuters/Corbis; **88/89** Stefan Rousseau/Pool/Reuters/Corbis; **90/91** Photoshot; **93** Justin Kase zninez/Alamy; **96** Angelo Hornak/Alamy; **98** Holmes Garden Photos/Alamy; **101** UPPA/Photoshot; **103** Howard Sayer/Getty Images; **104** Roger Cracknell/Travel Pictures Ltd; **107** Ian Patrick/Alamy; **108** Rolf Richardson/Alamy; **110** Arcaid Images/Alamy; **112/113** NTPL/Mike Williams (View across the Parterre garden at Blickling Hall, Norfolk); **114/115** Rod Edwards/Travel Pictures Ltd; **116/117** English Heritage Photo Library; **118** Rod Edwards/Travel Pictures Ltd; **120/121** Gary K Smith/Alamy; **122** Topham Picturepoint; **125** Travel Library Limited/SuperStock; **126** Mark Dyball/Travel Pictures Ltd; **129** VisitBritain/Rod Edwards/Getty Images; **130/131** Peak Images/Alamy (Chatsworth House, Derbyshire); **133** Robert Harding Picture Library/SuperStock; **135** DGB/Alamy; **136** Getty Images/Stringer; **138/139** Tim Graham/Corbis; **141** AA/M Birkitt; **142** The National Trust Photolibrary/Alamy; **144** John Smaller/Alamy; **146** Homer W Sykes/Alamy; **150/151** English Heritage Photo Library; **153** Imagestate Media Partners Limited – Impact Photos/Alamy; **155** Glyn Thomas/Alamy; **157** Courtesy Worcester Porcelain Museum/JOHN EVERETT PHOTOGRAPHY; **158/159** Dae Sasitorn & Adrian Warren/www. lastrefuge.co.uk (Kendal Castle, Cumbria); **160/161** travelib prime/Alamy; **162/163** Keith Wood/Getty Images; **166/167** Monica Wells/Travel Pictures Ltd; **168** Andy Stothert/Getty Images; **170/171** Chris Warren/4Corners Images (Durham Cathedral Durham); **173** Emma Durnford/ LatitudeStock; **174** Rainer Mirau/Huber/4Corners Images; **177** Courtesy York Minster; **179** Travel Library Limited/SuperStock; **180** English Heritage Photo Library; **182/183** Granville Harris/LOOP IMAGES/Loop Images/Corbis (Caernarfon Castle, Gwynedd); **185** Riccardo Spila/ SIME/4Corners Images; **186/187** Roy Rainford/Robert Harding World Imagery; **188/189** NTPL/Andreas von Einsiedel; **192/193** David Hughes/ Robert Harding World Imagery; **194** Elizabeth Whiting & Associates/Corbis; **196/197** Ronnie Weir/Travel Pictures Ltd (Blair Castle, Perthshire); **199** South West Images Scotland/Alamy; **201** Sandro Vannini/Corbis; **202/203** Tim Graham/Getty Images; **205** Ian Stewart/AFP/Getty Images; **207** A1 Images/Travel Pictures Ltd; **210/211** Courtesy Bert Kaufmann; **213** gmsphotography/Getty Images; **215** Arterra Picture Library/Alamy

Every effort has been made to find and credit the copyright holders of images in this book. We will be pleased to rectify any errors or omissions in future editions. Email us at gbeditorial@readersdigest.co.uk

Contributors

Project Editor Jo Bourne
Art Editor Julie Bennett
Designer Martin Bennett
Sub-editor Marion Paull
Cartographic Consultant Alison Ewington
Picture Researcher Wilf Matos
Proofreader Deirdre Headon
Indexer Marie Lorimer
Maps Map Graphics Limited

Writer Rose Shepherd

FOR VIVAT DIRECT

Editorial Director Julian Browne
Art Director Anne-Marie Bulat
Managing Editor Nina Hathway
Trade Books Editor Penny Craig
Picture Resource Manager
　Sarah Stewart-Richardson
Pre-press Account Manager Dean Russell
Product Production Manager Claudette Bramble
Production Controller Jan Bucil

Origination by FMG
Printing and binding Arvato Iberia, Portugal

Front cover Hampton Court Palace, London
Back cover Beefeater, Tower of London

The Most Amazing Royal Places in Britain is published
in 2012 in the United Kingdom by Vivat Direct Limited
(t/a Reader's Digest), 157 Edgware Road, London W2 2HR

The Most Amazing Royal Places in Britain is owned and
under licence from the Reader's Digest Association, Inc.
All rights reserved.

We are committed both to the quality of our products and
the service we provide to our customers. We value your
comments, so please do contact us on **0871 351 1000**
or via our website at **www.readersdigest.co.uk**

If you have any comments or suggestions about the content
of our books, email us at **gbeditorial@readersdigest.co.uk**

ISBN 978 1 78020 099 6
Book Code 400-582 UP0000-1